CONSUMER GUIDE®
AUTO SERIES

4x4s, PICKUPS & VANS
BUYING 1994 GUIDE

All rights reserved under International and Pan American copyright conventions. Copyright © 1994 Publications International, Ltd. This publication may not be reproduced or quoted in whole or in part by mimeograph or any other printed or electronic means, or for presentation on radio, television, videotape, or film without written permission from Louis Weber, C.E.O. of Publications International, Ltd., 7373 North Cicero Ave., Lincolnwood, Illinois 60646. Permission is never granted for commercial purposes. Printed in U.S.A.

CONTENTS

Ford Explorer

Chevrolet Lumina Minivan

Dodge Ram Pickup Laramie

Toyota T100 2WD

Choosing the Right Vehicle 4
How Trucks Measure Up 5
4-Wheel-Drive Systems 7
Light Trucks and Safety 8
Shopping for a New Truck 11
Warranties and Service Contracts 13
Best Buys and Recommended 15

Chevrolet Astro 19
Chevrolet Blazer 22
Chevrolet Lumina Minivan 24
Chevrolet C/K Pickup 27
Chevrolet Sportvan/Van 32
Chevrolet Suburban 37
Chevrolet S10 Blazer 39
Chevrolet S10 Pickup 42
Chrysler Town & Country 45
Dodge Caravan 46
Dodge Dakota 50
Dodge Ram Pickup 54
Dodge Ram Wagon/Van 58
Eagle Summit Wagon 62
Ford Aerostar 64
Ford Bronco 67
Ford Club Wagon/Econoline Van 69
Ford Explorer 74
Ford F-Series 76
Ford Ranger 83
1995 Ford Windstar 86
Geo Tracker 88
GMC Jimmy 90
GMC Rally/Vandura 93
GMC Safari 98
GMC Sierra 101
GMC Sonoma 106

GMC Suburban	108
GMC Yukon	110
Honda Passport	111
Isuzu Amigo	113
Isuzu Pickup	115
Isuzu Rodeo	116
Isuzu Trooper	118
Jeep Cherokee	120
Jeep Grand Cherokee	122
Jeep Wrangler	125
1995 Kia Sportage	127
Land Rover/Range Rover	128
Mazda B-Series Pickup	130
Mazda MPV	132
Mazda Navajo	134
Mercury Villager	135
Mitsubishi Expo	138
Mitsubishi Mighty Max	140
Mitsubishi Montero	142
Nissan Pathfinder	144
Nissan Quest	146
Nissan Truck	148
Oldsmobile Bravada	150
Oldsmobile Silhouette	152
Plymouth Colt Vista	154
Plymouth Voyager	156
Pontiac Trans Sport	159
Suzuki Samurai	161
Suzuki Sidekick	162
Toyota Land Cruiser	164
Toyota Pickup	166
Toyota Previa	169
Toyota T100	171
Toyota 4Runner	173
Volkswagen EuroVan	175

Chevrolet S10 Pickup

Honda Passport EX

Ford F-150 XLT regular-cab

Dodge Caravan ES

CHOOSING THE RIGHT VEHICLE

Which light truck is best for you? The answer starts with "Choosing the Right Vehicle."

Car sales rebounded during the 1993 model year, increasing 3.3 percent over 1992, to 8.42 million. Sales of light trucks, however, jumped a robust 16.3 percent, to 5.2 million—and that on top of a 12.4-percent gain the year before.

In fact, five of the 10 best-selling vehicles in America are trucks: the Ford F-Series and Chevrolet C/K pickups led all vehicles, with the Ford Explorer and Ranger, and the Dodge Caravan also placing.

Why the healthy demand for light trucks? Explanations include concerns about safety, the growth of active lifestyles and two-income households, baby boomers settling down to start families, even a dissatisfaction with today's downsized cars.

Whatever your reason for shopping the truck market, finding the vehicle that best suits your needs—and that might turn out to be a car rather than a truck—requires you to do some homework. *Consumer Guide*'s *4x4s, Pickups & Vans* is a great resource for information on your prospective truck purchase. But it's also vital that you test drive a variety of models *before* you buy. The differences in ride and handling qualities can be dramatic among different models or equipment levels in the same line, let alone among different brands.

Here's how we classify the different kinds of light trucks and some of the pros and cons of each.

Passenger Vans

The minivan has effectively replaced the family station wagon. And full-size vans are increasingly popular as aftermarket conversions.

Minivans generally measure 170 to 190 inches in overall length and have curb weights under 4000 pounds. The Dodge Caravan is a textbook example.

Full-size vans, such as the Ford Econoline, can exceed 200 inches and weigh more than 5000 pounds.

- **Advantages:** Minivans are efficient space users, offering seating for up to eight within the wheelbase of a 4- or 5-passenger mid-size car. A sliding side door makes minivans easy to get into and out of, you can move around once inside, and the seats usually fold or remove for additional cargo space. Minivans are available from just about every manufacturer. And with front-, rear-, or 4-wheel-drive—they're all-weather versatile.

Full-size vans are not nearly as car-like to drive as minivans. But, being true trucks, they have more brawn for load-carrying or towing. And when used for passengers, they can hold a dozen people or more and still have room for luggage.

- **Disadvantages:** A drawback to minivans, particularly the regular-length models, is that they can carry several people or lots of cargo—but seldom both at the same time. Another is that their fuel mileage is generally worse than a family car's. And with more weight, they're often slower to accelerate.

The big vans are cumbersome and consume more fuel still. Only Ford, General Motors, and Dodge build them, and all come with front-mounted engines and rear-wheel drive.

Cargo Vans

Full-size vans dominate this category because this is where size, weight, and strength count most.

About 85 percent of full-size vans are sold in cargo form. Though all the domestic automakers and most of the Japanese manufacturers offer cargo versions of their minivans, only 15 percent of minivans are sold as cargo haulers.

Most cargo vans come with just one or two front seats and bare-metal interiors. They often have fewer windows than passenger vans, though additional glass usually is an option. Cargo models are popular for aftermarket conversions to luxury passenger vans.

4WD Vehicles

Also called sport-utility vehicles, these are passenger wagons with a rear liftgate or tailgate and usually 4WD capability.

We call a sport-utility vehicle with two side doors a "3-door" design and those with four side doors a "5-door" design. Sport-utility vehicles come in three size categories.

Mini sport-utility vehicles are smaller than most passenger cars and generally have wheelbases under 90 inches and bodies no longer than 145 inches. A typical example is the Geo Tracker.

Compact sport-utilities span a broader range of sizes and prices. Generally, wheelbases are 100-110 inches and overall-length is under 180 inches. Ford Explorer and Jeep Grand Cherokee are the sales leaders in this class.

Full-size sport-utilities, typified by the Ford Bronco, weigh over 4000 pounds in base form and measure more than 180 inches overall.

- **Advantages:** Most sport-utility buyers choose 4WD models—even if they seldom venture off-road. Even on-road, 4WD eliminates the tire slippage in rain or snow that can be a problem when sport-utilities are in 2WD (read rear-wheel drive). And for those who do wander from the beaten path, 4WD is a necessity.

Sport-utility vehicles have more towing ability than the typical automobile. And their tall ride height and weight imparts a sense of security for some buyers. Also, 4x4s have a certain character that for many people makes them attractive alternatives to cars.

- **Disadvantages:** Size and weight make most sport-utilities less fuel efficient and less maneuverable than a family sedan. Their stout suspensions

Introduction

can be jarring over bumps. And the added ride height necessary for off-road clearance makes these 4x4s more susceptible to flipping over in turns (see the "Light Trucks and Safety" section). It also makes them more difficult to climb into and out of, and makes servicing more costly.

Pickup Trucks

Pickups divide into two groups: compact and full-size, both of which have become popular substitutes for cars.

Compact pickup trucks generally have a curb weight of under 3000 pounds and wheelbases that range from about 105 inches to around 123 for extended-cab models. The Ford Ranger is the top-seller.

Wheelbases on full-size models such as the Ford F-Series and Chevrolet C/K models start at about 115 inches and range up to 156, with curb weights of 3600 pounds or more.

The Dodge Dakota and the Toyota T100 fall between these categories.

- **Advantages:** Pickup trucks are immensely popular as "second cars" and in some cases as substitutes for cars. As with sport-utility vehicles, pickups fit today's recreation-oriented buyer, can carry and tow more than many cars, offer a feeling of security for some drivers, and have a rugged appeal.

- **Disadvantages:** While vans and 4WD vehicles are usually treated as cars under state and local laws, pickups are almost always considered trucks. For instance, many states and localities restrict trucks to the right-hand lanes or to separate sections of expressways. Some boulevards and urban roads are off limits to trucks entirely. Also, trucks carry higher license fees in some states. To avoid the higher fees and highway-use restrictions, owners in some states must purchase an aftermarket camper top to classify their pickup as a "recreational vehicle."

In general, all light trucks—pickups, vans, and 4WD vehicles—have ride, handling, and braking characteristics that are different from most cars. Most pickup trucks are driven with an empty bed the majority of the time. This puts nearly all of the truck's weight over the front axle. That means that in acceleration or braking, the lightly loaded rear end is prone to axle hop, which reduces traction. It also means the tail will easily slide sideways in turns on wet pavement.

Under the best of conditions, pickup trucks generally don't ride as comfortably as cars, and fuel mileage is substantially lower. True, some pickup cabins are quite plush, but even the most luxurious pickup was designed foremost to haul heavy loads or to negotiate off-road terrain, not to coddle its occupants.

One note: The EPA figures in our specifications tables list the *maximum* mpg rating for each engine. This is usually achieved in the lightest-weight model and with 2WD. For example, Ford's 2WD F-150 pickup with the 5.0-liter V-8 and 4-speed automatic is EPA rated at 15 mpg city/20 highway. But this powertrain is also available in the heavier F-250 model, where it's rated at 13/18.

HOW TRUCKS MEASURE UP

Exterior Dimensions

Dimensions may differ according to the equipment on a specific model.

The dimensions we list are supplied by the manufacturers and are for the base version of each body style. They generally hold true for all variants of that body style. However, there are cases where they will be slightly different. For example, most 4WD models will have a higher overall height than their 2WD counterparts, mainly because of the extra ground clearance added to 4x4s. Optional step bumpers can add to overall length, fender flares to overall width.

Space limitations prevent us from listing all variations of every model. If dimensions are vital to your buying decision, check the detailed brochures published by the manufacturer.

Curb Weight

This is the weight of the vehicle as ready for the road, including fuel, but without occupants or cargo.

We list curb weights for base models without optional equipment and generally equipped with 2WD. However, in cases where 4WD accounts for the vast majority of sales, such as with a compact sport-utility vehicle, the curb weight of the 4x4 version is given.

Four-wheel drive can add between 100 and 500 pounds to curb weight. Options such as a larger engine, automatic transmission, and additional seats also will increase a vehicle's curb weight. These distinctions are important when figuring how much a vehicle can safely haul. (See "Payload Capacity" and "Trailer-Towing Capacity.")

Gross Vehicle Weight Rating

This is the sum of the vehicle's curb weight and the weight it can carry in passengers and cargo.

Our reports sometimes discuss the gross vehicle weight rating (GVWR), but we do not include it in our specifications since we list curb weights and payloads separately.

GVWRs often are expressed as a general weight class, such as "over 8500 pounds GVWR." On some trucks, certain engines, transmissions, and suspension components are available only on vehicles in specific GVWR classes. Some manufacturers also specify a Combined Gross Vehicle Weight Rating, which includes the weight of a trailer.

CONSUMER GUIDE®

Introduction

Payload Capacity

This is how much weight a vehicle can carry, including passengers, cargo, fluids, and certain equipment—but not trailers.

We list the *maximum* payload for each body style. Adding equipment or occupants subtracts from the payload an amount equal to the weight of the equipment or occupants. For instance, if you squeeze three 200-pound men into the cab of a small pickup truck with a 1200-pound payload, then you have effectively reduced your payload capacity—or its ability to carry additional weight—to a net 600 pounds. Sometimes a model with a smaller engine will have a higher payload rating than the same model with a larger, more powerful engine simply because the bigger engine weighs more and uses up more payload capacity.

Some notes: Payload figures are provided by the manufacturers. Our charts usually list the payload of a cargo model when one is offered. This figure is typically higher than it is for the passenger counterpart. Also, you may have to order a special payload package or certain tires and suspension options to obtain the maximum payload.

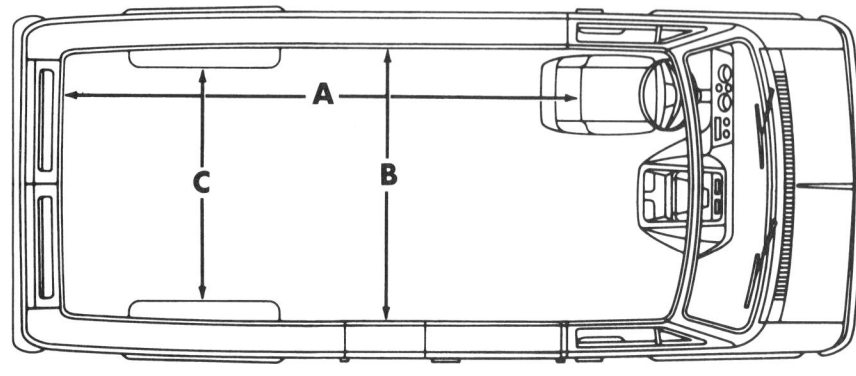

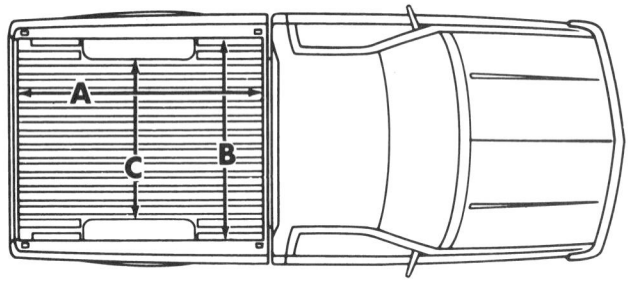

These illustrations show how we measure the dimensions of a cargo area.
A: *Length of the cargo bed at the floor. Note that on vans, the length is measured from the base of the front seat rearward.*
B: *Maximum width of the cargo bed at the floor of the bed.*
C: *Width between the wheel housings of the cargo bed, at the floor.*

Cargo Area Dimensions

These are measured differently for vans and pickup trucks.

The dimensions we list are supplied by the manufacturers. Note that charts for vans and sport-utility wagons also list the cargo volume in cubic feet.

Here's how we measure the cargo hold:

- **Length:** In pickup trucks, it's the length of the cargo-bed floor with the tailgate closed. In sport-utilities, it's the length of the cargo area with the rear seat or seats folded or removed when possible. In vans, it is the length of the cargo floor from the base of the front seat or seats to the rear doors. Since seatbacks slant rearward, the length of a van's cargo hold may be slightly less if you measure from above the floor.

- **Width:** the maximum width at the floor. Interior walls of vans are concave, so width may increase by a few inches at the beltline.

- **Width between the wheels:** maximum width, at the floor, between the wheel housings. This shows the minimum space for laying cargo flat on the floor.

- **Height:** Most manufacturers list the vertical opening of the tailgate as cargo-area height. Once inside, however, the height may be several inches greater.

- **Cubic feet:** The maximum cargo volume of enclosed vehicles. For vans, it's usually for the cargo model, when one is available, and is calculated with only the front seats in place. For vehicles with seats that can't be removed, we list the volume with all folding seats folded away for maximum cargo volume. To carry this much cargo, there probably is room only for a driver and front passenger.

Trailer-Towing Capacity

We list maximum trailer-towing weights, which frequently require an optional towing package or other optional equipment to accomplish.

Towing packages typically include specific powertrains, chassis reinforcements, and hitches. And often, the manufacturers calculate towing limits based on trailers that have their own brakes. Models without towing packages or those pulling unbraked trailers often have lower maximum towing capacity.

As with payload, the amount a vehicle can tow is reduced by the weight of passengers, cargo, and optional equipment. Check your owner's manual for towing restrictions. Most manufacturers publish towing guides that give detailed information about specific equipment needed to safely pull trailers.

4-WHEEL DRIVE SYSTEMS

Four-wheel-drive systems improve traction by supplying power to all four wheels of a vehicle. They accomplish this through a variety of technologies.

Here's how we describe the various systems and their associated components:

On-demand 4WD: The simplest and most widely used system. It allows 4WD to be engaged when it's needed. When 4WD is not needed, the vehicle goes about its business in 2-wheel drive, which means rear-wheel drive since there are no front-wheel-drive vehicles with on-demand 4WD.

With an on-demand system, the driver engages 4WD by shifting a floor-mounted transfer-case lever (see below) or by activating a switch on the dashboard or transmission shift lever.

"Shift-on-the-fly" on-demand systems allow 4WD to be engaged while the vehicle is moving. Others require that the vehicle be stopped to change between 2WD and 4WD. There are two kinds of on-demand 4WD: part-time and full-time.

Part-time 4WD: The vehicle normally operates in 2WD and will shift to 4WD when a transfer case is engaged to send the engine's power to the other two wheels. It's called part-time because it is designed to be used only in slippery conditions—snow, mud, loose gravel—not on dry pavement.

Using a part-time system on smooth, dry pavement can result in damage to the tires and the drive system. Here's why: On a vehicle that normally operates in rear drive, there is a rear differential that allows the rear wheels to rotate at different speeds in turns (when the outside wheel travels a greater distance than the inside wheel). With a part-time 4WD system, there is hardware that drives the front wheels, but no differential action. Thus, when powered, the front tires are not able to rotate at different speeds in turns. Using 4WD on dry pavement results in tire scrubbing and excessive wear on the front driving components. Since this system cannot be left permanently engaged, it often is referred to as an "on-demand, part-time" system.

Full-time 4WD: has front differential action that allows 4WD to be used on smooth, dry pavement without damaging the tires or drive system. Why use 4WD on dry, paved roads? Convenience is the main reason. If you intermittently go from paved roads to muddy, unpaved surfaces—or between plowed and snow-covered patches of roadway—then you won't have to shift in and out of 4WD to match the surface. Also, if you forget to disengage 4WD once you're on dry pavement, you won't damage the drive system.

Some sources use the term "full-time 4WD" to describe a permanently engaged 4WD system. We treat "Permanently engaged 4WD" as separate system (see below).

Shift-on-the-fly: allows 4WD to be engaged and disengaged while the vehicle is moving. The most versatile systems allow shifting between 2WD and 4WD High up to 55 mph or so.

Other systems may allow you to shift into 4WD up to certain speeds, such as 25 mph, but then require that you stop the vehicle to disengage 4WD. Still others may also require that you reverse directions for a short distance to fully disengage 4WD. A few systems have no shift-on-the-fly capability; you have to stop the vehicle to engage or disengage 4WD.

Shift-on-the-fly applies only to changing in or out of 4WD High, which usually can be used up to about 55 mph. Shifting in or out of 4WD Low, which is designed to operate at lower speeds, always requires that the vehicle be stopped.

Permanently engaged 4WD: All four wheels are constantly being powered without any special action by the driver. This works two ways: Power is either split between the front and rear wheels at a constant ratio, say 50-50, or there is a mechanical or electrical coupling that apportions power between front and rear for best traction.

This latter arrangement is the more sophisticated since it can vary distribution of the engine's power depending on traction conditions.

Transfer cases: Most on-demand 4WD systems have a transfer case that must be engaged to transmit engine power to the front wheels. The case is located beneath the floorboards and contains gears that are usually idle in 2WD. It typically is engaged by shifting a floor-mounted lever. Some vehicles have a button or switch to electrically engage the transfer case.

Transfer cases have two speeds. One speed is 4WD High, which allows running in 4WD at normal road speeds. The other is 4WD Low, which has lower gearing for maximum traction in severe conditions and often has a much lower speed limit, typically 25 mph or less.

Manual locking front hubs: When vehicles with on-demand 4WD are operated in 2WD, the front wheels are disconnected from the drive axles. For power to be delivered to the front wheels and achieve 4WD, the front drive axles must be engaged, or locked to the hubs.

Manual locking front hubs require that this be done by hand from outside the vehicle—an inconvenience in foul weather or when changing frequently from 2WD to 4WD. On most vehicles, once the manual hubs are locked, the 4WD system then has shift-on-the-fly capability, though the hubs still have to be unlocked by hand to return to 2WD operation. Some serious off-road enthusiasts prefer manual locking front hubs because they can confirm firsthand whether the hubs are free or locked without trusting the automatic system.

Automatic locking front hubs: This locks the front wheels to the drive axles automatically when the driver shifts into 4WD. Automatic front hubs also unlock when the driver disengages 4WD, allowing the front wheels to rotate freely again. Even with automatic locking front hubs, some vehicles must be stopped to lock the front hubs or engage 4WD, and then stopped and reversed to unlock them and disengage 4WD. Thus, auto locking hubs do not insure shift-on-the-fly 4WD.

Introduction

Is 4WD for You?

If you use 4WD only occasionally, you won't get your money's worth.

No less a 4WD mainstay than Jeep has found that only 5 percent of its vehicles ever get off road. Why then do so many people who seldom go off road buy 4WD vehicles?

Part of the answer is that 4WD vehicles appeal to buyers for reasons that have nothing to do with venturing from the pavement. Flashy 4x4 pickups with their big tires and extra ground clearance are the essence of macho to some. Sporty small convertibles, such as the Suzuki Sidekick, are just downright "cute" to another category of shopper. Still other drivers take comfort in the notion that in their 4WD vehicle they could escape to the wilderness if they really wanted to. And finally, more and more buyers recognize that 4WD gives them added control in poor weather.

But a 4WD vehicle is more expensive to purchase than a comparable 2WD vehicle. The difference may be less than $1000, or more than $3000. A 4WD vehicle also costs more to operate: There's more mechanical equipment to service and repair; and the extra weight of 4WD and the higher ride height of most 4x4s combine to reduce gas mileage and put a greater strain on the engine and tires, which probably won't last as long as in a lighter 2WD model.

Another penalty is on-road performance and comfort. Adding weight is the same as taking off horsepower, which results in slower acceleration. And the stiffer suspension needed to stand up to the rigors of off-road duty or to support the extra 4WD hardware results in diminished ride quality.

We're not trying to talk you out of 4WD. On the contrary, we think 4WD makes a vehicle easier and safer to drive in bad road conditions. Just think seriously about what you're paying for, and whether you'll get your money's worth.

LIGHT TRUCKS AND SAFETY

How safe any vehicle is depends in large measure on how it is driven and on whether its occupants use safety belts. But different types of trucks do have some inherent safety differences.

Many truck owners feel safer in a truck than in a car. They argue that trucks and vans weigh more than most cars, and weight provides more protection in a collision. Plus, you sit higher in a truck or a van, so you can see trouble coming better than in a car. And it is simply a secure feeling to peer down on surrounding traffic.

But what do studies of real-world crashes show? According to the National Highway Traffic Safety Administration (NHTSA), trucks as a class are no more dangerous than cars; the fatality rate for both automobiles and trucks is about 180 per million on the road.

Mirroring these findings are the number of crash-related personal-injury insurance claims made by truck occupants. The Highway Loss Data Institute, an insurance-industry trade group, says that as a group, occupants of light trucks—vans, pickups, and 4WD utility vehicles—actually have fewer personal-injury claims than do occupants of cars.

Not all the news about truck safety is good, however. Your chances of dying or being injured in a small pickup truck or small sport-utility are higher than in most any other vehicle on the road. Trucks, we'll see, pose some safety problems that cars don't.

Safety Variables

Size and weight play a role in survivability, but the way a vehicle is built and driven are vitally important, too.

Statistics support the notion that larger and heavier vehicles indeed have the lowest injury and fatality rates. NHTSA's most recent figures cover the 123 million cars and 45 million trucks and vans on the road in 1991.

The lightest vehicles—small cars and small pickup trucks—generally had the highest fatality rates compared to all vehicles. This follows a basic law of physics, in which heavier objects, with their mass and momentum, fare better than lighter ones in collisions.

But weight isn't everything. The way a truck is built gives it some advantages in a crash. For example, the lowest edge of a truck or van body—usually where it is joined to the frame—is one of the truck's most important safety features. When a striking vehicle—most often a passenger car—hits a truck from the side, it first hits this "sill" of the truck. The sill acts as a side-door beam to block intrusion into the truck's passenger area.

Sure enough, side crashes are where trucks hold their most significant safety edge over cars. The fatality rate for truck occupants involved in side collisions in 1991 was less than half the rate for car occupants (see chart).

The weight and ride-height of trucks and vans also works to their advantage in frontal collisions. Trucks often ride up and over smaller vehicles in frontal collisions. The same is true of vans, even though front-seat occupants in vans seldom have much impact-absorbing mass in front of them. Again, fatality rates for frontal collisions were lower for trucks than cars (see chart).

The effects of ride height and weight are further emphasized when you look at fatalities by types of trucks. Small pickup trucks—the lightest and lowest riding of all trucks—had the highest frontal-crash death rates of all trucks: 77.7 deaths for every one million of them on the road.

Vulnerable Trucks

Not everything about the way a truck is built makes it safer than a car.

CONSUMER GUIDE®

Introduction

No class of car or truck suffers a higher rate of fatal accidents or personal-injury claims than do small pickups. NHTSA figures show the overall death rate for small pickups in 1991 was 226 per million vehicles. That's 18 percent higher than the average for all trucks and vans, and 21 percent higher than the average for all cars. And personal injury claims are traditionally higher for small pickups than any other type of vehicle—aside from mini sport utilities, which we'll focus on in a moment.

A key reason for these high death and injury rates is that while small pickups are engineered as cargo-transport vehicles, the majority are instead driven unloaded, in place of cars as daily transportation. This results in several problems. Unladen, a small pickup's cargo bed is extremely light, increasing chances that the rear brakes will lock prematurely. And without a load to compress the suspension, stability is compromised because the center of gravity is higher than is optimal.

Small pickups seldom enjoy the height advantage typical of other trucks, and so their occupants face increased risk in frontal and side collisions, similar to that in small cars.

Making matters worse, is that no small pickup has a driver-side air bag (though the mid-size Dodge Dakota gets one for 1994). Finally, small pickups are often low-cost, entry-level vehicles, and their younger buyers are in the demographic group most at risk on the road.

Risk of Rollovers

By far the deadliest risk facing trucks is an accident in which the vehicle rolls over.

NHTSA puts a traffic death in the "rollover fatality" category when a rollover is the first and most significant cause of the death. Rollovers are directly related to a vehicle's stability in turns. This stability is influenced by the relationship between the vehicle's center of gravity and its track, or width between wheels on the same axle. A high center of gravity and a narrow track can make a vehicle unstable in turns or sharp changes of direction and increase the chances it will tip over once it begins to skid sideways.

The problem is most pronounced in pickup trucks and especially in sport-utility vehicles. Sport-utilities need extra ground clearance to maneuver off-road. And their narrow track helps them slip through backwoods obstacles. But on dry pavement—where the majority of 4WD vehicles spend most of their time—their off-road advantages become disadvantages.

Fatality rates tell the tale. NHTSA figures show the largest single cause of fatal truck crashes is rollovers, with a death rate of 86.9 per million light trucks on the road. That's twice the rollover death rate of automobiles.

Other factors besides height and track are at work in rollover crashes, however, not the least of which is how a vehicle typically is driven. Large and medium-sized cars share with vans a rather conservative owner population of families and older drivers. And they see much suburban and rural use. By contrast, small cars, small pickups, and 4WD vehicles are frequently purchased by younger, less-experienced drivers and often are driven in riskier ways. Once again, NHTSA's study of real-world crashes illustrates the point.

Medium- and full-size cars had the lowest rollover fatality rates. Among trucks, standard-size vans were the least risky, followed by compact vans.

The rollover death count grows frighteningly high for trucks with both a high center of gravity and with a particular attraction for younger buyers. The rollover fatality rate for standard-size pickups was 92.8 per one million vehicles. It was 102.5 per million for small pickups. And 113 per million for all 4WD utility vehicles.

Charges that vehicles such as the Suzuki Samurai, Jeep CJ, and Ford Bronco II tip too easily grabbed headlines over the past few years. NHTSA found that these vehicles behave no differently from most other 4x4s and said the real issue is that rollovers are a problem common to all 4WD vehicles—and not just because of their typically high center of gravity and narrow track, but because of the way they are driven.

Most fatal 4WD rollovers are single-vehicle accidents occurring on weekend nights, NHTSA says. The drivers are most frequently males under 25 years of age. Alcohol is usually involved. And in two of every three fatal rollover crashes, the person killed was ejected from the vehicle—indicating the victim probably was not wearing a seat belt.

WHICH VEHICLES ARE MOST DANGEROUS?

These charts show the fatality rate per one million registered vehicles by type of vehicle and by type of collision. The figures are for the 1991 calendar year and were compiled by the National Highway Traffic Safety Administration, the federal body that establishes automotive safety standards.

Fatalities per one million light trucks

	Small vans	Standard vans	Small pickup trucks	Standard pickup trucks	4WD vehicles	All light trucks
Frontal impact	44.5	36.7	79.1	77.7	47.7	64.3
Side impact	17.3	11.6	36.4	28.6	19.3	25.7
Rear impact	4.2	3.0	2.4	3.1	2.4	2.9
Rollover	46.2	40.6	102.5	92.8	113.0	86.9

Fatalities per one million automobiles

	Small cars	Medium cars	Large cars	All cars
Frontal impact	82.6	73.7	51.6	74.6
Side impact	61.0	53.0	30.3	53.3
Rear impact	5.9	4.5	3.2	5.0
Rollover	50.7	40.9	21.4	42.9

Introduction

Making Trucks Safer

The government is moving to make safety regulations for trucks similar to those for cars.

Here is a rundown of some significant safety items and how regulations regarding them may differ between cars and trucks:

- **Front-seat passive restraints.** For the 1995 model year, 20 percent of a manufacturer's light trucks must have passive restraints for both front-seat positions. The requirement rises to 50 percent of trucks for 1996 and 90 percent for 1997.

  These restraints can take the form of two automatic front seat belts or dual air bags. However, to encourage the installation of driver-side air bags, a manufacturer that installs just a driver-side air bag may use a manual passenger-side safety belt.

  For model-year 1998, 80 percent of a manufacturer's light trucks must have a driver-side air bag, and for the 1999 model year, all light trucks must have dual air bags and manual front safety belts.

  Regulations for passenger cars require that all have passive restraints for the two outboard front passenger seats—either air bags, automatic safety belts, or a combination. For the 1998 model year, all cars must have dual air bags.

  Even though the air-bag requirement for trucks is being phased in over several years, several manufacturers have already responded to the demand for this important safety feature.

  Minivans from Chrysler Corporation, Ford, and Toyota now have dual front air bags, and most other minivans have driver-side air bags. Driver-side air bags also can be found in Ford and General Motors full-size vans, in Ford and Toyota full-size pickups, and in full-size and compact-size pickups from Dodge, and in the Jeep Grand Cherokee, Mitsubishi Montero, and Ford Bronco sport-utility vehicles.

  Passive restraints are particularly important in trucks, because relatively few truck occupants use manual seat belts. Nationally, about 62 percent of automobile front-seat occupants wear seat belts; the figure for trucks is about 50 percent. NHTSA says full seat-belt usage would save the lives of an additional 2000 truck occupants annually; dual air bags would increase that savings to 2400 lives.

- **Center high-mounted stoplamp.** This feature is required for the 1994 model year on all light trucks below 10,000 pounds gross vehicle weight, which includes virtually all minivans and sport-utilities, and most pickups and full-size vans. Cars already are required to have this light.

  NHTSA says its studies show that the accidents prevented by the lamps are low-speed collisions. It says their presence on trucks probably will save no lives, but that it will eliminate 60,000 to 90,000 rear-end crashes annually, saving $100 million to $140 million in property damage and preventing 19,000 to 27,000 injuries per year.

- **Side door guard beams.** These are reinforced members inside the door designed to limit intrusion into the passenger compartment during a collision.

  They are required on automobiles and are required on 90 percent of light trucks for model-year 1994 and on 100 percent for 1995. The regulation mandates beams on all doors within 12 inches of a seating position. This requires them on the sliding side doors of minivans, though not all full-size vans are covered.

  NHTSA says truck fatalities in side crashes are relatively rare, but that the beams will prevent an estimated 60 to 85 deaths and 1500 serious injuries annually.

- **Roof-crush standard.** Car roofs must be capable of supporting 1.5 times the vehicle weight, up to 5000 pounds. Beginning with the 1995 model year, truck roofs must also be capable of supporting 1.5 times the unloaded vehicle weight. The truck standard will not apply to "convertibles," such as the Geo Tracker.

  NHTSA says the roof-crush standard for trucks probably will not result in the saving of any lives. The agency says most trucks and vans already satisfy the roof-crush regulations.

- **Rear lap/shoulder belts.** As with all automobiles, all light trucks, vans, utility vehicles, and small buses must have rear lap/shoulder belts. The regulation for passenger vans applies to all passenger seats 12 inches or less from an outside wall. This effectively waives the requirement for aisle seats, usually the right-side of the middle seat on passenger vans.

- **Front-seat head restraints.** The outboard front seats of trucks are required to have head restraints—the same requirement applied to passenger cars.

  Though many manufacturers install head restraints on the rear seats of both cars and trucks, there is no federal regulation requiring them to do so. In fact, NHTSA maintains that there is a tradeoff between the potential whiplash injuries prevented by rear-seat head restraints and the negative effect the restraints have on rearward visibility.

- **Rollover standards.** NHTSA is studying standards that would apply to both cars and light trucks and would address the vehicle's basic stability in terms of height, track, and other important variables. Most vehicles that roll over first skid out of control and then strike a curb or a ditch, NHTSA says. Anti-lock brakes help prevent some skids, so one possibility is that NHTSA may eventually require that anti-lock brakes be made standard.

  NHTSA also notes that two-thirds of the deaths in rollover accidents occur when the occupant is ejected. So another area of study involves a requirement that vehicle glass be better able to contain occupants during a rollover.

  The government requires that all sport-utility vehicles carry warnings inside the cabin and in the owner's manual warning that these vehicles handle and maneuver differently from passenger cars both on road and off. Sudden sharp turns or abrupt maneuvers may cause the vehicle to go out of control and rollover or crash, they warn. On soft-top sport-utilities, it also is noted that the roof and doors are designed only for protection against the elements and not to rely on them to contain occupants within the vehicle or to protect against injury during an accident.

  Finally, NHTSA says that the risk of injury or death in any kind of motor-vehicle accident can be reduced nearly by half if drivers and passengers of all vehicles simply wore their safety belts.

Introduction
SHOPPING FOR A NEW TRUCK

Research which vehicles best suit your needs and visit several dealerships to test drive your choices before deciding.

Take the process in steps.

• Determine what you can afford. Since most people have to borrow money to buy a new vehicle, shop for a loan before you shop for a truck. Have your eyes on a $25,000 extended-length leather-upholstered minivan? A 20-minute session with a loan officer at your bank may convince you that what you can afford is a regular-length $15,000 base model. Better to find this out at the bank than in a dealer's showroom, where they can juggle numbers faster than you can count.
• Arm yourself with information about the new truck you want and how much it costs. You'll be less likely to get ripped off than one who buys before doing sufficient research.
• Estimate the value of your old car or truck by checking with your bank's loan department, consulting used-car price guides in libraries, and checking prices in used-car or truck advertisements. You're likely to get the most money by selling your old car or truck yourself. But is the difference worth the hassle of temporarily becoming a used-car dealer?
• Test drive the vehicle with the equipment you think you want. Crave a 5-speed manual transmission and the off-road suspension? A 15-minute test drive might convince you to go with automatic transmission and a softer suspension.
• Size up supply and demand. A good deal on a slow-selling model might be below dealer invoice. A good deal on a hot-seller might be full suggested retail price.
• Price is important, but it shouldn't be your only consideration. A dealer on the other side of town may sell you a minivan for $200 less than the dealer down the street, but may not give you the best service in the long run. Ask friends and relatives and call the Better Business Bureau for information on dealers in your area.

Dealing with Dealers

Once you've settled on a truck, shop at least two dealers—more if you can—to compare prices.

• Make dealers bid for your business through lower prices. Let them know you'll go elsewhere to get a lower price or better service.
• There are no formulas for calculating a "good deal." You can't just "knock 10 percent off the sticker." It all depends on the market conditions for that model in your area and how much competition there is among dealers. Again, the only way you'll know whether you're getting a good deal is to shop for prices on the same model with the same equipment at two or more dealers and make them compete for your business.
• Have the dealer quote you a price; don't make the dealer an offer. If he accepts, your offer was probably too high. Even if you argue him down to your figure, how do you know he wouldn't have gone lower? Neither should you tell Dealer A how much Dealer B quoted you on the vehicle you want. A better strategy is to keep price quotes to yourself—and tell all the dealers that the one who gives you the lowest price and the best treatment gets your business.
• Shop elsewhere if a dealer won't give you a written price that's good next week and the week after. Take your time and think about it at home. Don't be pressured into making a snap decision in the showroom.
• Don't put a deposit on a vehicle just to get a price quote or a test drive. Deposits constitute a commitment and you're less likely to keep shopping. Go to another dealer instead.
• Take the "bottom line" approach. Rather than arguing over individual charges or options prices, ask for a final price showing how much you're going to pay for the truck you want. That's what really counts, the amount on the bottom line of the sales contract. Compare that figure to what other dealers are charging for the same truck and you'll know who's giving you the best deal.
• Keep your trade-in out of the new-truck price. If you're thinking about trading in your old vehicle, get a written trade-in value after you settle on a price for the new one. Some dealers try to lure you with the offer of a high trade-in allowance and then inflate the price of the new vehicle.
• Have loan quotes from a bank or other lender in hand when you go shopping. When a dealer offers to finance your purchase, you'll have something to compare it with. If the first interest rate isn't lower than your bank's, ask the dealer if he can do better.

Price Labeling

Price stickers hold a wealth of valuable information. However, a pickup truck doesn't have to have one.

Manufacturers are required by law to affix a price sticker called a Monroney label to every new car, passenger van, and sport-utility vehicle. They must include:
• The manufacturer's suggested retail price for the vehicle and all its factory-installed options.
• A destination charge for shipping from final assembly point (or port of importation) to the dealer.
• Environmental Protection Agency fuel economy estimates.

Pickup trucks escape the requirement because the law still treats them as commercial vehicles. Some automakers do paste Monroney-type stickers on their pickup trucks, but there's no law stipulating that the information be complete. Still, there are a variety of sources through which shoppers can establish a benchmark price for a specific truck. They include this book, computer buying services, and advertisements.

The Second Sticker

Many dealers add a second sticker. Beware!

Dealers make enormous profits on dealer-installed options such as rust-

Introduction

LEASE OR BUY?

Talk to an accountant or financial adviser—not the guy next door—about whether leasing is right for you. Leasing may be a great deal for your next-door neighbor but of no real benefit to you. Here's an overview of leasing's ins and outs.

• A big advantage of leasing is that a large down payment isn't needed, though some leases require a substantial initial payment, sometimes called "capital cost reduction." Also, monthly lease payments are generally lower than the monthly loan payment for an equivalent truck or van.

• The major disadvantage to leasing is that unless you eventually buy a truck and complete the payments on it, you'll always be making a monthly payment. At the end of a lease you have the option of giving the vehicle back to the leasing company or buying it. Either way, you're going to have to dig into your pocket again to keep a vehicle in your driveway.

• Monthly payments may be lower on a lease, but it is usually cheaper in the long run to buy if you keep a vehicle five years or longer. For example, if you pay off a truck loan in four years and keep the truck another three years, your only expenses once the truck is paid for will be for maintenance and repairs.

• On the other hand, would you rather drive a 7-year-old truck or a much newer one? A 2- or 3-year lease gives you the option of having a new truck more often. The truck you drive will always be under warranty and you don't have the hassle of selling or trading in an old car. After two or three years, you simply turn it in to the leasing agent.

• The major automakers have national lease programs through their dealers. You'll pay the same for that "No money down, $249 a month" lease whether you're in Philadelphia or Portland. But there will be little room if any for negotiation on the monthly payment or other costs.

Questions to Ask

• Most leases allow 15,000 miles a year, with a penalty of 10 to 15 cents a mile over that. Is a lower penalty negotiable?

• Most states require the lessee—that's you—to pay sales tax on the full suggested retail price of the vehicle. Do you have the option of rolling the sales tax into your monthly payment?

• Can you terminate the lease early? How much of a penalty must you pay to do so? It might cost thousands to get out of a lease.

• At the end of the lease, are you liable for "excessive wear" and must you pay to have the truck prepped for resale? It pays to take good care of a leased vehicle.

• If you move to another state, where do you turn the truck in at the end of the lease? If you lease from a franchised new-car dealer, verify whether you can turn the truck into any dealer that sells that brand.

• Independent leasing agents can't get trucks for less than a dealer, yet some advertise lower monthly payments than the manufacturer or dealer. Are they advertising the payment on a truck without air conditioning, automatic transmission, or another feature you might want?

---

proofing, "protection packages," and extended service contracts. The situation is compounded by dealers who routinely put these items on new vehicles, denying shoppers a choice and forcing customers to bargain down from a sticker price that already includes these grossly inflated charges. Challenge everything you see on a dealer's window sticker—before you sign the contract. The dealer won't take them off? Don't sign the contract. Here are some typical items included on second stickers:

• **Rustproofing:** Manufacturers provided enough high-tech factory rustproofing to back their products with a multiyear, multi-thousand-mile corrosion warranty. Additional dealer-installed or aftermarket rustproofing may not only void this warranty, but may actually reduce a truck's corrosion protection.

• **Protection packages:** These usually consist of dealer-applied paint sealers and fabric protectors. They duplicate substances applied at the factory or those you can apply yourself for a fraction of this cost.

• **Dealer prep charge:** Domestic manufacturers include this expense in the price of the truck; some imports—but not all—also include prep in the price. Don't pay it twice.

• **Documentary fees:** Title, tax, and license-transfer charges are legitimate, but other "documentary" or "computer" fees should not be borne by the consumer. Some states limit how much the dealer can charge for title, tax, and license. Check with local consumer protection agencies before paying any of them.

Advertising Fees

Challenge any extra fee for "advertising."

Many manufacturers do charge dealers a per-vehicle advertising fee. And dealers do share costs of regional advertising—though not every dealer participates. In either case, ad fees usually are a percentage of the invoice price: typically 1 to 1.5 percent for domestic models, others as high as 3 percent.

In most cases, the ad fee has been incorporated into the invoice price—the amount the dealer has paid for the truck. So it's already taken into account when the dealer determines the lowest selling price he'll accept.

But you really have no way of knowing whether an ad fee has in fact been levied on the vehicle you're considering. Nor can you be certain a posted "advertising fee" accurately reflects the amount paid into the fund.

The bottom line is that all businesses factor in advertising costs when setting a retail price. Why should you pay it as a separate additional charge?

Before You Sign

Understand the contract before you sign. Rushing to complete a deal is inviting the dealer to take advantage of you.

Before you sign, read the entire contract. Be certain you understand exactly what you're buying. The dealership isn't the best place to do this. The salesperson will likely pressure you to sign and lock in the terms of your purchase. Worse, you may be in a hurry because you're eager to drive off in your new truck or van. Once you sign, you're legally bound to the contract terms.

Take the contract home. Go over it at your own pace, and don't be afraid to call the dealer with questions. If a dealer doesn't want you to take the contract home, get a written purchase agreement that spells out all the details. Once you're satisfied it can be written into a contract.

Here's what a contract should spell out:

Introduction

- **Sale price:** The amount you've agreed to pay for the vehicle and optional equipment, plus any dealer-installed accessories.

- **Down payment:** How much you have to pay immediately, either in cash or with your trade-in.

- **Trade-in value:** The amount you're getting for your old car.

- **Destination charge:** The cost of shipping the vehicle to the dealer. Dealers get no discount; they pay the amount listed on the window sticker. Don't pay this charge twice; some dealers hide the destination charge in the sale price and then add it again as a separate item, pocketing the money.

- **Sales tax:** Check your state or local governments to determine how tax is assessed in your area. Most states levy sales tax on the full purchase price of the new vehicle. In some states, it's calculated on the net price after trade-in value has been deducted.

- **Loans:** Lenders must by law disclose all charges. Be sure you know how much you're actually borrowing, the interest rate, your monthly payment, the length of the loan, and the total amount you will pay over the course of the loan.

- **Total cost:** Be certain the "bottom line" is filled in, so you know your total price including options, accessories, destination charge, dealer prep, and taxes.

Rebates and Incentives

Incentives can save you money, but there may be "catches."

Customer-direct cash rebates are usually well advertised and take the form of a check made out from the automaker to the buyer. You'll usually have a choice between the cash rebate or a manufacturer-arranged cut-rate loan, typically from 2.9 percent to 4.9 percent annual percentage rate. Some calculation is necessary to determine whether the cash or the loan is best for you. In some states, if you sign a rebate over to the dealer as a down payment, you may not have to pay sales tax on that amount.

Dealer incentives are trickier. It may be difficult to find out if a manufacturer is offering dealers cash to sell certain models. And since these incentives often are keyed to the number of vehicles sold or to some quota, even the dealer doesn't always know how much the incentive will turn out to be. If you learn that a dealer incentive is in effect, try to negotiate the price of the vehicle down by that sum.

Our Price Lists

Every effort is made to see that the prices in this issue are accurate and the latest available.

Some price lists in this book contain only the vehicle's suggested retail price because the dealer invoice and fair price weren't available at the time of publication.

The invoice prices in this issue are what the dealer pays to buy the vehicle from the factory. Destination charges are the same on both the retail and invoice level.

The fair price listed for most trucks is an estimate of what you should expect to pay for a particular model based on national market conditions. The actual selling price for any vehicle depends on market conditions and supply and demand for that particular vehicle in your immediate area. So the fair price should be used only as a guide. You will have to determine the best price in your area by shopping for the same vehicle at two or more dealers.

Cash rebates and dealer incentives aren't included in the prices.

Automakers sometimes change their prices after we have gone to press. Also, dealers sometimes tell our readers that the prices we publish are incorrect.

If a dealer claims that our prices are incorrect or if the information in this issue doesn't match what you see in dealer showrooms, contact us and we'll do our best to help you out.

Consumer Guide®
7373 N. Cicero Ave.
Lincolnwood, IL 60646

WARRANTIES AND SERVICE CONTRACTS

A warranty is the manufacturer's pledge to absorb certain repair or replacement costs over a specific period.

Factory warranties are divided into specific areas of coverage.

- **Basic warranty:** Covers the entire truck, except for tires and battery, which are warranted by their manufacturers. Other important exclusions are: normal wear and maintenance items (oil, filters, brake linings); damage from the environment (hail, floods, other "acts of God"); damage due to improper maintenance (incorrect fuel or lubricants); and damage caused by the owner.

- **Extended warranty:** Coverage for a specific period beyond the basic warranty. Usually applies to the truck's powertrain, which consists of such major components as the engine, transmission, fuel system, drive shafts and related parts, and the transfer case on 4WD vehicles. Excluded are the same sorts of damage and maintenance items as under the basic warranty.

- **Corrosion:** Warranty protection against perforation rust, in which sheetmetal is eaten through. Typical exclusions include surface corrosion caused by hail, stone chips, and industrial pollution.

- **Transfers:** Most manufacturers allow factory warranties to be transferred from owner to owner at no

CONSUMER GUIDE®   13

Introduction

charge for as long as the warranty is in effect. Chrysler charges a $150 transfer fee on its domestically built trucks and minivans.

Service Contracts

Sure, you're eager to protect your investment, but proceed cautiously.

The automakers and other companies who write extra-cost service contracts or extended warranties expect to make a profit from them. They're betting they'll pay out less in repairs than you did to buy the contract. The odds are in their favor.

Extra-cost warranties and service contracts cover items not protected by factory warranties, or they provide longer coverage. Most of what they cover probably won't need repair or replacement during the duration of the contract. If you pay $500 to $1000 or more for a service contract, you'll need at least that amount in repairs to make it worthwhile.

All but the most expensive service contracts carry deductibles for each repair, usually $25 to $75 per visit. Some specify where you can get your truck repaired, limiting your choices and perhaps making repairs more costly or inconvenient. Extra-cost contracts issued by automakers may require that repairs be done at an authorized dealership, which could also be costly or inconvenient. And some service contracts require that you pay for repairs when they're made and then file for reimbursement, which can be a lengthy process. Finally, a host of aftermarket service-contract providers have recently gone out of business, complicating the process under which their clients can obtain repair payments.

Give any service contract careful scrutiny at home, not in the dealer's showroom. Get a copy of the contract, not just a brochure summarizing the coverage. Don't be in a hurry; you don't always have to buy a service contract at the time you buy your car. And you can back out of some of them for a small fee.

1994 Manufacturers' Warranties

MAKE/MODEL	BASIC WARRANTY (YRS/MILES)	EXTENDED WARRANTY (YRS/MILES)	CORROSION WARRANTY (YRS/MILES)	TRANSFERABLE?
Chevrolet	3/36,000	None	6/100,000	Yes, no cost
Chrysler	1/12,000	7/70,000 powertrain	7/100,000	Yes, $150
Chrysler (alternate)	3/36,000	None	7/100,000	Yes, $150
Dodge	1/12,000	7/70,000 powertrain	7/100,000	Yes, $150
Dodge (alternate)	3/36,000	None	7/100,000	Yes, $150
Eagle Summit, wagon	3/36,000	5/60,000 powertrain	7/100,000	Yes, no cost[1]
Ford	3/36,000	None	6/100,000	Yes, no cost
Geo	3/36,000	None	6/100,000	Yes, no cost
GMC	3/36,000	None	6/100,000	Yes, no cost
Honda	3/36,000	None	3/unltd.	Yes, no cost
Isuzu	3/50,000	5/60,000	6/100,000	Yes, no cost
Jeep	1/12,000	7/70,000 powertrain	7/100,000	Yes, $150
Jeep (alternate)	3/36,000	None	7/100,000	Yes, $150
Kia	3/36,000	5/60,000 powertrain	3/50,000	NA
Land Rover	3/42,000	None	6/unltd.	Yes,
Mazda	3/50,000	None	5/unltd.	Yes, no cost
Mercury	3/36,000	None	6/100,000	Yes, no cost
Mitsubishi	3/36,000	5/60,000 powertrain	7/100,000	Yes, no cost
Nissan	3/36,000	5/60,000 powertrain & major systems	5/unltd.	Yes, no cost
Oldsmobile	3/36,000	None	6/100,000	Yes, no cost
Plymouth	1/12,000	7/70,000 powertrain	7/100,000	Yes, $150
Plymouth (alternate)	3/36,000	None	7/100,000	Yes, $150
Plymouth Colt/Vista	3/36,000	5/60,000 powertrain	7/100,000	Yes, no cost[1]
Pontiac	3/36,000	None	6/100,000	Yes, no cost
Suzuki	3/36,000	None	3/unltd.	Yes, no cost
Toyota	3/36,000	5/60,000 powertrain	5/unltd.	Yes, no cost
Volkswagen	2/24,000	10/100,000	6/unltd.	Yes, no cost

1. *Chrysler Corp. imports, like domestic models, have choice of warranty shown or 1/12,000 basic and 7/70,000 powertrain coverage.*

Introduction

BEST BUYS AND RECOMMENDED

The Auto Editors of Consumer Guide® select Best Buys by comparing vehicles of comparable size, price, and market position. Road-test results, cost of ownership, warranty coverage, reputation for reliability and durability, and safety record are considered. Recommended choices also are worthy of attention.

COMPACT 4WD VEHICLES

BEST BUY

Jeep Grand Cherokee
The only sport-utility available with both a driver-side air bag and a V-8 engine.

RECOMMENDED

Ford Explorer
Roomy and still the best-selling sport-utility, but lacks a driver-side air bag.

Jeep Cherokee
Older companion to the Grand Cherokee still offers good value for the money.

FULL-SIZE 4WD VEHICLES

BEST BUY

Ford Bronco
For '94, becomes the first big 4x4 with a driver-side air bag. Anti-lock brakes are standard.

RECOMMENDED

Chevrolet Blazer
Turbodiesel engine is a new option and center high-mount stoplamp is standard for '94.

GMC Yukon
A twin of the Blazer, shares that model's new diesel engine and standard anti-lock brakes.

CONSUMER GUIDE® 15

Introduction

COMPACT PICKUP TRUCKS

BEST BUY

Dodge Dakota
Only pickup in this class with a driver-side air bag and the only one available with a V-8 engine.

RECOMMENDED

Ford Ranger
Top-selling compact pickup features the only flareside cargo box in the class.

Mazda B-Series
Madza uses a Ranger platform and running gear—but no flareside box—and adds own trim.

Chevrolet S10 Pickup
Redesigned for '94 with a roomier cab and much-improved dashboard layout.

GMC Sonoma
Like its Chevy S10 Pickup twin, redesigned for '94 and gains much refinement.

Introduction

FULL-SIZE VAN

BEST BUY

Ford Club Wagon/Econoline
Passenger models add 4-wheel anti-lock brakes. All but heavy-duty models have a driver-side air bag.

FULL-SIZE PICKUPS

BEST BUY

Ford F-Series
F-150 versions of America's top-selling vehicle gain a driver-side air bag.

RECOMMENDED

Chevrolet C/K Pickup
Turbocharged diesel V-8s are new options for General Motors' most-popular vehicle line.

GMC Sierra
Like the near-duplicate Chevy C/K, also gains side door guard beams and center stoplamp.

Dodge Ram Pickup
Redesigned with a driver-side air bag and optional V-10 engine. Stretched-cab not yet offered.

CONSUMER GUIDE®

Introduction

MINIVANS

BEST BUYS

Dodge Caravan
The top-selling minivan gains a passenger-side air bag and an optional 3.8-liter V-6.

Plymouth Voyager
As with its Caravan twin, now has dual air bags and meets all passenger-car safety standards.

RECOMMENDED

Nissan Quest
A driver-side air bag is new and anti-lock brakes are now standard on the GXE model.

Mercury Villager
Built from the same design as the Quest. Also gets a driver-side air bag, plus a new luxury model.

Chevrolet Lumina Minivan
Gets a new name, a shorter nose, driver-side air bag, and optional child safety seats.

Oldsmobile Silhouette
Shares its design with the Lumina and Trans Sport. Gets an air bag, but keeps the old nose.

Pontiac Trans Sport
As with the similar Olds and Chevy versions, a power sliding side door is newly optional.

Toyota Previa
Adds a passenger-side air bag to driver-side air bag and gains a supercharged engine option.

Chevrolet Astro

Chevrolet Astro CL Extended Length

A driver-side air bag, introduced as an option last spring, is standard for 1994 on all versions of these rear- and 4-wheel-drive minivans. The air bag also is standard this year on Astro's GMC-brand version, the Safari (see separate report).

Body Styles/Chassis

Both the passenger and cargo versions use a 111-inch wheelbase, but there are two body lengths, 176.8 inches and 186.8. The extended model's extra 10 inches are behind the rear wheels and add 18.6 cubic feet of storage space. Two of every three Astros sold are Extended models.

Passenger models, which account for about 65 percent of Astro sales, come in a single base price level tabbed CS, but decor groups labeled CL and LT are among available option packages. Cargo vans come in a single trim line. Cargo models come without side or rear windows, but options make possible a variety of glass arrangements.

All models have a sliding side door and dual swing-out rear doors. A "Dutch door" option features a one-piece glass liftgate with separately opening split panel doors below. The liftgate, which raises on gas struts, can be opened via an electronic release left of the steering column.

Four-wheel anti-lock brakes (ABS) are standard on all Astros.

In addition to the air bag, new safety features include side door guard beams in both front doors and the sliding side door, and a center high-mounted rear stoplamp in the roof. Also, all windows now have solar-control tinted glass.

Chevy lists the maximum cargo volume of Astro's cargo model at 181.5 cubic feet for the regular-length version and 200.1 cubic feet for the extended; capacity for passenger models with all rear seats removed is 151.8 and 170.4, respectively.

Maximum payload, 1922 pounds, is found on the 2WD extended-body model. The lowest payload rating, 1697 pounds, is on the 4WD regular-length Astro.

Powertrains

Standard with 2WD is a 4.3-liter V-6 rated at 165 horsepower. Optional on 2WD models and standard with 4WD is a 200-horsepower version of the 4.3.

A 4-speed overdrive automatic is the only transmission. It has electronic shift controls and a feature that allows it to start out in second gear for improved slippery-surface traction.

All-wheel-drive models of both body lengths account for about 15 percent of Astro sales. They feature a permanently engaged 4WD system instead of the standard rear-wheel drive. The 4WD system normally splits engine power 65-percent rear wheels/35-percent front. It automatically transfers more power to the axle with the best grip when there's wheel slip.

Specifications	4-door van	4-door van
Wheelbase, in.	111.0	111.0
Overall length, in.	176.8	186.8
Overall width, in.	77.5	77.5
Overall height, in.	76.2	76.2
Turn diameter, ft.	39.5	39.5
Curb weight, lbs.	3897	3987
Fuel capacity, gal.	27.0	27.0

Passenger Area Dimensions

Seating capacity	8	8
Front head room, in.	39.2	39.2
Rear head room, in.	37.9	37.9
Front leg room, in.	41.6	41.6
Rear leg room, in.	36.5	36.5

Available Seating

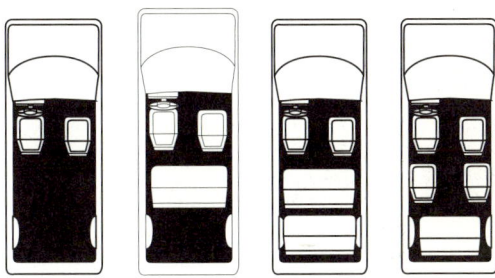

Cargo Dimensions and Payloads

Cargo area length, in.	88.9	98.9
Cargo area width, in.	57.0	57.0
Cargo area width between wheels, in.	51.6	51.6
Cargo area height, in.	51.4	51.4
Cargo vol., cu. ft.	181.5	200.1
Max. payload, lbs.	1720	1922
Max. trailer weight, lbs.	5500	5500

Engines	ohv V-6	ohv V-6
Size, liters/cu. in.	4.3/262	4.3/262
Horsepower @ rpm	165 @ 4000	200 @ 4400
Torque (lbs./ft.) @ rpm	235 @ 2000	260 @ 3600
Availability	S	O[1]

EPA city/highway mpg

4-speed OD automatic	16/21	15/20

1. Std. 4WD models.

Built in Baltimore, Md.

KEY: Dimensions and capacities are supplied by the manufacturers. **Curb Weight:** base models, not including optional equipment. **Max. payload, lbs.** = gross amount; net payload may be lower due to optional equipment. **Engines: ohv** = overhead valve; **ohc** = overhead cam; **I** = inline cylinders; **V** = cylinders in V configuration; **flat** = horizontally opposed cylinders; **rpm** = revolutions per minute; **OD** = overdrive transmission; **S** = standard; **O** = optional; **NA** = not available.

CONSUMER GUIDE®

Chevrolet

Any Astro model can tow a 2000-pound trailer. With the heavy-duty trailering package, 2WD Astros can tow up to 5500 pounds, 4WD models up to 5000 pounds.

Accommodations

Passenger models have standard seating for five—two front buckets and a removable 3-place bench seat; 7- and 8-passenger arrangements are optional. The middle and rear bench seats on passenger models have quick-release latches that allow them to be removed without hand tools.

Cargo models come with only a driver's seat; a front passenger seat is optional.

For 1994, the carpeting is treated with Scotchgard-brand fabric protection. There also are new graphics for the analog gauges, and air conditioners use CFC-free refrigerant.

Evaluation

Astro and Safari—along with the Ford Aerostar—have a truck-based chassis and full-frame design. This makes them better suited to heavy-duty work than front-drive minivans. For example, Astro's 5500-pound trailer-towing capacity is nearly double that of the front-drive Chevrolet Lumina Minivan.

The penalty for this brawn is ride and handling that are less car-like than the front-drive minivans. And Astro's strong engines consume lots of fuel: Expect to average around 15 mpg in daily driving.

The 200-horsepower version of the 4.3 makes its extra power felt mostly in low-speed acceleration, as well as in towing muscle.

The transmission's second-gear-start feature should help traction in bad weather or algae-covered boat ramps (though it's not to be used when trailering). Four-wheel drive is better still. Astro's system goes about its business unobtrusively, requiring no action from the driver, but adds nearly another inch to the body's already-high step-up. Full 4-wheel ABS is a valuable safety feature.

Astro's standard instrumentation is much improved this year, switching from hard-to-read hockey-stick-shaped gauges to easy-to-read circular ones. The optional electronic instrumentation uses a green digital speedometer readout and blue bar graphs to keep track of fuel level and other information.

The front footwells are uncomfortably narrow, but passenger space is otherwise good. Regular-length models with seven or eight seats have little rear cargo room, which explains why extended bodies account for the lion's share of Astro sales.

If you do much towing, the Dutch doors allow easy access to the rear because a trailer hitch cuts into the space needed to open the standard full doors. And the Dutch doors' one-piece glass liftgate also enhances rear visibility by eliminating the standard doors' vertical middle bar and making available an optional rear defogger and wiper.

We welcome the addition of a driver-side air bag, but some rivals—such as the Chrysler minivans and the Toyota Previa—now have dual air bags.

Still, if you're looking for a minivan to haul and tow, consider the Astro/Safari twins, as well as the Aerostar. If you want one for passenger use, put the Dodge Caravan/Plymouth Voyager twins at the top of your list. Also look at the Lumina, the Pontiac Trans Sport and Oldsmobile Silhouette, and the Mercury Villager and Nissan Quest.

Prices

Chevrolet Astro	Retail Price	Dealer Invoice	Fair Price
CS	$16525	*	*
CS extended	16827	*	*
CS extended (California)	17995	*	*
CS AWD	18854	*	*
CS AWD extended	19156	*	*
Destination charge	545	545	545

California CS extended includes destination charge.

Standard Equipment:

4.3-liter V-6 engine (high-output V-6, AWD), 4-speed automatic transmission, 4-wheel anti-lock brakes, driver-side air bag, power steering, coolant temperature and oil pressure gauges, voltmeter, trip odometer, solar-control tinted glass, intermittent wipers, AM radio, highback front bucket seats, 3-passenger bench, front door map pockets, front and rear passenger-side assist handles, dual manual outside mirrors, full carpeting, remote fuel door release, 205/75R15 tires (extended has 215/75R15). **California model** adds: front air conditioning, rear defogger, AM/FM cassette player, tilt steering wheel, 8-passenger seating with reclining front bucket seats, power windows and door locks, deep-tinted glass, alloy wheels. **AWD** models have permanent 4-wheel drive.

Optional Equipment:

4.3-liter high-output V-6, 2WD	500	430	445
Front air conditioning	845	727	752

Left: A driver-side air bag is a new standard feature on all Astros. Above: The Dutch door option.

*Some dealer invoice and fair prices not available at time of publication.

Chevrolet

	Retail Price	Dealer Invoice	Fair Price
Front and rear air conditioning	$1368	$1176	$1218
w/Group 2, 3, 4, or 5	523	450	465
Rear heater	205	176	182
Locking differential	252	217	224
7-passenger seating, w/Group 2	1043	897	928
w/CL Decor Group	955	821	850
w/LT Decor Group	852	733	758
w/Group 3 or 4	429	369	382
w/Group 3 or 4 and CL	315	271	280
w/Group 3 or 4 and LT (credit)	(25)	(22)	(22)
8-passenger seating,			
w/Group 2 or CL	395	340	352
w/Group 2 and LT	877	754	781
w/Group 5 (credit)	(429)	(369)	(369)
w/Group 5 and CL (credit)	(315)	(271)	(271)
w/Group 5 and LT	25	22	22
Reclining seats w/armrests	245	211	218
6-way power driver's seat	240	206	214
CS Value Pkg.	465	400	414

Deluxe bodyside moldings and grille, color-keyed bumpers, rally wheels and floormats.

CL Decor Group	1086	934	967

Front air dam with fog lamps, swing-out glass on sliding side, left front quarter, and rear doors, driver- and passenger-side sunshades with passenger-side lighted visor mirror, storage compartment, dome lights, black grille, bodyside and wheel opening moldings, color-keyed bumpers, rally wheels, door trim panels, and floormats.

LT Decor Group	2896	2491	2577
w/Group 4 or 5	1804	1551	1606

CL Decor Group plus complete body glass, deep-tinted side windows, reclining front bucket seats with dual fold-down armrests, adjustable split second bench seat with fold-down center console (includes convenience tray and cup holders), velour upholstery, rear quarter storage compartment, striping.

Preferred Equipment Group 2,			
CS	505	434	449
w/CL Decor Group	348	299	310

Front air conditioning, dual black mirrors, AM/FM radio, complete body glass.

Preferred Equipment Group 3, CS	1493	1284	1329
w/CL Decor Group	1028	884	915

Group 2 plus ZQ3 Convenience Group, CS Value Pkg., 8-passenger seating, seat recliners with dual armrests.

Preferred Equipment Group 4, 2WD			
w/CL Decor Group	2700	2322	2403
2WD w/LT Decor Group	2780	2391	2474
2WD extended and AWD			
w/CL Decor Group	2692	2315	2396
2WD extended and AWD			
w/LT Decor Group	2772	2384	2467

Air conditioning, AM/FM cassette, complete body glass, ZQ2 and ZQ3 Convenience Groups, 8-passenger seating, seat recliners with dual armrests, power mirrors, underseat storage compartment, 205/75R15 tires (base 2WD), 215/75R15 tires (others).

Preferred Equipment Group 5,			
2WD CS	3724	3203	3314
2WD w/CL Decor Group	3479	2992	3096
2WD w/LT Decor Group	3219	2768	2865
2WD extended and AWD CS	3716	3196	3307
2WD extended and AWD			
w/CL Decor Group	3471	2985	3089
2WD extended and AWD			
w/LT Decor Group	3211	2761	2858

Group 4 plus 7-passenger seating, luggage rack, roof console, power driver's seat, alloy wheels.

Rear door liftgate	364	313	324

Includes rear wiper/washer and electric release.

Deluxe bumpers, CS	128	110	114
w/CL and LT Decor Pkgs. or			
CS Value Pkg.	76	65	68
Luggage rack	126	108	112
Cold Climate Pkg.	46	40	41

	Retail Price	Dealer Invoice	Fair Price
Rear defogger	$154	$132	$137
Requires rear door liftgate.			
Roof console, CS	83	71	74
w/CL and LT Decor Pkgs.	50	43	45
Storage compartment	30	26	27
ZQ2 Convenience Group	434	373	386
Power windows and locks.			
ZQ3 Convenience Group	383	329	341
Cruise control, tilt steering wheel.			
Power locks	223	192	198
Heavy-duty cooling system	198	170	176
Complete body glass	157	135	140
Deep-tinted glass	161	138	143
w/complete body glass	290	249	258
Electronic instrumentation	195	168	174
Auxiliary lighting	127	109	113
CS w/roof console	94	81	84
Deluxe outside mirrors	52	45	46
Power mirrors	150	129	134
w/Group 2 or 3	98	84	87
Deluxe 2-tone paint	476	409	424
w/CL Decor Pkg. or			
CS Value Pkg.	251	216	223
Special 2-tone paint	172	148	153
Custom 2-tone paint	329	283	293
w/CL and LT Decor Pkgs.			
or CS Value Pkg.	104	89	93
AM/FM radio	151	130	134
AM/FM cassette	273	235	243
w/Group 2 or 3	122	105	109
AM/FM cassette w/equalizer	423	364	376
w/Group 2 or 3	272	234	242
w/Group 4 or 5	150	129	134
AM/FM CD player	557	479	496
w/Group 2 or 3	406	349	361
w/Group 4 or 5	284	244	253
Radio delete (credit)	(95)	(82)	(82)
205/75R15 whitewall tires	72	62	64
205/75R15 white letter tires	96	83	85
215/75R15 whitewall tires	60	52	53
215/75R15 white letter tires	88	76	78
w/Group 4 or 5	(NC)	(NC)	(NC)
Trailering Special Equipment,			
heavy duty	507	436	451
w/high-output V-6	309	266	275
Alloy wheels	340	292	303
w/CL or LT Decor Pkg.	248	213	221
Rally wheels	92	79	82

Chevrolet Astro Cargo Van

	Retail Price	Dealer Invoice	Fair Price
Astro cargo van	$15661	*	*
Astro cargo van, extended	16064	*	*
Astro AWD cargo van	17910	*	*
Astro AWD cargo van, extended	18383	*	*
Destination charge	545	545	545

Standard Equipment:

4.3-liter V-6, 4-speed automatic transmission, anti-lock brakes, driver-side air bag, power steering, vinyl highback left front seat, remote fuel door release, tinted glass, dual outside mirrors, AM radio, coolant temperature and oil pressure gauges, voltmeter, trip odometer, intermittent wipers, 205/75R15 tires (215/75R15 on extended models).

Optional Equipment:

Air conditioning	845	727	752
Rear heater	205	176	182
Preferred Group 2, base	1181	1016	1051
extended	1111	955	989

Air conditioning, front bucket seats, dual below-eyeline mirrors, heavy duty rear springs (std. extended).

Some dealer invoice and fair prices not available at time of publication.

Chevrolet

	Retail Price	Dealer Invoice	Fair Price
Optional axle ratio	NC	NC	NC
Locking differential	252	217	224
Front passenger seat	214	184	190
Seatback recliner and armrests	245	211	218
Cloth seat trim	NC	NC	NC
Color-keyed bumpers	52	45	46
Rear defogger	154	132	137
Requires dutch doors.			
Dutch doors	364	313	324
Includes rear wiper/washer power release. Replaces standard swing-out rear doors.			
Cold Climate Pkg.	46	40	41
Engine block heater, coolant protection.			
Roof console	83	71	74
Includes map and reading lights, two storage compartments. Requires auxiliary lighting.			
Auxiliary lighting	127	109	113
with roof console	94	81	84
Front and rear dome lights, reading lights, courtesy light switches on all doors, glove box light, stepwell lights. Requires front passenger seat.			
ZQ2 Convenience Group	434	373	386
Power windows and locks.			
ZQ3 Convenience Group	383	329	341
Cruise control and tilt steering wheel.			
Power locks	223	192	198
Heavy duty cooling system	198	170	176
Engine and transmission oil cooler.			
Deep tinted glass	NC	NC	NC
Complete body glass	368	316	328
with deep tinted glass	630	542	561
Rear panel door glass	87	75	77
with deep tinted glass	141	121	125
Side door and rear panel door glass	155	133	138
with deep tinted glass	262	225	233
Swing-out rear door glass	136	117	121
Deluxe grille	27	23	24
Electronic instrumentation	195	168	174
Heavy Duty Trailering Special Equipment	507	436	451
Platform trailer hitch, wiring harness, heavy duty cooling system.			
Deluxe black outside mirrors	52	45	46
Power mirrors	150	129	134
with Group 2	98	84	87
AM/FM radio	96	83	85
AM/FM cassette	218	187	194
Radio delete (credit)	(95)	(82)	(82)
Heavy duty rear springs, base	70	60	62
Underseat storage compartment	30	26	27
Requires front passenger seat.			
215/75R15 all-season whitewall tires, extended	60	52	53
215/75R15 all-season white letter tires, extended	88	76	78
Rally wheels	92	79	82

Chevrolet Astro CL Extended Length

Chevrolet Blazer

RECOMMENDED

Chevrolet Blazer Silverado

Chevrolet's full-size sport-utility vehicle has a 6.5-liter turbocharged diesel engine as a new option, and side door guard beams and a center high-mounted stoplamp as new standard features. These changes also apply to the Yukon, a similar vehicle sold by GMC dealers (see separate report).

Body Styles/Chassis

A 3-door wagon is Blazer's only body style. Blazer is built from the same design as General Motors' big C/K pickups, though Blazer has a full-length metal roof with a tailgate and top-hinged rear window.

Anti-lock brakes that work on all four wheels in both 2- and 4-wheel drive are standard.

The base trim level is called Cheyenne. An optional Silverado Package includes dressier interior appointments and exterior trim, while a Sport option package adds wheel flares.

New safety features include side door guard beams for both front doors and, in the roof, a center high-mounted stoplamp. Deep-tinted solar-control glass, which reduces the amount of heat reaching the interior, replaces "privacy glass" as an option for side windows. Maximum payload is 1540 pounds.

Powertrains

A 210-horsepower 5.7-liter gasoline V-8 returns as the standard engine.

The new optional engine is Blazer's first turbocharged diesel. It's a 6.5-liter V-8 and is rated at 180 horsepower.

The gas engine is available with a standard 5-speed manual transmission or optional 4-speed electronic automatic. The diesel comes only with a heavy-duty 4-speed automatic.

All Blazers have GM's Insta-Trac 4WD, a part-time system that's not for use on dry pavement. It has automatic locking front hubs and allows shifting between 2WD and 4WD High at any speed.

Towing capacity is 6500 pounds with the optional trailering package.

Accommodations

A pair of low-back front bucket seats is standard. A 3-place 40/60 split front bench is part of the extra-cost Silverado package, and high-back buckets are a stand-alone option. A folding 3-place rear bench is standard.

The air conditioning now uses a CFC-free refrigerant.

Chevrolet

Evaluation

We have not test-driven a Blazer with the new turbodiesel engine, but with a healthy 360 pounds/feet of torque at just 1700 rpm, it should appeal to those who do a lot of trailering. The diesel also should deliver better fuel economy than an equivalent gas engine.

Now that the Dodge Ramcharger is discontinued, Blazer's only rival is the Ford Bronco. Bronco doesn't offer a diesel engine, though it does come with a driver-side air bag for 1994.

Acceleration with Blazer's gas V-8 is robust, and it can pull heavy trailers without protest. The electronically controlled automatic shifts smoothly, though it isn't quick to change down a gear in passing situations. All this muscle will cost you at the gas pump. We averaged just 12.5 mpg over 300 miles in an automatic transmission Silverado, though much of that was city driving.

Body lean is the rule in turns, but it is not unnerving and grip in corners is reassuring. The steering is a bit overassisted, but it's precise and requires relatively few corrections to stay on course. We're pleased to see anti-lock braking control on all wheels, though the nose dips severely in hard stops.

Unladen, Blazer's tail judders sideways on closely spaced bumps, but the big 4x4 is otherwise nicely damped over irregularities.

Though engine noise is prominent, Blazer is quieter overall than the Bronco. Its full steel roof and fixed rear side windows reduce the squeaks and wind noise you get over time with the Ford's add-on rear-roof panel.

The step-up into the interior is quite truck-like, and at nearly 28 inches, the distance from the ground to the rear load floor is higher than in most 2WD pickups. Though the right-front seat slides forward, getting in or out of the rear seat is a chore for all but the very limber.

Once aboard, there's king-size head and leg room all around, with three-abreast capacity on the bench seats. The buckets are comfortable, especially with the available fold-down armrests, though they're short on lumbar bolstering.

Blazer has large, unobstructed analog gauges. But the radio and climate controls suffer too many haphazardly arranged lookalike buttons. The optional automatic heating and air conditioning unit has finicky adjustments. And the extra-cost cassette and graphic equalizer are to the right of center of the dash—more than an arm's reach from the driver's position. Similarly, it's a long stretch to the floor-mounted 4WD transfer-case lever.

More than half of all Blazers are sold in Silverado trim, with power accessories and alloy wheels additional items of choice. That means a list price of over $23,000. Sales are relatively healthy and there were no incentives on Blazers (as there were on Bronco) as calendar 1993 closed, so there's obviously a demand. But unless you require this much size and muscle most of the time, a more sensible and economical daily vehicle would be a compact 4x4.

Specifications

	3-door wagon
Wheelbase, in.	111.5
Overall length, in.	188.0
Overall width, in.	76.4
Overall height, in.	71.0
Turn diameter, ft.	41.5
Curb weight, lbs.	4608
Fuel capacity, gal.	30.0

Passenger Area Dimensions

Seating capacity	6
Front head room, in.	40.2
Rear head room, in.	38.0
Front leg room, in.	41.7
Rear leg room, in.	37.6

Cargo Dimensions and Payloads

Cargo area length, in.	74.6
Cargo area width, in.	64.0
Cargo area width between wheels, in.	48.3
Cargo area height, in.	39.9
Cargo vol., cu. ft.	99.4
Max. payload, lbs.	1540
Max. trailer weight, lbs.	6500

Engines

	ohv V-8	Turbodiesel ohv V-8
Size, liters/cu. in.	5.7/350	6.5/400
Horsepower @ rpm	210 @ 4000	180 @ 3400
Torque (lbs./ft.) @ rpm	310 @ 2400	360 @ 1700
Availability	S	O

EPA city/highway mpg

5-speed OD manual	13/16	15/19
4-speed OD automatic	12/16	

Built in Janesville, Wisc.

KEY: Dimensions and capacities are supplied by the manufacturers. **Curb Weight:** base models, not including optional equipment. **Max. payload, lbs.** = gross amount; net payload may be lower due to optional equipment. **Engines: ohv** = overhead valve; **ohc** = overhead cam; **I** = inline cylinders; **V** = cylinders in V configuration; **flat** = horizontally opposed cylinders; **rpm** = revolutions per minute; **OD** = overdrive transmission; **S** = standard; **O** = optional; **NA** = not available.

Top: Optional high-back bucket seats with center console.
Above: Blazer comes with standard 4WD and V-8 power.

Chevrolet

Prices

Chevrolet Blazer	Retail Price	Dealer Invoice	Fair Price
Cheyenne 4WD 3-door wagon	$21330	*	*
Destination charge	600	600	600

Standard Equipment:
5.7-liter V-8 engine, 5-speed manual transmission, automatic locking front hubs, part-time 4-wheel drive with 2-speed transfer case, 4-wheel anti-lock brakes, power steering, vinyl front bucket seats, 3-passenger rear bench seat, solar-control glass, AM/FM radio, trip odometer, voltmeter, oil pressure and engine temperature gauges, remote tailgate release, dual outside mirrors, intermittent wipers, front air dam, front tow hooks, 225/75R16C all-season tires.

Optional Equipment:
6.5-liter turbodiesel engine	2825	2430	2514
4-speed automatic transmission	930	800	828
Air conditioning	845	727	752
Optional axle ratio	(NC)	(NC)	(NC)
Locking differential	252	217	224
Silverado Group 2	1855	1595	1651

Silverado Decor (40/60 cloth split bench seat, floor console with storage, front and rear map lights, lighted visor mirrors, upgraded door and rear quarter panel trim, door map pockets, chrome mirrors, grille and bumpers, carpet, floormats), air conditioning, tilt steering wheel, cruise control.

Silverado Group 3	2407	2070	2142

Silverado Group 2 plus power mirrors, AM/FM cassette, power windows and locks, deep-tinted glass, alloy wheels.

Sport Silverado Group 4	3056	2628	2720

Silverado Group 3 plus Sport Pkg. (2-tone paint, gray bumpers and wheel flare trim, black mirrors).

Heavy Duty Trailering Special Equipment	408	351	363
with diesel engine	210	181	187

Includes trailer hitch and platform, wiring harness, engine and transmission oil cooler, heavy duty radiator. Requires automatic transmission.

Skid Plate Pkg.	225	194	200
Appearance Pkg.	191	164	170

Includes chrome grille, composite halogen headlights, dual horns.

Cold Climate Pkg. (NA diesel engine)	33	28	29

Includes engine block heater.

Off-Road Chassis Pkg.	400	344	356

Includes Skid Plate Pkg. Requires 265/75R16 tires.

Convenience Group ZQ2	367	316	327

Power front windows, power locks. Requires Silverado Group 2.

Convenience Group ZQ3	383	329	341

Cruise control and tilt steering wheel.

Tachometer	59	51	53
Engine oil cooler	135	116	120
Engine oil and transmission cooler	198	170	176
Deep-tinted glass	215	185	191
Rear wiper/washer and defogger,			
Cheyenne and Group 2	279	240	248
without defogger	125	108	111
Power driver's seat	240	206	214

Requires Silverado Decor trim.

Power mirrors, painted	98	84	87
AM/FM cassette	122	105	109
AM/FM cassette with equalizer,			
base and Silverado Group 2	272	234	242
with Silverado Group 3	150	129	134
Custom cloth reclining bucket seats	341	293	303
Heavy duty front springs	63	54	56
Rally wheels	60	52	53
Alloy wheels	310	267	276
with Silverado Group 2	250	215	223
Deluxe 2-tone paint	290	249	258
Wheel flare moldings	180	155	160

Requires LT245 or LT265 tires.

Roof carrier	126	108	112

Chevrolet Lumina Minivan

Chevrolet Lumina Minivan

Chevy's front-drive minivan gets a restyled nose and an optional power side door. On the safety front, a driver-side air bag is newly standard and child seats are new options.

The name is changed also, from Lumina APV (All Purpose Vehicle) to Lumina Minivan, but its design is still shared with the Oldsmobile Silhouette and Pontiac Trans Sport (see separate reports).

Body Styles/Chassis

Like its Olds and Pontiac cousins, the Lumina Minivan comes in a single wheelbase and body length, but the Chevy is the only one to offer a cargo version. All three are built of fiberglass-like composite exterior panels bonded to a steel frame and have a transverse-mounted engine accessible only through the front hood.

Lumina's blunter new nose reduces overall length by nearly three inches. In addition to two front doors, there's a sliding right-side door and a one-piece rear liftgate.

A single price series is offered, but several tiers of optional equipment are available on passenger models. In addition, a one-price model is being offered to California buyers that adds a host of features and includes the destination charge for $17,695.

Anti-lock brakes are standard on all Lumina Minivans.

The power sliding side door is available only on passenger models as a $295 option on top of the $2843 Preferred Equipment Group 3. It's activated by switches inside the vehicle or by the remote entry system. A power motor slides the door open only when the shift lever is in park and the door is unlocked; it closes it regardless of gear position. If the sliding door senses an obstruction when closing, it will automatically reverse to the open position.

Other new features are an automatic door-locking system integrated with the optional power door locks, and a remote keyless entry system.

Chevy lists a maximum payload on the APV cargo van of 1257 pounds.

Powertrains

A 120-horsepower 3.1-liter V-6 coupled to a 3-speed automatic transmission is standard. Optional is a 170-horsepower 3.8-liter V-6 with a 4-speed overdrive automatic.

An optional traction control system is due later in the model year.

*Some dealer invoice and fair prices not available at time of publication.

Chevrolet

Lumina Minivans with the 3.8 and optional trailering package can tow up to 3000 pounds, 1000 more than with the 3.1 V-6.

Accommodations

The cargo van comes with two front buckets. Passenger models have two front buckets and a 3-place middle bench. Gone is last year's 6-bucket option, leaving a 7-bucket arrangement as the only seating alternative.

Second- and third-row seats in 7-passenger models have been revised to fold and tilt forward to improve cargo capacity and rear-seat entry and exit.

The new integral child seats are optional on 7-passenger models. The two outboard second-row seats have fold-down child restraint seats with five-point safety belts. The seats are designed for use by children who weigh between 20 and 40 pounds. A child over 40 pounds can use the restraint seat with the standard three-point lap and shoulder belts.

Cargo capacity for the cargo model is 115.4 cubic feet. It is 112.6 cubic feet for the passenger model with all rear seats removed.

Evaluation

The addition of a driver's air bag is among several key improvements to these minivans since their introduction as 1990 models. In sum, the advances make the Lumina and its Pontiac and Olds cousins worthy of consideration by any minivan shopper—something we couldn't say a year ago.

Among key competitors, the Dodge Caravan, Plymouth Voyager, Ford Windstar, and Toyota Previa now come with dual air bags. Lumina, however, has standard anti-lock brakes, which are optional on the Dodge, Plymouth, and Toyota. And Chevy offers a special value model in California.

The 3.8-liter V-6 and 4-speed automatic were made available for '92, and give the Chevy performance on a par with any of its rivals. The 3.1 V-6 feels weak with even a moderate load of passengers and cargo aboard.

A car-like driving feel and flexible seating and cargo arrangements are continued high points, and the controls are improved for '94, principally by replacing the undersized climate-system buttons with larger ones. The driver still must look away from the road to reach the radio and climate system, however.

The power side door is unique to the GM vans. It is a convenience, but parents will want to test the door's ability to stop and reverse direction when it encounters an obstacle.

This year's shorter snout reduces the amount of body hidden from the driver beyond the windshield. But some effort still is required to get used to the compromised forward visibility caused by the sloped nose, clutter of roof pillars, and expansive dash-top shelf.

We recommend the optional 3.8 V-6. The 3.1 feels underpowered, especially with the air conditioner on and several passengers aboard. The 3.8 helps the nearly 3500-pound minivan get away from a stop, pass on the highway, and climb hills without drama. It can tow more than the 3.1, and its overdrive automatic makes for more relaxed freeway cruising.

There's no engine hump to interfere with passage between the front seats, though the 7-bucket setup does not allow passage to the rearmost seats from inside the vehicle. Head and leg room in the middle and front are good; the rear seats are cramped for anyone over about 5-foot-6. A variety of passenger and cargo configurations is possible, though with only 12 inches of floor space between the rear-

most seats and the hatch door on 7-passenger models, there's little cargo room in back with all seats in place. However, no competitor has seats that are lighter or easier to remove than the middle and rear buckets on these GM vans, which weigh just 34 pounds each.

Like its corporate cousins, the Lumina Minivan has dent- and rust-resistant fiberglass-like exterior panels. Its styling breaks from the traditional minivan box. And it's priced to compete. But we'd look first at the Dodge Caravan or Plymouth Voyager.

Specifications

	4-door van
Wheelbase, in.	109.8
Overall length, in.	191.5
Overall width, in.	73.9
Overall height, in.	65.7
Turn diameter, ft.	43.1
Curb weight, lbs.	3554
Fuel capacity, gal.	20.0

Passenger Area Dimensions

Seating capacity	7
Front head room, in.	39.2
Rear head room, in.	38.7
Front leg room, in.	40.1
Rear leg room, in.	36.9

Available Seating

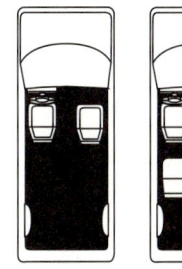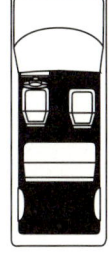

Cargo Dimensions and Payloads

Cargo area length, in.	86.0
Cargo area width, in.	56.0
Cargo area width between wheels, in.	42.5
Cargo area height, in.	41.3
Cargo vol., cu. ft.	115.4
Max. payload, lbs.	1257
Max. trailer weight, lbs.	3000

Engines

	ohv V-6	ohv V-6
Size, liters/cu. in.	3.1/189	3.8/231
Horsepower @ rpm	120 @ 4200	170 @ 4800
Torque (lbs./ft.) @ rpm	175 @ 2200	225 @ 3200
Availability	S	O

EPA city/highway mpg

3-speed automatic	19/23	
4-speed OD automatic		19/25

Built in Tarrytown, N.Y.

KEY: Dimensions and capacities are supplied by the manufacturers. **Curb Weight:** base models, not including optional equipment. **Max. payload, lbs.** = gross amount; net payload may be lower due to optional equipment. **Engines: ohv** = overhead valve; **ohc** = overhead cam; **I** = inline cylinders; **V** = cylinders in V configuration; **flat** = horizontally opposed cylinders; **rpm** = revolutions per minute; **OD** = overdrive transmission; **S** = standard; **O** = optional; **NA** = not available.

Chevrolet

Prices

Chevrolet Lumina Minivan

	Retail Price	Dealer Invoice	Fair Price
4-door van	$17015	*	*
4-door van (California)	17695	*	*
Destination charge	530	530	530

California model includes destination charge.

Standard Equipment:
3.1-liter V-6, 3-speed automatic transmission, anti-lock brakes, driver-side air bag, power steering, reclining front bucket seats, 4-way manual driver's seat, 3-passenger middle seat, tinted glass with solar-control windshield, lockable center console with cup holders, front and rear reading lights, rear auxiliary power outlet, left remote and right manual mirrors, AM/FM radio, intermittent wipers, rear wiper/washer, 205/70R15 tires, wheel covers. **California** model adds: front air conditioning, cruise control, tilt steering wheel, AM/FM cassette player, rear defogger, power windows, door locks and mirrors, remote keyless entry system, deep-tinted glass, 7-passenger seating with reclining front bucket seats, child safety seats, cargo area net, 205/70R15 touring tires, alloy wheels.

Optional Equipment:

	Retail	Dealer	Fair
3.8-liter V-6	619	532	551

Requires 4-speed automatic transmission and air conditioning.

4-speed automatic transmission	200	172	178

Requires 3.8-liter V-6 engine.

Top: A driver-side air bag is now standard on the Lumina Minivan. Above: Optional 7-passenger seating with buckets that fold down or can be removed.

	Retail Price	Dealer Invoice	Fair Price
Front air conditioning	$830	$714	$739
Front and rear air conditioning	1280	1101	1139

Requires 3.8-liter V-6 engine and Preferred Equipment Group 2 or 3.

Preferred Equipment Group 1	778	669	692

Front air conditioning, cruise control, tilt steering wheel, power door/tailgate locks with side door delay, power mirrors.

Preferred Equipment Group 2	2323	1998	2067

Group 1 plus cassette player, power windows with driver-side express down, rear defogger, remote keyless entry, deep-tinted glass, 7-passenger seating, cargo area net.

Preferred Equipment Group 3	2843	2445	2530

Group 2 plus LS Trim Pkg. (includes body-color bumpers and rocker panels, upgraded cloth upholstery) and 6-way power driver's seat.

7-passenger seating	660	568	587

Two front bucket seats and five modular rear seats.

Trailering Pkg.	320	275	285

Includes load leveling suspension. Requires 3.8-liter V-6 engine and Preferred Equipment Group 2 or 3.

Traction Control	350	301	312

Requires Group 3.

Manual sunroof (NA base or with Group 1)	300	258	267
Luggage rack (NA base)	145	125	129
Rear defogger	170	146	151
Deep-tinted glass	245	211	218
Power door/tailgate locks	300	258	267
Power windows (NA base)	275	237	245

Includes driver-side express down.

Power mirrors	78	67	69
6-way power driver's seat (NA base or with Group 1)	270	232	240
Child safety seats	225	194	200

Requires 7-passenger seating.

Power sliding side door	295	254	263

Requires Group 3.

Remote keyless entry	125	108	111
Load leveling suspension (NA base or with Group 1)	170	146	151

Requires 205/70R15 tires (3.1-liter); 205/70R15 tires and Trailering Pkg. (3.8-liter).

Cruise control	225	194	200
Tilt steering wheel	145	125	129
Cassette player	140	120	125
CD player	396	341	352
w/Group 2 and 3	256	220	228
Custom 2-tone paint	148	127	132
Cargo area net	30	26	27
205/70R15 touring tires	35	30	31
205/70R15 self-sealing tires	150	129	134
Alloy wheels	275	237	245
Engine block heater	20	17	18

Chevrolet Lumina Cargo Van

	Retail Price	Dealer Invoice	Fair Price
Cargo van	$15685	*	*
Destination charge	530	530	530

Standard Equipment:
3.1-liter V-6, 3-speed automatic transmission, anti-lock brakes, driver-side air bag, power steering, vinyl front bucket seats, left remote and right manual mirrors, rear wiper/washer, center console with storage and cupholder, tinted glass with solar-control windshield, carpet (front area), rubber floormats, AM/FM radio, digital clock, intermittent wipers, trip odometer, 205/70R15 tires.

Optional Equipment:

Front air conditioning	830	714	739
Cloth highback bucket seats	182	157	162
Rear defogger	170	146	151
Deep-tinted glass	107	92	95
Power locks	300	258	267
Engine block heater	20	17	18

Some dealer invoice and fair prices not available at time of publication.

Chevrolet C/K Pickup

Chevrolet K1500 Extended Cab

Chevrolet's full-size pickups—the best-selling vehicle line at General Motors—gain side door guard beams and a center high-mounted stoplamp as new standard features, and two 6.5-liter diesel V-8 engines as new options for 1994.

GMC dealers sell a similar line of full-size pickups as the Sierra (see separate report).

Body Styles/Chassis

These pickups are identified by their drive system and payload. Rear-drive models carry a "C" designation and 4-wheel-drive models a "K" designation. Payload designations are 1500 for a half-ton rating, 2500 for a three-quarter ton rating, and 3500 for a one-ton rating.

All series are available in regular-length cab body styles or with an extended-cab for additional interior seating and storage. Models with flared rear fenders are called Sportside; those with slab-sided cargo boxes are called Fleetside.

Short-bed regular-cab models are available in the 1500-series only and have a 117.5-inch wheelbase and 6.5-foot bed.

Long-bed models are available in all three series and have a 131.5-inch wheelbase and 8-foot bed.

Extended cab models also are available in all three series. They have either a 141.5-inch wheelbase and the short bed, or a 155.5-inch wheelbase and the long bed. (The short-bed extended-cab model is not available in the 3500 series.)

Sportside models come in both cab styles, but only with the short cargo bed.

Dual-rear-wheel models are offered in the 2500- and 3500-series.

A Crew Cab with four side doors comes as a C/K3500 with a 168.6-inch wheelbase and 8-foot bed. Crew Cabs are only a fraction of C/K pickup sales and are not covered in our specifications chart.

Anti-lock rear brakes, which work in 2WD only, continue standard on all models.

Cheyenne remains the base-level C/K trim and Silverado returns at the top of the line.

A special model, the W/T, or Work Truck, is offered as a no-frills C/K1500 regular-cab long- and short-bed.

Discontinued for '94 is the 454 SS option package, which was a C1500 regular-cab short-bed with the performance handling package and the 7.4-liter V-8 engine. However, several special option groups remain, including the Sport Handling and Off-Road packages.

A 3-place front bench seat is standard on all models and front buckets are optional when the Silverado package is ordered. Extended-cab models get a 3-place rear bench for 6-passenger capacity. Crew Cab models come standard with a 3-place rear bench.

In an effort to improve entry and exit to the rear seats on extended-cab models, the front passenger seat on extended-cabs gains 7.8 inches of travel and the seatback recliners get a memory feature.

Maximum payloads are carried by the 2WD regular-cab, long-bed model. In the 1500 series, it's 2298 pounds, in the 2500 series it's 3853 pounds, and in the 3500 series, it's 5024 pounds.

Powertrains

Standard in most 1500s and 2500s is a 4.3-liter V-6 with 165 horsepower. Again available on C/K 2500 models over 8600 pounds gross vehicle weight is a 4.3 V-6 with 10 fewer horsepower than the regular 4.3, but with a lower compression ratio and a low-restriction exhaust system designed to improve performance in heavy-duty applications.

Two V-8s are optional on 1500s and 2500s: a 5.0-liter with 175 horsepower and a 5.7-liter with 200. A lower-compression 5.7 with 190 horsepower is available in heavy-duty 2500s and is the standard engine for 3500-series C/K pickups. Also available on all models is a 5.7-liter V-8 that can run on compressed natural gas or propane.

A 7.4-liter V-8 with 230 horsepower is optional in heavy-duty 2500-series models and in all 3500-series pickups. This engine had been standard in the 454 SS, where it was rated at 255 horsepower.

Gone is last year's 6.2-liter naturally aspirated diesel V-8, which had 140 horsepower, or 150 in heavy-duty form. It is replaced by a naturally aspirated 6.5-liter diesel V-8 rated at 155 horsepower. This engine is optional in all 1500 and 2500 models except for the W/T.

Newly available for all 1500 and 2500 models (except the W/T) is a new 180-horsepower turbocharged 6.5-liter diesel V-8. Chevy says it's the first turbodiesel ever offered in trucks with gross vehicle weight ratings under 8500 pounds.

Carried over as an option for heavy-duty C/K 2500 models over 8500 pounds GVWR and in C/K 3500 pickups is a turbocharged 6.5-liter diesel V-8 of 190 horsepower.

A 5-speed manual transmission is standard with all gasoline engines and with the naturally aspirated diesel V-8.

A 4-speed overdrive automatic with electronic controls is optional with those engines and is the only transmission available with the turbodiesels.

"K" models have Chevy's Insta-Trac on-demand 4WD, a part-time system that's not for use on dry pavement. It has automatic locking front hubs and can be shifted between 2WD and 4WD-high at any speed via a floor-mounted transfer-case lever. It also includes a 4WD-low gear.

Maximum towing weight without a fifth wheel kingpin hitch is: 1500 series models, 8500 pounds (K1500 with 5.7-liter V-8); 2500 series, 10,000 pounds (C2500 with the 5.7-liter V-8 and K2500 with the 7.4-liter V-8); 3500 series, 10,000 pounds (C/K3500 with the 7.4 V-8).

With a kingpin hitch, the 1500 series can tow up to 8500 pounds, 2500 series can tow 11,500 pounds, and the 3500 series can tow 13,500 pounds.

Evaluation

Chevy's C/K series perennially finishes a close second to Ford's F-Series as the top-selling vehicle in the United States.

Chevrolet

The Chevy actually is the newer truck, the C/K having replaced the R/V platform in 1988. Ford introduced its current F-Series as a 1980 model, with sheetmetal facelifts for '87 and '92. But the rivals remain closely matched in powertrain, body style, trim, and payload choices.

Both manufacturers have dropped "muscle" versions of their full-size pickups, the 454 SS at Chevy and the F-150 Lightning at Ford. Chevy, however, now offers a turbodiesel in C/K pickups under 8500 pounds GVWR, while Ford's naturally aspirated and turbocharged diesels are confined to over-8500-pound GVWR F-Series models. Ford counters with a standard driver-side air bag in its half-ton models.

And while Chevy and Ford will continue to dominate the big-pickup market, Dodge's redesigned 1994 Ram Pickup is vastly improved and offers some unique features, such as unmatched regular-cab storage space and an available V-10 engine. The Ram also has a driver-side air bag on all models, plus anti-lock brakes that work on all four wheels.

Still, for the majority of big-pickup shoppers, the buying decision will continue to come down to brand preference and the kind of deal they can get.

Most C/Ks are purchased in the Southern states, and 76 percent of owners drive them for personal use, working around the home, hunting, and fishing. Overall, the best-selling C/K is the regular-cab C1500 with the 8-foot cargo bed. The most popular engine is the 5.7-liter V-8. And Silverado is the most popular trim level. Such a truck ought to meet most hauling needs—with a good dose of luxury, to boot. We're leery of doing much heavy work with the base V-6, though it feels adequate with manual transmission.

We recently tested a K1500 extended-cab with the 5.7 and automatic. It had ample power, with strong low-end grunt and good passing response on the open road, though we averaged just 13.1 mpg in a mix of city and expressway driving.

We also tested a 5.7-liter 5-speed C1500 Sportside. It sprinted to 60 mph in a bit over 10 seconds, impressive for a truck. However, unladen stopping distances averaged more than 200 feet from 60 mph, poor for a modern full-size pickup. Also, rear-wheel locking was difficult to avoid, despite the standard anti-lock system.

These pickups have a wide, spacious-feeling cab with ample room for even the largest occupants. However, their radios and climate systems are controlled by a collection of fussy buttons rather than simple switches. Order the optional cassette player or graphic equalizer and it's mounted to the right-of-center of the dash—a long stretch from the driver's position.

As for ride quality, only the short-wheelbase 4x4 with the off-road suspension is too harsh, though on others, the more you raise the payload capacity, the more jouncing and bouncing you'll experience with an empty cargo box.

Big pickups offer power and hauling capacity unavailable on compact pickups, though they drink much more fuel, are harder to manage in traffic, and cost more. If you decide you need a full-size pickup, be prudent with extras. A $15,000, base price can easily swell to $20,000 under a healthy load of options. We like the C/K trucks, but give both the Chevy and GMC models, as well as the F-Series and Ram, a close look before buying.

Specifications

	Short bed	Long bed	Extended cab	Extended cab
Wheelbase, in.	117.5	131.5	141.5	155.5
Overall length, in.	194.0	212.6	218.0	237.0
Overall width, in.	76.8	76.8	76.8	76.8
Overall height, in.	70.4	70.4	70.4	74.9
Turn diameter, ft.	40.3	44.4	47.1	52.9
Curb weight, lbs.	3775	3915	4160	4297
Fuel capacity, gal.	25.0	34.0	34.0	34.0

Passenger Area Dimensions

Seating capacity	3	3	6	6
Front head room, in.	40.0	40.0	40.0	40.0
Rear head room, in.	–	–	NA	NA
Front leg room, in.	41.7	41.7	41.7	41.7
Rear leg room, in.	–	–	32.1	32.1

Cargo Dimensions and Payloads

Cargo area length, in.	78.7	97.6	78.7	97.6
Cargo area width, in.	64.4[1]	64.4	64.4[1]	64.4
Cargo area width between wheels, in.	49.1	49.1	49.1	49.1
Cargo area height, in.	19.3	19.3	19.3	19.3
Max. payload, lbs.	2240	5024	2916	4758
Max. trailer weight, lbs.	8500	13,500	11,000	13,500

1. 49.1 on Sportside.

Engines

	ohv V-6	ohv V-8	ohv V-8	ohv V-8	Diesel ohv V-8
Size, liters/cu. in.	4.3/262	5.0/305	5.7/350	7.4/454	6.5/400
Horsepower	165 @	175 @	200 @	230 @	155 @
@ rpm	4000	4200	4000	3600	3400[1]
Torque (lbs./ft.)	235 @	265 @	310 @	385 @	275 @
@ rpm	2000	2800	2400	1600	1900[2]
Availability	S	O	S	O	O

EPA city/highway mpg

5-speed OD manual	17/22	14/19	14/19	NA	19/24
4-speed OD automatic	17/21	14/19	14/18	NA	17/23

1. 6.5-liter turbodiiesel, 180 @ 3400. 2. 6.5-liter turbodiesel, 360 @ 1700.

Built in Ft. Wayne, Ind.; Pontiac, Mich.; and Canada.

KEY: Dimensions and capacities are supplied by the manufacturers. **Curb Weight:** base models, not including optional equipment. **Max. payload, lbs.** = gross amount; net payload may be lower due to optional equipment. **Engines: ohv** = overhead valve; **ohc** = overhead cam; **I** = inline cylinders; **V** = cylinders in V configuration; **flat** = horizontally opposed cylinders; **rpm** = revolutions per minute; **OD** = overdrive transmission; **S** = standard; **O** = optional; **NA** = not available.

Prices

Chevrolet CK 1500 Pickup

	Retail Price	Dealer Invoice	Fair Price
C Sportside, short bed, 4.3	$14690	$12854	$13354
C Fleetside, short bed, 4.3	14027	12274	12774
C Fleetside, long bed, 4.3	14307	12519	13019
C Fleetside, W/T short bed, 4.3	12354	11180	11680
C Fleetside, W/T long bed, 4.3	12554	*	*
K Sportside, short bed, 4.3	17031	14902	15402
K Fleetside, short bed, 4.3	16469	14410	14910
K Fleetside, long bed, 4.3	16768	14672	15172
K Fleetside, W/T short bed, 4.3	15446	13979	14479
K Fleetside, W/T long bed, 4.3	15646	*	*
C Sportside extended cab short bed, 4.3	16266	14233	14733
C Fleetside extended cab short bed, 4.3	15854	13872	14372
C Fleetside extended cab long bed, 5.0	16697	14610	15110
K Sportside extended cab short bed, 4.3	18591	16264	16764
K Fleetside extended cab short bed, 4.3	18179	15903	16403
K Fleetside extended cab long bed, 5.0	18953	16580	17080
Destination charge	595	595	595

C denotes 2WD; K denotes 4WD. California model dealer invoice and fair price not available at time of publication. California model includes destination charge.

Standard Equipment:

4.3-liter V-6 engine (5.0-liter V-8 engine, C/K Fleetside extended cab long bed), 5-speed manual transmission, anti-lock rear brakes, power steering, fold-down 3-passenger vinyl bench seat (regular cab), 60/40 split fold-down

Some dealer invoice and fair prices not available at time of publication.

Chevrolet

3-passenger vinyl bench seat (extended cab), fold-down rear seat (extended cab), solar-control glass, intermittent wipers, dual outside mirrors, cloth headliner (extended cab), AM radio (except W/T), under dash cup holders, coolant temperature and oil pressure gauges, voltmeter, front tow hooks (4WD), full-size spare tire (except W/T). **California C Fleetside W/T short bed** adds: air conditioning, AM/FM cassette player, chrome grille, composite halogen headlamps, dual horns, painted rear bumper, rally wheels. Tires, C regular cab: 225/75R15; C extended cab: 235/75R15; K regular cab: LT225/75R16; K extended cab: LT245/75R16.

Chevrolet K1500 Sportside

Optional Equipment:

	Retail Price	Dealer Invoice	Fair Price
5.0-liter V-8 (std. extended cab long bed)	$575	$495	$512
5.7-liter V-8	865	744	770
with extended cab long bed	270	232	240
6.5-liter V-8 diesel	2870	2468	2554
with extended cab long bed	2295	1973	2043
Includes heavy duty chassis, 235/75R15 tires (regular cab).			
6.5-liter V-8 turbo diesel	3670	3156	3266
with ext. cab long bed	3095	2661	2755
Includes heavy duty chassis, 235/75R15 tires (regular cab). Requires bumper guards.			
Alternative fuel conversion, 2WD regular cab long bed, and 4WD regular cab, long bed	125	108	111
Requires 5.7-liter engine and 4-speed automatic transmission.			
4-speed automatic transmission	930	800	828
Heavy duty 5-speed manual transmission	98	84	87
Air conditioning	805	692	716
Optional axle ratio	(NC)	(NC)	(NC)
Locking differential	252	217	224
Work Truck Group 2, 2WD W/T	162	139	144
K W/T	223	192	198
Rear step bumper, AM radio, rally wheel trim, spare tire.			
Cheyenne Group 1, 2WD Fleetside regular cab (credit)	(890)	(765)	(765)
Includes 4-speed automatic transmission.			
Cheyenne Group 2, regular cab	475	409	423
Fleetside regular cab with 4-speed automatic transmission (credit)	(415)	(356)	(356)
extended-cab	575	495	512
Air conditioning, AM/FM radio.			
Silverado Group 3	1262	1085	1123
with 4.3- or 5.0-liter engine and 4-speed automatic transmission	762	655	678
Silverado Decor Pkg. (includes chrome front bumper, deluxe front appearance with dark argent grille and bright trim, black bodyside moldings with bright trim, bright wheel opening moldings (Fleetside), rally wheel trim, Silverado nameplate, rear quarter swing-out windows (extended cloth or vinyl 3-passenger bench seat with head restraints and folding backrest (regular cab), 60/40 split bench seat or bucket seat with center console (extended), carpeting, floormats, sport steering wheel, storage tray, passenger-side visor mirror), air conditioning, AM/FM radio, auxiliary lighting, dual below-eye-line stainless steel mirrors.			
Silverado Group 4	2084	1792	1855
with 4.3- or 5.0-liter engine and 4-speed automatic transmission	1584	1362	1410
Group 3 plus cassette player, power windows and locks, tilt steering column, cruise control.			
Sport Preferred Equipment Group,			
2WD Sportside regular cab	2428	2088	2161
with Sport Handling Pkg.	2048	1761	1823
4WD Sportside regular cab	2608	2239	2321
Sport Pkg. (Includes color-keyed mirrors, bumpers, and grille, front air dam with fog lights (2WD; tow hooks 4WD), tailgate Chevrolet decal, 235/75R15 all-season tires (2WD), LT265/75R16 on-off road tires (4WD), alloy wheels. Deletes bodyside molding.), air conditioning, Silverado Decor Pkg. interior trim, power door locks and windows, tilt steering wheel, cruise control, AM/FM cassette, auxiliary lighting.			
Cold-Climate Pkg.	33	28	29
Engine block heater.			
Appearance Pkg.	191	164	170
Chrome grille, composite halogen headlights, dual horns.			
Convenience Group ZQ2	367	316	327
Power windows and locks.			

	Retail Price	Dealer Invoice	Fair Price
Convenience Group ZQ3	$383	$329	$341
Cruise control and tilt steering column.			
Off-Road Chassis Pkg., 4WD regular and extended	270	232	240
Bilstein gas shocks absorbers, skid plate.			
Sport Handling Pkg.	1065	916	948
with Silverado Group 3 or 4	974	838	867
Bilstein gas shock absorbers, chrome wheels, 275/60R15 tires.			
Heavy Duty Trailering Special Equipment, with heavy duty 5-speed manual transmission	385	331	343
with Snow Plow Prep Pkg., Off-Road Chassis Pkg. or Sport Handling Pkg.	345	297	307
with 4-speed automatic transmission	448	385	399
with Snow Plow Prep Pkg., Off-Road Chassis Pkg. or Sport Handling Pkg.	408	351	363
With 6.5-liter diesel or turbo diesel engine	250	215	223
with Off-Road Chassis Pkg.	210	181	187
Trailer hitch, wiring harness.			
Snow Plow Prep Pkg.	158	136	141
with Off-Road Chassis Pkg.	55	47	49
Bedliner	225	194	200
Chrome rear step bumper	229	197	204
Chrome front bumper	26	22	23
Painted rear step bumper	130	112	116
Heavy duty chassis, 4WD extended cab	230	198	205
Engine oil cooler	135	116	120
Requires manual transmission.			
Heavy duty engine and transmission oil coolers	198	170	176
Requires automatic transmission.			
Rear defogger, extended cab	154	132	137
Requires Silverado Trim.			
Tachometer	59	51	53
Dome and reading lights	33	28	29
Roof marker lights	52	45	46
Auxiliary lighting	94	81	84
Dome and reading lights, glovebox light, underhood light.			
Bright bodyside moldings, Fleetside	107	92	95
Sportside or with Sport Handling Pkg.	76	65	68
Conventional 2-tone paint	132	114	117
Deluxe 2-tone paint	243	209	216
AM radio, W/T	162	139	144
AM/FM radio	170	146	151
W/T	332	286	295
AM/FM cassette	292	251	260
with Cheyenne Group 2 or Silverado Group 3	122	105	109
W/T	454	390	404
WT with Group 2	292	251	260
AM/FM cassette with equalizer	442	380	393
with Cheyenne Group 2 or Silverado Group 3	272	234	242
with Silverado Group 4 or Sport Preferred Equipment Group	150	129	134
Not available W/T.			

CONSUMER GUIDE® 29

Chevrolet

	Retail Price	Dealer Invoice	Fair Price
Radio delete	(117)	(101)	(101)
Power driver's seat, extended cab	$240	$206	$214
Requires Silverado Decor Pkg., cloth bench or buckets seats.			
Cloth bench seat regular cab	NC	NC	NC
extended cab	174	150	155
Cloth reclining highback bucket seats with			
Silverado Decor Pkg., regular cab	490	421	436
extended cab	291	250	259
Vinyl split bench seat with			
Silverado Decor Pkg.	174	150	155
Rear seat delete, extended (credit)	(395)	(340)	(340)
Heavy duty shock absorbers	40	34	36
Skid plate, 4WD	95	82	85
Heavy duty front springs, 4WD	63	54	56
Front tow hooks (std. 4WD)	38	33	34
Deep tinted glass, extended cab	150	129	134
with Silverado Group 3 or 4	107	92	95
with sliding rear window or rear defogger	115	99	102
with Silverado Group 3 or 4 and sliding rear window or rear defogger	72	62	64
Sliding rear window	113	97	101
Swing-out rear quarter window, extended	43	37	38
Auxiliary battery	134	115	119
Bright wheel covers	42	36	37
Rally wheel trim	60	52	53
Alloy wheels	310	267	276
with Siverado Group 3 or 4	250	215	223
Cast alloy wheels, 4WD	299	257	266
with Silverado Group 3 or 4	250	215	223
Chrome wheels, 2WD	299	257	266
with Silverado Group 3 or 4	257	221	229
Tires: 225/75R15 white letter, each axle	50	43	45
Spare	25	22	22
225/75R15 spare, W/T	160	138	142
235/75R15, each axle	28	24	25
Spare	14	12	12
Spare, W/T	174	150	155
LT 225/75R16 spare, 4WD W/T	221	190	197
LT225/75R16C on/off road, each axle 4WD	22	19	20
Spare	11	9	10
Spare, 4WD W/T	232	200	206
235/75R15 whitewall, each axle	64	55	57
with diesel engine or extended cab	36	31	32
Spare	32	28	28
with diesel engine or extended cab	18	15	16
235/75R15 white letter, each axle	78	67	69
with diesel engine or extended cab	50	43	45
Spare	39	34	35
with diesel engine or extended cab	25	22	22
LT225/75R16C on/off road outline white letter, each axle 4WD	72	62	64
Spare	36	31	32
LT265/75R16C, each axle 4WD	134	115	119
Spare	67	58	60
Extended cab	76	65	68
Spare	38	33	34
LT265/75R16C outline white letter, each axle 4WD	184	158	164
Spare	92	79	82
Extended cab	126	108	112
Spare	63	54	56
LT245/75R16C on/off road, each axle extended cab 4WD	23	20	20
Spare	12	10	11
LT245/75R16C white letter on/off road, each axle extended cab 4WD	73	63	65
Spare	37	32	33

Chevrolet C/K 2500 Pickup

	Retail Price	Dealer Invoice	Fair Price
C regular cab long bed, 4.3	$14914	★	★
C regular cab long bed heavy duty, 5.7	16583	★	★
K regular cab long bed, 4.3	$16943	★	★
K regular cab long bed heavy duty, 5.7	19035	★	★
C extended cab short bed, 5.0	17642	15437	15937
C extended cab long bed heavy duty, 5.7	18330	★	★
K extended cab short bed, 5.0	19459	17024	17524
K extended cab long bed heavy duty, 5.7	20802	★	★
Destination charge	600	600	600

C denotes 2WD; K denotes 4WD.

Standard Equipment:

4.3-liter V-6 engine (regular cab), 5.0-liter V-8 (extended cab), 5.7-liter V-8 (heavy duty models), 5-speed manual transmission (heavy duty 5-speed manual transmission on heavy duty models), anti-lock rear brakes, power steering, vinyl front fold down bench seat (regular cab), 60/40 split fold-down vinyl front bench (extended cab), fold-down rear seat (extended cab), chrome front bumper, engine oil cooler (heavy duty models), solar-control glass, dual outside mirrors, AM radio, front tow hooks (4WD), painted silver wheels, intermittent wipers. LT225/75R16D tires (regular cab), LT245/75R16C tires (extended cab), LT245/75R16E (heavy duty models).

Optional Equipment:

	Retail Price	Dealer Invoice	Fair Price
5.0-liter V-8	575	495	512
5.7-liter V-8	865	744	770
extended cab	290	249	258
6.5-liter V-8 diesel	2870	2468	2554
extended cab	2295	1974	2043
6.5-liter turbo diesel	3670	3156	3266
extended cab	3095	2662	2755
heavy duty	2825	2430	2514
7.4-liter V-8	605	520	538
Not available extended cab short bed.			
Alternative fuel conversion	125	108	111
Requires 5.7-liter engine and 4-speed automatic transmission.			
Heavy duty 5-speed manual transmission	98	84	87
Standard on heavy duty models.			
4-speed automatic transmission	930	800	828
Air conditioning	805	692	716
Optional axle ratio	NC	NC	NC
Locking differential	252	217	224
Cheyenne Group 2	575	495	512
Air conditioning, AM/FM radio.			
Silverado Group 3	1412	1214	1257
extended cab	1312	1128	1168
Silverado Decor Pkg. (includes chrome front bumper, deluxe front appearance with dark argent grille and bright trim, black bodyside moldings with bright trim, bright wheel opening moldings (Fleetside), rally wheel trim, Silverado nameplate, rear quarter swing-out windows, extended cloth or vinyl 3-passenger bench seat with head restraints and folding backrest (regular cab), 60/40 split bench seat or bucket seat with center console (extended), carpeting, floormats, sport steering wheel, storage tray, passenger-side visor mirror, air conditioning, AM/FM radio, auxiliary lighting, dual below-eye-line stainless steel mirrors.			
Silverado Group 4	2184	1878	1944
extended cab	2084	1792	1855
Group 3 plus cassette player, power windows and locks, tilt steering column, cruise control.			
Cold-Climate Pkg.	33	28	29
Engine block heater.			
Appearance Pkg.	191	164	170
Chrome grille, composite halogen headlights, dual horns.			
Convenience Group ZQ2	367	316	327
Power windows and locks.			
Convenience Group ZQ3	383	329	341
Cruise control and tilt steering column.			
Heavy Duty Trailering Special Equipment, with heavy duty 5-speed manual transmission	345	297	307
with diesel or 7.4-liter engine, or optional axle ratio	210	181	187
with 4-speed automatic transmission	408	351	363
Trailer hitch, wiring harness.			

Some dealer invoice and fair prices not available at time of publication.

Chevrolet

	Retail Price	Dealer Invoice	Fair Price
Snow Plow Prep Pkg., 4WD regular cab	$118	$101	$105
Heavy duty front springs.			
Camper Special Chassis Equipment	233	200	207
with Silverado Group 3 or 4	188	162	167
with diesel engine	99	85	88
with Silverado Group 3 or 4	54	46	48
Camper style stainless steel mirrors, camper wiring harness. Gasoline models include heavy duty auxiliary battery.			
Bedliner	225	194	200
Chrome rear step bumper	229	197	204
Requires Silverado Decor Pkg.			
Painted rear step bumper	130	112	116
Front bumper guards	32	28	28
Requires Silverado Decor Pkg.			
Engine oil cooler	135	116	120
Requires manual transmission.			
Heavy duty engine and transmission oil coolers	198	170	176
Requires automatic transmission.			
Rear defogger, extended cab	154	132	137
Requires Silverado Decor Pkg.			
Tachometer	59	51	53
Dome and reading lights	33	28	29
Roof marker lights	52	45	46
Auxiliary lighting	94	81	84
Dome and reading lights, glovebox light, underhood light.			
Stainless steel mirrors	45	39	40
Camper-type mirrors	53	46	47
with Siverado Group 3 or 4	8	7	7
Bright bodyside moldings	107	92	95
4WD heavy duty	76	65	68
Includes bright wheel opening moldings.			
Conventional 2-tone paint	132	114	117
Deluxe 2-tone paint	243	209	216
AM/FM radio	170	146	151
AM/FM cassette	292	251	260
with Cheyenne Group 2 or Silverado Group 3	122	105	109
AM/FM cassette with equalizer	442	380	393
with Cheyenne Group 2 or Silverado Group 3	272	234	242
with Silverado Group 4	150	129	134
Radio delete	(117)	(101)	(101)
Power driver's seat, extended cab	240	206	214
Requires Silverado Trim Pkg., cloth bench or bucket seats.			
Cloth bench seat regular cab	NC	NC	NC
Cloth reclining bench seat, regular cab	174	150	155
extended cab	NC	NC	NC
Cloth reclining highback bucket seats with Silverado Decor Pkg., regular cab	490	421	436
extended cab	291	250	259
Vinyl split bench seat	174	150	155
Rear seat delete, extended (credit)	(395)	(340)	(340)
Skid plate, 4WD	95	82	85
Heavy duty front springs, 4WD	63	54	56
Front tow hooks (std. 4WD)	38	33	34
Deep tinted glass, extended cab	150	129	134
with Silverado Group 3 or 4	107	92	95
with sliding rear window or rear defogger	115	99	102
with Silverado Group 3 or 4 and sliding rear window or rear defogger	72	62	64
Sliding rear window	113	97	101
Swing-out rear quarter window, extended	43	37	38
Auxiliary battery	134	115	119
Bright wheel covers	42	36	37
Rally wheel trim	60	52	53
Tires: LT225/75R16D spare tire	289	249	257
LT225/75R16D on/off road tires, each axle	22	19	20
spare	300	258	267
LT245/75R16C on/off road, each axle			
4WD extended cab	23	19	20
spare	312	268	278
LT245/75R16C on/off road outline white letter, each axle extended cab 4WD	72	62	64
spare	337	290	300
LT245/75R16E, each axle	92	79	82
spare	335	288	298
LT245/75R16E on/off road tires, each axle	114	98	101
heavy duty models	22	19	20
spare (all models)	346	298	308

Chevrolet C/K 3500 Pickup

	Retail Price	Dealer Invoice	Fair Price
C regular cab, 5.7	$16648	*	*
K regular cab, 5.7	19259	*	*
C extended cab, 5.7	19892	*	*
K extended cab, 5.7	22291	19504	20004
Destination charge	600	600	600

C denotes 2WD; K denotes 4WD. All 3500s are long bed.

Standard Equipment:

5.7-liter V-8 engine, heavy duty 5-speed manual transmission, anti-lock rear brakes, power steering, fold-down vinyl bench seat (regular cab), 60/40 split fold down vinyl bench and fold-down rear bench (extended cab), chrome front bumper, solar-control glass, dual outside mirrors, AM radio, trip odometer, wheel opening flares (4WD), front tow hooks (4WD), painted silver wheels, intermittent wiper, dome and roof marker lights (extended cab), LT245/75R16E tires (regular cab), LT225/75R16D tires (extended cab). Extended cab models have dual rear wheels.

Optional Equipment:

6.5-liter turbo diesel	2825	2430	2514
7.4-liter V-8	470	404	418
Alternative fuel conversion	125	108	111
Requires 5.7-liter engine and 4-speed automatic transmission.			
Heavy duty 4-speed automatic transmission	930	800	828
Air conditioning	805	692	716
Optional axle ratio	NC	NC	NC
Locking differential	252	217	224
Cheyenne Group 2	575	495	512
Air conditioning, AM/FM radio.			
Silverado Group 3	1512	1300	1346
extended cab	1312	1128	1168
Silverado Decor Pkg. (includes chrome front bumper, deluxe front appearance with dark argent grille and bright trim, black bodyside moldings with bright trim, bright wheel opening moldings (Fleetside), rally wheel trim, Silverado nameplate, rear quarter swing-out windows (extended cloth or vinyl 3-passenger bench seat with head restraints and folding backrest (regular cab), 60/40 split bench seat or bucket seat with center console (extended), carpeting, floormats, sport steering wheel, storage tray, passenger-side visor mirror, air conditioning, AM/FM radio, auxiliary lighting, dual below-eye-line stainless steel mirrors.			
Silverado Group 4	2184	1878	1944
extended cab	2084	1792	1855
Group 3 plus cassette player, power windows and locks, tilt steering column, cruise control.			
Cold-Climate Pkg.	33	28	29
Engine block heater.			
Appearance Pkg.	191	164	170
Chrome grille, composite halogen headlights, dual horns.			
Convenience Group ZQ2	367	316	327
Power windows and locks.			
Convenience Group ZQ3	383	329	341
Cruise control and tilt steering column.			
Heavy Duty Trailering Special Equipment	210	181	187
Trailer hitch, wiring harness.			
Snow Plow Prep Pkg., 4WD regular cab	118	101	105
Heavy duty front springs.			
Camper Special Chassis Equipment	233	200	207
with Silverado Group 3 or 4	188	162	167
with diesel engine	99	85	88
with Silverado Group 3 or 4	54	46	48
Camper style stainless steel mirrors, camper wiring harness. Gasoline models include heavy duty auxiliary battery.			

Some dealer invoice and fair prices not available at time of publication.

Chevrolet

	Retail Price	Dealer Invoice	Fair Price
Bedliner	$225	$194	$200
Chrome rear step bumper	229	197	204
Requires Silverado Decor Pkg.			
Painted rear step bumper	130	112	116
Front bumper guards	32	28	28
Requires Silverado Decor Pkg.			
Rear defogger, extended cab	154	132	137
Requires Silverado Decor Pkg.			
Tachometer	59	51	53
Dome and reading lights (std. extended cab)	33	28	29
Roof marker lights (std. extended cab)	52	45	46
Auxiliary lighting	94	81	84
Dome and reading lights, glovebox light, underhood light.			
Stainless steel mirrors	45	39	40
Camper-type mirrors	53	46	47
with Siverado Group 3 or 4	8	7	7
Bright bodyside moldings	107	92	95
4WD heavy duty	76	65	68
Includes bright wheel opening moldings.			
Conventional 2-tone paint	132	114	117
Deluxe 2-tone paint	243	209	216
AM/FM radio	170	146	151
AM/FM cassette	292	251	260
with Cheyenne Group 2 or Silverado Group 3	122	105	109
AM/FM cassette with equalizer	442	380	393
with Cheyenne Group 2 or Silverado Group 3	272	234	242
with Silverado Group 4	150	129	134
Radio delete	(117)	(101)	(101)
Power driver's seat, extended cab	240	206	214
Requires Silverado Trim Pkg., cloth bench or bucket seats.			
Cloth bench seat regular cab	NC	NC	NC
Cloth reclining bench seat, regular cab	174	150	155
extended cab	NC	NC	NC
Cloth reclining highback bucket seats with Silverado Decor Pkg., regular cab	490	421	436
extended cab	291	250	259
Vinyl split bench seat	174	150	155
Rear seat delete, extended (credit)	(395)	(340)	(340)
Skid plate, 4WD	95	82	85
Heavy duty front springs, 4WD	63	54	56
Front tow hooks (std. 4WD)	38	33	34
Deep tinted glass, extended cab	150	129	134
with Silverado Group 3 or 4	107	92	95
with sliding rear window or rear defogger	115	99	102
with Silverado Group 3 or 4 and sliding rear window or rear defogger	72	62	64
Sliding rear window	113	97	101
Swing-out rear quarter window, extended	43	37	38
Auxiliary battery	134	115	119
Bright wheel covers	42	36	37
Not available with dual rear wheels.			
Rally wheel trim	60	52	53
Dual rear wheels, regular cab	955	821	850
Includes roof marker lights and tailgate light.			
Tires: LT225/75R16C tires (front), 2WD regular cab (credit)	(104)	(88)	(88)
LT225/75R16D tires (front), regular cab (credit)	(70)	(58)	(58)
rear	428	368	381
spare	300	258	267
LT225/75R16D on/off road tires (front), regular cab (credit)	(48)	(40)	(40)
front extended cab	22	19	20
dual rear, regular cab	472	406	420
dual rear, extended cab	44	38	39
spare	311	267	277
LT245/75R116E spare tire, regular cab	335	288	298
LT245/75R16E on/off road tires, 4WD regular cab each axle	22	19	20
spare	346	298	308

Chevrolet Sportvan/Van

Chevrolet Sportvan Beauville

Safety improvements head the additions for 1994 to the Sportvan, Chevrolet's full-size passenger van. A driver-side air bag is standard on all models with a gross vehicle weight rating (GVWR) below 8500 pounds, and all models have side guard beams in the front doors and a center high-mounted stoplamp.

The passenger version is again called the Sportvan and the cargo model is the Chevy Van. GMC Truck dealers sell similar models under the GMC Rally and Vandura labels (see separate report).

Body Styles/Chassis

Chevy offers the Sportvan in two body lengths and the Van in three.

The 110-inch wheelbase Van has a 180.1-inch-long body. Last year, this size was offered in Sportvan trim, as well.

Cargo and passenger models are offered with a 125-inch wheelbase and 204.0-inch body, and a 146-inch wheelbase with a 223.2-inch body.

Series numbers correspond to the general payload category: G10 is a half-ton; G20 is a three-quarter ton; and G30 is a one-ton. In addition, there are heavy-duty G30s with GVWRs (the combined weight of the vehicle and all it can carry) of 8600 and 9200 pounds.

The 110-inch wheelbase model comes in the G10 series only. The 125-inch wheelbase version comes in all three weight classes. The 146-inch-wheelbase model is a G30 only.

All have two swing-out rear doors. Buyers may choose between 60/40 swing-open side doors or a single sliding side door. Passenger models have windows all around; cargo models come without side or rear glass, though a variety of window options is offered. All glass comes with Solar-Ray tinting.

Four-wheel anti-lock brakes are standard for all models.

On Sportvans, the maximum payload is 2142 pounds for the G20 and 3951 for the G30 in Heavy-Duty form. Payload ratings for Vans are 2039 for the G10, 2697 for the G20, and 4288 for the G30 with a Heavy Duty chassis.

Powertrains

Four gasoline engines and one diesel are offered.

A 155-horsepower 4.3-liter V-6 is standard on G10 and

Chevrolet

G20 Sportvans and Vans and also on G30 Vans.

A 170-horsepower 5.0-liter V-8 is optional on G20 and G30 models.

A 200-horsepower 5.7-liter V-8 is standard on G30 Sportvans. This engine is optional on G20 Sportvans and on G20 and G30 Vans.

Two V-8s designed for heavy-duty work are optional on G30 models equipped with the extra-cost heavy-duty chassis: a 190-horsepower version of the 5.7-liter, and a 7.4-liter rated at 230 horsepower.

The diesel is a 6.2-liter V-8. A 155-horsepower version is optional on G20 Sportvans and Vans, and a 160-horsepower version is optional on heavy-duty G30 models. The 6.5-liter diesel replaces a 6.2-liter diesel V-8 that was rated at 145 horsepower and, in heavy-duty applications, 155 horsepower.

The only transmission is a 4-speed overdrive automatic. It has electronic shift controls and can be locked in second gear for better traction in start-ups on slippery surfaces.

On Sportvans, G20 models can tow up to 7000 pounds and G30s up to 10,000. Tow ratings for Vans may differ slightly; consult your dealer for details.

Accommodations

Sportvans come in base or upscale Beauville trim; Vans are offered in a single trim level.

On Sportvans, G20 models come standard with seats for eight, with seats for five available as a credit option. G30 models in both wheelbases come standard with seats for 12. Credit-option 8-passenger seating is available for the 125-inch wheelbase G30. On the long-wheelbase G30, 15-passenger seating is a $371 option. The driver-side air bag is included on models with a GVWR below 8500 pounds, which includes all Sportvans and Vans except heavy-duty G30 models.

Cargo models come with a driver's seat standard; an auxiliary front seat is optional.

Evaluation

Only Ford, Dodge, and GM compete in the full-size van class, where nearly three out of four vehicles sold is a cargo model. That demonstrates how well-suited these vehicles are for commercial tasks, where heavy-duty use—and abuse—is the rule. A portion of these cargo models are sold for aftermarket conversion to plush family touring vans, which, after addition of the usual captains chairs, wood cabinetry, and other amenities, constitutes another heavy-duty use.

Among Sportvans, the most popular are the 125-inch-wheelbase G20 and the 146-inch-wheelbase G30. That's one reason both the Chevy and GMC versions of this van no longer offer the 110-inch wheelbase version. The other reason is that a similar package was available in GM's own Chevrolet Astro and GMC Safari minivans, which have a 111-inch wheelbase.

Most Sportvan buyers order the swing-out side doors and Beauville trim, and 80 percent opt for the 5.7-liter V-8. In this form, you get a G20 capable of carrying a large family or a G30 with the ability to haul a band of 15. At maximum seating capacity, neither will have much room at the rear for luggage, but delete the rearmost bench, and you begin to create a cargo hold that can boarder on cavernous. Plus, the rear-drive layout and brawny V-8s allow towing some pretty big boats or travel trailers.

Carting around lots of people and cargo and pulling a large trailer is where the big vans have an advantage over even the truck-based compact vans such as the Astro/Safari and the Ford Aerostar, which have lower payloads, more limited towing ability, and seat a maximum of seven.

But you pay the price at the gas pump; even a V-6 G20 won't average more than about 14 mpg in daily driving. Compared to minivans, full-size vans are harder to maneuver in traffic and unlike the aforementioned minivans, which

Specifications

	5-door van	5-door van	5-door van
Wheelbase, in.	110.0	125.0	146.0
Overall length, in.	180.1	204.0	223.2
Overall width, in.	79.1	79.5	79.5
Overall height, in.	80.0	79.7	82.3
Turn diameter, ft.	41.3	46.0	54.0
Curb weight, lbs.	3926	4067	4931
Fuel capacity, gal.	22.0	33.0	33.0

Passenger Area Dimensions

Seating capacity	2	12	15
Front head room, in.	40.8	40.8	40.8
Rear head room, in.	40.9	40.9	40.9
Front leg room, in.	39.5	39.5	39.5
Rear leg room, in.	37.2	37.2	37.2

Available Seating

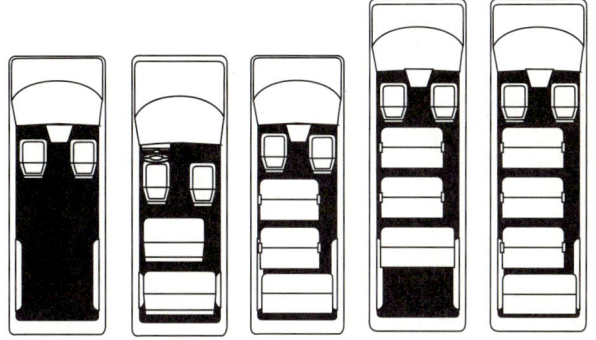

Cargo Dimensions and Payloads

Cargo area length, in.	102.5	126.3	147.5
Cargo area width, in.	70.8	70.8	70.8
Cargo area width between wheels, in.	53.5	53.5	53.5
Cargo area height, in.	49.2	49.2	49.2
Cargo vol., cu. ft.	207.0	260.0	306.0
Max. payload, lbs.	2039	4101	4288
Max. trailer weight, lbs.	6000	10,000	10,000

Engines

	ohv V-6	ohv V-8	ohv V-8	ohv V-8	Diesel ohv V-8
Size, liters/cu. in.	4.3/262	5.0/305	5.7/350	7.4/454	6.2/379
Horsepower @ rpm	155 @ 4000	170 @ 4000	200 @ 4000	230 @ 3600	155 @ 3600
Torque (lbs./ft.) @ rpm	230 @ 2000	265 @ 2400	310 @ 2400	385 @ 1600	275 @ 1700
Availability	S	O	O[1]	O	O

EPA city/highway mpg

4-speed OD automatic	15/18	13/18	13/17	NA	16/20

1. 190-horsepower HD 5.7 is standard on G30 Sportvan and long-wheelbase Van.

Built in Flint, Mich.

KEY: Dimensions and capacities are supplied by the manufacturers. **Curb Weight:** base models, not including optional equipment. **Max. payload, lbs.** = gross amount; net payload may be lower due to optional equipment. **Engines: ohv** = overhead valve; **ohc** = overhead cam; **I** = inline cylinders; **V** = cylinders in V configuration; **flat** = horizontally opposed cylinders; **rpm** = revolutions per minute; **OD** = overdrive transmission; **S** = standard; **O** = optional; **NA** = not available.

Chevrolet

are available with 4-wheel-drive, the big vans are limited to rear-drive, which increases chances that their rear tires will slip and slide on wet or snowy roads.

The Chevys and their GMC cousins certainly do the job of a full-size van. They now match the Ford Club Wagon and Econoline in having a driver-side air bag, and GM is alone in offering diesel power in a GVWR below 8500 pounds.

Still, if you need a full-size van, look first to the more modern and refined Ford Club Wagon. It was redesigned for 1992, while GM's design dates to 1970.

Prices

Chevrolet Sportvan G20

	Retail Price	Dealer Invoice	Fair Price
125-inch wheelbase	$18875	*	*
Destination charge	580	580	580

Standard Equipment:
4.3-liter V-6, 4-speed automatic transmission, anti-lock brakes, driver-side air bag, power steering, vinyl front bucket seats, two removable 3-passenger rear bench seats, swing-out side doors (sliding side door may be substituted at no additional cost), chrome bumpers, swing-out front qaurter and rear door windows, intermittent wipers, solar-control glass, heavy duty shock absorbers and rear springs, black bodyside moldings, coolant temperature and oil pressure gauges, voltmeter, trip odometer, digital clock, dual outside mirrors, rubber floor covering, AM radio, 225/75R15 tires.

Optional Equipment:

5.0-liter V-8	575	495	512
5.7-liter V-8	865	744	770
6.5-liter V-8 diesel	2870	2468	2554
Front air conditioning	975	839	868
Front & rear air conditioning	1574	1354	1401
with Group 2 or 3	599	515	533
Rear heater	205	176	182
Optional axle ratio	NC	NC	NC
Locking differential	252	217	224
Base Equipment Preferred Group 2	966	831	860
Front air conditioning, AM/FM radio.			
Beauville Preferred Group 3	1777	1528	1582
Base Group 2 plus Beauville Trim (includes chrome grille and wheel opening moldings, halogen headlamps, Beauville nameplate, carpeting, passenger-side visor mirror, upgraded door trim panels, cloth headliner, locking underseat storage compartment, spare tire cover, rear coathooks, front and rear color-keyed floormats, cruise control, tilt steering wheel, power windows and door locks, auxiliary lighting.			
Beauville Preferred Group 4	3225	2774	2870
Group 3 plus cassette player, reclining cloth front bucket seats with armrests, front and rear air conditioning, deep-tinted glass, power stainless steel mirrors, rally wheels.			
Cold Climate Pkg.	48	41	43
Engine block heater.			
ZQ2 Convenience Group	434	373	386
Power windows and door locks.			
ZQ3 Convenience Group	383	329	341
Cruise control and tilt steering wheel.			
Rear defogger	95	82	85
Includes fixed rear windows.			
Heavy duty cooling system	198	170	176
Engine and transmission oil coolers, heavy duty radiator.			
Power door locks	223	192	198
Remote keyless entry system	175	151	156
Includes headlamp delay. Requires auxiliary lighting and ZQ2 Convenience Group.			
Deep-tinted glass	380	327	338
Auxiliary lighting	156	134	139
Front and rear dome/reading lights, underhood light.			
Power stainless steel mirrors	98	84	87
Requires ZQ2 Convenience Group.			

	Retail Price	Dealer Invoice	Fair Price
Lighted visor mirrors	$75	$65	$67
Requires Group 3 or 4.			
Two-tone paint	269	231	239
with Group 3 or 4	137	118	122
AM/FM radio	141	121	125
AM/FM cassette	263	226	234
with Group 2 or 3	122	105	109
AM/FM cassette with equalizer	413	355	368
with Group 2 or 3	272	234	242
with Group 4	150	129	134
CD player	537	462	478
with Group 2 or 3	396	341	352
with Group 4	274	236	244
Power antenna	85	73	76
Radio delete (credit)	(95)	(82)	(82)
Leather-wrapped steering wheel	60	52	53
Custom cloth bucket seats, with Group 3 or 4	NC	NC	NC
Custom cloth reclining bucket seats, with Group 3	402	346	358
Rear seat delete (credit)	(371)	(319)	(319)
Deletes third 3-passenger seat for 5-passenger seating.			
Heavy duty trailering special equipment	508	437	452
with 6.5-liter diesel engine	310	267	276
Platform-mounted trailer hitch, heavy duty flasher, wiring harness.			
Light duty trailering special equipment	132	114	117
Bumper-mounted trailer hitch, heavy duty flasher, wiring harness.			
6875 lbs. GVWR, 5.7-liter engine	319	274	284
with 6.5-liter diesel engine	NC	NC	NC
Rally wheels	121	104	108
225/75R15 spare tire	137	118	122
225/75R15 whitewall tires, each axle	36	31	32
spare	155	133	138
225/75R15 white letter tires, each axle	50	43	45
spare	162	139	144
235/75R15 spare	151	130	134

Chevrolet Sportvan G30

	Retail Price	Dealer Invoice	Fair Price
125-inch wheelbase	$20227	*	*
Extended, 146-inch wheelbase	21383	*	*
Destination charge	580	580	580

Standard Equipment:
5.7-liter V-8, 4-speed automatic transmission, anti-lock brakes, power steering, vinyl front bucket seats, two removable 3-passenger middle bench seats, 4-passenger rear bench seat, swing-out side doors (sliding side door may be substituted at no additional cost on base model), chrome bumpers, swing-out front quarter and rear door windows, intermittent wipers, solar-control glass, heavy duty shock absorbers and rear springs, black bodyside moldings, coolant temperature and oil pressure gauges, voltmeter, trip odometer, digital clock, dual outside mirrors, rubber floor covering, AM radio, LT225/75R16D tires (base), LT 225/75R16E tires (extended).

A driver-side air bag is standard on all Sportvans and Vans with a gross vehicle weight under 8500 pounds.

*Some dealer invoice and fair prices not available at time of publication.

Optional Equipment:

	Retail Price	Dealer Invoice	Fair Price
7.4-liter V-8	$605	$520	$538
6.5-liter heavy duty V-8 diesel	1655	1423	1473
Alternative fuel conversion	125	108	111
Requires std. 5.7-liter engine. Base also requires 8600 lbs. or 9200 lbs. GVWR.			
Front air conditioning	975	839	868
Front & rear air conditioning	1574	1354	1401
with Group 2 or 3	599	515	533
Rear heater	205	176	182
Optional axle ratio	NC	NC	NC
Locking differential	252	217	224
Base Equipment Preferred Group 2	966	831	860
Front air conditioning, AM/FM radio.			
Beauville Preferred Group 3	1777	1528	1582
Base Group 2 plus Beauville Trim (includes chrome grille and wheel opening moldings, halogen headlamps, Beauville nameplate, carpeting, passenger-side visor mirror, upgraded door trim panels, cloth headliner, locking underseat storage compartment, spare tire cover, rear coathooks, front and rear color-keyed floormats), cruise control, tilt steering wheel, power windows and door locks, auxiliary lighting.			
Beauville Preferred Group 4	3146	2706	2800
Group 3 plus cassette player, reclining cloth front bucket seats with armrests, front and rear air conditioning, deep-tinted glass, power stainless steel mirrors, rally wheels.			
Cold Climate Pkg.	48	41	43
Engine block heater.			
ZQ2 Convenience Group	434	373	386
Power windows and door locks.			
ZQ3 Convenience Group	383	329	341
Cruise control and tilt steering wheel.			
Rear defogger	95	82	85
Includes fixed rear windows.			
Heavy duty cooling system	198	170	176
Engine and transmission oil coolers, heavy duty radiator.			
Power door locks	223	192	198
Remote keyless entry system	175	151	156
Includes headlamp delay. Requires auxiliary lighting and ZQ2 Convenience Group.			
Deep-tinted glass	380	327	338
Auxiliary lighting	156	134	139
Front and rear dome/reading lights, underhood light.			
Power stainless steel mirrors	98	84	87
Requires ZQ2 Convenience Group.			
Lighted visor mirrors	75	65	67
Requires Group 3 or 4.			
Two-tone paint	269	231	239
with Group 3 or 4	137	118	122
AM/FM radio	141	121	125
AM/FM cassette	263	226	234
with Group 2 or 3	122	105	109
AM/FM cassette with equalizer	413	355	368
with Group 2 or 3	272	234	242
with Group 4	150	129	134
CD player	537	462	478
with Group 2 or 3	396	341	352
with Group 4	274	236	244
Power antenna	85	73	76
Radio delete (credit)	(95)	(82)	(82)
Leather-wrapped steering wheel	60	52	53
Custom cloth bucket seats, with Group 3 or 4	NC	NC	NC
Custom cloth reclining bucket seats, with Group 3	402	346	358
Additional 3-passenger middle bench seat for 15-passenger seating, extended	371	319	330
Rear seat delete, base (credit)	(371)	(319)	(319)
Deletes rear 4-passenger seat for 8-passenger seating.			
Heavy duty trailering special equipment	508	437	452
with 7.4-liter or 6.5-liter diesel engine	310	267	276
Platform-mounted trailer hitch, heavy duty flasher, wiring harness.			
Light duty trailering special equipment	132	114	117
Bumper-mounted trailer hitch, heavy duty flasher, wiring harness.			
8600 lbs. GVWR, base	251	216	223

Chevrolet

	Retail Price	Dealer Invoice	Fair Price
9200 lbs. GVWR, base	$371	$319	$330
extended	240	206	214
Bright wheel covers	42	36	37
LT225/75R16E tires, each axle	34	29	30
8600 lbs. or 9200 lbs. GVWR	NC	NC	NC
spare (all)	224	193	199
LT225/75R16D, spare tire	207	178	184

Chevrolet Van G10

	Retail Price	Dealer Invoice	Fair Price
110-inch wheelbase	$15936	*	*
125-inch wheelbase	16120	*	*
Destination charge	580	580	580

Standard Equipment:

4.3-liter V-6, 4-speed automatic transmission, anti-lock brakes, driver-side air bag, power steering, vinyl bucket driver's seat, coolant temperature and oil pressure gauges, voltmeter, trip odometer, solar-control glass, heavy duty shock absorbers, intermittent wipers, parcel tray, AM radio, digital clock, black bodyside moldings, swing-out side doors (sliding side door may be substituted at no charge), 215/75R15 tires.

Optional Equipment:

	Retail	Dealer	Fair
5.0-liter V-8 engine	575	495	512
Front air conditioning	975	839	868
Front and rear air conditioning	1574	1354	1401
with Group 2	599	515	533
Rear heater	205	176	182
Optional axle ratio	NC	NC	NC
Locking differential	252	217	224
Preferred Equipment Group 2	1118	961	995
Front air conditioning, auxiliary front seat, AM/FM radio.			
Deluxe front appearance	142	122	126
Dark argent grille with bright trim, rectangular headlamps.			
Chrome bumpers	76	65	68
Cold Climate Pkg.	48	41	43
Engine block heater.			
ZQ2 Convenience Group	434	373	386
Power windows and locks.			
ZQ3 Convenience Group	383	329	341
Cruise control and tilt steering wheel.			
Remote keyless entry	175	151	156
Includes headlamp delay. Requires auxiliary lighting and ZQ2 Convenience Pkg.			
Power door locks	223	192	198
Power mirrors	98	84	87
Requires ZQ2 Convenience Group, Swing-Out Glass Pkg. or Fixed Glass Pkg.			
Swing-Out Glass Pkg.	226	194	201
Swing-out glass for rear and side doors.			
Fixed Glass Pkg.	90	77	80
Fixed rear and side door glass.			
Full body glass (six windows)	144	124	128
Requires Swing-Out Glass Pkg.			
Right rear bodyside glass	52	45	46
Requires Swing-Out Glass Pkg. or Fixed Glass Pkg.			
Fixed rear door glass	50	43	45
Swing-out rear door glass	109	94	97
with full body glass	59	51	53
Rear defogger, with Swing-Out Glass Pkg.	95	82	85
with Fixed Glass Pkg. or fixed rear door glass	154	132	137
Heavy duty cooling system	198	170	176
Engine and transmission oil coolers, heavy duty radiator.			
Auxiliary lighting	156	134	139
Front and rear dome/reading lights, underhood light.			
Leather-wrapped steering wheel	60	52	53
Carpet	157	135	140
Requires auxiliary front seat.			
Auxiliary front seat	187	161	166
AM/FM radio	96	83	85

*Some dealer invoice and fair prices not available at time of publication.

Chevrolet

	Retail Price	Dealer Invoice	Fair Price
AM/FM cassette	$218	$187	$194
with Group 2	122	105	109
AM/FM cassette with equalizer	368	316	328
with Group 2	272	234	242
CD player	517	445	460
with Group 2	421	362	375
Radio delete (credit)	(95)	(82)	(82)
Power antenna	85	73	76
33-gallon fuel tank, 125-inch WB	96	83	85
Trailering Special Equipment	132	114	117
Bumper-mounted trailer hitch, wiring harness, heavy duty flasher.			
Rally wheels	121	104	108
215/75R15 whitewall tires, each axle	30	26	27
spare	15	13	13

Chevrolet Van G20

	Retail Price	Dealer Invoice	Fair Price
110-inch wheelbase	$15905	*	*
125-inch wheelbase	16110	*	*
Destination charge	580	580	580

Standard Equipment:
4.3-liter V-6, 4-speed automatic transmission, anti-lock brakes, driver-side air bag, power steering, vinyl bucket driver's seat, coolant temperature and oil pressure gauges, voltmeter, trip odometer, solar-control glass, heavy duty shock absorbers, intermittent wipers, parcel tray, AM radio, digital clock, black bodyside moldings, swing-out side doors (sliding side door may be substituted at no charge), 225/75R15 tires.

Optional Equipment:

	Retail	Dealer	Fair
5.0-liter V-8 engine	575	495	512
5.7-liter V-8 engine, 125-inch WB	865	744	770
6.5-liter diesel engine, 125-inch WB	2870	2468	2554
Front air conditioning	975	839	868
Front and rear air conditioning	1574	1354	1401
with Group 2	599	515	533
Rear heater	205	176	182
Optional axle ratio	NC	NC	NC
Locking differential	252	217	224
Preferred Equipment Group 2	1118	961	995
Front air conditioning, auxiliary front seat, AM/FM radio.			
Deluxe front appearance	142	122	126
Dark argent grille with bright trim, rectangular headlamps.			
Chrome bumpers	76	65	68
Cold Climate Pkg.	48	41	43
Engine block heater.			
ZQ2 Convenience Group	434	373	386
Power windows and locks.			
ZQ3 Convenience Group	383	329	341
Cruise control and tilt steering wheel.			
Remote keyless entry	175	151	156
Includes headlamp delay. Requires auxiliary lighting and ZQ2 Convenience Pkg.			
Power door locks	223	192	198
Power mirrors	98	84	87
Requires ZQ2 Convenience Group, Swing-Out Glass Pkg. or Fixed Glass Pkg.			
Swing-Out Glass Pkg.	226	194	201
Swing-out glass for rear and side doors.			
Fixed Glass Pkg.	90	77	80
Fixed rear and side door glass.			
Full body glass (six windows)	144	124	128
Requires Swing-Out Glass Pkg.			
Right rear bodyside glass	52	45	46
Requires Swing-Out Glass Pkg. or Fixed Glass Pkg.			
Fixed rear door glass	50	43	45
Swing-out rear door glass	109	94	97
with full body glass	59	51	53
Rear defogger, with Swing-Out Glass Pkg.	95	82	85
with Fixed Glass Pkg. or fixed rear door glass	154	132	137
Heavy duty cooling system	198	170	176
Engine and transmission oil coolers, heavy duty radiator.			
Auxiliary lighting	156	134	139
Front and rear dome/reading lights, underhood light.			
Leather-wrapped steering wheel	60	52	53
Carpet	157	135	140
Requires auxiliary front seat.			
Auxiliary front seat	187	161	166
AM/FM radio	96	83	85
AM/FM cassette	218	187	194
with Group 2	122	105	109
AM/FM cassette with equalizer	368	316	328
with Group 2	272	234	242
CD player	517	445	460
with Group 2	421	362	375
Radio delete (credit)	(95)	(82)	(82)
Power antenna	85	73	76
33-gallon fuel tank, 125-inch WB	96	83	85
Trailering Special Equipment	132	114	117
Bumper-mounted trailer hitch, wiring harness, heavy duty flasher.			
Heavy Duty Trailering Special Equipment	508	437	452
with 6.5-liter diesel engine	310	267	276
Platform-mounted trailer hitch, wiring harness, heavy duty flasher.			
6875 lbs. GVWR, 125-inch WB	319	274	284
with 6.5-liter engine	NC	NC	NC
Requires 5.7-liter or 6.5-liter diesel engine.			
Rally wheels	121	104	108
225/75R15 spare tire	137	118	122
225/75R15 whitewall tires, each axle	36	31	32
spare	155	133	138
225/75R15 white letter tires, each axle	50	43	45
spare	162	139	144
235/75R15 tires, each axle	NC	NC	NC
spare	162	139	144
Requires 6875 GVWR.			
235/75R15 whitewall tires, each axle	36	31	32
spare	169	145	150
Requires 6875 GVWR.			

Chevy Van G30

	Retail Price	Dealer Invoice	Fair Price
125-inch wheelbase	$16237	*	*
Extended, 146-inch wheelbase	18357	*	*
Destination charge	580	580	580

Standard Equipment:
4.3-liter V-6 engine (base), 5.7-liter V-8 engine (extended), 4-speed automatic transmission, anti-lock brakes, driver-side air bag, power steering, vinyl bucket driver's seat, coolant temperature and oil pressure gauges, voltmeter, trip odometer, solar-control glass, heavy duty shock absorbers, intermittent wipers, parcel tray, AM radio, digital clock, black bodyside moldings, swing-out side doors, 30-gallon fuel tank (extended), LT225/75R16 tires (base), LT225/75R16E tires (extended).

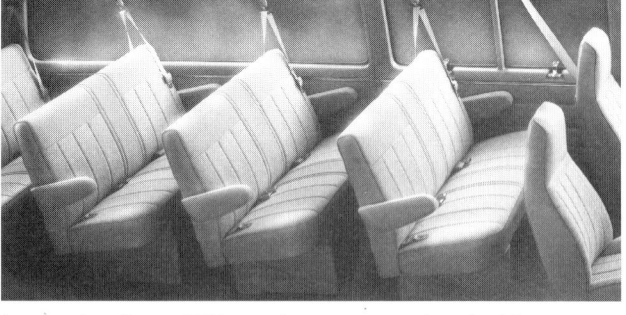

Long-wheelbase G30 sportvans can seat up to 15 passengers.

Some dealer invoice and fair prices not available at time of publication.

Chevrolet

Chevrolet Suburban

Chevrolet Suburban C1500

Side door guard beams, a center high-mounted stoplamp, and an optional 6.5-liter turbocharged diesel V-8 are the key changes on the Suburban, a 4-door wagon based on the full-size Chevy pickup.

Suburban is sold in nearly identical form by GMC Truck dealers (see separate report).

Body Styles/Chassis

Suburban comes with four side doors and two swing-open rear doors. A tailgate with a top-hinged rear window is a no-cost option. In addition to gaining side door guard beams and a high-mount stoplamp, Suburban's grille has been slightly revised for 1994.

Anti-lock brakes that work on all four wheels in both 2WD and 4WD are standard on all models.

Rear-drive Suburbans carry the "C" designation, 4-wheel-drive models use a "K" designation. The 1500-series Suburbans have a half-ton payload rating and the 2500 series a three-quarter ton rating.

Maximum payload, 3430 pounds, is found on the C2500.

Powertrains

A 5.7-liter V-8 is the standard engine. It's rated at 210 horsepower in 1500-series models and, due to a heavier-duty application, 190 horsepower in the 2500s.

Optional on 2500-series models is a 230-horsepower 7.4-liter V-8.

A 6.5-liter turbocharged diesel V-8 rated at 190 horsepower is a new option for 2500-series Suburbans. It is the first diesel offered since Suburban was redesigned on the C/K pickup platform for the 1992 model year.

A 4-speed overdrive automatic is the only transmission. It has electronic shift controls and a second-gear start feature for increased traction on slippery surfaces.

Suburban 4x4s use GM's Insta-Trac 4WD system, which allows shifting in and out of 4WD High at any speed. It comes with automatic locking front hubs, but is a part-time system and is not for use on dry pavement.

Maximum towing capacity is 6500 pounds on the 1500-series and 10,000 pounds on the 2500s.

Accommodations

Cheyenne is the name for the base trim level, with Silverado again the label for the uplevel option packages.

A 3-place front bench is standard in Cheyenne. A 3-place split/folding middle bench is optional on Cheyenne and standard on Silverado. Also optional are front bucket seats, as well as a removable 3-place third seat.

Optional Equipment:	Retail Price	Dealer Invoice	Fair Price
7.4-liter V-8 engine, extended	$845	$727	$752
6.5-liter heavy duty diesel engine	2870	2468	2554
Alternative fuel conversion	125	108	111
Requires 5.7-liter engine. Base requires 8600 lbs. or 9200 lbs. GVWR. Front air conditioning	975	839	868
Front and rear air conditioning	1574	1354	1401
with Group 2	599	515	533
Rear heater	205	176	182
Optional axle ratio	NC	NC	NC
Locking differential	252	217	224
Preferred Equipment Group 2	1118	961	995
Front air conditioning, auxiliary front seat, AM/FM radio.			
Deluxe front appearance	142	122	126
Dark argent grille with bright trim, rectangular headlamps.			
Chrome bumpers	76	65	68
Cold Climate Pkg.	48	41	43
Engine block heater.			
ZQ2 Convenience Group	434	373	386
Power windows and locks.			
ZQ3 Convenience Group	383	329	341
Cruise control and tilt steering wheel.			
Remote keyless entry	175	151	156
Includes headlamp delay. Requires auxiliary lighting and ZQ2 Convenience Pkg.			
Power door locks	223	192	198
Power mirrors	98	84	87
Requires ZQ2 Convenience Group, Swing-Out Glass Pkg. or Fixed Glass Pkg.			
Swing-Out Glass Pkg.	226	194	201
Swing-out glass for rear and side doors.			
Fixed Glass Pkg.	90	77	80
Fixed rear and side door glass.			
Full body glass (six windows)	144	124	128
Requires Swing-Out Glass Pkg.			
Right rear bodyside glass	52	45	46
Requires Swing-Out Glass Pkg. or Fixed Glass Pkg.			
Fixed rear door glass	50	43	45
Swing-out rear door glass	109	94	97
with full body glass	59	51	53
Rear defogger, with Swing-Out Glass Pkg.	95	82	85
with Fixed Glass Pkg. or fixed rear door glass	154	132	137
Heavy duty cooling system	198	170	176
Engine and transmission oil coolers, heavy duty radiator.			
Auxiliary lighting	156	134	139
Front and rear dome/reading lights, underhood light.			
Leather-wrapped steering wheel	60	52	53
Carpet	157	135	140
Requires auxiliary front seat.			
Auxiliary front seat	187	161	166
AM/FM radio	96	83	85
AM/FM cassette	218	187	194
with Group 2	122	105	109
AM/FM cassette with equalizer	368	316	328
with Group 2	272	234	242
CD player	517	445	460
with Group 2	421	362	375
Radio delete (credit)	(95)	(82)	(82)
Power antenna	85	73	76
33-gallon fuel tank, 125-inch WB	96	83	85
Trailering Special Equipment	132	114	117
Bumper-mounted trailer hitch, wiring harness, heavy duty flasher.			
Heavy Duty Trailering Special Equipment	508	437	452
with 7.4-liter engine or 6.5-liter diesel engine	310	267	276
Platform-mounted trailer hitch, wiring harness, heavy duty flasher.			
7400 lbs. GVWR, base	837	720	745
Requires 5.7-liter engine.			
8600 lbs. GVWR, base	1012	870	901
9200 GVWR, base	1252	1077	1114
extended	240	206	214
Base requires 5.7-liter, 7.4-liter or diesel engine.			

CONSUMER GUIDE®

Chevrolet

Evaluation

Suburban sales have climbed steadily since the '92 redesign. The vehicle is particularly popular in southern states, and the typical order is for a C1500 with Silverado Preferred Equipment Group 3. That creates a rather lavishly equipped $25,000 full-size wagon that virtually defines its own market segment.

Granted, a full-size van will provide similar power, accommodations, and interior volume. And a van will have easier entry and exit via the sliding side door, plus room to move about once inside. Even the stretched versions of the compact Chevy Astro and Ford Aerostar vans offer interior space similar to a Suburban, with available 4WD, and a less-steep sticker price.

But no compact van can match Suburban's towing or payload, and the full-size vans that do match it certainly don't have the particular blend of prestige and style that Suburban buyers want.

Acceleration with the 5.7-liter V-8 is only adequate around town and it takes a very deliberate stab at the throttle to induce a downshift for passing. Fuel economy is awful. We averaged 10.7 mpg in 750 miles of mixed city/highway driving in a K1500 with the 5.7.

Once up to speed, Suburban proves a smooth, capable highway cruiser. Bumps are absorbed well and there's only moderate floating over freeway dips, though turns at any speed are accompanied by noticeable body lean. Simulated panic stops induce pronounced nose dive, and in the model we tested, rear-wheel locking, despite the 4-wheel anti-lock brakes.

It's a chore to get in or out of the back doors because the opening between the door pillar and the seat is so narrow. And Suburban is high enough off the ground that most rear-seaters will need to use the grab handle on the roof. The right-side portion of the split middle bench slides forward a few inches, but access to the optional third seat requires some serious stooping.

Once aboard, there's not as much room for adults to stretch out in the rear seats as this vehicle's size would suggest. There's plenty of width for fitting three abreast, and head room is no problem even in the rear-most seats. But neither rear seat affords a surplus of leg room for those over 6-feet.

Cargo room is cavernous and the rear load floor is 25.9 inches off the ground, so it's not a major strain to hoist in heavy objects. Folding the 70/30 split middle bench is a two-step procedure, but there's a handy carpeted panel that hinges down to create a flat load floor from the front seatbacks to the front of the rear-most bench. Unfortunately, the rear bench's seatback does not fold flat, and while that seat is removable, it's heavy and cumbersome.

The driver enjoys good visibility, a car-like seating position, and an easy reach to the controls, though the climate system and radio buttons use the haphazard layout we criticize on the Chevy Blazer.

Suburban loyalists are quite happy with this truck, but unless you're one of them, a van or a compact sport-utility vehicle is likely to be a better value.

Specifications

	4-door wagon
Wheelbase, in.	131.5
Overall length, in.	219.5
Overall width, in.	76.4
Overall height, in.	68.8
Turn diameter, ft.	45.8
Curb weight, lbs.	4657
Fuel capacity, gal.	42.0

Passenger Area Dimensions

Seating capacity	9
Front head room, in.	39.9
Rear head room, in.	38.8
Front leg room, in.	41.7
Rear leg room, in.	36.3

Cargo Dimensions and Payloads

Cargo area length, in.	99.6
Cargo area width, in.	64.0
Cargo area width between wheels, in.	48.5
Cargo area height, in.	40.8
Cargo vol., cu. ft.	149.5
Max. payload, lbs.	3430
Max. trailer weight, lbs.	10,000

Engines

	ohv V-8	ohv V-8	Turbodiesel ohv V-8
Size, liters/cu. in.	5.7/350	7.4/454	6.5/400
Horsepower @ rpm	210 @ 4000[1]	230 @ 3600	190 @ 3400
Torque (lbs./ft.) @ rpm	300 @ 2800	385 @ 1600	385 @ 1700
Availability	S	O[2]	O[2]
EPA city/highway mpg			
4-speed OD automatic	13/17	NA	15/19

1. 190 horsepower in 2500 series 2. 2500 series

Built in Janesville, Wisc.

KEY: Dimensions and capacities are supplied by the manufacturers. **Curb Weight:** base models, not including optional equipment. **Max. payload, lbs.** = gross amount; net payload may be lower due to optional equipment. **Engines: ohv** = overhead valve; **ohc** = overhead cam; **I** = inline cylinders; **V** = cylinders in V configuration; **flat** = horizontally opposed cylinders; **rpm** = revolutions per minute; **OD** = overdrive transmission; **S** = standard; **O** = optional; **NA** = not available.

Prices

Chevrolet Suburban	Retail Price	Dealer Invoice	Fair Price
C1500 4-door wagon	$20406	*	*
K1500 4-door wagon	22657	*	*
C2500 4-door wagon	21638	*	*
K2500 4-door wagon	23858	*	*
Destination charge	640	640	640

C denotes 2WD; K denotes 4WD.

Standard Equipment:

5.7-liter V-8 engine, 4-speed automatic transmission, 4-wheel anti-lock brakes, power steering, front bench seat, dual outside mirrors, intermittent wipers, coolant temperature and oil pressure gauges, voltmeter, trip odometer, Solar-Ray glass, AM/FM radio. **4WD** adds front tow hooks, trans-

Seating for up to seven is available on the Suburban. Front bucket seats and rearmost bench are options.

*Some dealer invoice and fair prices not available at time of publication.

mission oil cooler. 235/75R15 tires (C1500), LT225/75R16D tires (K1500), LT245/75R16E tires (2500).

Optional Equipment:	Retail Price	Dealer Invoice	Fair Price
7.4-liter V-8 engine, 2500	$605	$520	$538
6.5-liter turbodiesel V-8, 2500	2825	2430	2514
Front air conditioning	845	727	752
Front and rear air conditioning	1295	1114	1153
with Group 2	450	387	401
Optional axle ratio	NC	NC	NC
Locking differential	252	217	224
Tailgate body	NC	NC	NC
Silverado Preferred Equipment Group 2	3876	3333	3450
with tailgate	3812	3278	3393

Front air conditioning, tilt steering column, cruise control, power windows and locks, power mirrors, Silverado Decor (cloth upholstery, folding rear seat, lighted visor mirrors, trim, carpeting, floormats, auxiliary lighting, sport steering wheel, deluxe exterior trim, chrome mirrors, bumper guards, rally wheels).

Silverado Preferred Equipment Group 3,			
1500	5581	4800	4967
1500 with tailgate	5517	4745	4910
2500	5331	4585	4745
2500 with tailgate	5267	4530	4688

Group 2 plus: rear air conditioning, deep-tinted glass, cassette player, center and rear seats, alloy wheels.

Cold Climate Pkg.	33	28	29
Engine block heater.			
Convenience Pkg. ZQ2	NC	NC	NC
Power windows and locks.			
Convenience Pkg. ZQ3	383	329	341
Cruise control and tilt steering column.			
Appearance Pkg.	191	164	170
Trailer Towing Pkg.	408	351	363
with diesel engine or 7.4-liter V-8	210	181	187
Engine and transmission oil cooling	198	170	176
with Trailer Towing Pkg.	NC	NC	NC
Rear defogger	154	132	137
Rear defogger and wiper/washer	279	240	248
Rear wiper/washer	125	108	111
Deep-tinted glass	305	262	271
Rear heater	205	176	182
Roof marker lamps	52	45	46
Camper type stainless steel mirrors	45	39	40
with Group 2 or 3 (credit)	(45)	(39)	(39)
Power mirrors, 2500	NC	NC	NC
Conventional two-tone paint	180	155	160
Deluxe two-tone paint	290	249	258
AM/FM cassette	122	105	109
AM/FM cassette w/equalizer	272	234	242
with Group 3	150	129	134
Premium speakers	85	73	76
Radio delete (credit)	(287)	(247)	(247)
Center seat	585	503	521
with Group 2 or 3	NC	NC	NC
Center and rear seats	1095	942	975
with Group 2	578	497	514
Custom cloth reclining split front seat	174	150	155
Custom cloth reclining bucket seats	540	464	481
Leather reclining front bucket and center seats	1555	1337	1384
with center and rear seats	1920	1651	1709
Power driver's seat	240	206	214
Skid Plate Pkg.	225	194	200
Heavy duty front springs	63	54	56
Tow hooks	38	33	34
Roof rack	126	108	112
Tachometer	59	51	53
Wheel flares molding, 1500	180	155	160
Rally wheels	60	52	53
with Group 2	NC	NC	NC
Alloy wheels, 1500	310	267	276
with Group 2	250	215	223

Chevrolet

Chevrolet S10 Blazer

Chevrolet S10 Blazer 5-door 4WD

Chevy's compact sport-utility enters its twelfth season with few changes. It is due to be redesigned next year along the lines of the new S10 pickup. A nearly identical vehicle is sold by GMC dealers as the Jimmy, and it too will be redesigned next year. The Oldsmobile Bravada is also similar to the S10 Blazer and Jimmy. The Jimmy and Bravada are covered in separate reports.

Body Styles/Chassis

S10 Blazer rides a chassis derived from that used for General Motors' compact pickup trucks. It comes in 3- and 5-door body styles. The wheelbase of the 5-door model is 6.5 inches longer than the 3-door's, and its body is longer by 6.5 inches, also. Both body styles have a fold-down tailgate with a separate window that is hinged at the top.

Four-wheel anti-lock brakes that work both in 2- and 4-wheel drive are standard on both body styles. New safety features for '94 include side door guard beams and a center high-mounted stoplamp.

Maximum payload for 2WD models is 1129 pounds on the 3-door and 1453 on the 5-door; for 4WD models, it's 1164 on the 3-door and 1324 on the 5-door.

Powertrains

Two powertrain choices are offered. Standard is a 4.3-liter V-6 rated at 165 horsepower and coupled to a 5-speed manual transmission. Optional is 200-horsepower "enhanced" variant of the 4.3 mated to a 4-speed electronic automatic transmission. For better starts on slippery surfaces, the automatic can be manually locked into second gear.

Rear-wheel drive is standard. Optional with either powertrain combination is GM's Insta-Trac on-demand 4WD. It has automatic locking front hubs and shift-on-the-fly capability between 2WD and 4WD High. An optional electronic transfer case engages or disengages 4WD via a dash button, as opposed to moving the standard floor-mounted lever.

Maximum towing capacity is 5500 pounds on 2WD models and 5500 on 4x4s.

CONSUMER GUIDE®

Chevrolet

Accommodations

Three-door S10s come in base, Tahoe, and Tahoe LT trim. The 5-door continues in Tahoe and Tahoe LT form.

Standard seating for 3-door models consists of front bucket seats only; a 2-place rear bench with folding seatback is optional. Rear shoulder belts come with the rear seat.

Newly standard on 5-door models is a 60/40 split front seat that includes a folding center armrest with dual cup holders. Models with the optional front buckets have a storage tray. A 3-place fold-down rear bench is standard on 4WD models, optional on 2WDs.

A new Driver Convenience option package includes cruise control and tilt steering wheel.

Evaluation

Blazer bowed for 1983 and shows its age against the newer, roomier, and more refined Ford Explorer and Jeep Grand Cherokee.

Explorer is the runaway sales leader in the compact sport-utility class, though even it hasn't kept pace by furnishing a driver-side air bag, as do the Grand Cherokee (which also offers a V-8 option) and the Mitsubishi Montero. It is expected that the redesigned '95 S10 Blazer and Jimmy will have a driver-side air bag.

To the S10's credit, the 4.3-liter V-6 is a strong if noisy engine, with the enhanced version furnishing excellent power off the line. Payload and towing ratings are competitive, and are higher than on most imported compact sport-utilities. We averaged 18.4 mpg with our recent S10 5-door with the enhanced 4.3. That fuel economy is unremarkable, but about par for this class.

The 4-wheel anti-lock brakes and shift-on-the-fly 4WD are other appealing features. S10 Blazer's convenient electronic transfer case mimics the system used on the Ford 4x4s. An advantage to GM's Insta-Trac is that you don't have to stop and back up to fully disengage 4WD, as Ford recommends you do on the Explorer. Neither Ford nor Chevy match the available 4WD system in Jeep Cherokee and Grand Cherokee, which allows 4WD running on dry pavement. (Bravada, however, comes with a permanently engaged 4WD system.)

With a 107-inch wheelbase—6.5 inches longer than the 3-door's—the 5-door S10 boasts vastly improved access to the rear seats. Rear leg room is identical in either body style, but the 5-doors have 15 inches more rear hip room because the seat is positioned in front of the wheel wells rather than between them. The 5-door's longer wheelbase also improves the ride quality, but the Blazer/Jimmy suspension is still among the least compliant in the class. As a result, you'll bounce and bang over bumpy roads. Don't get the off-road suspension unless you do a lot of off-road driving; its on-road ride is punishing. The Tahoe LT, with its softer suspension settings and less-aggressive tires, has a noticeably more comfortable ride.

Gauges and controls don't match the Explorer or Grand Cherokee for overall ease of operation, but the only real shortfall is in hiding the antiquated climate-system slide levers behind the steering wheel rim.

The S10 has some good features, but it can't match the Jeep Grand Cherokee for ride or handling, nor the Explorer for all-round appeal. Factory incentives and dealer discounts are frequent, though there are good reasons that Explorer and Grand Cherokee sell well without such inducements.

Specifications

	3-door wagon	5-door wagon
Wheelbase, in.	100.5	107.0
Overall length, in.	170.3	176.8
Overall width, in.	65.4	65.4
Overall height, in.	64.1	64.1
Turn diameter, ft.	34.6	35.4
Curb weight, lbs.	3221	3397
Fuel capacity, gal.	20.0	20.0

Passenger Area Dimensions

Seating capacity	4	6
Front head room, in.	39.1	39.1
Rear head room, in.	38.7	38.8
Front leg room, in.	42.5	42.5
Rear leg room, in.	35.5	36.5

Cargo Dimensions and Payloads

Cargo area length, in.	68.6	76.1
Cargo area width, in.	50.0	52.5
Cargo area width between wheels, in.	38.4	38.4
Cargo area height, in.	39.1	39.1
Cargo vol., cu. ft.	62.7	74.3
Max. payload, lbs.	1164	1453
Max. trailer weight, lbs.	5500	5500

Engines

	ohv V-6	ohv V-6
Size, liters/cu. in.	4.3/262	4.3/262
Horsepower @ rpm	165 @ 4000	200 @ 4500
Torque (lbs./ft.) @ rpm	235 @ 2400	260 @ 3600
Availability	S	O

EPA city/highway mpg

5-speed OD manual	16/21	
4-speed OD automatic		16/22

Built in Pontiac, Mich.; Moraine, Ohio; and Shreveport, La.

KEY: Dimensions and capacities are supplied by the manufacturers. **Curb Weight:** base models, not including optional equipment. **Max. payload, lbs.** = gross amount; net payload may be lower due to optional equipment. **Engines: ohv** = overhead valve; **ohc** = overhead cam; **I** = inline cylinders; **V** = cylinders in V configuration; **flat** = horizontally opposed cylinders; **rpm** = revolutions per minute; **OD** = overdrive transmission; **S** = standard; **O** = optional; **NA** = not available.

Prices

Chevrolet S10 Blazer

	Retail Price	Dealer Invoice	Fair Price
3-door wagon, 2WD	$15641	*	*
3-door wagon, 4WD	17437	*	*
5-door wagon, 2WD	16931	*	*
5-door wagon, 4WD	19165	*	*
Destination charge	475	475	475

Standard Equipment:

3-door: 4.3-liter V-6, 5-speed manual transmission, anti-lock brakes, power steering, solar-control tinted glass, coolant temperature and oil pressure gauges, voltmeter, AM radio, tow hooks (4WD), dual outside mirrors, front armrests, trip odometer, highback vinyl front reclining bucket seats with folding seatbacks, door map pockets, intermittent wipers, day/night rearview mirror, 205/75R15 tires, full-size spare tire. **5-door** adds: 60/40 reclining cloth front bench seat with storage armrest and cup holders, folding rear bench seat (4WD), Tahoe trim (includes reading lights and illuminated entry, lighted visor mirrors, chrome bumpers and grille, bright bodyside and wheel opening moldings, bright wheel trim rings [4WD], floormats, upgraded interior trim). 4WD models have Insta-Trac part-time 4WD.

Some dealer invoice and fair prices not available at time of publication.

Chevrolet

Optional Equipment:

	Retail Price	Dealer Invoice	Fair Price
RY8 Enhanced Powertrain Pkg.	$1160	$998	$1032

High output 4.3-liter V-6, 4-speed automatic transmission, engine and transmission oil coolers.

	Retail Price	Dealer Invoice	Fair Price
Optional axle ratio	(NC)	(NC)	(NC)
Locking differential	252	217	224
Electronic shift transfer case, 4WD	123	106	109
Air conditioning	805	692	716
Tahoe Equipment Group 2,			
2WD 3-door	1378	1185	1226
4WD 3-door	1346	1158	1198

Chrome bumpers and grille, bright bodyside and wheel opening moldings, bright wheel trim rings (4WD), upgraded interior trim, seat separator console, reading lights, lighted visor mirrors, cargo net, tilt steering wheel, cruise control, AM/FM radio, cloth reclining bucket seats with manual lumbar adjustment, folding rear seat, deep-tinted side glass with light-tinted rear window, 205/75R15 white-letter tires.

Tahoe Equipment Group 2,			
2WD 5-door	651	560	579
4WD 5-door	190	163	169

Cruise control, tilt steering wheel, cloth reclining bucket seats with manual lumbar support, folding rear seat (std. 4WD), AM/FM radio, deep-tinted side glass with light-tinted rear window, 205/75R15 white letter tires.

Tahoe Equipment Group 3, 2WD 3-door	2943	2531	2619
4WD 3-door	2943	2531	2619
2WD 5-door	2365	2034	2105
4WD 5-door	1962	1687	1746

Group 2 plus air conditioning, cassette player, Driver Convenience Pkg. ZM8 (remote tailgate release and rear defogger), Operating Convenience Pkg. (power door locks and windows), rear wiper/washer, luggage carrier, alloy wheels.

Tahoe LT Preferred Equipment Group,			
2WD 3-door	4245	3651	3778
4WD 3-door	4410	3793	3925
2WD 5-door	3776	3247	3361
4WD 5-door	3538	3043	3149

LT trim adds to Tahoe trim reclining leather bucket seats with power lumbar adjustment, 6-way power driver's seat, overhead console, remote keyless entry system, 205/75R15 white letter tires (2WD), 235/75R15 white letter tires (4WD), 2-tone paint, air conditioning, tilt steering wheel, cruise control, power tailgate release, rear defogger, cassette player, deep-tinted glass with light-tinted rear window, rear wiper/washer.

Folding cloth rear seat (std. 4WD 5-door)	435	374	387
with vinyl trim	409	352	364
Deluxe cloth 60/40 reclining			
bench seat, 5-door	(NC)	(NC)	(NC)
5-door with Tahoe			
Group 2 or 3 (credit)	(237)	(203)	(203)

Credit when 60/40 reclining cloth bench seat replaces standard reclining cloth bucket seats.

Custom highback vinyl bucket seats			
(NA 5-doors)	(NC)	(NC)	(NC)
Deluxe cloth highback reclining bucket seats with manual lumbar adjustment,			
3-door	221	190	197
5-door	211	181	188
Deluxe cloth highback reclining bucket seats with power lumbar adjustment and 6-way power driver's seat, 3-door	366	315	326
5-door	501	431	446
3- and 5-door with Tahoe Group 2 or 3	290	249	258
3- and 5-door with Tahoe LT Group (credit)	(650)	(559)	(559)

Requires Operating Convenience Pkg.

Operating Convenience Pkg., 3-door	367	316	327
5-door	542	466	482

Includes power windows with driver-side express down and automatic power door locks.

Driver Convenience Pkg. ZQ3	383	329	341

Includes cruise control and tilt steering wheel.

Driver Convenience Pkg. ZM8	197	169	175

Includes rear defogger and remote tailgate release.

Remote keyless entry system	135	116	120

Front bucket seats with center console and electronic instrumentation are among the S10 Blazer options.

	Retail Price	Dealer Invoice	Fair Price
Electronic instrumentation	$195	$168	$174
Air dam with fog lamps	115	99	102
Power mirrors	83	71	74
Heavy duty shock absorbers	40	34	36
Heavy duty front springs	63	54	56

Includes heavy duty shock absorbers.

Heavy duty battery	56	48	50
Heavy duty cooling system, with 5-speed manual transmission	135	116	120
Spare wheel and tire carrier	159	137	142
Cold Climate Pkg., 5-door	109	94	97
3-door	179	154	159
Front console	145	125	129
Overhead console	83	71	74
Luggage carrier, base and Tahoe Group 2	126	108	112
Deep-tinted glass	225	194	200
Tahoe Group 2 and 3, Tahoe LT	81	70	72
with light-tinted rear window (std. Tahoe LT)	144	124	128
Rear wiper/washer	125	108	111

Requires Driver Convenience Pkg. ZM8.

Sliding side window, 3-door	257	221	229

Requires deep-tint glass.

Radio delete (credit)	(95)	(82)	(82)
AM/FM radio	131	113	117
AM/FM cassette	253	218	225
with Tahoe Group 2	122	105	109
AM/FM cassette with equalizer	403	347	359
with Tahoe Group 2	272	234	242
with Tahoe Group 3 and Tahoe LT	150	129	134
AM/FM CD player	537	462	478
with Tahoe Group 2	406	349	361
with Tahoe Group 3 and Tahoe LT	284	244	253
Shield Pkg. (NA 2WD)	75	65	67

Includes transfer case, front differential skid plates, fuel tank and steering linkage shield.

Off-road suspension	182	157	162
with Tahoe Group 2 or 3	122	105	109
Trailering Special Equipment (heavy duty)			
with Enhanced Powertrain Pkg.	210	181	187
with 5-speed manual transmission	345	297	307
Trailering Special Equipment (light duty),			
with Enhanced Powertrain Pkg.	109	94	97
with 5-speed manual transmission	300	258	267
Special 2-tone paint	227	195	202
Custom 2-tone (std. Tahoe LT)	275	237	245
Wheel opening moldings, 3-door	43	37	38
5-door	13	11	12
Rally wheels, 3-door	92	79	82
Alloy wheels	340	292	303
5-door or Tahoe Group 2	248	213	221
Special alloy wheels, 5-door or with Tahoe Group 2	280	241	249
205/75R15 on/off road white letter tires	170	146	151
with Tahoe Group 2 or 3	49	42	44

CONSUMER GUIDE®

Chevrolet

Chevrolet S10 Pickup

RECOMMENDED

Chevrolet S10 Pickup Extended Cab 4WD

The S10 compact pickup has been redesigned for 1994 with new styling, more powerful engines, and available 4-wheel anti-lock brakes. The S10 is again available with rear- or 4-wheel drive, regular or extended cabs, and 4-cylinder or V-6 power.

The similar GMC Sonoma also has been redesigned (see separate report).

Body Styles/Chassis

The 1994 S10 uses a modified version of the previous-generation platform, so wheelbases are unchanged at 108.3 inches for the regular-cab short-bed, 117.9 for the regular-cab long-bed, and 122.9 for the extended-cab.

However, body lengths increase significantly: The regular-cab short-bed gains 10.6 inches, the regular-cab long bed 9.9 inches, and the extended-cab 10 inches. Length of the standard cargo bed remains at six feet. Long-bed models retain a 7.5-foot box.

A center high-mounted stoplamp and side door guard beams are newly standard.

Rear anti-lock brakes are standard on 4-cylinder S10s. V-6 models have 4-wheel anti-lock brakes that work in both rear- and 4WD. Last year, rear anti-lock brakes were standard and worked only in 2WD.

Though the cab is just one inch wider on the outside, there is three inches more shoulder room this year. Chevy claims the new S10 is larger than the rival Ford Ranger (the best-selling compact pickup) in nine interior dimensions.

Regular-cab models come with a 3-place bench seat; extended-cabs add two rear jump seats. Front buckets are optional on both.

The redesigned dashboard has round analog gauges and rotary climate controls. A new center console contains two cupholders. And two auxiliary 12-volt power outlet are available.

Base and uplevel LS models are offered. Two new option packages debut. The new Super Sport package, available only with rear-wheel drive as a regular-cab short-bed model, includes the 195-horsepower 4.3-liter V-6, 4-speed automatic, and sport suspension package. An off-road package called the ZR2 gives the 4WD regular-cab a 4-inch-wider track, a 3-inch higher stance, and an off-road suspension/tire package. The ZR2 is available with either V-6.

Payload ceilings are 1703 pounds for the regular-cab short-bed, 1743 for the regular-cab long-bed, and 1519 for the extended-cab model.

Powertrains

The base engine is a new 118-horsepower 2.2-liter 4-cylinder and is available with either a 5-speed manual or a 4-speed automatic transmission with electronic shift controls. The 2.2 replaces a 105-horsepower 2.5-liter four.

Gone is last year's 125-horsepower 2.8-liter V-6, which was available only with manual transmission.

Again optional on 2WD models and standard on 4WD models is a 165-horsepower 4.3-liter V-6. It's available with either transmission.

Optional on all models and mandatory with the Super Sport package is a 195-horsepower "enhanced" version of the 4.3-liter V-6. With the ZR2 package, the enhanced V-6 uses only the 5-speed manual; in all other applications, it uses the automatic transmission.

The available 4WD system is again Chevrolet's Insta-Trac setup. It's an on-demand, part-time 4WD system that's not for use on dry pavement. It has automatic locking front hubs and shift-on-the-fly between 2WD and 4WD High.

Again optional on all 4WD models is an electronic-shift transfer case. Instead of a floor-mounted transfer-case lever, this option allows shifting into and out of 4WD and between 4WD High and 4WD Low with the push of a dashboard button.

Base models can tow up to 2000 pounds. A heavy-duty towing package, which requires the 165-horsepower 4.3 V-6, allows 2WD models to tow up to 6000 pounds and enables 4x4s to pull up to 5500 pounds.

Evaluation

General Motors' redesign of the S10 and GMC Sonoma has put these compact pickups among the very best in overall performance, ergonomics, and refinement. These last two areas of improvement are significant since, as with other small pickups, about 90 percent of S10s are purchased for personal use.

GM's new models lack the driver-side air bag of the Dodge Dakota, a mid-size pickup that also offers an available V-8 engine. But the S10 LS 2WD extended-cab model we tested was a fine match in all areas for its main competitor, the Ford Ranger. That's something we couldn't say about the previous S10, which felt crude compared to the Ranger.

The S10's new sense of polish begins with the cabin. It feels much roomier than its predecessor, especially in the regular-cab version, which now has noticeably more rearward seat travel and more storage space. The extended-cab's rear jump seats remain best-suited to children. And both cab styles suffer a hump in the floor that intrudes on the leg room of the front passenger.

But with 20 percent more glass area, the cabins feel airier, and visibility is top-notch, helped by large, well-placed outside mirrors. Wind noise is reduced, as well, and is now no louder than many cars at highway speeds.

A new dashboard with softer, rounded forms replaces the old squared-off, hard-edged design. Adding to the sense of refinement are new soft-touch rotary controls for the climate system. They're simpler than the previous collection of notchy levers. The door-mounted power window and lock switches and the radio controls are more inviting, as well. The center console on bucket-seat models contains dual

CONSUMER GUIDE®

Chevrolet

cupholders and several covered and open bins, and all models have door map pockets.

When it was cold, the 165-horsepower V-6 in our test model ran rough and its fan was intrusively loud. But both became quieter as the truck warmed up and the V-6 provided good acceleration. The automatic transmission generally changed gears smoothly, though it did not consistently shift down promptly for more power in low-speed passing situations. In a mix of city, highway, and suburban driving, we averaged 18.4 mpg.

Brief test drives in a 4-cylinder model showed that it provided best performance with a manual transmission, while the new enhanced V-6 furnished outstanding power with either gearbox. Running on modest 15-inch all-season tires and benefitting from a long wheelbase, our test LS had a smooth, car-like ride. It easily absorbed most bumps and took dips and swells with minimal bouncing. Different tire and suspension setups are sure to have different ride characteristics, and the S10 brochure in fact warns that higher-payload and off-road suspensions are much firmer than the base arrangement.

Though body lean was evident in turns, our test LS felt balanced and poised in changes of direction, with a natural feel to the power steering and fine resistance to gusty crosswinds. The standard anti-lock brakes prevented lock-up during simulated panic stops, but the brake pedal felt uncomfortably squishy in everyday use.

Like the old S10, the new one is competitive with the Ranger in pricing. But unlike the old one, it's competitive in comfort, design, and evident attention to assembly quality, too.

Prices

Chevrolet S10 Pickup

	Retail Price	Dealer Invoice	Fair Price
2WD regular cab, short bed	$9655	$9124	$9424
2WD regular cab, short bed (California Pkg.)	11495	—	—
2WD regular cab, long bed	9955	9407	9707
LS 2WD regular cab, short bed	10790	9765	10265
LS 2WD regular cab, long bed	11366	10286	10786
4WD regular cab, short bed	14155	13376	13876
4WD regular cab, long bed	14455	13660	14160
LS 4WD regular cab, short bed	15290	13837	14337
LS 4WD regular cab, long bed	15866	14359	14859
LS 2WD extended cab, short bed	11790	10670	11170
LS 4WD extended cab, short bed	16310	14761	15261
Destination charge	470	470	470

California Pkg. 2WD regular cab short bed dealer invoice and fair price not available at time of publication.

Standard Equipment:

2.2-liter 4-cylinder engine, 5-speed manual transmission, anti-lock rear brakes, power steering, intermittent wipers, cloth or vinyl fold-down bench seat with head restraints, AM radio, solar-control glass, coolant temperature and oil pressure gauges, voltmeter, trip odometer, passenger-side visor mirror, door map pockets, vinyl full floor covering, rear step bumper, 205/75R15 all-season tires, full-size spare tire. **California Pkg.** adds: air conditioning, AM/FM cassette, tachometer, sliding rear window, alloy wheels. **LS** adds: 60/40 reclining split bench seat with armrest, vinyl jump seat (extended cab), upgraded door trim, reading lights, AM/FM radio, full carpet, lighted visor mirrors, chrome grille, wheel trim rings. **LS regular cab, long bed** adds: Exterior Appearance Pkg. (color-keyed bumpers, gray bodyside moldings with bright insert, bright wheel opening moldings). **4WD** has 4.3-liter V-6, 4-wheel anti-lock brakes, front tow hooks.

Specifications

	Short bed	Long bed	Extended cab
Wheelbase, in.	108.3	117.9	122.9
Overall length, in.	188.8	204.1	202.8
Overall width, in.	67.9	67.9	67.9
Overall height, in.	60.5	60.5	60.5
Turn diameter, ft.	36.9	39.9	41.6
Curb weight, lbs.	2822	2874	3081
Fuel capacity, gal.	20.0	20.0	20.0

Passenger Area Dimensions

Seating capacity	3	3	5
Front head room, in.	39.5	39.5	39.5
Rear head room, in.	—	—	NA
Front leg room, in.	42.4	42.4	42.4
Rear leg room, in.	—	—	NA

Cargo Dimensions and Payloads

Cargo area length, in.	72.6	88.6	72.6
Cargo area width, in.	56.5	56.5	56.5
Cargo area width between wheels, in.	39.5	39.5	39.5
Cargo area height, in.	16.8	16.8	16.8
Max. payload, lbs.	1703	1743	1519
Max. trailer weight, lbs.	6000	6000	6000

1. 49.1 on Sportside.

Engines

	ohv I-4	ohv V-6	ohv V-6
Size, liters/cu. in.	2.2/134	4.3/262	4.3/262
Horsepower	118 @ 5200	165 @ 4000	195 @ 4500
Torque (lbs./ft.)	130 @ 2800	235 @ 2400	260 @ 3600
Availability	S	O[1]	O[2]

EPA city/highway mpg

5-speed OD manual	23/28	18/23	18/25
4-speed OD automatic	19/25	18/23	17/24

1. Standard on 4WD models. 2. Required on Super Sport model.

Built in Shreveport, La., and Linden, N.J.

KEY: Dimensions and capacities are supplied by the manufacturers. **Curb Weight:** base models, not including optional equipment. **Max. payload, lbs.** = gross amount; net payload may be lower due to optional equipment. **Engines: ohv** = overhead valve; **ohc** = overhead cam; **I** = inline cylinders; **V** = cylinders in V configuration; **flat** = horizontally opposed cylinders; **rpm** = revolutions per minute; **OD** = overdrive transmission; **S** = standard; **O** = optional; **NA** = not available.

Optional Equipment:

4.3-liter V-6, 2WD	850	731	757
Includes 4-wheel anti-lock brakes.			
4.3-liter high output (HO) V-6, 2WD	1409	1212	1254
4WD	559	481	498
Includes 4-wheel anti-lock brakes (std. 4WD), tachometer, engine oil and transmission oil coolers, heavy duty radiator.			
4-speed automatic transmission	927	797	825
Optional axle ratio	NC	NC	NC
Locking differential	252	217	224
Electronic shift transfer case, 4WD	123	106	109
Air conditioning	805	692	716
Preferred Equipment Group 1, base regular cab (credit)	(150)	(129)	(129)
Credit for deletion of AM radio and rear step bumper.			
Preferred Equipment Group 6, LS 2WD regular and extended cab with 4.3-liter or 4.3-liter HO engine, LS 4WD regular and extended cab	235	202	209
Includes AM/FM cassette, sliding rear window.			
Preferred Equipment Group Bonus Value, LS 2WD regular and extended cab with 2.2-liter engine, LS 4WD regular and extended cab with 4-speed automatic transmission	235	202	209
Preferred Equipment Group 6 plus alloy wheels.			

Chevrolet

	Retail Price	Dealer Invoice	Fair Price
Exterior Appearance Pkg., LS (std. LS regular cab, long bed)	$276	$237	$246

Includes color-keyed bumpers, gray bodyside moldings with bright inserts, bright wheel trim rings.

	Retail	Dealer	Fair
SS Pkg., LS 2WD regular cab, short bed	629	541	560

LS trim, locking differential, fog lamps, body-color grille, leather-wrapped steering wheel, alloy wheels. Requires 4.3-liter HO engine, 4-speed automatic transmission, 3.42 axle ratio, Sport Suspension, solid paint.

Air dam with fog lamps	115	99	102
Rear step bumper, base regular cab with Preferred Equipment Group 1	130	112	116
Cold-Climate Pkg.	109	94	97

Heavy duty battery, engine block heater.

ZQ6 Convenience Group	475	409	423

Power windows door locks and mirrors.

ZQ3 Convenience Group	383	329	341

Cruise control, tilt steering wheel.

ZR2 Sport Performance Pkg., LS 4WD regular cab, short bed	1685	1449	1500

Includes Shield Pkg., Bilstein shock absorbers, heavy duty springs, wheel opening flares, 31 x 10.5R15 on/off road tires, modified jack and spare tire storage winch, chassis enhancements for increased height and width.

Heavy Duty Suspension Pkg.,			
2WD regular cab, short bed	664	571	591
4WD regular cab	217	187	193

Includes heavy duty rear springs and shock absorbers. 4WD adds 235/75R15 tires.

Off-road Pkg., 4WD regular			
cab short bed	481	414	428
4WD regular cab, long bed	417	359	371
4WD extended cab	328	282	292

Heavy duty front springs, Bilstein shock absorbers, stabilizer bar, upsized torsion bar, jounce bumpers, 235/75R15 white letter tires.

Sport Pkg., LS 2WD regular cab,			
short bed	316	272	281
LS 2WD regular cab, long bed	252	217	224

Heavy duty rear springs and shock absorbers, 215/65R15 white letter tires.

Carpet	55	47	49
5-lead wiring harness	41	35	36
Below eye line black mirrors	52	45	46
Special 2-tone paint, LS with Exterior Appearance Pkg.	227	195	202

Includes striping.

Sport 2-tone paint, LS	172	148	153
AM radio, base regular cab with Group 1	95	82	85
AM/FM radio	226	194	201
AM/FM cassette	122	105	109
AM/FM cassette, base regular cab with Group 1	348	299	310
AM/FM cassette with equalizer	272	234	242
with Group 6	150	129	134
Base regular cab with Group 1	498	428	443
AM/FM CD player	406	349	361
with Group 6	284	244	253
Base regular cab with Group 1	632	544	562
Vinyl or cloth bench seat	NC	NC	NC

Requires base regular cab with Group 1.

Cloth 60/40 bench seat	NC	NC	NC
Cloth reclining bucket seats with center console, regular cab	181	156	161
extended cab	156	134	139
Shield Pkg., 4WD	126	108	112

Includes transfer case and front differential skid plates, fuel tank and steering linkage shields.

Trailering Special Pkg., 4.3-liter engine and 4-speed automatic transmission	408	351	363
with 4.3-liter engine and 5-speed manual transmission	345	297	307
with 4.3-liter HO engine	210	181	187

Includes 7-lead wiring harness, weight distributing hitch platform, heavy duty flasher. 4.3-liter HO engine also includes heavy duty cooling system. Base regular cab with Group 1 requires rear step bumper. 2WD regular cab with 5-speed manual transmission requires 3.08 axle ratio. 4WD regular cab with 5-speed manual transmission requires 3.42 axle ratio.

Tachometer	59	51	53
Leather-wrapped steering wheel, LS	54	46	48
Sliding rear window	113	97	101
Heavy duty battery	56	48	50
Heavy duty cooling system	135	116	120
with 4-speed automatic transmisson	198	170	176
Sport striping	69	59	61
Argent alloy wheels, LS	280	213	249
Cast alloy wheels, LS	248	213	221
205/75R15 white letter all-season tires	121	104	108
215/65R15 white letter on/off road tires	170	146	151
235/75R15 white letter on/off road tires, 4WD with Heavy Duty Suspension Pkg.	182	157	162

Top: The S10 pickup's redesigned interior is spacious and ergonomically pleasing. Middle: The sporty new SS package for 2WD regular-cab models. Above: A base 2WD regular-cab long-bed.

44

CONSUMER GUIDE®

Chrysler

Chrysler Town & Country

Chrysler Town & Country

A passenger-side air bag and a larger engine top changes to Town & Country, the luxury version of Chrysler Corporation's minivan.

Town & Country is built from the same design as the Dodge Caravan and Plymouth Voyager, which are covered in separate reports. All three gain side door guard beams and other changes that allow them to meet all U.S. passenger-car safety standards through 1998.

Body Styles/Chassis

Caravan and Voyager come in regular- and extended-length bodies, but Town & Country is available only as an extended-length model. Four-wheel anti-lock brakes are standard on both 2- and 4-wheel-drive versions of the Town & Country.

Maximum payload is 2000 pounds.

Powertrains

Town & Country's standard engine is now a 162-horsepower 3.8-liter V-6, a new engine for Chrysler's minivans. It replaces a 150-horsepower 3.3-liter V-6.

The standard 4-speed automatic transmission gains a switch that allows locking out the overdrive fourth gear.

Front-wheel drive is standard; optional is the same all-wheel-drive (AWD) system offered on the Caravan and Voyager. It's permanently engaged and normally sends 90 percent of the engine's power to the front wheels. When tire slip occurs, the system automatically sends power to the wheels with the most grip.

Standard towing capacity is 2000 pounds, though an optional Towing Package raises that to 3500 pounds.

Accommodations

Seven-passenger seating is standard and includes four bucket seats and a 3-passenger bench seat in back. A new no-charge option replaces the middle buckets with a bench seat incorporating two child safety seats that fold from the backrest. The child seats previously were offered only on the Caravan and Voyager.

Town & Country's dashboard has been redesigned to accommodate the passenger-side air bag and a knee bolster. The glove box has been moved lower on the dashboard and the radio, in the center, has been moved higher to make it easier to reach.

Evaluation

Even though the Town & Country comes loaded with features, there's little of substance here that can't be had for less money on Dodge and Plymouth models.

Still, dual air bags are just part of an impressive array of safety features that includes anti-lock brakes, side door guard beams, and available child safety seats and AWD.

The Chrysler badge does bespeak luxury, however, and Town & Country won't disappoint on the road. It's stable in turns, its ride soft and controlled, and wind and road noise are lower than ever thanks to improved sound insulation.

Specifications

	4-door van
Wheelbase, in.	119.3
Overall length, in.	192.8
Overall width, in.	72.0
Overall height, in.	68.8
Turn diameter, ft.	43.0
Curb weight, lbs.	3929
Fuel capacity, gal.	20.0[1]

1. 18.0 gal with AWD.

Passenger Area Dimensions

Seating capacity	7
Front head room, in.	39.1
Rear head room, in.	38.4
Front leg room, in.	41.5
Rear leg room, in.	37.7

Available Seating

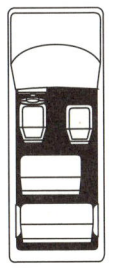

Cargo Dimensions and Payloads

Cargo area length, in.	96.4
Cargo area width, in.	58.0
Cargo area width between wheels, in.	50.9
Cargo area height, in.	NA
Cargo vol., cu. ft.	141.3
Max. payload, lbs.	2000
Max. trailer weight, lbs.	3500

Engines

	ohv V-6
Size, liters/cu. in.	3.8/230
Horsepower @ rpm	162 @ 4400
Torque (lbs./ft.) @ rpm	213 @ 3600
Availability	S

EPA city/highway mpg

4-speed OD automatic	16/22

Built in St. Louis, Mo.

KEY: Dimensions and capacities are supplied by the manufacturers. **Curb Weight:** base models, not including optional equipment. **Max. payload, lbs.** = gross amount; net payload may be lower due to optional equipment. **Engines: ohv** = overhead valve; **ohc** = overhead cam; **I** = inline cylinders; **V** = cylinders in V configuration; **flat** = horizontally opposed cylinders; **rpm** = revolutions per minute; **OD** = overdrive transmission; **S** = standard; **O** = optional; **NA** = not available.

Chrysler • Dodge

Acceleration also improves with the new 3.8-liter V-6 engine, and a fully ladened Town & Country no longer feels taxed. Fuel economy will likely be in the 15-17 mpg range on surface streets, and maybe the low 20s on the highway with front-wheel drive (and a little less with AWD).

Rivals such as the Oldsmobile Silhouette, Mercury Villager, and Nissan Quest now have a driver-side air bag, but none has dual air bags or as much cargo space behind the rear seat as Town & Country.

Prices

Chrysler Town & Country	Retail Price	Dealer Invoice	Fair Price
4-door van with Pkg. 29X	$27284	$24700	$25600
AWD 4-door van with Pkg. 29X	29380	26544	27444
Destination charge	560	560	560

Standard Equipment:

Pkg. 29X: 3.8-liter V-6, 4-speed automatic transmission, anti-lock brakes, power steering, driver- and passenger-side air bags, front and rear air conditioning, 7-passenger seating (bucket seats in front and middle rows and 3-passenger rear bench seat), power driver's seat, cloth and leather upholstery, power front door and rear quarter vent windows, programmable power locks, forward storage console, overhead console (with compass, outside temperature readout, and front and rear reading lights), rear defogger, intermittent wipers, rear wiper/washer, cruise control, leather-wrapped tilt steering wheel, illuminated remote keyless entry system, remote fuel door and decklid releases, tinted windshield and front door glass, sunscreen glass (other windows), electronic instruments (tachometer, coolant temperature and oil pressure gauges, trip odometer), floormats, luggage rack, heated power mirrors, lighted visor mirrors, AM/FM cassette with six Infinity speakers, imitation woodgrain exterior trim, fog lamps, 205/70R15 tires, alloy wheels. **AWD** has permanent all-wheel drive.

Optional Equipment:

Leather seat trim	NC	NC	NC
Pkg. 29Y	NC	NC	NC
Substitutes gold stripe and gold painted alloy wheels for woodgrain exterior trim.			
7-passenger bench seating	NC	NC	NC
Front bucket seats, reclining 2-passenger middle and folding 3-passenger rear bench seats. Includes integrated child seats.			
Trailer Towing Group	270	230	236
AWD	201	171	176
CD player with equalizer and six Infinity speakers	170	145	149
Extra cost paint	97	82	85
Whitewall tires, with Pkg. 29X	69	59	60
Alloy wheels, gold painted, with Pkg. 29X	NC	NC	NC
Alloy wheels, white painted, with Pkg. 29Y	NC	NC	NC

Cargo space is good even with all seats in place.

Dodge Caravan

✓ **BEST BUY**

Dodge Caravan ES

Dodge's version of the Chrysler Corporation minivan has a new passenger-side air bag, side door guard beams, and other changes that enable it to meet all passenger car safety requirements through 1998. It also gets a larger optional V-6 engine.

The similar Chrysler Town & Country and Plymouth Voyager also get those features and are covered in separate reports.

Body Styles/Chassis

Regular-length Caravans have a wheelbase of 112 inches and a body length of 178. Grand Caravans add seven inches to the wheelbase and 14 inches to the body length. Both versions come in base, SE, LE, and ES form. A cargo version, called the C/V, also is available in both body styles.

A sliding side door and a one-piece tailgate are standard; dual swing-out rear doors are optional on cargo models.

All Caravans come standard with front-wheel drive. This year, the optional all-wheel drive (AWD) is available only on Grand models. Four-wheel anti-lock brakes are optional only on Caravans with either the 3.3- or 3.8-liter engines.

Among other changes for '94; the dashboard has been redesigned, the optional bench seat with two integrated child safety seats gets a reclining seatback, and all models have new bumper fascias and body moldings.

Maximum payload on CV models of both body lengths is 2000 pounds.

Powertrains

A 100-horsepower 2.5-liter 4-cylinder engine is standard on the base Caravan.

Optional on base Caravans and standard on SE, LE, ES, and base Grand models is a 142-horsepower 3.0-liter V-6.

A 3.3-liter V-6 with 162 horsepower—up 12 from last year—is standard on Grand SE, LE, and ES and optional on regular SE, LE, and ES models.

The new 3.8-liter V-6 is optional only on Grand LE and ES. It's also rated at 162 horsepower, but has more torque than the 3.3, 213 pounds/feet to 194.

A 5-speed manual transmission is standard on the base model. A 3-speed automatic is used with the 2.5 and 3.0 engines. A 4-speed overdrive automatic is mandatory with

Dodge

the 3.3- and 3.8-liter V-6s and optional with the 3.0. The 4-speed automatic gains a new switch that locks out overdrive.

Grand Caravan's optional permanently engaged AWD system normally sends 90 percent of the engine's power to the front wheels. If they start to slip, it automatically increases power to the rear wheels until traction is restored.

Specifications

	4-door van	4-door van
Wheelbase, in.	112.3	119.3
Overall length, in.	178.1	192.8
Overall width, in.	72.0	72.0
Overall height, in.	66.0	66.7
Turn diameter, ft.	40.5	42.5
Curb weight, lbs.	3275	3602[1]
Fuel capacity, gal.	20.0	20.0[2]

1. 4008 lbs., AWD. 2. 18.0 AWD.

Passenger Area Dimensions

Seating capacity	5-7	7
Front head room, in.	39.1	39.1
Rear head room, in.	38.5	38.4
Front leg room, in.	41.5	41.5
Rear leg room, in.	37.6	37.7

Available Seating

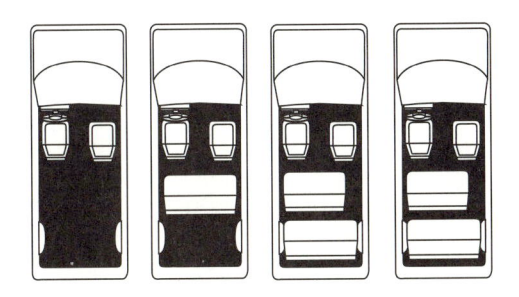

Cargo Dimensions and Payloads

Cargo area length, in.	81.9	96.4
Cargo area width, in.	59.0	59.0
Cargo area width between wheels, in.	50.9	50.9
Cargo area height, in.	48.0	48.4
Cargo vol., cu. ft.	133.0	160.0
Max. payload, lbs.	2000	2000
Max. trailer weight, lbs.	3500	3500

Engines

	ohv V-6	ohc V-6	ohv V-6	ohv V-6
Size, liters/cu. in.	2.5/153	3.0/181	3.3/201	3.8/230
Horsepower @ rpm	100 @ 4800	142 @ 5000	162 @ 4800	162 @ 4400
Torque (lbs./ft.) @ rpm	135 @ 2800	173 @ 2400	194 @ 3600	213 @ 3600
Availability	S	O	O[1]	O[2]

EPA city/highway mpg

5-speed OD manual	20/27			
3-speed automatic	20/24	19/23		
4-speed OD automatic		18/23	NA	16/22

1. Std., Grand Caravan and AWD. 2. Optional, Grand Caravan LE and ES.

Built in St. Louis, Mo., and Canada.

KEY: Dimensions and capacities are supplied by the manufacturers. **Curb Weight:** base models, not including optional equipment. **Max. payload, lbs.** = gross amount; net payload may be lower due to optional equipment. **Engines: ohv** = overhead valve; **ohc** = overhead cam; **I** = inline cylinders; **V** = cylinders in V configuration; **flat** = horizontally opposed cylinders; **rpm** = revolutions per minute; **OD** = overdrive transmission; **S** = standard; **O** = optional; **NA** = not available.

Standard towing capacity is 2000 pounds. The optional Heavy Duty Trailer Towing Group raises that to 3500 pounds.

Accommodations

Five-passenger seating is standard on the base model; all others come with seating for seven. The Quad-Command option replaces the middle bench with a pair of reclining bucket seats on 7-passenger models.

A pair of integrated child safety seats is an option on 7-passenger models. So equipped, the 2-place middle bench seat can be used as a regular seat or converted for use by youngsters weighing between 20 and 40 pounds by folding out sections of the backrest. Youngsters are secured by a built-in 5-point lap/shoulder harness.

The CV comes with two front buckets.

Evaluation

In combined sales, the Caravan, Voyager, and Town & Country account for nearly 50 percent of the minivan market and boast a high percentage of repeat buyers. And with good reason. Their car-like road manners, efficient use of interior space, and combination of features set the standard for this class. Additional sound insulation makes them quieter than ever, and the revamped dash puts the radio and climate systems within easier reach.

Avoid the weak 4-cylinder engine and go with one of the V-6s. The 4-cylinder doesn't have enough power for vehicles this heavy. Though we're glad Chrysler offers optional anti-lock brakes, it's a shame they're not available on all models.

Regular-length versions can seat seven people, though it gets crowded if all are adults. And regular-length Caravans don't have much cargo room with all seats in place.

The Grand Caravan has more passenger space and plenty of cargo room at the rear. Choose the 4-bucket Quad Command option and you get a middle-seat tilt feature that eases passage to the rear bench from the side door, but none of Caravan's seats are light enough to be easily removed. Hauling out the 3-place rear bench seat is a backbreaker for one person.

Standard front-wheel drive furnishes good traction. The unobtrusive AWD system is a boon in the snow belt, but it makes the ride rougher over bumps and costs some acceleration and fuel economy because it adds 300 pounds or more to the curb weight. With any V-6 model, you'll be lucky to break 20 mpg even on the highway.

Ford's new front-drive Windstar, which is sized like the Grand Caravan and comes with dual air bags, looks to be the strongest threat yet to the Dodge and Plymouth minivans. Chrysler is taking the Windstar seriously. It continues to fine-tune its Caravan and Voyager, and discounts ought to become even more readily available on these high-value minivans as Windstar makes its presence felt.

Prices

Dodge Caravan

	Retail Price	Dealer Invoice	Fair Price
Base SWB	$14919	$13629	$14329
Base Grand	18178	16522	17222
SE SWB	18139	16462	17162
Grand SE	19304	17513	18413
Grand SE AWD	21982	19869	20769
LE SWB	21963	19827	20727
Grand LE	22883	20662	21562

Dodge

	Retail Price	Dealer Invoice	Fair Price
Grand LE AWD	$25560	$23017	$23917
ES SWB	22472	20275	21175
Grand ES	23392	21110	22010
Grand ES AWD	26069	23466	24366
Destination charge	560	560	560

SWB denotes standard wheelbase; AWD denotes All-Wheel Drive.

Standard Equipment:

Base: 2.5-liter 4-cylinder engine, 5-speed manual transmission, driver- and passenger-side air bags, power steering, cloth front bucket seats, 3-passenger middle bench seat, tinted glass, trip odometer, coolant temperature gauge, dual outside mirrors, visor mirrors, AM/FM radio, intermittent wipers, rear wiper/washer, 195/75R14 tires, wheel covers. **Base Grand** adds: 3.0-liter V-6 engine, 3-speed automatic transmission, 7-passenger seating (front buckets and 2-place middle and 3-place rear bench seats), rear trim panel storage and cup holders, 205/70R15 tires. **SE** adds to Base: 3.0-liter V-6 engine, 3-speed automatic transmission, cruise control, power mirrors, cassette player, power remote tailgate release, tilt steering wheel, front passenger lockable underseat storage drawer, striping, dual note horn. **Grand SE** adds to Base Grand: 3.3-liter V-6 engine, 4-speed automatic transmission, cruise control, power mirrors, cassette player, power remote tailgate release, tilt steering wheel, front passenger lockable underseat storage drawer, striping, dual note horn. **LE** adds to SE: front air conditioning, front storage console, overhead console with trip computer, rear defogger, power rear quarter vent windows, power door locks, remote keyless entry system, tachometer, oil pressure gauge, voltmeter, heated power mirrors, lighted visor mirrors, illuminated entry system, headlamp time delay, floormats, 205/70R15 tires. **Grand LE** adds to Grand SE: front air conditioning, front storage console, overhead console with trip computer, rear defogger, power rear quarter vent windows, power door locks, remote keyless entry system, tachometer, oil pressure gauge, voltmeter, heated power mirrors, lighted visor mirrors, illuminated entry system, headlamp time delay, floormats. **ES** adds to LE and Grand LE: ES Decor Group. **AWD** models have permanently engaged all-wheel drive.

Quick Order Packages:

Pkgs. 21T, 22T, 24T Base SWB and 26T Base SWB, Base Grand	213	181	196

Front air conditioning, map and cargo lights, power remote liftgate release, front passenger underseat lockable storage drawer, bodyside molding, dual horns. Pkg. 22T requires 3-speed automatic transmission; Pkg. 24T requires 3.0-liter engine and 3-speed automatic transmission; Pkg. 26T requires 3.0-liter engine and 4-speed transmission.

Pkg. 26B SE SWB and Pkg. 28B SE SWB, Grand SE, Grand SE AWD	213	181	196

Pkgs. 24B-28B add to SE standard equipment front air conditioning, map and cargo lights, rear defogger. SE SWB Pkg. 24B requires 4-speed automatic transmission; SE SWB Pkg. 28B requires 3.3-liter engine and 4-speed automatic transmission.

Pkg. 26D SE SWB, and Pkg. 28D SE SWB, Grand SE, Grand SE AWD	1159	985	1066

Pkgs. 26D-28D add to Pkgs. 26-28B forward and overhead consoles, oil pressure and voltage gauges, tachometer, lighted visor mirrors, Light Group, power door locks and rear quarter vent windows, floormats, deluxe insulation. SE SWB Pkg. 26D requires 4-speed automatic transmission; SE SWB Pkg. 28D requires 3.3-liter engine and 4-speed automatic transmission.

Pkg. 26K LE SWB, and Pkg. 28K LE SWB, Grand LE, Grand LE AWD and Pkg. 29K Grand LE, Grand LE AWD	306	260	282

Pkgs. 26K-29K add to LE standard equipment: power driver's seat, power windows, AM/FM radio with cassette player, equalizer and six Infinity speakers, sunscreen glass. LE SWB Pkg. 26K requires 4-speed automatic transmission; LE SWB Pkg. 28K requires 3.3-liter engine and 4-speed automatic transmission; Grand LE and Grand LE AWD require 3.8-liter engine.

Pkg. 28L and 29L Grand LE, Grand LE AWD	962	818	885

Pkgs. 28L-29L add to 28K-29K: Woodgrain Decor Group (woodgrain trim and moldings, front and rear body-color fascias, luggage rack, whitewall tires, alloy wheels). Requires 3.8-liter engine.

Pkg. 26M and ES SWB, and Pkg. 28M ES SWB, Grand ES and Pkg. 29M, Grand ES	$431	$366	$397
Pkg. 28 and 29M, Grand ES AWD	306	260	282

Pkgs. 26M-29M add to 26K-29K, ES SWB, Grand ES SWB: ES Decor Group (body-color fascia, cladding, and grille, fog lamps, alloy wheels), Sport Handling Group (heavy duty brakes, firmer front and rear sway bars, upgraded front struts and rear shocks, 205/70R15 tires, alloy wheels). Pkgs. 28M-29M add to 28K-29K Grand ES AWD: ES Decor Pkg. with Sport Handling Suspension, 205/70R15 tires, alloy wheels. (Sport Handling Group not available with AWD); deletes 2-tone paint. ES SWB Pkg. 26M requires 4-speed automatic transmission; ES SWB Pkg. 28M requires 3.3-liter engine and 4-speed automatic transmission; Grand ES and Grand ES AWD require 3.8-liter engine.

Individual Options:

3.0-liter V-6, Base SWB	767	652	706

Requires 3-speed automatic transmission.

3.3-liter V-6, SE, LE, and ES SWB	102	87	94

Requires 4-speed automatic transmission.

3.8-liter V-6, Grand LE, ES	302	257	278

Includes 4-speed transmission.

3-speed automatic transmission, Base SWB	601	511	553
4-speed automatic transmission, SE, LE ES, SWB and Base Grand	198	168	182
Anti-lock brakes: SE SWB with Pkgs. 26-28B or 26-28D	687	584	632
SE SWB with Pkgs. 26-28B or 26-28D and alloy wheels, Trailer Tow, Sport Handling, Gold Special Edition, or Sport Wagon Groups; Grand SE with Pkgs. 28B or 28D	599	509	551
LE SWB with Pkgs. 26-28K or 26-28M; Grand LE with Pkgs. 26-28K, 26-28L, or 26-28M	599	509	551
Front air conditioning, Base SWB and Base Grand	857	728	788
Front air conditioning with sunscreen glass, Base SWB with Pkg. 26T, SE SWB with Pkg. 26-28B and 26-28D, Base Grand with Pkg. 26T and SE Grand with Pkg. 28B and 28D	414	352	381

Not available with Sport Wagon Decor Group.

Sunscreen glass, Grand SE AWD with Pkg. 28B and 28D	414	352	381
Rear air conditioning with rear heater and sunscreen glass, Base Grand with Pkg. 26T, Grand SE with Pkg. 28B, Grand SE AWD with Pkg. 28B	988	840	909
Grand SE and Grand SE AWD with Pkg. 28B and Sport Wagon Decor Group	574	488	528
with Trailer Towing Group	925	786	851
with Sport Wagon Decor Group and Trailer Towing Group	511	434	470
Grand SE and Grand SE AWD with Pkg. 28D	880	748	810
with Sport Wagon Decor Group	466	396	429
with Trailer Towing Group	818	695	753
with Sport Wagon Decor Group and Trailer Towing Group	404	343	372
Grand LE and Grand LE AWD with Pkgs. 28-29K, 28-29L, or 28-29M	466	396	429
with Trailer Towing Group	404	343	372

Requires rear defogger.

Rear bench seat, Base SWB	346	294	318
7-passenger seating with integrated child seat, Base SWB	570	485	524
SE, LE and ES SWB, Grand, Grand AWD	225	191	207
Quad Command Seating, SE, LE, and ES	597	507	549

Two front and two middle bucket seats, 3-passenger rear bench seat.

Converta-Bed 7-passenger seating, SE, LE, and ES	553	470	509

Dodge

Top: A passenger-side air bag joins the driver-side air bag in a revamped dashboard. Middle: Fold-out child safety seats are optional. Above: A Grand Caravan ES.

	Retail Price	Dealer Invoice	Fair Price
Leather trim, ES	$865	$735	$796
Not available with integrated child seat.			
Heavy Duty Trailer Towing Group, SE SWB with Pkgs. 26-28B and 26-28D	556	473	512
with Gold Special Edition Group	442	376	407
LE SWB with Pkgs. 26-28K, Grand SE with Pkgs. 28B and 28D and Grand LE with Pkgs. 28-29K and 28-29L	442	376	407
SE SWB with Pkgs. 26-28B and 26-28D, LE SWB with Pkgs. 26-28K, ES SWB with Pkgs. 26-28M, Grand SE with Pkgs. 28B and 28D, Grand LE with Pkgs. 28-29K and 28-29L, Grand ES with Pkgs. 26-28M	410	349	377

	Retail Price	Dealer Invoice	Fair Price
Grand SE AWD with Pkgs. 28B and 28D, Grand LE AWD with Pkgs. 28-29K, 28-29L, and 28-29M	$373	$317	$343
Heavy duty brakes, battery, load suspension and radiator, trailer towing wiring harness, 205/70R15 all-season tires, conventional spare tire.			
Sport Handling Group, SWB SE with Pkg. 26-28B and 26-28D	239	203	220
Grand SE with Pkg. 28B and 28D, Grand LE with Pkg. 28-29L	125	106	115
Heavy duty brakes, front and rear sway bars, 205/70R15 tires. Not available with Sport Wagon Decor Pkg.			
LE SWB with Pkg. 26-28K and Grand LE with Pkg. 28-29K	488	415	449
Heavy duty brakes, front and rear sway bars, 205/70R15 tires, alloy wheels.			
Convenience Group I, Base SWB and Base Grand	372	316	342
Cruise control, tilt steering wheel.			
Convenience Group II, Base SWB and Base Grand	694	590	638
SE SWB with Pkg. 26-28B and Grand SE with Pkg. 28B..............................	265	225	244
Convenience Group I plus power mirrors and door locks.			
Convenience Group III, SE SWB with Pkg. 26-28B and Grand SE with Pkg. 28B	673	572	619
SE SWB with Pkg. 26-28D and Grand SE with Pkg. 28D	408	347	375
Convenience Group II plus power windows and remote keyless entry system.			
AWD Convenience Group I, Grand SE AWD with Pkg. 28B	265	225	244
Power mirrors and door locks.			
AWD Convenience Group II, Grand SE AWD with Pkg. 28B	673	572	619
with Pkg. 28D	408	347	375
AWD Convenience Group I plus power windows and remote keyless entry system.			
Gold Special Edition Group, SE	250	213	230
Gold striping, moldings and badging, 205/70R15 tires, gold-color alloy wheels.			
Sport Wagon Decor Group, SE	750	638	690
Sunscreen glass, front and rear fascias, leather-wrapped steering wheel, fog lamps, Sport Handling Group, alloy wheels.			
Rear defogger	168	143	155
Power door locks	265	225	244
Luggage rack	143	122	132
Cassette player	170	145	156
AM and FM stereo with CD player, equalizer and six Infinity speakers SE SWB with Pkg. 26-28D, Grand SE with Pkg. 28D, Grand SE AWD with Pkg. 28D	501	426	461
LE SWB with Pkg. 26-28K and 26-28L, Grand LE with Pkg. 28-29K, 28-29L and 28-29M, Grand LE AWD with Pkg. 28-29K, 28-29L, 28-29M, ...	170	145	156
Infinity speaker system, SE	202	172	186
Firm Ride Heavy Load Suspension, 2WD	178	151	163
with Sport Handling Group	146	124	134
Includes conventional spare tire.			
205/70R14 whitewall tires, Base SWB and SE SWB	143	122	132
205/70R15 whitewall tires, SWB SE, SWB LE, Base Grand, Grand SE, Grand LE, Grand SE AWD, Grand LE AWD	69	59	63
Not available with Sport Handling, Gold Special Edition, Sport Wagon Groups.			
Conventional spare tire	109	93	100
15-inch alloy wheels, LE SWB with Pkg. 26-28K, Grand LE with Pkg. 28-29K, Grand LE AWD with Pkg. 28-29K	363	309	334
Extra-cost paint	97	82	89

CONSUMER GUIDE®

Dodge

Dodge Caravan CV

	Retail Price	Dealer Invoice	Fair Price
Base	$14412	$13108	$13760
Extended	16866	15267	16067
Destination charge	560	560	560

Standard Equipment:
2.5-liter 4-cylinder engine, 5-speed manual transmission (base), 3.3-liter V-6, 4-speed automatic transmission (extended), driver- and passenger-side air bags, power steering, vinyl front bucket seats, variable-speed intermittent wipers, rear wiper/washer, tinted glass, remote liftgate release, rubber floor covering, cup holders, AM/FM radio, digital clock, color-keyed grille, front and rear fascias, sport steering wheel, dual fold-away mirrors, 195/75R14 tires (base), LT195/75R15 tires (extended), full-size spare (extended).

Optional Equipment:

3.0-liter V-6, base	694	590	611
Requires 3-speed automatic transmission.			
3-speed automatic transmission, base	601	511	529
Anti-lock brakes, extended	599	509	527
Includes cargo dome light.			
Air conditioning	857	728	754
Commercial Pkg. 22/24B, base	278	236	245
Heavy duty battery, 2000 lbs. GVWR, gauge cluster (includes tachometer, oil pressure, voltmeter, diagnostic warning lights), LT195/75R14 tires. Pkg. 22B requires 3-speed automatic transmission. Pkg. 24B requires 3.0-liter engine and 3-speed automatic transmission.			
Commercial Pkg. 22/24Z,	1177	1000	1036
Commercial Pkg. 22/24B plus air conditioning, cruise control, tilt steering column, cassette player, Light Group (front map/reading lights, cargo area light, illuminated entry system), lockable storage drawer under front passenger seat. Pkg. 22Z requires 3-speed automatic transmission. Pkg. 24Z requires 3.0-liter engine and 3-speed automatic transmission.			
Conversion Pkg. 24C, base	1267	1077	1115
Commercial Pkg. 24Z plus temporary plastic driver's seat, vented body-side and rear quarter glass, dual visor mirrors. Requires 3.0-liter engine and 3-speed automatic transmission.			
Conversion Pkg. 24D, base	2082	1770	1832
Conversion Pkg. 24C plus sunscreen glass, deluxe sound insulation, power locks, windows and mirrors, power liftgate release. Requires 3.0-liter engine and 3-speed automatic transmission.			
Commercial 28B, extended	66	56	58
Heavy duty battery, gauge cluster (includes tachometer, oil pressure, voltmeter, diagnostic warning lights).			
Commercial Pkg. 28Z, extended	965	820	849
Commercial 28B plus air conditioning, cruise control, tilt steering wheel, cassette player, Light Group (front map/reading lights, cargo area light, illuminated entry system), lockable stroge drawer under front passenger seat.			
Conversion Pkg. 28C, extended	955	812	840
Commercial Pkg. 28Z plus temporary plastic driver's seat, vented body-side and rear quarter glass, dual visor mirrors.			
Conversion Pkg. 28D, extended	1970	1675	1734
Conversion Pkg. 28C plus sunscreen glass, deluxe sound insulation, power locks, windows and mirrors, power liftgate release.			
Deluxe Convenience Pkg.	372	316	327
Cruise control, tilt steering column.			
Power Convenience Group	730	621	642
Power windows, door locks, and mirrors, remote keyless entry system. Requires Pkg. 24C (base) and 28C (extended).			
5790 lbs. GVWR Pkg., base	312	265	275
Heavy duty suspension, LT195/75R14 tires.			
Heavy Duty Trailer Towing Pkg., extended	264	224	232
with 28B/28Z/28C, or 28D	144	122	127
Heavy duty alternator, battery, radiator, flasher, and transaxle cooler, wiring harness.			
Vinyl bucket seats, with Conversion Pkg.	70	60	62
Deluxe reclining cloth bucket seats	48	41	42
Rear defogger	168	143	148
Sunscreen glass	256	218	225
with Conversion Pkg.	414	352	364
Vented side door glass	118	100	104

Dodge Dakota

✓ BEST BUY

Dodge Dakota Club Cab 4WD

Dakota, Dodge's mid-size pickup, gets a standard driver-side air bag, center high-mount stoplamp, side door guard beams, and other safety features for 1994.

Dakota was introduced for 1987 as the industry's only mid-size pickup, but Toyota's similarly sized T100 joined it last year in the niche between the compact- and full-size categories.

Body Styles/Chassis

Regular-cab models come in two sizes: a 111.9-inch wheelbase with a 6.5-foot cargo bed; and a 123.9-inch wheelbase with an 8-foot bed.

The extended Club Cab, which adds 19 inches of length to the standard cab, has a 130.9-inch wheelbase and 6.5-foot cargo bed. Regular-cab models come in WS (Work Special), Base, and Sport form; Club Cabs come in Base and Sport models. The uplevel decor group option available on both body styles is now called SLT, rather than LE.

Anti-lock rear brakes are standard, but 4-wheel anti-lock brakes are optional for all Dakotas. The 4-wheel anti-lock system is operative in both 2- and 4-wheel drive, though it retains the standard front-disc/rear-drum setup.

A 3-place front bench seat is standard on all Dakotas and a pair of front buckets is optional on all Base and Sport models. A 3-place rear bench seat is optional on the Base Club Cab and standard on the Sport and SLT versions of the Club Cab. Two storage compartments are located beneath the hinged rear cushions; the driver-side compartment can be locked.

Dakota is the first compact pickup to get a driver-side air bag and the safety feature is accompanied by a new padded knee bolster on the lower edge of the dashboard. In addition to the new door beams and stoplamp, new safety features include reinforcements in the windshield pillars and other areas that allow Dakota to meet passenger-car standards for roof-crush resistance in a rollover. Dodge says a new adhesive-bonded rear window contributes to the roof-crush resistance.

Maximum payload rating is 2600 pounds for conventional-cab models and 2000 for the Club Cab.

Powertrains

The base engine for 2WD models is a 99-horsepower 2.5-liter 4-cylinder.

Dodge

Standard on all 4WD models and optional on all 2WDs is a 3.9-liter V-6. This engine is rated at 175 horsepower, down 5 horsepower from 1993.

Optional on all Dakotas is a 5.2-liter V-8. It's rated at 220 horsepower, 10 fewer than last year, but torque increases from 280 pounds/feet to 295.

The 4-cylinder engine comes only with a 5-speed manual transmission. The 3.9-liter V-6 has a 5-speed manual as standard and offers an optional 4-speed automatic. The V-8, which last year was available only with the automatic transmission, is this year offered with either gear box.

Dakota's 4WD system is on-demand and part-time (not for use on dry pavement). Its automatic locking front hubs and floor-mounted transfer-case lever allow changing between 2WD and 4WD High up to 55 mph.

Maximum trailer-towing weight is 6800 pounds on the regular-cab models and 6600 on the Club Cab.

Evaluation

From its inception, Dakota was pitched as the only pickup to combine the nimbleness of a compact with the heavy-duty design of a full-size. Most shoppers, however, considered Dakota the answer to a question nobody had asked, and sales languished.

That began to change for 1991, when Dodge added the Club Cab, a body style that Dakota's rivals already had and one in high demand among personal-use buyers. Just as significant, the 1991 Dakota became the only non-full-size pickup with an available V-8 engine.

Those changes translated into record-high sales for Dakota in 1992, and sales were up again for model-year 1993. Club Cabs account for 55 percent of sales—the highest share of any pickup truck—while the V-8 is ordered in 50 percent of the Club Cab models and in 20 percent of the regular-cabs.

For '94, the WS is an advance over last year's "work" model in that it can be ordered with any engine, long-bed or short, and 2- or 4WD. Last year's work model was a 2WD 4-cylinder long-bed.

Also note that in some cases, higher-contented Dakotas cost less than lesser-equipped models. For example, the list price of a Base 4WD Club Cab is $257 more than a Sport 4WD Club Cab, even though the Sport version adds such features as power steering, cassette player, tachometer, and other amenities.

Dakota's popular V-8 does indeed furnish robust acceleration; Dodge says 0-60 mph takes only 8.3 seconds. That's about one second quicker than the V-6, but in everyday driving, the six never lacks responsiveness or feels overmatched, though its exhaust noise is more intrusive than the V-8's.

Where the V-8 gives Dakota a decided advantage over compacts is in towing: Its 6800-pound limit is 800 pounds more than Ford Ranger's and Chevrolet S10's. And Dakota's payload capacity is 857 pounds more than the S10's and 950 more than the Ranger's.

Dakota's exterior dimensions are similar to the Toyota T100, though the Japanese competitor doesn't offer a V-8 or an extended-cab body. And while the T100 can't tow more than 5000 pounds, it does have a cab that comfortably seats three across and a spacious cargo bed that accommodates a 4x8 plywood sheet between the wheelhousings—something neither Dakota nor the compacts can match.

Dakota has a clear advantage with its driver-side air bag and available 4-wheel ABS, a combination not offered by any other compact pickup.

Dakota handles competently, though like most pickups, when the bed is unloaded, the ride is too bouncy. We'd avoid the base 4-cylinder engine unless you carry nothing but light loads.

Drivers face a straightforward control layout, though on 4WD models, the floor-mounted transfer-case lever is too low and too far forward for easy use. The automatic transmission's fourth-gear overdrive is activated by a dashboard button. A nice 2-cup beverage holder slides out of the dashboard.

The bucket seats are comfortable, but the bench seat is too upright. Getting into and out of the Club Cab's rear seat is a chore. Only the passenger seat slides forward, and neither front seatback returns to place after being tipped. The back seat really is too small for three adults, though head room is good for two grown-ups. Knee room, however, is limited. Storage bins beneath the back seats are a useful touch.

Overall, Dakota has come a long way in a few years and now offers enough features, power, and safety to qualify as a must-see for pickup-truck shoppers.

Specifications

	Short bed	Long bed	Club Cab
Wheelbase, in.	111.9	123.9	130.9
Overall length, in.	189.0	201.0	208.0
Overall width, in.	69.3	69.3	69.3
Overall height, in.	64.2	64.2	64.2
Turn diameter, ft.	39.8	43.5	46.6
Curb weight, lbs.	2991	3080	3508
Fuel capacity, gal.	15.0	15.0	15.0

Passenger Area Dimensions

Seating capacity	3	3	6
Front head room, in.	39.6	39.6	39.8
Rear head room, in.	—	—	38.0
Front leg room, in.	41.6	41.6	41.6
Rear leg room, in.	—	—	26.7

Cargo Dimensions and Payloads

Cargo area length, in.	78.1	96.6	78.1
Cargo area width, in.	59.6	59.6	59.6
Cargo area width between wheels, in.	45.0	45.0	45.0
Cargo area height, in.	17.5	17.5	17.5
Max. payload, lbs.	2600	2600	2000
Max. trailer weight, lbs.	6800	6800	6600

Engines

	ohc I-4	ohv V-6	ohv V-8
Size, liters/cu. in.	2.5/153	3.9/239	5.2/318
Horsepower @ rpm	99 @ 4500	175 @ 4800	220 @ 4400
Torque (lbs./ft.) @ rpm	132 @ 2800	225 @ 3200	295 @ 3200
Availability	S	O[1]	O

EPA city/highway mpg

5-speed OD manual	23/27	17/22	15/20
4-speed OD automatic		16/20	14/18

1. Standard on 4WD models.

Built in Warren, Mich.

KEY: Dimensions and capacities are supplied by the manufacturers. **Curb Weight:** base models, not including optional equipment. **Max. payload, lbs.** = gross amount; net payload may be lower due to optional equipment. **Engines: ohv** = overhead valve; **ohc** = overhead cam; **I** = inline cylinders; **V** = cylinders in V configuration; **flat** = horizontally opposed cylinders; **rpm** = revolutions per minute; **OD** = overdrive transmission; **S** = standard; **O** = optional; **NA** = not available.

Dodge

Prices

Dodge Dakota

	Retail Price	Dealer Invoice	Fair Price
WS 2WD short bed	$9560	$9160	$9460
WS 2WD long bed	11085	10563	10863
Base 2WD short bed	11432	10425	10725
Base 2WD long bed	12282	11173	11473
Sport 2WD short bed	10742	10033	10333
Base 2WD Club Cab	14299	12948	13448
2WD Club Cab	14042	12722	13222
WS 4WD short bed	14704	13933	14233
WS 4WD long bed	14878	14093	14393
Base 4WD short bed	15798	14307	14607
Base 4WD long bed	15973	14461	14761
Sport 4WD short bed	15280	14157	14457
Sport 4WD Club Cab	17471	16779	17279
Base 4WD Club Cab	17728	16006	16506
Destination charge	495	495	495

Standard Equipment:

WS and Base: 2.5-liter 4-cylinder engine (2WD short bed), 3.9-liter V-6 (2WD long bed and 4WD models), 5-speed manual transmission, anti-lock rear brakes, driver-side air bag, power steering (WS 2WD long bed and 4WD models), AM/FM radio (base), digital clock (base), trip odometer, tinted glass, vinyl bench seat, dual black outside mirrors, stabilizer bar (4WD), painted front bumper, front air dam (4WD), 195/75R15 tires (WS and base 2WD models and 4WD short bed), 205/75R15 tires (WS and base 4WD long bed), full-size spare tire. **Sport** adds: power steering, cassette player, intermittent wipers, cloth/vinyl upholstery, carpet, tachometer, color-keyed upper bodyside moldings and wheel flares (4WD), painted rear step bumper, five 215/75R15 outline white letter tires (2WD), five 235/75R15 outline white letter tires (4WD), alloy wheels. **Base Club Cab** adds to base: 3.9-liter V-6 engine, 60/40 split reclining bench seat with center armrest, cloth/vinyl upholstery, flip-out quarter vent windows, behind-seat storage compartments, front stabilizer bar, 215/75R15 tires (4WD). **Sport Club Cab** adds to Base Club Cab: power steering, cassette player, tachometer, 60/40 split flip-type rear seat, cloth upholstery, upgraded door trim panels, carpet, 22-gallon fuel tank, intermittent wipers, painted rear step bumper, color-keyed bodyside moldings and wheel flares, 215/75R15 outline white letter tires (2WD), 235/75R15XL outline white letter tires (4WD), alloy wheels.

Quick Order Packages:

Pkg. 23/24D, SLT Base 2WD	845	718	744
SLT Base 4WD	817	694	719

SLT Decor Group (bright front bumper with air dam, bright grille and headlamp bezels, bodyside and wheel flare opening moldings, bodyside and tailgate striping, aero headlamps, capeting, upgraded door trim panels, dual manual remote mirrors, tachometer, woodtone instrument panel, driver-side visor mirror, cloth sunvisors with map pockets, deluxe sound insulation, Light Group, intermittent wipers, storage tray, jack cover, chrome wheels, carpeted floormats), power steering (std. 4WD), cassette player, bright rear step bumper, cloth/vinyl upholstery, sliding rear window, 22-gallon fuel tank, 215/75R15 tires. Pkg. 23D requires 3.9-liter V-6 engine. Pkg. 24D requires 3.9-liter V-6 engine and 4-speed automatic transmission.

Pkg. 23/24/25/26E, Special SLT Base 2WD	1411	1199	1242
Special SLT Base 4WD short bed	1314	1117	1156
Special SLT Base 4WD long bed	1253	1065	1103

Pkg. 23/24D plus air conditioning. Pkg. 23E short bed requires 3.9-liter V-6 engine. Pkg. 24E short bed requires 3.9-liter V-6 engine and 4-speed automatic transmission. Pkg. 24E long bed requires 4-speed automatic transmission. Pkg. 25E requires 5.2-liter V-8 engine. Pkg. 26E requires 5.2-liter engine and 4-speed automatic transmission.

Pkg. 23/24/25/26F, Super SLT			
Base 2WD Club Cab	917	779	807
Super SLT Base 4WD Club Cab	798	678	702

SLT Decor Group (Club Cab adds dark-tint swingout rear quarter windows, Rear Seat Group, premium cloth upholstery), air conditioning, cruise control, tilt steering column, cassette player, 60/40 split flip-type rear seat, bright rear step bumper, sliding rear window, 22-gallon fuel tank, 215/75R15 outline white letter tires (2WD), 235/75R15XL outline white letter tires (4WD).

Optional Equipment:

	Retail Price	Dealer Invoice	Fair Price
3.9-liter V-6, WS and Base 2WD short bed	$531	$451	$467
WS requires power steering and 22-gallon fuel tank.			
5.2-liter V-8, Sport 2WD	1118	950	984
Sport 4WD, Sport Club Cab and WS long bed	587	499	517
WS 4WD short bed	648	551	570
WS short bed includes 205/75R15 tires.			
4-speed automatic transmission	897	762	789
Not available with 2.5-liter engine.			
4-wheel anti-lock brakes	500	425	440
Air conditioning	797	677	701
2WD models require power steering.			
Power steering, WS 2WD short bed, Base 2WD	281	239	247
Not available with 2.5-liter engine.			
Optional axle ratio	39	33	34
Anti-slip differential	257	218	226
Bright Group, Sport	249	212	219
Bright front bumper with sport air dam and fog lights, bright rear step bumper.			
Off-Road Appearance Group, Sport	659	560	580
Bright front bumper with air dam and fog lights, bright step rear bumper, elliptical light bar, dual spotlights.			
Protection Group, 4WD models	129	110	114
Fuel tank, front axle and transfer case skid plates, front deflector shield.			
Deluxe Convenience Group, Sport and Base with SLT or Special SLT Pkg.	353	300	311
Cruise control, tilt steering column, sport steering wheel, intermittent wipers.			
Power Convenience Group, Sport and Base with Quick Order Pkg.	371	315	326
Power windows and door locks.			
Overhead Convenience Group, Sport and Base with Quick Order Pkg.	281	239	247
Overhead console with compass, temperature display, map/reading lights and storage compartment, automatic dimming rearview mirror.			
Power Overhead Convenience Group, Sport and Base with Quick Order Pkg.	552	469	486
Overhead Convenience Group plus Power Convenience Group.			
Light Group	78	66	69
Ignition switch light with time delay, instrument panel courtesy light, ashtray, glove box and underhood lights.			
Rear Seat Group, Base Club Cab	245	208	216
Rear seatback and corner bolsters, cloth lower backlight molding, rear seat and rear seatbelts.			
Heavy Duty Suspension Group	41	35	36
Heavy duty front and rear gas shock absorbers.			
Heavy Duty Electrical Group	120	102	106
Heavy Duty alternator and battery.			
Snow Plow Preparation Group, 4WD short bed with 5-speed: WS and Base	756	643	665
Base with SLT or Special SLT Pkg.	399	339	351
4WD short bed with 4-speed automatic:			
WS and Base	819	696	721
Base with SLT or Special SLT Pkg.	462	393	407
4WD long bed with 5-speed: WS and Base	695	591	612
Base with SLT or Special SLT Pkg.	399	339	351
4WD long bed with 4-speed automatic:			
WS and Base	758	644	667
Base with SLT or Special SLT Pkg.	462	393	407
4WD Club Cab with 5-speed: Base	583	496	513
Base with Super SLT Pkg.	343	292	302
4WD Club Cab with 4-speed automatic: Base	646	549	568
Base with Super SLT Pkg.	406	345	357
Heavy Duty Electrical Pkg., transmission oil cooler and temperature warning light (with automatic), maximum engine cooling, 235/75R15XL tires, 2000 lbs. Payload Pkg. (base cab), 1800 lbs.			
Payload Pkg. (Club Cab). GVWR Payload Pkgs.:			
1800 lbs., WS and Base 2WD	193	164	170
Base with SLT or Special SLT Pkg.	132	112	116
Includes 205/75R15 tires; requires power steering. Not available with 2.5-liter engine.			

Dodge

Top: Dakota is the only non-full-size pickup with a driver-side air bag. Above: Dakota Sport regular-cab 2WD.

	Retail Price	Dealer Invoice	Fair Price
Base Club Cab 4WD	$311	$264	$274
with Super SLT Pkg.	127	108	112
Includes 235/75R15 tires.			
2000 lbs., WS and Base 4WD			
short bed	433	368	381
Base with SLT or Special SLT Pkg.	127	108	112
WS and Base 4WD long bed	372	316	327
Base with SLT or Special SLT Pkg.	127	108	112
Includes 235/75R15XL tires.			
Base 4WD Club Cab	489	416	430
with Super SLT	249	212	219
Includes 205/75R15 tires; requires power steering. Not available with 2.5-liter engine. 2600 lbs.,			
2WD: WS and Base	596	507	524
Base with SLT or Special SLT Pkg.	474	403	417
Includes LT215/75R15 tires; requires power steering. Not available with 2.5-liter engine.			
Trailer Towing Prep Group:			
WS with 5-speed	276	235	243
WS with 4-speed automatic	339	288	298
Sport with 5-speed	270	230	238
Sport with 4-speed automatic.	333	283	293
Sport Club Cab with 5-speed	218	185	192
Sport Club Cab with 4-speed automatic	281	239	247
Base with 5-speed	328	279	289
Base with 4-speed automatic.	391	332	344
Base with 5-speed and Quick Order Pkg.	218	185	192
Base with 4-speed automatic and Quick Order Pkg.	281	239	247

	Retail Price	Dealer Invoice	Fair Price
with Snow Plow Preparation Group: WS	$99	$84	$87
Base	151	128	133
Base with Quick Order Pkg.	41	35	36
Heavy Duty Electrical Group, 22-gallon fuel tank, maximum engine cooling, heavy duty flashers, 5-lead trailer towing wiring harness, tachometer. Not available with 2.5-liter engine.			
Cloth and vinyl bench seat, WS and Base	53	45	47
Vinyl bench seat, Base with SLT or Special SLT Pkg.	NC	NC	NC
Cloth/vinyl bucket seats, Sport	379	322	334
Sport Club Cab	55	47	48
Base	305	259	268
Base Club Cab	109	93	96
Includes center console.			
Painted rear step bumper	133	113	117
Rear delete, Sport (credit)	NC	NC	NC
with Quick Order Pkg.	(101)	(86)	(86)
Maximum engine cooling	57	48	50
with 4-speed automatic	120	102	106
Intermittent wipers, WS and Base	70	60	62
Remote mirrors	51	43	45
Bright mirrors, WS and Base	89	76	78
Power bright mirrors, with Quick Order Pkg.	107	91	94
22-gallon fuel tank, Base and Sport	52	44	46
AM/FM radio, WS	194	165	171
AM/FM cassette, WS	404	343	356
Base	210	179	185
AM/FM cassette with equalizer, Sport and Base with Quick Order Pkg.	300	255	264
Includes four Infinity speakers.			
Infinity speaker system, Sport and Base with Quick Order Pkg.	171	145	150
AM/FM radio delete (credit)	(122)	(104)	(104)
Tilt steering column, WS and Base	204	173	180
Sport, Base with Quick Order Pkg.	134	114	118
Includes intermittent wipers.			
Tachometer, WS and Base	58	49	51
Not available with 2.5-liter engine.			
Engine block heater	34	29	30
Sliding rear window	115	98	101
Carpeting, Base Club Cab	58	49	51
2-tone center band paint, with Quick Order Pkg.	173	147	152
Includes lower bodyside moldings and wheel flare openings.			
2-tone lower break paint, with Quick Order Pkg.	168	143	148
Extra cost paint	77	65	68
Not available Sport.			
Bodyside and wheel flare moldings delete, Sport (credit)	NC	NC	NC
Styled chrome wheels, Sport	NC	NC	NC
Cast alloy wheels, Base with Quick Order Pkg.	NC	NC	NC
Wheel trim rings, WS and Base	61	52	54
Tires, 2WD: 215/75R15, WS and Base	122	104	107
with 1800 lbs. Payload Pkg.	61	52	54
215/75R15 OWL, 2WD with Quick Order Pkg.	118	100	104
Tires, 4WD: 215/75R15, WS and Base short bed	122	104	107
WS and Base long bed	61	52	54
235/75R15XL, WS and Base short bed	306	260	269
WS and Base long bed	245	208	216
Base Club Cab	184	156	162
Sport	NC	NC	NC
235/75R15XL all-terrain, WS and Base short bed	362	308	319
WS long bed	301	256	265
Base with Quick Order Pkg.	56	48	49
Club Cab	240	204	211
Club Cab with 1800 lbs. Payload Pkg.	56	48	49
235/75R15XL all-terrain, Base with Quick Order Pkg.	179	152	158
OWL denotes outlined white letter.			

CONSUMER GUIDE® 53

Dodge

Dodge Ram Pickup

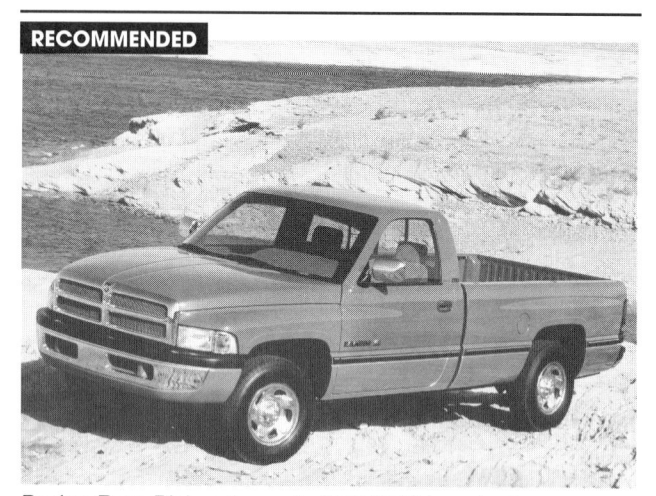

RECOMMENDED

Dodge Ram Pickup Laramie SLT 1500 long-bed

Dodge shelves a 22-year old pickup design and replaces it with a redesigned Ram for 1994. Highlighted by dramatic front-end styling, a standard driver-side air bag, and an available V-10 engine, the 1994 Ram is the newest entry in the full-size pickup market dominated by Ford and General Motors.

Dodge says it hopes to sell 250,000 Ram Pickups in the 1994 model year. That number would double Dodge's current 7-percent share of the big-pickup class.

Body Styles/Chassis

Ram bowed with just a regular-cab body but offers short- and long-bed cargo boxes. An extended Club Cab is due in June 1994, but Dodge says it has no plans to offer a crew cab body style or a flare-fender cargo box.

The short-bed Ram has a 118.7-inch wheelbase and a 6.5-foot cargo bed. The long-bed has a wheelbase of 134.7 inches and an 8-foot cargo bed. Compared to the same body styles of the previous design, the 1994 Rams are 3.7 inches longer in wheelbase and four inches longer overall.

The new trucks also are about two inches taller than the old, and base-model curb weights increase by 226 pounds on the short-bed model and 290 pounds on the long-bed.

Both the short- and long-bed are available with 2- or 4-wheel drive and in three series: 1500 (half-ton), 2500 (three-quarter-ton), and 3500 (one-ton), which comes with standard dual rear wheels.

The base price level is called Work Special and is available only in the 1500 series with either bed length. There also is a Base-level long-bed model. Higher-priced versions are designated LT, ST, and Laramie SLT and are offered in all series and bed lengths.

Front-disc and rear-drum brakes with rear-wheel anti-lock control are standard. Optional on 1500 and 2500 models is a 4-wheel anti-lock system. It retains the rear drum brakes, but works in both 2WD and 4WD. No other full-size pickup offers 4-wheel anti-lock brakes.

A three-place bench seat is standard on all Rams. Available on all models except the Work Special is a 40/20/40 split bench with dual recliners and a folding center armrest/storage bin Dodge calls a "business console." The covered bin is large enough to hold cellular phones and other mobile office equipment. Bucket seats are not offered.

All Ram models come with a driver-side air bag and a padded knee bolster on the bottom edge of the dashboard. The only other full-size pickup with a driver-side air bag is the Ford F-Series, though Ford includes the air bag only on its light-duty models. The Toyota T100, which is not as large as the domestic full-size pickups, also has a driver-side air bag.

Ram pickups also have a center high-mounted stoplamp and side door guard beams.

Maximum payloads are found on the 2WD Rams. The 1500-series limit is 2365 pounds, the 2500-series limit is 4104 pounds, and the 3500-series limit is 5288 pounds.

Powertrains

Ram's engines are carried over from the previous generation, except for addition of the V-10 to the lineup.

A 175-horsepower 3.9-liter V-6 is standard on 1500-series models and is the only engine offered in the Work Special version. Horsepower is down by 5 from last year, but torque increases by 10 pounds/feet, to 230.

Specifications

	Short bed	Long bed
Wheelbase, in.	118.7	134.7
Overall length, in.	204.1	224.3
Overall width, in.	78.4	78.4
Overall height, in.	72.0	72.0
Turn diameter, ft.	40.6	45.2
Curb weight, lbs.	3958	4121
Fuel capacity, gal.	26.0	35.0

Passenger Area Dimensions

Seating capacity	3	3
Front head room, in.	40.2	40.2
Rear head room, in.	—	—
Front leg room, in.	41.0	41.0
Rear leg room, in.	—	—

Cargo Dimensions and Payloads

Cargo area length, in.	77.4	97.6
Cargo area width, in.	64.5	64.5
Cargo area width between wheels, in.	50.0	50.0
Cargo area height, in.	19.1	19.1
Max. payload, lbs.	2365	5288
Max. trailer weight, lbs.	8100	13,600

Engines

	ohv V-6	ohv V-8	ohv V-8	Turbodiesel ohc I-6	ohv V-10
Size, liters/cu. in.	3.9/239	5.2/318	5.9/360	5.9/360	8.0/488
Horsepower @ rpm	175 @ 4800	220 @ 4400	230 @ 4000	175 @ 2500[3]	300 @ 4000
Torque (lbs./ft.) @ rpm	230 @ 3200	300 @ 3200	330 @ 3200	420 @ 1600[4]	450 @ 2400
Availability	S	O[1]	O[2]	O	O
EPA city/highway mpg					
5-speed OD manual	17/21	14/19	13/16	NA	NA
4-speed OD automatic	15/19	13/17	12/16	NA	NA

1. Standard, 4WD and 2500-series models. 2. Standard, 3500-series models.
3. 160 @ 2500, automatic transmission. 4. 400 @ 1750, automatic transmission.

Built in Warren, Mich. and Mexico.

KEY: Dimensions and capacities are supplied by the manufacturers. **Curb Weight:** base models, not including optional equipment. **Max. payload, lbs.** = gross amount; net payload may be lower due to optional equipment. **Engines: ohv** = overhead valve; **ohc** = overhead cam; **I** = inline cylinders; **V** = cylinders in V configuration; **flat** = horizontally opposed cylinders; **rpm** = revolutions per minute; **OD** = overdrive transmission; **S** = standard; **O** = optional; **NA** = not available.

Dodge

A 220-horsepower 5.2-liter V-8 is standard on 4x4s and on 2500-series Rams and optional on 1500-series models. Horsepower is down by 10 from last year, but torque increases by 20 pounds/feet, to 300.

A 230-horsepower 5.9-liter V-8 is standard on 3500-series models and optional on 1500s and 2500s. This engine gains 5 pounds/feet of torque, to 330.

A 5.9-liter inline 6-cylinder turbocharged diesel engineered by Cummins is optional on 2500- and 3500-series Rams. The turbodiesel is rated at 175 horsepower with manual transmission, 15 more than last year, and 160 with automatic, which was not offered last year.

The new V-10 displaces 8.0 liters and was designed for the Ram Pickup, but made its first appearance in the Dodge Viper sports car, where an aluminum version is rated at 400 horsepower. The iron version in the Ram has 300 horsepower.

Dodge offers a 5-speed manual transmission and a 4-speed automatic with each of these engines, though the transmissions themselves differ depending on the application. Last year, the automatic used with the 3.9-liter V-6 was a 3-speed.

Ram 4x4s have an on-demand, part-time 4WD system (not for use on dry pavement). Standard are automatic-locking front hubs that allow shift-on-the-fly between 2WD and 4WD High up to 55 mph.

Maximum towing capacity is found on the 2WD models. The limit is 8100 pounds on the 1500 series, 13,600 pounds on the 2500 series, and 13,200 on the 3500 series.

Evaluation

"Long on function, short on frills, Dodge's full-size pickups are basic, durable trucks best suited for work, not pleasure."

That was our summation of the previous-generation Ram. The 1994 models seem equally well-suited for work, but now they also generate a good deal of pleasure.

In fact, Dodge expects the most popular model to be the 1500 Laramie SLT, which includes cruise control, leather-wrapped tilt steering wheel, power windows and locks, chrome wheels, and other amenities.

The model we test drove was a 2WD 1500 long-bed with ST Package 24C, the 5.2-liter V-8, and automatic transmission. Without features like power windows or a cassette player, it leaned more toward the work end of the spectrum. Even so, it was as accommodating and refined as any Ford or General Motors rival we've driven, and a quantum leap ahead of the previous Ram in all areas.

Dodge claims to have the largest interior of any regular-cab pickup. Our test model had plenty of room for three-across seating, but the big bonus was in space behind the seat. There is enough room to recline the seatbacks, a luxury in itself in a big pickup. And Dodge has cleverly fitted a series of sturdy plastic bins, shelves, and a net that maximizes the space by allowing efficient stowage of tools, briefcases, and other gear.

When not in use, the center 20 percent of the seatback folds down to become an armrest with useful compartments inside. To get at the compartments, however, you must open the large padded lid, which proves cumbersome while driving.

More inviting was the dashboard. All gauges are plainly marked. Controls are unobstructed, close by, and logical in operation. Special credit is due the climate system, which is governed by three simple knobs. All controls are nicely illuminated with the exception of a dashboard button that disengages the automatic transmission's overdrive gear. It's hard to find at night. Above the radio is a slide-out holder large enough for two 16-ounce beverage containers.

The 5.2-liter V-8 provided more-than-adequate acceleration and ran smoothly. We averaged 14.4 mpg over 735 miles on a variety of roads, with a high of 16.1 mpg on one highway trip.

Based on our experience with the previous model, we wouldn't recommend the V-6 engine for constant heavy-duty work. The Cummins turbodiesel is a real powerhouse, and it has even more muscle this year. A brief test drive in a 3500 4x4 with manual transmission showed the V-10 to be extremely strong, also. And it has more torque than the diesel engine.

Even though our test Ram 1500 had the base suspension and tires, the ride was quite jouncy over dips and bumps with the bed empty. Turns could be taken at a moderate pace with good grip and balance, and gusty crosswinds had little effect on directional stability. The 4-wheel anti-lock brakes stopped this truck with fine control, but some test drivers said pedal action was spongy, others felt it was sufficiently firm.

Engine and road noise are low for a truck, though the wind roared loudly around the front roof pillars at highway speeds on one model we drove.

Sales of the 1994 Ram got off to a brisk start, so Dodge has gotten the Ram's message across. We're impressed by the truck, and advise any full-size pickup shopper, regardless of brand loyalty, to test drive one.

Prices

Dodge Ram 1500 Pickup

	Retail Price	Dealer Invoice	Fair Price
1500 Work Special short bed	$12734	$11661	—
1500 LT short bed	14389	12689	—
1500 Work Special long bed	13006	11900	—
1500 Base long bed	14661	12917	—
1500 4WD LT short bed	17376	15250	—
1500 4WD LT long bed	17696	15522	—
Destination charge	600	600	600

Fair price not available at time of publication.

Standard Equipment:

3.9-liter V-6 engine (5.2-liter V-8 with 4WD), 5-speed manual transmission, anti-lock rear brakes, driver-side air bag, power steering, vinyl bench seat, trip odometer, voltmeter, oil pressure and engine temperature gauges, tinted glass, dual outside mirrors, intermittent wipers, AM/FM radio (except Work Special), digital clock, vinyl floormat, five 225/75R16 tires.

Quick Order Packages:

Pkg. 22A, LT/Base	927	788	—
Adds automatic transmission.			
Pkg. 23A, LT/Base	587	499	—
Adds 5.2-liter V-8.			
Pkg. 24A, LT/Base	1514	1287	—
5.2-liter V-8, automatic transmission.			
ST Pkg. 21C	504	428	—
4WD ST	204	173	—
40/20/40 split cloth bench seat, carpeting, behind seat storage, cargo lamp, bright bumpers and wheel trim rings.			
Pkg. 22C, ST	927	788	—
Adds automatic transmission. Requires Pkg. 21C.			
Pkg. 23C, ST	587	499	—
Adds 5.2-liter V-8. Requires Pkg. 21C.			
Pkg. 24C, ST	1514	1287	—
4WD ST	927	788	—
Adds 5.2-liter V-8 (std. 4WD), automatic transmission. Requires Pkg. 21C.			

Dodge

	Retail Price	Dealer Invoice	Fair Price
Pkg. 26C, ST	$1784	$1516	—
4WD ST	1197	1017	—
Adds 5.9-liter V-8, automatic transmission. Requires Pkg. 21C.			
Laramie SLT Pkg. 21G	2145	1823	—
Laramie SLT 4WD	2155	1832	—
Air conditioning, cruise control, tilt steering wheel, power windows and locks, Premium Decor Group, Light Groups, bodyside moldings, cassette player, cloth 40/20/40 split bench seat, front bumper shields, leather-wrapped steering wheel, striping, tachometer, bright bumpers, carpeting, behind seat storage, cargo lamp, five 245/75R16 tires, chrome wheels.			
Pkg. 22G, Laramie SLT	927	788	—
Adds automatic transmission. Requires Pkg. 21G.			
Pkg. 23G, Laramie SLT	587	499	—
Adds 5.2-liter V-8. Requires Pkg. 21G.			
Pkg. 24G, Laramie SLT	1514	1287	—
4WD Laramie SLT	927	788	—
Adds 5.2-liter V-8 (std. 4WD), automatic transmission. Requires Pkg. 21G.			
Pkg. 26G, Laramie SLT	1784	1516	—
4WD Laramie SLT	1197	1017	—
Adds 5.9-liter V-8, automatic transmission. Requires Pkg. 21G.			

Optional Equipment:

5.2-liter V-8 (std., 4WD)	587	499	—
5.9-liter V-8	857	728	—
4WD	270	230	—
Anti-lock brakes	500	425	—
Cargo lamp, Work Special	38	32	—
4-speed automatic transmission	927	788	—
Optional axle ratio	39	33	—
Sure Grip Axle	257	218	—
Air conditioning	797	677	—
Deluxe Convenience Group	353	300	—
Tilt steering wheel, cruise control.			
Heavy Duty Service Group, 2WD			
w/5-speed	277	235	—
4WD w/5-speed	321	273	—
2WD w/automatic transmission	341	290	—
4WD w/automatic transmission	385	327	—
Heavy duty alternator, battery, engine cooling and transmission oil cooler, skid plates (4WD).			
Light Group, 2WD LT/Base,			
2WD ST	164	139	—
4WD ST	126	107	—
Overhead console, cloth headliner, misc. lights.			
Trailer Tow Load Equalizing Hitch/Harness			
(N/A Work Special)	242	206	—
Requires rear bumper, Heavy Duty Service Group.			
Snow Plow Prep Group, 4WD	NC	NC	NC
Requires Heavy Duty Service Group, Trailer Tow Group, rear step bumper, upsized tires.			
Travel Convenience Group, ST, Laramie	$231	$196	—
Overhead console with compass and thermometer, reading lamps, power mirrors, automatic day/night rearview mirror, full headliner.			
Cloth bench seat, Work Special	72	61	—
Cloth 40/20/40 split back bench seat,			
LT/Base, ST	261	222	—
Power driver's seat, Laramie	296	252	—
Includes 40/20/40 split bench seat.			
Tachometer, ST	76	65	—
Cab clearance lights	52	44	—
Bright 7-inch x 10-inch mirrors			
(N/A Work Special)	48	41	—
Power 6-inch x 9-inch mirrors			
(N/A Work Special)	99	84	—
Sliding rear window	134	114	—
AM/FM radio with two speakers,			
Work Special	190	162	—
Four speaker system	50	43	—
AM/FM cassette with four speakers,			
LT/Base, ST	210	179	—
Work Special	400	340	—
six Infinity speakers	202	172	—
AM/FM cassette with equalizer and six			
Infinity speakers, Laramie	331	281	—
Radio delete (credit),			
LT/Base, ST	(122)	(104)	(104)
Bodyside moldings, ST	102	87	—
Extra-cost paint	77	65	—
2-tone lower paint	132	112	—
Painted rear step bumper, Work Special,			
LT/Base	133	113	—
Bright rear step bumper delete (credit),			
ST, Laramie	(234)	(199)	(199)
Engine block heater	34	29	—
Carpeting delete (credit),			
ST, Laramie	NC	NC	NC
Conventional spare tire and wheel,			
Work Special	160	136	—
2WD Tire Options Five 245/75R16C tires,			
LT/Base, ST	130	111	—
Five 245/75R16C outlined white letter tires, ST	255	217	—
Laramie SLT	126	107	—
4WD Tire Options Five LT245/75R16C tires,			
4WD LT, ST	140	119	—
Five LT245/75R16C all-terrain tires, LT, ST	280	238	—
Laramie SLT	140	119	—
Five LT245/75R16C all-terrain outlined white letter tires, LT, ST	405	344	—
Laramie SLT	265	225	—
Five LT265/75R16C all-terrain outlined white letter tires, ST	545	463	—
Laramie SLT	405	344	—
Four chrome wheels, ST	322	274	—
Bright wheel trim, LT/Base	60	51	—

Dodge Ram 2500/3500 Pickup

	Retail Price	Dealer Invoice	Fair Price
2500 LT light duty	$15916	$13984	—
2500 LT heavy duty	17102	14992	—
3500 LT dual rear wheel	18417	16109	—
2500 4WD LT light duty	18194	15945	—
2500 4WD LT heavy duty	19638	17172	—
3500 4WD LT dual rear wheel	20867	18217	—
Destination charge	600	600	600

Fair price not available at time of publication.

Standard Equipment:

5.2-liter V-8 engine (light duty; heavy duty and 3500 have 5.9-liter PFI V-8), 5-speed manual transmission, anti-lock rear brakes, driver-side air bag, power steering, vinyl bench seat, trip odometer, voltmeter, oil pressure and

A driver-side air bag is Standard on all Ram Pickups.

Dodge

engine temperature gauges, tinted glass, dual outside mirrors, intermittent wipers, AM/FM radio, digital clock, heavy duty battery, painted front bumper, bright grille, heavy duty shock absorbers, automatic locking front hubs (4WD models), shift-on-the-fly transfer case (4WD models), vinyl floormat, clearance lamps (3500), 225/75R16 tires (2500 2WD light duty), 245/75R16 tires (2500 2WD heavy duty), 225/75R16D tires (2500 4WD light duty), 225/75R16E (2500 4WD heavy duty), LT215/85R16 tires (3500). 2500

Quick Order Packages:

	Retail Price	Dealer Invoice	Fair Price
ST Pkg. 23/24/25/26C, light duty	$404	$343	—
ST Pkg. 25/26D, heavy duty	404	343	—
ST Pkg., 2WD heavy duty with 8.0-liter V-10 engine	1151	978	—
ST Pkg., 4WD heavy duty with 8.0-liter V-10 engine	1195	1016	—
ST Pkg., 2WD heavy duty with 5.9-liter 6-cylinder diesel engine	4823	4100	—
ST Pkg., 4WD heavy duty with 5.9-liter 6-cylinder diesel engine	4867	4137	—

40/20/40 split cloth bench seat, carpeting, behind seat storage, dome and cargo lights, bright bumpers and wheel trim rings, Heavy Duty Service Group (8.0-liter and diesel engines). Pkg. 24C and 26D require 4-speed automatic transmission. Pkg. 25C requires 5.9-liter engine. Pkg. 26C requires 4-speed automatic transmission and 5.9-liter engine.

Laramie SLT Pkg. 23/24/25/26G, light duty	2665	2265	—
Laramie SLT Pkg. 25/26H, heavy duty	2665	2265	—
Laramie SLT Pkg., 2WD heavy duty with 8.0-liter V-10 engine	3412	2900	—
Laramie SLT Pkg., 4WD heavy duty with 8.0-liter V-10 engine	3456	2938	—
Laramie SLT Pkg., 2WD heavy duty with 5.9-liter 6-cylinder diesel engine	7008	5957	—
Laramie SLT Pkg., 2WD heavy duty with 5.9-liter 6-cylinder diesel engine	7052	5994	—

Air conditioning, cruise control, tilt steering wheel, power windows and door locks, Premium Decor Group (40/20/60 split cloth bench seat, carpeting, door map pockets, upgraded door trim, bright front step bumper, underhood insulation, black sport leather-wrapped steering wheel, black tailgate trim, black bodyside moldings, bodyside striping, covered passenger-side visor mirror, floormats), Light Group, cassette player, front bumper shields, tachometer, behind seat storage, chrome wheels, Heavy Duty Service Group (8.0-liter and diesel engines). Pkg. 24G and 26H require 4-speed automatic transmission. Pkg. 25G requires 5.9-liter engine. Pkg. 26G requires 4-speed automatic transmission and 5.9-liter engine.

3500 Quick Order Packages:

ST Pkg. 25/26C	649	552	—
ST Pkg., 2WD 8.0-liter V-10 engine	1396	1187	—
ST Pkg., 4WD 8.0-liter V-10 engine	1440	1224	—
ST Pkg., 2WD with 5.9-liter 6-cylinder diesel engine	5068	4308	—
ST Pkg., 4WD heavy duty with 5.9-liter 6-cylinder diesel engine	5112	4345	—

40/20/40 split cloth bench seat, carpeting, behind seat storage, dome and cargo lights, bright bumpers and wheel trim rings, Heavy Duty Service Group (8.0-liter and diesel engines). Pkg. 26C requires 4-speed automatic transmission.

Laramie SLT Pkg. 25/26G	2588	2200	—
Laramie SLT Pkg., 2WD with 8.0-liter V-10 engine	3335	2835	—
Laramie SLT Pkg., 4WD with 8.0-liter V-10 engine	3379	2872	—
Laramie SLT Pkg., 2WD with 5.9-liter 6-cylinder diesel engine	6931	5891	—
Laramie SLT Pkg., 2WD with 5.9-liter 6-cylinder diesel engine	6975	5929	—

Top: Ram 3500 models have dual rear wheels. This 2WD version has a V-10 engine. Above: A V-8 powered 1500 long-bed 4WD.

Air conditioning, cruise control, tilt steering wheel, power windows and door locks, Premium Decor Group (40/20/60 split cloth bench seat, carpeting, door map pockets, upgraded door trim, bright front step bumper, underhood insulation, black sport leather-wrapped steeing wheel, black tailgate trim, black bodyside moldings, bodyside striping, covered passenger-side visor mirror, floormats), Light Group, cassette player, front bumper shields, tachometer, behind seat storage, chrome wheels, Heavy Duty Service Group (8.0-liter and diesel engines). Pkg. 26G requires 4-speed automatic transmission.

Optional Equipment:

	Retail Price	Dealer Invoice	Fair Price
5.9-liter V-8 engine	$857	$728	—
5.9-liter 6-cylinder diesel engine	4142	3521	—

Includes maximum engine cooling, message center, air-manifold-mounted electric heater, extra sound insulation. Models with 4-speed automatic transmission also include auxiliary transmission oil cooler. 4WD models include transfer case skid plate. Requires Heavy Duty Service Group.

8.0-liter V-10 engine, 2500 heavy duty and 3500	470	400	—

Includes heavy duty battery and alternator, maximum engine cooling. Models with 4-speed automatic transmission also include auxiliary transmission cooler. 4WD models include transfer case skid plate. Requires Heavy Duty Service Group.

4-speed automatic transmission	927	788	—
Anti-lock brakes, 2500	500	425	—
Air conditioning	797	677	—
Optional axle ratio	39	33	—
Sure Grip Axle	257	218	—
Deluxe Convenience Group	353	300	—
Tilt steering wheel, cruise control.			
Heavy Duty Service Group, 2WD with 5-speed	277	235	—
4WD with 5-speed	321	273	—
2WD w/automatic transmission	341	290	—
4WD w/automatic transmission	385	327	—

Dodge

	Retail Price	Dealer Invoice	Fair Price
Heavy duty alternator, battery, engine cooling and transmission oil cooler, skid plates (4WD).			
Light Group	$164	$139	—
with ST Pkg.	126	107	—
Overhead console, cloth headliner, exterior cargo light, glove box and underhood lights, auxiliary 12-volt electrical outlet.			
Trailer Towing Prep Group	242	206	—
Class IV platform hitch receiver, wiring harness, heavy duty flashers. Requires rear bumper and Heavy Duty Service Group.			
Snow Plow Prep Group, 4WD	270	230	—
Heavy duty front springs, upgraded front suspension, warning light for transmission oil overheat. Requires Heavy Duty Service Group, Trailer Towing Prep Group, rear step bumper, conventional spare tire.			
Travel Convenience Group, ST, Laramie	231	196	—
Overhead console with compass and thermometer, reading lamps, power mirrors, automatic day/night rearview mirror, full headliner.			
Power driver's seat, Laramie SLT Pkg.	296	252	—
Cloth 40/20/40 split bench seat	261	222	—
Vinyl 40/20/40 split bench seat, with Quick Order Pkg.	(NC)	(NC)	(NC)
Tachometer, ST	76	65	—
Cab clearance lights, 2500	52	44	—
Bright 7-inch x 10-inch mirrors	48	41	—
Power 6-inch x 9-inch mirrors	99	84	—
Sliding rear window	134	114	—
AM/FM cassette with 4 speakers	210	179	—
AM/FM cassette with equalizer and 6 Infinity speakers, Laramie SLT	331	281	—
Two additional speakers	50	43	—
Four additional speakers, Laramie SLT Pkg.	202	172	—
Radio delete (credit)	(122)	(104)	(104)
Front air dam	12	10	—
Bodyside moldings, ST	102	87	—
Extra cost paint	77	65	—
2-tone lower-break paint	132	112	—
Includes bodyside moldings.			
2-tone center band paint, 2500	243	207	—
with Laramie SLT Pkg.	182	155	—
2-tone waterfall, 3500	215	183	—
4WD with Laramie SLT Pkg.	154	131	—
Painted rear step bumper	133	113	—
Bright rear step bumper delete (credit), with ST and Laramie SLT Pkg.	(234)	(199)	(199)
Engine block heater	34	29	—
Carpeting delete (credit)	NC	NC	NC
Four chrome wheels, 2500 with ST Pkg.	322	274	—
Wheel dress-up, 2500	60	51	—
Includes bright wheel trim rings and center hubs.			
Wheel dress-up (skins), 3500	305	259	—
2500 tire options: LT225/75R16D spare tire, light duty	289	246	—
LT245/75R16E tires, light duty	180	153	—
Spare tire	334	284	—
LT245/75R16 all-terrain tires, light duty	292	248	—
Heavy duty	112	95	—
Spare tire	362	308	—
LT245/75R16E outlined white letter tires, light duty	280	238	—
Heavy duty	100	85	—
Spare tire	359	305	—
LT265/75R16E all-terrain outlined white letter tires, Light duty	392	333	—
Heavy duty	212	180	—
Spare tire	387	329	—
3500 tire options: LT215/85R16D spare tire	248	211	—
LT215/85R16D all-terrain	168	143	—
Spare tire	276	235	—
LT215/85R16D outline white letter	150	128	—
Spare tire	273	232	—
LT215/85R16D all-terrain outline white letter	318	270	—
Spare tire	301	256	—

Dodge Ram Wagon/Van

Dodge B150 Ram Wagon

Dodge restyled its full-size passenger van and introduced it as an early 1994 model last spring, but there are still several changes this fall.

New safety features include guard beams for the front doors and a reinforced roof that meets the federal passenger-car standards for rollover protection.

Plus, all models have asbestos-free brake linings and the optional air conditioning now uses a CFC-free refrigerant.

Body Styles/Chassis

Passenger versions are called Wagons, cargo models Vans. Both are available in three body lengths on two wheelbases.

The 109.6-inch wheelbase carries a 187.2-inch-long body. The 127.6-inch wheelbase carries bodies of 205.2 and 231.2 inches. The last is called the Maxi Wagon or Maxi Van and all its extra length is grafted onto the rear of the body.

Dodge classes these vans according to payload categories: B150 (half-ton); B250 (three-quarter-ton); and B350 (one-ton).

B150 Wagons come only in the 109-inch wheelbase. B150 Vans come in both the 109- and 127.6-inch wheelbases.

All B250 and B350 models use the 127.6-inch wheelbase. The Maxi versions are available only in B250 and B350 weight classes.

Overall body lengths were up by about seven inches in the early '94 restyle, with most of the additional length attributed to the reshaped nose, which includes a new grille and bumper and aero headlamps and turn signals. Also added was a center high-mounted stoplamp.

Wagons come with a single side-opening rear door and a sliding side door. Dual swing-open rear and side doors are available.

Vans have dual swing-out side and rear doors as standard, with the single rear door and sliding side door optional.

Four-wheel anti-lock brakes (ABS) are newly optional on all models. Rear anti-lock brakes remain standard.

Van payload ratings are 1513 pounds for the B150 (found on the short-wheelbase model), 2276 pounds for the B250 (found on the short-wheelbase model), and 4252 pounds on the B350 (found on the regular-length body).

Dodge

Wagon payload ratings are 1876 pounds on the B150, 2030 on the B250, and 3934 on the B350—the last two being regular-length body styles.

Powertrains

A 175-horsepower 3.9-liter V-6 is standard on all B150 models and on all regular-length B250s.

A 220-horsepower 5.2-liter V-8 is standard on the B250 Maxi Van and on all B350 models. The 5.2 V-8 is optional on all B150 and all other B250 models.

A 5.9-liter V-8 is standard on the B350 Wagon and optional on all other B250 and B350 models.

The 5-speed manual transmission is dropped for 1994. A 3-speed automatic is mandatory with the V-6 engine and available with the 5.2-liter V-8. A 4-speed automatic is mandatory with the 5.9-liter V-8 and available with the 5.2-liter V-8.

B150 Vans can tow up to 6400 pounds, B250 Vans up to 8800 pounds, and B350 Vans up to 9000 pounds. Towing limits are some 300 less for each corresponding Ram Wagon model.

Accommodations

Cargo models come with two front bucket seats.

Seats for five are standard on passenger models. Short-wheelbase Wagons have optional seating for up to eight, long-wheelbase Wagons for up to 12, and Maxi Wagons for up to 15.

A travel seat option for 8-passenger B250 and B350 Wagons has a 6-place dinette table and bench seats that convert into a bed.

Evaluation

Though it still does not offer a diesel engine, as do the big vans from Ford and General Motors, Rams have the payload, towing power, and sheer carrying capacity to match anything in this class.

We recommend the 5.2-liter V-8 if you frequently carry several passengers or lots of cargo. And you probably should opt for the 5.9-liter V-8 if you're into serious hauling or towing. It's a good idea to spring for the optional 35-gallon gas tank, as well; the standard 22-gallon unit limits the cruising range of these fuel-thirsty vans.

Last spring's facelift did update the looks of these vans, but the basic platform still dates to the 1972 model year—just two years newer than full-size vans from GM. However, the Chevrolet and GMC vans gain a driver-side air bag for 1994. The Ford Econoline and Club Wagon, meanwhile was given a major revamp for 1992 and got a driver-side air bag for '93. The Ford is superior also in terms of driving refinement and in isolation from road noise.

It's interesting to note that passenger versions account for 20 percent of sales for the Ford vans and about 10 percent for the GM vans, but about 25 percent of sales for the Dodges. Competitive pricing makes the Dodge particularly attractive to non-commercial group owners, such as churches, and the best-selling Ram Wagon is in fact the 15-passenger Maxi model.

As with rivals from Ford and GM, Dodge's big van is great for hauling mobs of people or mounds of cargo. But beware that you're buying a truck-like vehicle of considerable bulk and a few significant inconveniences. Size and weight make the Dodge and its competitors cumbersome to drive in urban traffic and costly to feed because of poor fuel economy.

There's generous cargo room behind the rear bench in the 5-passenger Wagon and even in the long-wheelbase 12-passenger.

The seats are comfortable, but there's a distressing lack of front foot room. As with others of this ilk, the engine cover protrudes to cut space in the center, and the front wheel wells intrude from the flanks. There are only a few inches of pass-through room to squeeze past the engine to the middle or rear seats. Still, the engine cover has handy molded-

Specifications

	4-door van	4-door van	Maxi 4-door van
Wheelbase, in.	109.6	127.6	127.6
Overall length, in.	187.2	205.2	231.2
Overall width, in.	79.8	79.8	79.8
Overall height, in.	79.0	79.0	79.6
Turn diameter, ft.	40.5	46.2	52.4
Curb weight, lbs.	3734	3863	4064
Fuel capacity, gal.	22.0	22.0	22.0

Passenger Area Dimensions

Seating capacity	8	12	15
Front head room, in.	39.9	39.9	39.9
Rear head room, in.	39.3	39.4	39.4
Front leg room, in.	39.0	39.0	39.0
Rear leg room, in.	40.5	40.5	40.5

Available Seating

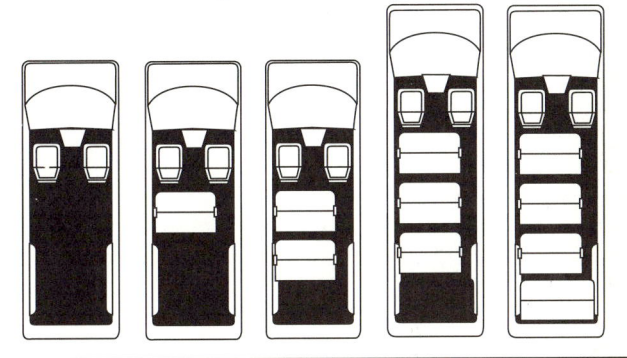

Cargo Dimensions and Payloads

Cargo area length, in.	92.9	110.9	134.9
Cargo area width, in.	72.2	72.2	72.2
Cargo area width between wheels, in.	50.0	50.0	50.0
Cargo area height, in.	53.2	53.2	53.2
Cargo vol., cu. ft.	206.6	246.7	304.5
Max. payload, lbs.	2276	4252	4126
Max. trailer weight, lbs.	6400	9000	9000

Engines

	ohv V-6	ohv V-8	ohv V-8
Size, liters/cu. in.	3.9/239	5.2/318	5.9/360
Horsepower @ rpm	175 @ 4800	220 @ 4400	230 @ 4000
Torque (lbs./ft.) @ rpm	225 @ 3200	295 @ 3600	330 @ 3200
Availability	S	O	O

EPA city/highway mpg

3-speed automatic	18/17	12/14	
4-speed OD automatic		13/17	12/16

Built in Canada.

KEY: Dimensions and capacities are supplied by the manufacturers. **Curb Weight:** base models, not including optional equipment. **Max. payload, lbs.** – gross amount; net payload may be lower due to optional equipment. **Engines: ohv** = overhead valve; **ohc** = overhead cam; **I** = inline cylinders; **V** = cylinders in V configuration; **flat** = horizontally opposed cylinders; **rpm** = revolutions per minute; **OD** = overdrive transmission; **S** = standard; **O** = optional; **NA** = not available.

Dodge

in cup holders and parcel bins, so Dodge makes the best of the situation.

We like the Ford Club Wagon and Econoline in this class, and so do buyers who have made it the best selling big van. The Ram Van and Wagon trail the Chevy and GMC brands in sales—and in our ranking. But the Dodge should be the easiest of all the big vans on which to negotiate a good price.

Prices

Dodge Ram Van

	Retail Price	Dealer Invoice	Low Price
B150 SWB	$12951	$11847	$12347
B150 LWB	15866	13936	14436
B250 SWB	15911	13974	14474
B250 LWB	16279	14287	14787
B250 Maxi Van	17266	15126	15626
B350 LWB	17559	15375	15875
B350 Maxi Van	18524	16195	16695
Destination charge	595	595	595

SWB and LWB denote short- and long-wheelbase models. All 350 models are LWB.

Standard Equipment:

3.9-liter V-6 (150/250), 5.2-liter V-8 (350), 3-speed automatic transmission (150/250), 4-speed automatic transmission (350), anti-lock rear brakes, power steering, vinyl front bucket seats, tinted glass, double hinged side and rear doors (sliding side door and single rear door may be substituted at no charge), AM/FM radio, digital clock, dual black fold-away mirrors, painted front and rear bumper, front stabilizer bar, black rubber floor covering, 205/75R15 tires with matching spare tire (150), 225/75R15 tires (250), 235/75R15XL tires (250 Maxi Van), LT225/75R16D tires (350), LT225/75R16E tires (350 Maxi Van).

Quick Order Pkgs.

Commercial Pkg. 150 SWB, 22/24/26C	186	158	164
150 LWB, 22/24/26C (credit)	(301)	(256)	(256)
250 SWB, 22/24/26C	143	122	126
250 LWB, 22/24/26C (credit)	(207)	(176)	(176)
250 Maxivan, 24/26C (credit)	(221)	(188)	(188)
350 LWB, 26/28C	15	13	13
350 Maxi Van, 26/28C	(482)	(410)	(410)

35-gallon fuel tank, GVW upgrade (150 and 350 Maxivan), black 6-inch x 9-inch outside mirrors, Van Window Group with rear door glass, maximum engine cooling and auxiliary transmission cooler (350), intermittent wipers, Heavy Duty Suspension Group (250 and 350), front and side door scuff pads, five 225/75R15 tires (250), five 235/75R15XL tires (250 Maxivan), five LT225/75R16D tires (350), five LT225/75R16E tires (350 Maxivan). Pkg. 24C requires 5.2-liter V-8 engine. Pkg. 26C requires 5.2-liter engine and 4-speed automatic transmission. Pkg. 28C requires 5.9-liter V-8 engine.

Dodge B150 Ram Van

	Retail Price	Dealer Invoice	Fair Price
Conversion Pkg. 250 SWB, 22/24/26E	$941	$800	$828

Commercial Pkg. plus air conditioning, heavy duty alternator and battery, Convenience Group (ashtray, glove box and underhood lights, ignition key light headlamp switch with time delay), Deluxe Convenience Groups, Exterior and Van Conversion Appearance Groups, styled steel wheels, Van Window Group with rear door and side window glass. Pkg. 24E requires 5.2-liter V-8 engine. Pkg. 26E requires 5.2-liter engine and 4-speed automatic transmission.

250 SWB, 22/24/26F	1791	1522	1576
250 LWB, 22/24/26F	1662	1413	1463
250 Maxi Van	1445	1228	1272

Conversion Pkg. E plus power mirrors, cassette player, Power Convenience Pkg., five 225/75R15 whitewall tires, alloy wheels. Pkg. 24F requires 5.2-liter V-8 engine. Pkg. 26F requires 5.2-liter engine and 4-speed automatic transmission. Pkg. 28F requires 5.9-liter V-8 engine and 4-speed automatic transmission.

Optional Equipment:

5.2-liter V-8, 150/250	587	499	517
5.9-liter V-8, 250 LBW	857	728	754
350	270	230	238
4-speed automatic transmission, 150/250	250	213	220
Anti-lock brakes	500	425	440
Air conditioning	970	825	854
Optional axle ratio	39	33	34
Anti-spin differential	257	218	226
Deluxe Convenience Group	400	340	352

Cruise control, tilt steering column, premium steering wheel. Requires Commercial Pkg.

Power Convenience Group, 250 SWB with Conversion Pkg.	628	534	553

Power windows and door locks, remote keyless entry system.

Heavy Duty Suspension Group (std. 250 Maxi Van)	37	31	33

Heavy duty front and rear gas shock absorbers.

Lock Group	8	7	7

Separate keys for ignition/front doors and side/rear doors.

Trailer Towing Prep Group: 250 with Commercial Pkg.	375	319	330
250 SWB with Conversion Pkg.	201	171	177
250 LWB with Conversion Pkg.	164	139	144
350	412	350	363
350 with Z3B GVWR Pkg.	375	319	330
350 with Commercial Pkg.	245	208	216
GVW Pkgs. Z1B (5300 lbs.), 150	87	74	77
Z2B (6400 lbs.), 250 LWB	217	184	191
with Commercial Pkg.	203	173	179
Z3B (8510 lbs.), 350	274	233	241
with Commercial Pkg.	254	216	224
Z3B (8510 lbs.), 350 Maxivan	123	105	108
with Commercial Pkg.	86	73	76
Z3D (9000 lbs.), 350 Maxivan	519	441	457
with Commercial Pkg. 28C	425	361	374
Exterior Appearance Group	373	317	328

Bright bumpers step caps, bright grille, rectangular halogen headlamps. Requires Commercial Pkg.

Temporary Plastic Seat Group	85	72	75
250 with Trailer Towing Group or Conversion Pkg. (credit)	(69)	(59)	(59)

Temporary plastic driver's seat, rear seatbelt shoulder harness reinforcement brackets, dual sunvisors, dual shoulder/lap seatbelts, accessory wiring harness, heavy duty alternator. Deletes front seats and right riser, interior paint, headliner, dome light, floormats. Requires heavy duty battery.

Van Window Groups: GHD glass	103	88	91
with Commercial Pkg.	43	37	38

Fixed glass for rear dual doors and right-side dual doors.

GHB rear door glass	60	51	53
GHJ glass	134	114	118
with Commercial Pkg.	74	63	65

Fixed glass for rear dual doors, right-side dual doors, and right rear quarter window.

Dodge

	Retail Price	Dealer Invoice	Fair Price
GHG All Window Glass Pkg.	$209	$178	$184
with Commercial Pkg.	149	127	131
Vented glass, with GHB	60	51	53
with GHD or GHJ	139	118	122
with GHG	217	184	191
Sunscreen glass, 150 with Commercial Pkg. and GHB	120	102	106
and GHD	241	205	212
and GHG or GHJ	409	348	360
250 with Commercial Pkg. and GHG or GHJ	409	348	360
and GHB	120	102	106
with Conversion Pkg. and GHD	241	205	212
350 with Commercial Pkg. and GHD	241	205	212
and GHG or GHJ	409	348	360
and GHB	120	102	106
Intermittent wipers	60	51	53
Delete front passenger seat (credit)	(184)	(156)	(156)
Upgraded vinyl upholstery	67	57	59
driver's seat only	34	29	30
Cloth and vinyl upholstery	152	129	134
Passenger-side seat riser	48	41	42
Requires Temporary Plastic Seat Group.			
Front and side door scuff pads	40	34	35
Door pull straps, 250 with Conversion Pkg.	37	31	33
Bright rear step bumper	216	184	190
with Exterior Appearance Group	59	50	52
Heavy duty battery	57	48	50
Heavy duty alternator	154	131	136
Engine cover console	153	130	135
Requires Commercial or Conversion Pkg.			
Maximum engine cooling	66	56	58
Transmission oil cooler	64	54	56
Requires maximum engine cooling.			
35-gallon fuel tank	113	96	99
Engine block heater	34	29	30
Black 6-inch x 9-inch mirrors	94	80	83
Power 6-inch x 9-inch mirrors, with Commercial Pkg.	64	54	56
250 with Conversion Pkg.	64	54	56
AM/FM cassette, with Commercial Pkg.	210	179	185
250 SWB with Conversion Pkg.	210	179	185
Premium AM/FM cassette with equalizer, 250 SWB with "E" Conversion Pkgs.	534	454	470
with "F" Conversion Pkgs.	153	130	135
250 LWB with Conversion Pkg.	153	130	135
Infinity Sound Speaker System, 250 SWB with Conversion Pkg.	171	145	150
Requires AM/FM cassette.			
Radio delete (credit)	(122)	(104)	(104)
Heavy duty front springs	15	13	13
Heavy duty rear springs	71	60	62
150 requires Commercial Pkg. and Z1B GVWR Pkg. 250/350 require Z3B GVWR Pkg.			
Tilt steering column, with Commercial Pkg.	134	114	118
Requires intermittent wipers.			
Tires: 225/75R15, 150	128	109	113
225/75R15 whitewall, 250 with "E" Conversion Pkg.	91	77	80
235/75R15XL outline white letter, 150 with Commercial Pkg.	367	312	323
250 SWB with Commercial Pkg. or "E" Conversion Pkg.	240	204	211
250 with "F" Conversion Pkg.	149	127	131
250 LWB with Conversion Pkg.	31	26	27
with Commercial Pkg.	240	204	211
250 Maxi Van with Commercial Pkg.	123	105	108
235/75R15XL, 250	94	80	83
250 LWB with Commercial Pkg.	117	99	103
LT225/75R16E, 350	151	128	133
with Commercial Pkg.	168	143	148
Conventional spare tires: 225/75R15, 250	144	122	127
235/75R15, 250	167	142	147

Dodge Ram Wagon

	Retail Price	Dealer Invoice	Fair Price
B150	$14491	$13252	$13552
B250	18260	16021	16321
B250 Maxi Wagon	19546	17114	17414
B350	19548	17116	17416
B350 Maxi Wagon	20565	17980	18280
Destination charge	595	595	595

Standard Equipment:

3.9-liter V-6 (150 and 250), 5.2-liter V-8 (250 Maxi Wagon 350), 5.9-liter V-8 (350 Maxi Wagon), 3-speed automatic transmission (150 and 250), speed automatic transmission (350), anti-lock rear brakes, power steering, vinyl front bucket seats, 3-passenger middle bench seat, tinted glass, AM/FM radio, digital clock, dual black fold-away mirrors, painted front and rear bumpers, front stabilizer bar, heavy shock absorbers (250 Maxi Wagon), black rubber floor covering, double hinged right side door with vented glass (sliding side door with vented glass may be substituted at no additional cost), single rear door with fixed glass, 205/75R15 tires (150), 225/75R15 tires (250), 235/75R15XL tires (250 Maxi Wagon), LT225/75R16D tires (350), LT225/75R16E tires (350 Maxi Wagon).

Quick Order Pkgs.:

Value Pkg. 150, 22/24/26C	500	425	440
250, 22/24/26/28C	1049	892	923

Air conditioning, single rear door with vented glass, heavy duty alternator, bright bumpers and grille, carpet, Convenience Group, 35-gallon fuel tank, manual remote mirrors, 8-passenger seating, Heavy Duty Suspension Group (250), 235/75R15XL tires with matching spare tire, spare tire cover, bright wheel covers. Pkg. 24C requires 5.2-liter V-8 engine. Pkg. 26C requires 5.2-liter engine and 4-speed automatic transmission. Pkg. 28C requires 5.9-liter 4-speed automatic transmission and 4-speed automatic transmission.

350, 26/28B	1166	991	1026
350 Maxi Wagon, 26/28B	1741	1480	1532

Air conditioning, single rear door with vented glass, heavy duty alternator, bright bumpers and grille, carpet, Convenience Group, 35-gallon fuel tank, manual remote mirrors, 12-passenger seating (350), 15-passenger seating (Maxiwagon), Heavy Duty Suspension Group (Maxiwagon), LT225/75R16E tires with matching spare tire, spare tire cover, bright wheel trim rings. Pkg. 28B requires 5.9-liter V-8 engine.

LE Pkg. 150, 22/24/26E	3209	2728	2824
250, 22/24/26/28E	3353	2850	2951
250 Maxi Wagon, 26E	3330	2831	2930
350, 26/28E	4023	3420	3540
350 Maxi Wagon, 26/28E	4448	3781	3914

Value Pkg. 22C (150 and 250) and Value Pkg. 26B (350) plus Deluxe Convenience Pkg., sunscreen glass, LE Decor Pkg. (bodyside moldings, bright bumpers and grille, reclining bucket seats, cloth and vinyl upholstery, cloth headliner, premium steering wheel, instrument panel woodgrain trim, upgraded door trim, carpeting, front floormats, dual horns, map and reading lamps, passenger-side lighted visor mirror, engine cover console), Power Convenience Group (power windows and locks, remote keyless entry system), cassette player, power mirrors, rear air conditioning with auxiliary heater (350 Maxi Wagon), 235/75R15XL whitewall tires with matching spare tire (250), styled steel wheels (150 and 250).

Optional Equipment:

5.2-liter V-8, 150 and 250	587	499	517
5.9-liter V-8, 250	857	728	754
350 Maxi Wagon	270	230	238
Requires 4-speed automatic transmission.			
4-speed automatic transmission, 150 and 250	250	213	220
Requires 5.2-liter engine.			
4-wheel anti-lock brakes	500	425	440
Optional axle ratio	39	33	34
Anti-spin differential	257	218	226
Front air conditioning	970	825	854
Rear air conditioning (NA 150)	611	519	538
250 with Value or LE Pkg., 350 with Value Pkg.	457	388	402
and Trailer Towing Pkg.	400	340	352

CONSUMER GUIDE® 61

Dodge • Eagle

	Retail Price	Dealer Invoice	Fair Price
Rear air conditioning with rear heater	$822	$699	$723
250 with Value or LE Pkg., 350 with Value Pkg.	668	568	588
and Trailer Towing Pkg.	611	519	538
Auxiliary rear heater, 150	365	310	321
150 with Value or LE Pkg.	211	179	186
250 and 350	365	310	321
250 with Value or LE Pkg., 350 with Value Pkg. and Trailer Towing Pkg.	211	179	186
Deluxe Convenience Group	400	340	352

Cruise control, tilt steering column, premium steering wheel. Requires intermittent wipers.

Convenience Group	110	94	97

Intermittent wipers, ashtray, glove box and underhood lights, ignition key light, time-delay headlight switch.

Heavy Duty Suspension Group (std. 250 Maxi Wagon)	37	31	33

Heavy duty front and rear gas shock absorbers.

Trailer Towing Prep Group: 350	412	350	363
250 with Z2B GVWR Pkg.	375	319	330
250 with Value or LE Pkg., 250 Maxi Wagon with LE Pkg.	221	188	194
350 with Value Pkg.	258	219	227
350 with LE Pkg.	201	171	177
350 with Z3B GVWR Pkg.	375	319	330
350 with Z3B GVWR Pkg. and Value Pkg.	221	188	194
350 with Z3B GVWR Pkg. and LE Pkg.	164	139	144

Heavy duty alternator and battery, maximum engine cooling, auxiliary transmission oil cooler, heavy duty flashers, trailer wiring harness, Heavy Duty Suspension Group (std. 250 Maxi Wagon). 250 requires 5.2-liter engine and 4-speed automatic transmission.

GVW Pkgs. Z1D (6010 lbs.), 150	332	282	292
Z2B (6400 lbs.), 250	217	184	191
Z3B (8510 lbs.), 350	238	202	209
350 with Value or LE Pkg.	255	217	224
350 Maxi Wagon	123	105	108

Pkg. Z1D and Z2B include 235/75R15XL tires. Pkg. Z1D adds matching spare tire. Pkg. Z3B includes 225/75R16E tires (std. Maxi Wagon). 350 with Value or LE Pkg. adds matching spare tire.

8-passenger seating	342	291	301
150 requires Z1D GVWR Pkg.			
8-passenger travel seating, 250 with LE Pkg.	913	776	803
350 with LE Pkg.	551	468	485
350 Maxi Wagon with LE Pkg.	266	226	234

Includes two 3-passenger rear bench seats with folding seatbacks for sleeper conversion and 6-place dinette table.

12-passenger seating, 350	704	598	620
350 Maxi Wagon with Value or LE Pkg. delete, (credit)	(285)	(242)	(242)
15-passenger seating, 350 Maxi Wagon	989	841	870
Requires Z3B GVWR Pkg.			
Cloth and vinyl seat trim	85	72	75
Heavy duty battery	57	48	50
Heavy duty alternator	154	131	136
Bright rear step bumper	216	184	190
with LE Pkg.	59	50	52
Center storage console	153	130	135
Requires Value Pkg. and 4-speed automatic transmission.			
Maximum engine cooling	66	56	58
Transmission oil cooler	64	54	56

Requires maximum engine cooling. Not available 150 with 3.9-liter engine and 3-speed automatic transmission.

Intermittent wipers	60	51	53
Rear defogger	110	94	97
Requires single rear door with vented glass.			
Single rear door with vented glass	69	59	61
Dual rear doors with vented glass	69	59	61
Sunscreen glass	409	348	360
Black manual remote mirrors	94	80	83
Tilt steering column	134	114	118
AM/FM cassette, with Value Pkg.	210	179	185
AM/FM cassette/equalizer, with LE Pkg.	153	130	135

	Retail Price	Dealer Invoice	Fair Price
35-gallon fuel tank	$113	$96	$99
Engine block heater	34	29	30
Heavy duty front springs	15	13	13
Heavy duty rear springs	71	60	62
Full width driver compartment carpet, 350 with Value Pkg.	58	139	51
Rear carpeting with silencers, 350 with Value Pkg.	99	139	87
2-tone center band paint	357	139	314
with LE Pkg.	243	139	214
Includes bodyside moldings and rear tape strip.			
2-tone lower break paint	304	139	268
with LE Pkg.	190	139	167
Includes bodyside moldings.			
Styled wheels, 150 and 250 with Value Pkg.	180	153	158
Alloy wheels, 150 and 250 with LE Pkg.	130	111	114
Bright wheel covers, 150 and 250	66	56	58
Wheel trim rings, 350	126	107	111
Tires: 235/75R15, 150	245	208	216

Eagle Summit Wagon

Eagle Summit Wagon AWD

Eagle Summit Wagon gains a driver-side air bag, adjustable-height driver's shoulder belt, and CFC-free air conditioning for 1994. Designed and built in Japan by Chrysler Corporation's partner, Mitsubishi, the Eagle Summit Wagon is duplicated as the Plymouth Colt Vista (see separate report). Both are nearly identical to Mitsubishi's own Expo LRV (covered under that heading).

Body Styles/Chassis

Slotted in size and market position between a subcompact station wagon and a minivan, Summit Wagon has a sliding curb-side door and a one-piece rear liftgate.

DL and upscale LX models are available with front-wheel drive. There also is an AWD-badged version with all-wheel drive and a level of standard equipment that falls between the two front-drive models.

Power steering is now standard on all models. Anti-lock brakes with 4-wheel discs are optional.

No payload rating is listed by the manufacturer.

Powertrains

A 113-horsepower 1.8-liter 4-cylinder engine remains standard on the DL. The AWD model joins the LX this year in getting a 136-horsepower 2.4-liter four as standard. The 2.4 is optional on the DL.

Both engines team with standard 5-speed manual transmission or optional 4-speed automatic.

Towing capacity with the 1.8 is 1500 pounds. With the 2.4, capacity is 2000 pounds on front-drive models, 2500 with AWD.

Accommodations

Standard are front bucket seats and a 3-person rear bench with a folding one-piece backrest. The LX has a split folding backrest. On all models, the rear seat can be tumbled forward or removed.

Cargo volume is 34.6 cubic feet behind the rear seat, 67.8 cubic feet with the seat folded, and 79 with it removed.

Evaluation

The Summit Wagon and its siblings succeed nicely in combining compact-wagon economy and maneuverability with minivan-style versatility.

Opt for the 2.4-liter engine if you routinely carry anything near a full passenger or cargo load. The 1.8 delivers no more than adequate acceleration on the flat—with automatic, 11.7 seconds 0-60 mph by our clock. And the 1.8 feels strained on even mild uphill grades—and that's with just the driver aboard.

The 2.4's extra displacement translates into appreciated extra pulling power, plus more relaxed cruising and little if any difference in overall fuel economy. Speaking of mileage, it's pretty good: We've averaged in the mid-20-mpg range in a fairly even city/highway driving mix with either engine.

The 5-speed manual shifts smoothly and is nicely matched by light clutch action. But it doesn't seem to provide a great performance advantage over the automatic, which is quick to change down a gear (sometimes two) to maintain speed on hills or to pass, though shifts are sometimes rather harsh.

The Summit Wagon is quite maneuverable at low speeds. In fast corners, though, its rather tall build and relatively narrow track result in lots of body lean. Grip isn't the best with the rather skinny tires supplied on front-drive versions, but the AWD with its wider tires is surprisingly poised.

Regardless of model, ride is smooth and relaxed over all surfaces. Braking feels balanced, even without the optional anti-lock system. There's generally good isolation from engine and wind noise, but the base model is noticeably louder in both respects, and unwanted tire noise afflicts any model, especially on patchy pavement.

For its size, the Summit Wagon rates high on utility. Step-in height is low, and the sliding right-side door opens and closes easily on a unique inner-rail mechanism that eliminates the bodyside channel used with traditional sliding doors. Seating positions are comfortably chair-like, and combine with ample glass areas for great outward vision.

Gauges are simple. The only control flaws are audio systems mounted too low for safe operation on the move and a power door lock button that's on the dash but should be on the driver's door.

The rear seat is none too plush, and there's only enough cargo space behind it for a couple of medium-size suitcases. But the rear backrest folds flat in a jiffy, and the entire seat tumbles forward to leave a flat load floor from tailgate almost to the front seats.

If a minivan is too big or too expensive for you and small conventional wagons too limited, the Summit Wagon makes appealing sense.

Eagle

Specifications

	4-door wagon
Wheelbase, in.	99.2
Overall length, in.	168.5
Overall width, in.	66.7
Overall height, in.	62.1
Turn diameter, ft.	33.5
Curb weight, lbs.	2734[1]
Fuel capacity, gal.	14.5

1. 3064 lbs., AWD.

Passenger Area Dimensions

Seating capacity	5
Front head room, in.	40.0
Rear head room, in.	38.6
Front leg room, in.	40.8
Rear leg room, in.	36.1

Available Seating

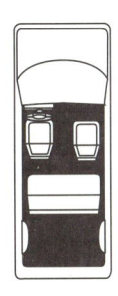

Cargo Dimensions and Payloads

Cargo area length, in.	67.8
Cargo area width, in.	41.3
Cargo area width between wheels, in.	39.0
Cargo area height, in.	43.4
Cargo vol., cu. ft.	79.0
Max. payload, lbs.	NA
Max. trailer weight, lbs.	2500

Engines

	ohc I-4	ohc I-4
Size, liters/cu. in.	1.8/112	2.4/143
Horsepower @ rpm	113 @ 6000	136 @ 5500
Torque (lbs./ft.) @ rpm	116 @ 4500	145 @ 4250
Availability	S	O[1]

EPA city/highway mpg

5-speed OD manual	24/29	22/27
4-speed OD automatic	24/29	20/26

1. Standard, LX, AWD.

Built in Japan.

KEY: Dimensions and capacities are supplied by the manufacturers. **Curb Weight:** base models, not including optional equipment. **Max. payload, lbs.** = gross amount; net payload may be lower due to optional equipment. **Engines: ohv** = overhead valve; **ohc** = overhead cam; **I** = inline cylinders; **V** = cylinders in V configuration; **flat** = horizontally opposed cylinders; **rpm** = revolutions per minute; **OD** = overdrive transmission; **S** = standard; **O** = optional; **NA** = not available.

Prices

Eagle Summit Wagon	Retail Price	Dealer Invoice	Fair Price
DL 4-door wagon	$12979	$12036	$12579
LX 4-door wagon	14194	13130	13694

Eagle • Ford

	Retail Price	Dealer Invoice	Fair Price
AWD 4-door wagon	$14884	$13751	$14384
Destination charge	430	430	430

Standard Equipment:

DL: 1.8-liter 4-cylinder engine, 5-speed manual transmission, driver-side air bag, motorized front passenger, shoulder belt, power steering, cloth/vinyl reclining front bucket seats with center console, folding and removable rear seat, coolant temperature gauge, trip odometer, remote fuel door release, dual outside mirrors, intermittent wipers, passenger-side visor mirrors, 185/75R14 tires. **LX** adds: 2.4-liter 4-cylinder engine, cloth seats, split folding and removable rear seat with reclining back, tilt steering column, power mirrors, tinted glass, driver-side visor mirror, power locks, remote tailgate lock, rear wiper/washer, rear seat heater ducts, two-tone paint, rear stabilizer bar, wheel covers. **AWD** adds to DL: full-time 4-wheel drive, 2.4-liter 4-cylinder engine, remote tailgate lock, power mirrors, rear wiper/washer, driver-side visor mirror, rear stabilizer bar, 205/70R14 tires, wheel covers.

Optional Equipment:

Pkg. 21C/22C, DL	1156	994	1017

Air conditioning, tinted glass, rear defogger, rear wiper/washer, power mirrors, AM/FM radio, power tailgate lock, rear stabilizer bar, wheel covers. Pkg. 22C requires automatic transmission.

Pkg. 21D/22D/24D, DL	1796	1545	1580

Pkg. 21C plus power locks, cruise control, cassette player, floormats. Pkg. 22D requires automatic transmission. Pkg. 24D requires 2.4-liter engine, automatic transmission.

Pkg. 23K/24K, LX	1609	1384	1416

Air conditioning, rear defogger, power windows, cruise control, remote keyless entry, cassette player, cargo area cover, floormats. Pkg. 24K requires automatic transmission.

Pkg. 23S/24S, AWD	673	579	592

Tinted glass, rear defogger, remote keyless entry, AM/FM radio, floormats, full cloth seats, split back reclining rear seat, upgraded interior trim. Pkg. 24S requires automatic transmission.

Pkg. 23W/24W, AWD	2138	1839	1881

Pkg. 23S plus air conditioning, power windows, cruise control, cassette player, tachometer. Pkg. 24W requires automatic transmission.

2.4-liter 4-cylinder engine, DL	181	156	159
4-speed automatic transmission	723	622	636
Anti-lock brakes	699	601	615
Includes rear disc brakes.			
Air conditioning, AWD	790	679	695
Rear defogger	66	57	58
Roof rack	151	130	133
AM/FM radio, DL and AWD	288	248	253
AM/FM cassette, DL and AWD	181	156	159
2-tone paint, LX and AWD	193	166	170
Floormats, DL and AWD	55	47	48

The rear seat folds to increase cargo space.

Ford Aerostar

Ford Aerostar XLT Extended Length

The addition of a high-mount third brake light is among the few changes to Ford's minivan for '94.

This is to be the last model year for the Aerostar. Ford plans to retire it in favor of the new Windstar minivan (see separate report).

Body Styles/Chassis

Aerostar continues in two basic forms. The version designed for commercial use and recreational-vehicle customizing is called the Van and is identified by solid sheet metal in place of rear side windows. Ford calls the passenger model the Aerostar Wagon and gives it full side windows.

Both have a 118.9-inch wheelbase and both Van and Wagon are available with a standard body that's 174.9 inches long, and in Extended form with 15.4 extra inches of length added to the tail. The added length is good for 30 additional cubic feet of cargo space.

Both the Van and Wagon have a sliding right-side door. Vans come with dual center-opening rear cargo doors. The Wagon has a one-piece liftgate, which is optionally available on the Van.

Wagons come in XL, XL Plus, XLT, and top-shelf Eddie Bauer models. The Van is offered in a single trim level.

Maximum payloads are with 2WD: 1950 pounds for the regular-length version, 1870 for the extended-body.

Powertrains

Aerostars are available with standard rear-wheel drive or optional permanently engaged 4-wheel drive.

A 135-horsepower 3.0-liter V-6 is standard on 2WD models. A 155-horsepower 4.0-liter V-6 is standard on 4WD models and on the Eddie Bauer 2WD extended-length. The 4.0 V-6 is optional on other extended-length 2WD models.

The 3.0 teams with 5-speed manual transmission or optional 4-speed overdrive automatic. The automatic is the only choice with the 4.0.

Aerostar's 4WD system is designed for on-road use only. It normally apportions engine torque on a 35/65 basis front/rear. However, should its electronics detect spinning or slippage at any wheel, a center differential locks in a 50/50 split that returns to normal once the front and rear axles are rotating at equal rates. Rear anti-lock brakes are standard on all models.

Van towing capacities are 4900 pounds for the standard 2WD model and up to 4800 pounds for the Extended version; 4WD limits are 4700 on the regular length and 4600 on the extended. Towing limits for the Wagon are 4800 pounds for the regular-length and 4700 for the Extended.

Accommodations

All Aerostars have a standard driver-side air bag. XL models have fixed-back front buckets and a 3-passenger middle bench seat. XL Plus and XLT have front captains chairs, a 2-place middle bench, and a 3-place rear bench for 7-passenger seating. Eddie Bauer models have the 7-passenger setup, but use a rearmost bench that can be folded into a bed.

The 7-passenger arrangement, including the seat/bed, is optional on the XLT model. A four-captains-chair layout with a rear bench is optional on all Wagons.

Optional integrated child seats are available with the 2-place middle bench. The two safety seats fold from the backrest padding and allow the seat to be used as a standard bench seat when the child seats are stowed. Each child seat has a 5-point restraint system.

Vans come with two high-back, non-reclining front bucket seats.

Evaluation

If a minivan replacement for a conventional family station wagon is what you seek, look to lighter-duty models like the front-drive Dodge Caravan/Plymouth Voyager and Chevrolet's Lumina Minivan, or even Ford's new Windstar.

Aerostar, like the similarly truck-based Chevrolet Astro/GMC Safari, is better suited to heavier-duty chores like hauling hefty payloads or towing trailers. The 2WD Aerostar Wagon's 4800-pound towing capacity, for example, is 1300 pounds more than a Dodge Caravan's.

Still, Aerostar scores points as a passenger vehicle with its driver-side air bag, modern interior design, and child safety seats. Though it's nice that Aerostar comes with standard rear-wheel anti-lock brakes, most competitors offer 4-wheel anti-lock brakes as either standard or optional.

Power is more than adequate with either V-6: Our 4.0-liter 4WD Extended model clocked a credible 10.4 seconds 0-60 mph.

Aerostar's truck-like brawn means a stiffish ride (especially with a trailer towing package), a high cabin step-up, and mediocre fuel economy. Don't expect more than 15 mpg city and low-20s highway.

Though bigger and burlier than front-drive minivans, Aerostar isn't unpleasantly "trucky" in everyday driving. It certainly runs smoother and quieter than the Astro/Safari.

If you regularly travel in snow, consider the no-fuss 4WD, particularly because rear-drive Aerostars tend to have relatively poor wet-weather traction when lightly loaded.

XLT and especially Eddie Bauer Aerostars can be quite plush, and passenger space is more than sufficient with either body, but cargo room in regular-length 7-seaters is unimpressive with all seats installed. Removing the third seat helps greatly, though that's a chore because the seat weighs about 100 pounds, as does the second seat. At least the third seat's backrest can be flopped forward to increase load volume without inviting back strain.

The driving position is comfortable, with accommodating gauges and controls. A handy mini floor console with dual cup holders is standard; we'd advise against the optional larger center console because it hampers passage from the front seats to the rear of the van. Other negatives are the postage-stamp sized horn buttons and power window switches located inconveniently beneath the front-door arm rests.

Specifications

	4-door van	4-door van
Wheelbase, in.	118.9	118.9
Overall length, in.	174.9	190.3
Overall width, in.	71.7	72.0
Overall height, in.	72.9	74.0
Turn diameter, ft.	39.8	39.8
Curb weight, lbs.	3481	3558
Fuel capacity, gal.	21.0	21.0

Passenger Area Dimensions

Seating capacity	7	7
Front head room, in.	39.5	39.5
Rear head room, in.	38.8	38.8
Front leg room, in.	41.4	41.4
Rear leg room, in.	39.5	40.5

Available Seating

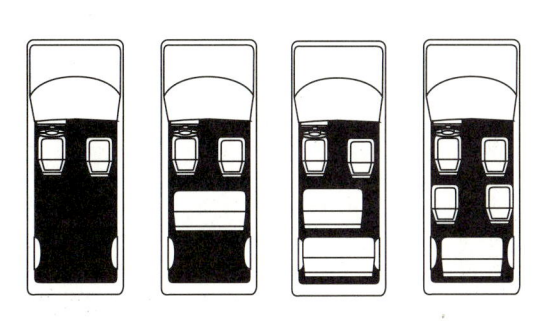

Cargo Dimensions and Payloads

Cargo area length, in.	86.0	100.5
Cargo area width, in.	65.5	65.5
Cargo area width between wheels, in.	48.2	48.2
Cargo area height, in.	48.1	49.0
Cargo vol., cu. ft.	140.0	170.0
Max. payload, lbs.	1950	1870
Max. trailer weight, lbs.	4900	4800

Engines

	ohv V-6	ohv V-6
Size, liters/cu. in.	3.0/182	4.0/245
Horsepower @ rpm	135 @ 4600	155 @ 4000
Torque (lbs./ft.) @ rpm	160 @ 2800	230 @ 2400
Availability	S	O[1]

EPA city/highway mpg

5-speed OD manual	19/25	
4-speed OD automatic	18/23	16/20

1. Standard Aerostar 4WD and Eddie Bauer Extended Length 2WD.

Built in St. Louis, Mo.

KEY: Dimensions and capacities are supplied by the manufacturers. **Curb Weight:** base models, not including optional equipment. **Max. payload, lbs.** = gross amount; net payload may be lower due to optional equipment. **Engines: ohv** = overhead valve; **ohc** = overhead cam; **I** = inline cylinders; **V** = cylinders in V configuration; **flat** = horizontally opposed cylinders; **rpm** = revolutions per minute; **OD** = overdrive transmission; **S** = standard; **O** = optional; **NA** = not available.

Ford

Prices

Ford Aerostar Wagon

	Retail Price	Dealer Invoice	Fair Price
XL regular length, 2WD	$15150	*	*
XL extended, 2WD	16595	*	*
XL regular length, 4WD	18620	*	*
XL extended, 4WD	19515	*	*
XL Plus regular length, 2WD	16685	*	*
XL Plus extended, 2WD	17725	*	*
XL Plus regular, 4WD	19695	*	*
XL Plus extended, 4WD	20520	*	*
XLT regular length, 2WD	20590	*	*
XLT extended, 2WD	21070	*	*
XLT regular length, 4WD	22145	*	*
XLT extended, 4WD	23010	*	*
Eddie Bauer regular length, 2WD	23470	*	*
Eddie Bauer extended, 2WD	24270	*	*
Eddie Bauer regular length, 4WD	25380	*	*
Eddie Bauer extended, 4WD	26290	*	*
Destination charge	535	535	535

Standard Equipment:

XL: 3.0-liter V-6 with 5-speed manual transmission 2WD (4WD models have 4.0-liter V-6 with 4-speed automatic transmission, permanent 4WD), anti-lock rear brakes, driver-side air bag, power steering, cloth and vinyl front bucket seats, 3-passenger fold-down bench seat, tinted glass, dual outside mirrors, right visor mirror, rear wiper/washer, intermittent wipers, remote fuel door release, AM/FM radio, 215/70R14 tires. **XL Plus** adds: dual captain's chairs, 2-passenger middle and 3-passenger rear bench seats, cloth upholstery, storage bin under right front seat. **XLT** adds: 4-speed automatic transmission, dual captain's with power lumbar support, front air conditioning, cruise control, tilt steering wheel, underseat storage bin, door and seatback map pockets, dual-note horn, 2-tone paint, liftgate convenience net, Light Group, leather-wrapped steering wheel. **Eddie Bauer** adds: 4.0-liter V-6 engine (ex. regular-length 2WD), front and rear air conditioning with auxiliary heater, Electronics Group, Power Convenience Group, luggage rack, mini console, AM/FM cassette, rear defogger, rear seat/bed, upgraded upholstery, 2-tone paint, floormats, forged alloy wheels.

Optional Equipment:

	Retail Price	Dealer Invoice	Fair Price
4.0-liter V-6, Ext. 2WD	300	255	262
4-speed automatic transmission, XL 2WD	750	637	656
Limited-slip axle	252	215	220
Optional axle ratio	38	32	33
Base Preferred Equipment Pkg. 400A, XL Base	37	31	32
Air conditioning, right underseat storage bin.			
XL Preferred Equipment Pkg. 401A, XL Plus	734	623	642
Deluxe paint stripe, air conditioning, privacy glass, cruise control, tilt steering wheel.			
XLT Preferred Equipment Pkg. 403A, XLT	315	267	275
Privacy glass, rear defogger, power windows and locks, power mirrors, cassette player.			
Eddie Bauer Pkg. 405A	$338	$287	$295
Privacy glass, floor console with storage and cup holders.			
Dual captain's chairs, XL Base	644	547	563
7-passenger seating: with front captain's chairs,			
XL Base	1043	886	912
with Pkg. 401A or 403A	552	470	483
with four captain's chairs, XLT	598	508	523
Four captain's chairs and seat/bed, XLT	622	528	544
Eddie Bauer	NC	NC	NC
with leather upholstery	848	720	742
Child safety seats	224	191	196
Front air conditioning, XL	857	729	749
High-capacity front air conditioning with rear heater	576	489	504
Floor console with storage and cup holders	174	147	152
Floor console delete (credit)	(61)	(52)	(52)
Rear defogger	168	142	147
Electronics Group, with Pkg. 403A	813	691	711
Electronic instruments, AM/FM stereo cassette with equalizer and clock, trip computer, autolamp and electrochromatic mirror.			
Exterior Appearance Group,			
with Pkg. 400A	576	522	504
with Pkg. 401A	174	147	152
with Pkg. 403A	94	79	82
XLT without privacy glass and Power Convenience Group	513	436	448
Styled wheel covers, privacy glass, 2-tone paint, swing-lock outside mirrors.			
Light Group	159	135	139
Underhood, glove box and instrument panel lights, illuminated entry system.			
Luggage rack (std. Eddie Bauer)	143	121	125
Swing-lock mirrors (NA XLT and Eddie Bauer)	52	45	45
with Exterior Appearance Group and Power Convenience Group	NC	NC	NC
Bodyside molding	63	53	55
Power Convenience Group	538	457	470
with Exterior Appearance Pkg.	485	413	424
Power windows and locks, power mirrors.			
Cruise control and tilt steering wheel	371	315	324
Sport Appearance Pkg.	733	623	641
High-gloss silver metallic treatment, color-keyed headlight frames and grille, striping, full wheel covers.			
Trailer Towing Pkg.	282	239	246
Class I wiring harness, heavy duty turn signal flasher, limited-slip axle with axle ratio upgrade.			
XL Plus Convenience Group, with Pkg. 401A	827	703	723
Privacy glass, cruise control, tilt steering wheel, deluxe paint stripe.			
XLT Convenience Group, with Pkg. 403A	901	766	788
with Exterior Appearance Group	849	721	742
Power Convenience Group, AM/FM cassette, rear defogger.			
Deluxe paint stripe	43	36	37
Delete for credit, XL Plus	(29)	(25)	(25)
Underseat storage bin	37	31	32
with captain's chairs	NC	NC	NC

Above: A driver-side air bag is standard. Right: Aerostar XL with Sport Appearance Package.

Some dealer invoice and fair prices not available at time of publication.

Ford Aerostar Van

	Retail Price	Dealer Invoice	Fair Price
RL cargo van, 2WD	$15320	*	*
EL cargo van, 2WD	15870	*	*
RL cargo van, 4WD	17815	*	*
EL cargo van, 4WD	18415	*	*
RL window van, 2WD	15615	*	*
EL window van, 2WD	16165	*	*
RL window van, 4WD	18115	*	*
EL window van, 4WD	18710	*	*
Destination charge	535	535	535

RL and EL denote regular-length and extended-length models.

Standard Equipment:
3.0-liter V-6 (2WD), 4.0-liter V-6 (4WD), 5-speed manual transmission (2WD), 4-speed automatic transmission (4WD), anti-lock rear brakes, driver-side air bag, power steering, vinyl front bucket seats, coolant temperature and oil pressure gauges, voltmeter, tinted glass, dual sliding bodyside windows (window van), front stabilizer bar, digital clock, front carpeting, rear floor liner, dual black aero foldaway mirrors, heavy duty battery, front black aero spoiler, remote fuel door release, AM radio, intermittent wipers, underbody spare tire (EL), inside mounted spare tire (RL), P215/70R14SL all-season tires, wheel covers.

Optional Equipment:

4.0-liter V-6, 2WD	316	268	278
Requires automatic transmission.			
4-speed automatic transmission, 2WD	750	638	660
Includes mini floor console and auxiliary transmission oil cooler.			
Limited-slip rear axle	252	214	222
Air conditioning	868	738	764
Preferred Equipment Pkg. 423A, cargo van	1212	1030	1067
Air conditioning, dashboard insulation, cruise control, tilt steering wheel, swing-lock mirrors, AM/FM radio.			
Preferred Pkg. 431A, window van	1362	1157	1199
Air conditioning, dashboard insulation, cruise control, tilt steering wheel, swing-lock mirrors, AM/FM radio.			
Bright Pkg.	104	88	92
Includes deluxe grille and bumpers.			
Power Convenience Pkg.	538	457	473
Power windows, door locks, and mirrors.			
Cloth captain's chairs	468	398	412
Includes under seat storage bin.			
Captain's chairs	98	83	86
Includes power lumbar support.			
Cruise control and tilt steering column	371	315	326
Floor console	174	148	153
Includes cup holders and storage bin.			
Underseat storage bin (passenger-side)	37	31	33
Rear defogger	168	143	148
Requires rear liftgate door.			
Privacy glass, window van	413	351	363
Rear liftgate door with glass	NC	NC	NC
Replaces std. dual rear doors.			
Fixed side-door window, cargo van	68	58	60
Engine block heater	33	28	29
Swing-lock mirrors	52	45	46
1950 lbs. and 1870 lbs. Payload Pkgs.	104	88	92
Trailer Towing Pkg.	282	239	248
Includes wiring harness, heavy duty turn signal flasher, limited-slip axle. Cargo van requires Preferred Equipment Pkg. 423A.			
Rear wiper/washer	139	118	122
Requires rear liftgate door.			
AM/FM radio	221	188	194
AM/FM cassette	343	292	302
with Preferred Equipment Pkg. 423A or 431A	122	104	107
Radio delete, (credit)	(61)	(52)	(52)
Forged alloy wheels	363	309	319
Underbody spare tire, 2WD	22	19	19

Some dealer invoice and fair prices not available at time of publication.

Ford Bronco

✓ BEST BUY

Ford Bronco XLT

Ford's full-size sport-utility vehicle has a driver-side air bag and side door guard beams as new standard features for 1994. Door guard beams are required this year on truck-based vehicles like the Bronco.

Body Styles/Chassis

Bronco is essentially a 4-wheel-drive Ford F-Series pickup truck with an expanded passenger area and an add-on rear-roof section. It's offered only in a 3-door body style with a 2-way tailgate that contains a power window.

Three price levels are offered. The base model this year is called XL instead of Custom. The XLT is a step up in price and equipment, and the Eddie Bauer is the top-of-the-line model.

Bronco is the only full-size sport-utility with a driver-side air bag. It shares its dashboard with the F-Series pickups, which also gain the air bag and side door guard beams for 1994.

Four-wheel anti-lock brakes (ABS) are standard and act on all wheels in both 2WD and 4WD.

Payload is 1200 pounds on 6-passenger versions and 1050 pounds on 5-seat Broncos.

Powertrains

The standard engine is a 5.0-liter V-8 rated at 205 horsepower, 20 more than last year due to internal modifications. Standard with this engine is a 5-speed manual transmission; a 4-speed automatic is optional and standard on the Eddie Bauer model.

Optional on all models except the XL is a 5.8-liter V-8. Internal modifications increase its horsepower to 210 from 200 and its torque rating from to 325 pounds/feet from 300. Automatic transmission is mandatory with this engine.

All Broncos have an on-demand, part-time 4WD system that's not for use on dry pavement. It has a floor-mounted transfer-case shift lever and automatic-locking front hubs. Manual locking hubs are a credit option on XL and XLT models.

Optional on XLT and Eddie Bauer Broncos is Touch Drive, an electrically operated 4WD system that allows changing in or out of 4WD on the move at the push of a dashboard button. Touch Drive requires automatic transmission.

Ford

Bronco is the only big 4x4 with a driver-side air bag.

With either 4WD system, Bronco must be backed up a few feet to disengage the auto-locking hubs.

Automatic-transmission Broncos can tow up to 6600 pounds with the 5.0-liter engine and up to 7000 with the 5.8. With manual transmission, the towing limit is 3000 pounds.

Accommodations

Bucket seats and a 3-place folding/removable rear bench are standard. A 3-place front bench seat is an extra-cost item on LX models and a credit option on XLT models.

For 1994, a cargo net and retractable cargo cover are new standard features on the Eddie Bauer and new options on the XLT. A premium audio system with either a cassette player or a CD player is optional on all models, while a Security Group with remote keyless entry and an anti-theft alarm is newly available on the XLT and Eddie Bauer.

Other new standard features for the Eddie Bauer model are an overhead console and an illuminated visor mirror.

Evaluation

Bronco's current design dates from 1979, though it has received several important equipment changes since. Last year, it got 4-wheel ABS, a safer system than rear-only ABS. That improvement kept Bronco abreast of its only rival, the Chevrolet Blazer/GMC Yukon, which was redesigned for 1992 and included 4-wheel ABS as standard. (Dodge has discontinued its full-size Ramcharger sport-utility.)

But Bronco edges ahead of the GM brands for 1994 with the driver-side air bag, a safety feature not available on the Blazer or Yukon. Ford engineers say tests showed the air bag would not unintentionally deploy in tough off-road use.

Like Bronco, Blazer and Yukon have full shift-on-the fly 4WD convenience, though unlike Ford's Touch Drive, GM's doesn't require that you stop and reverse to fully disengage 4WD.

Capping the rear portion of Bronco's cabin with an add-on shell promotes squeaks and offers much less isolation from road and wind noise than the full-metal body of the Blazer/Yukon.

Minus points in common with its big brethren include a jouncy ride and an unwieldy size that renders Bronco clumsy in urban driving. In addition, there's a rather tall step up into the interior. And with only two side doors, Bronco is less convenient for family use than 5-door compact sport-utilities.

Room for six adults, ample cargo space, heavy-duty towing power, and rugged off-road capabilities are Bronco's main attractions.

Bronco's 5.0-liter V-8 is a better all-around choice than the 5.8. Neither is a quiet engine, but the 5.0 costs less and provides satisfying get-up and relaxed cruising. And while the 5.0 uses a bit less fuel than the 5.8, mileage with either of these engines is poor. It takes a light throttle foot to keep from dipping into single-digit mpg in city driving, and 20 mpg on the open road is the best most drivers can hope for.

If you don't regularly pull large trailers, you might find that Ford's own 5-door Explorer will do many of the jobs you expect of the Bronco—with more civility and economy.

If you absolutely need a 4x4 this big, the Bronco's standard air bag is an important consideration against the newer, quieter Blazer/Yukon.

Specifications

	3-door wagon
Wheelbase, in.	104.7
Overall length, in.	183.6
Overall width, in.	79.1
Overall height, in.	74.4
Turn diameter, ft.	36.6
Curb weight, lbs.	4616
Fuel capacity, gal.	32.0

Passenger Area Dimensions

Seating capacity	6
Front head room, in.	41.2
Rear head room, in.	39.3
Front leg room, in.	41.1
Rear leg room, in.	37.7

Cargo Dimensions and Payloads

Cargo area length, in.	63.3
Cargo area width, in.	63.5
between wheels, in.	50.8
Cargo area height, in.	43.7
Cargo vol., cu. ft.	101.4
Max. payload, lbs.	1200
Max. trailer weight, lbs.	7000

Engines

	ohv V-8	ohv V-8
Size, liters/cu. in.	5.0/302	5.8/351
Horsepower @ rpm	205 @ 4000	210 @ 3600
Torque (lbs./ft.) @ rpm	275 @ 3000	325 @ 2800
Availability	S	O

EPA city/highway mpg

5-speed OD manual	14/17	
4-speed OD automatic	13/18	13/17

Built in Wayne, Mich.

KEY: Dimensions and capacities are supplied by the manufacturers. **Curb Weight:** base models, not including optional equipment. **Max. payload, lbs.** = gross amount; net payload may be lower due to optional equipment. **Engines: ohv** = overhead valve; **ohc** = overhead cam; **I** = inline cylinders; **V** = cylinders in V configuration; **flat** = horizontally opposed cylinders; **rpm** = revolutions per minute; **OD** = overdrive transmission; **S** = standard; **O** = optional; **NA** = not available.

Prices

Ford Bronco	Retail Price	Dealer Invoice	Fair Price
XL 3-door 4WD wagon	$21725	*	*
XLT 3-door 4WD wagon	23965	*	*
Eddie Bauer 4WD wagon	26800	*	*
Destination charge	600	600	600

Some dealer invoice and fair prices not available at time of publication.

Standard Equipment:

XL: 5.0-liter V-8 engine, 5-speed manual transmission, anti-lock brakes, driver-side air bag, power steering, automatic locking front hubs, vinyl front bucket seats, vinyl folding rear 3-passenger bench seat, AM/FM radio, digital clock, chrome bumpers and grille, coolant temperature and oil pressure gauges, voltmeter, tinted glass, dual black mirrors, front stabilizer bar, intermittent wipers, floormats, fuel tank and transfer case skid plates, trip odometer, argent steel wheels, bright hub caps, pivoting front vent windows, power tailgate window, 235/75R15XL tires, matching spare tire, black spare tire cover. **XLT** adds: carpet, upgraded interior trim, cloth reclining captain's chairs with power lumbar support, cruise control, tilt steering column, leather-wrapped steering wheel, door map pockets, passenger-side visor mirror, tachometer, door courtesy and rear cargo lights, brushed aluminum tailgate applique, additional sound insulation, lower bodyside moldings, dual bright mirrors, styled steel wheels. **Eddie Bauer** adds to XLT: 4-speed automatic transmission, air conditioning, rear defogger, automatic-dimming rearview mirror, lighted visor mirrors, underhood light, dual beam map/dome lights, floor console, overhead storage console with compass and outside temperature display, cargo net, privacy glass, heavy duty battery, carpeted floormats, headlamps-on warning buzzer, two-tone rocker panel paint, bright wheel opening moldings, striping, bronze spare tire cover, deep-dish alloy wheels. Deletes lower bodyside moldings.

Optional Equipment:

	Retail Price	Dealer Invoice	Fair Price
5.8-liter V-8	$220	$187	$194
Requires 4-speed automatic transmission. Not available XL.			
4-speed automatic transmission	926	786	815
Touch Drive 4WD electric shift, XLT and Eddie Bauer	125	106	110
Includes automatic locking hubs. Requires automatic transmission. XLT requires Preferred Pkg. 684A.			
Manual locking hubs (credit), XL and XLT	(60)	(51)	(51)
Limited-slip axle	250	213	220
Cloth/vinyl bench seat, XL	100	85	88
XLT (credit)	(350)	(298)	(298)
Leather captain's chairs, XLT and Eddie Bauer	645	548	568
Includes power lumbar support. XLT requires Pkg. 684A.			
XL Preferred Equipment Pkg. 680A	995	846	876
Climate Control Group, Wheel Group.			
XLT Preferred Equipment Pkg. 683A	485	413	427
Climate Control Group, Wheel Group with chrome styled wheels.			
XLT Preferred Equioment Pkg. 684A	970	824	873
Pkg. 683A plus Luxury Group.			
Eddie Bauer Preferred Equipment Pkg. 686A	270	230	238
Wheel Group and Luxury Group.			
Climate Control Group (std. Eddie Bauer)	985	838	867
Air conditioning, rear defogger.			
Light and Convenience Group, XLT	205	174	180
Automatic dimming rearview mirror, lighted visor mirrors. Requires Pkg. 684A.			
Wheel Group, XL	310	263	273
XLT	400	340	352
Eddie Bauer	165	140	145
Includes outside swing-away spare tire carrier, black spare tire cover (bronze cover and lock on Eddie Bauer), argent styled wheels with bright hub covers (XL), chrome styled steel wheels (XLT).			
Luxury Group, XLT with Pkg. 684A	985	838	867
Eddie Bauer with Pkg. 686A	605	514	532
Includes privacy glass on quarter windows (std. Eddie Bauer), power windows and door locks, bright power mirrors, AM/FM cassette with four speakers, Light and Convenience Group (underhood light, dual-beam dome/map light, headlight-on warning buzzer. Std. Eddie Bauer), floor console (deleted if bench seat is selected).			
Security Group, XLT and Eddie Bauer	255	217	224
Remote keyless entry system, anti-theft alarm. XLT requires Pkg. 684A. Eddie Bauer requires Pkg. 686A.			
Trailer Towing Pkg., XL and XLT	360	306	317
XLT with 265/75R15SL tires	320	272	282

	Retail Price	Dealer Invoice	Fair Price
Eddie Bauer	$305	$259	$268
Eddie Bauer with 265/75R15SL tires	265	225	233
Includes trailer wiring harness, heavy duty turn signal flasher, rear stabilizer bar, quad front and heavy duty rear shock absorbers, heavy duty battery (std. Eddie Bauer), super engine cooling.			
Retractable cargo cover, XLT	80	68	70
Requires Pkg. 683A or 684A.			
Cargo net, XLT	30	26	26
Requires Pkg. 683A or 684A.			
Deluxe 2-tone paint, XLT	245	208	216
Incudes wheel opening moldings.			
AM/FM cassette, XLT with Pkg. 683A	215	182	189
XLT with Pkg. 684A and Eddie Bauer with Pkg. 686A	80	67	70
AM/FM CD player, XLT with Pkg. 683A	510	433	449
XLT with Pkg. 684A and Eddie Bauer with Pkg. 686A	375	318	330
Deep dish alloy wheels, XLT	235	200	207
235/75R15XL outline white letter all-terrain tires, XLT and Eddie Bauer	200	170	176
265/75R15SL outline white letter all-terrain tires, XLT and Eddie Bauer	800	680	704
XLT with Pkg. 684A and Eddie Bauer with Pkg. 686A	635	540	559

Ford Club Wagon/ Econoline Van

✓ BEST BUY

Ford Club Wagon Chateau

Four-wheel anti-lock brakes are now standard on all passenger models and optional on all cargo versions of Ford's full-size vans.

Previously, all models came with rear anti-lock brakes. Front door guard beams also are newly standard for all versions of these vans. These are the best-selling full-size vans. Ford redesigned them for 1992, their first alteration since 1975. The redesign brought a standard driver-side air bag, the first in any full-size van.

Body Styles/Chassis

Passenger models are called Club Wagons, cargo versions Econolines. On Econolines, which account for most of Ford's big-van sales, series designations represent payload categories: E-150 (half-ton); E-250 (three-quarter-ton); and E-350 (one-ton). In addition, there are E-250 Heavy Duty models with an 8500-pound gross vehicle weight.

Club Wagons are also are divided by categories that correspond roughly to those of the Econoline, except Ford des-

Ford

ignates them the Regular Club Wagon, Heavy Duty Regular, and Super Club Wagon.

All of these vans ride a 138-inch wheelbase, but two body lengths are offered.

Regular-body models measure 211.8 inches long overall. Super Wagon and Super Van models add 20 inches to the tail for a 231.8-inch overall length. The Super-length body is available on all models except E-150 Econolines and Regular and Heavy Duty Club Wagons.

All Econolines and Club Wagons come with 60/40 hinged side doors. A one-piece sliding side door is available at no additional cost on all but the Super Wagon and Super Van. These side doors get guard beams, as well.

Econolines come with solid metal side and rear body panels, but a variety of window arrangements is optionally available, from glass only in the rear doors to glass all around.

On Econolines, payload limits are 2030 pounds on the E-150, 3455 pounds on the regular-length E-250 HD Van, and 4195 on the regular-length E-350 Heavy Duty Van.

Ford does not specify payload ratings for Club Wagons, listing instead their maximum passenger capacity (see Accommodations).

Powertrains

A 4.9-liter inline-6-cylinder engine rated at 145 horsepower is standard on all models.

A 5.0-liter V-8 is optional on E-150s and on Regular Club Wagon models. This engine gains 10 horsepower, to 195, for 1994.

A 5.8-liter V-8 is optional on all models. It, too, gains 10 horsepower, to 210, for '94.

A 245-horsepower 7.5-liter V-8 is optional on E-350 models and on Heavy Duty and Super Club Wagons.

A 7.3-liter diesel V-8 rated at 185 horsepower is available on the same models as the 7.5 gasoline V-8.

A 3-speed automatic transmission comes standard with the 6-cylinder in all states but California. A 4-speed automatic is standard with the 6-cylinder in California and optional with it elsewhere. The 4-speed automatic is the only transmission with the gasoline V-8 engines.

The maximum towing limit for the E-150 is 6600 pounds and for the regular-length Club Wagon is 6400 pounds. The E-250 can tow up to 7500 pounds and the regular-length Heavy Duty Club Wagon can tow up to 10,000 pounds. E-350 models and the Super Club Wagon also can tow up to 10,000 pounds.

Accommodations

Econolines come in base and XL trim levels and as models suited for conversion to recreational vehicles.

Econolines come with two front seats.

Club Wagons are available in XL and XLT price levels, with a top-line Chateau trim offered on regular-length models. Last year, the XL price level was called Custom.

Regular Club Wagons seat eight in XL and XLT trim. Seats for seven are standard on the Chateau, optional on the XLT. The 7-seat setup includes four captain's chairs and a rear bench that folds into a bed.

Heavy Duty Wagons in XL and XLT trim seat 12, with the 7-seat arrangement standard in the Chateau and optional in the XLT.

Super Club Wagons seat 15 in LX and LXT form, with seating for 12 an XL-model option.

A driver-side air bag is standard on all Club Wagons except the Super model and on all Econolines except the E-350. Club Wagon outboard rear seats have lap/shoulder belts.

Specifications

	4-door van	4-door van
Wheelbase, in.	138.0	138.0
Overall length, in.	211.8	231.8
Overall width, in.	79.5	79.5
Overall height, in.	80.7	83.4
Turn diameter, ft.	46.5	47.8
Curb weight, lbs.	4470[1]	4972
Fuel capacity, gal.	35.0	35.0

1. Econoline E-150; 5022 lbs., base Club Wagon.

Passenger Area Dimensions

Seating capacity	12	15
Front head room, in.	41.5	41.5
Rear head room, in.	NA	NA
Front leg room, in.	39.5	39.5
Rear leg room, in.	NA	NA

Available Seating

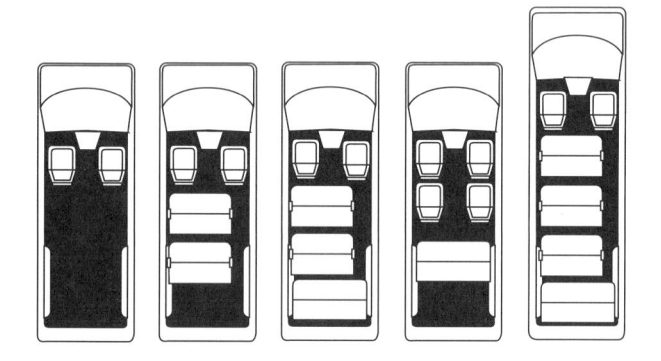

Cargo Dimensions and Payloads

Cargo area length, in.	120.7	140.7
Cargo area width, in.	75.0	75.0
Cargo area width between wheels, in.	52.2	52.2
Cargo area height, in.	53.2	53.2
Cargo vol., cu. ft.	260.8	299.8
Max. payload, lbs.	4195	3925
Max. trailer weight, lbs.	10,000	10,000

Engines	ohv I-6	ohv V-8	ohv V-8	ohv V-8	Diesel ohv V-8
Size, liters/cu. in.	4.9/300	5.0/302	5.8/351	7.5/460	7.3/444
Horsepower @ rpm	145 @ 3400	195 @ 4000	210 @ 3600	245 @ 4000	185 @ 3000
Torque (lbs./ft.) @ rpm	265 @ 2000	270 @ 3000	325 @ 2800	400 @ 2200	360 @ 1400
Availability	S	O	O	O	O
EPA city/highway mpg					
3-speed auto.	14/16				NA
4-speed OD automatic	14/18	13/18	12/16	NA	NA

Built in Lorain, Ohio.

KEY: Dimensions and capacities are supplied by the manufacturers. **Curb Weight:** base models, not including optional equipment. **Max. payload, lbs.** = gross amount; net payload may be lower due to optional equipment. **Engines: ohv** = overhead valve; **ohc** = overhead cam; **I** = inline cylinders; **V** = cylinders in V configuration; **flat** = horizontally opposed cylinders; **rpm** = revolutions per minute; **OD** = overdrive transmission; **S** = standard; **O** = optional; **NA** = not available.

Ford

Evaluation

Ford is the big-van sales leader. The Econoline outsells the Club Wagon by nearly 5-1 and alone outsells the combined passenger and cargo models of any of its competitors.

The strongest of those competitors are the Chevrolet Sportvan and Van and the GMC Rally and Vandura.

Ford beat them to market with a driver-side air bag, but comparable GM versions get that important safety feature for 1994. And while the GM vans got 4-wheel anti-lock brakes first, the Fords catch up this year.

The big Dodge Ram van, the slowest-seller in the big-van field, gets 4-wheel anti-lock brakes as a new option for '94, but offers neither a driver-side air bag nor the variety of engines available in the Ford and GM vans.

Adding the air bag earns the big Chevy and GMC vans some points for 1994, but the Fords still rank as our only Best Buy choice in this category.

The Regular Club Wagon in Chateau trim we tested was downright plush and a good factory-built alternative to some of those cushy aftermarket conversions.

We like the 60/40 swing-out side door; it's easier to open than the heavy sliding door. Wind noise is less than on rivals, there's more isolation from mechanical vibration and road harshness, and steering feel is better, too. Plus, the Club Wagon's dashboard is the most car-like of any big van.

Ford's big vans do share many traits with the GM and Dodge competitors, however.

Their good points stem mainly from size, weight, and muscular engines.

Minuses include low fuel economy—we averaged just 11.9 mpg with our 5.8-liter Chateau. And these being genuine trucks, ride, handling, and maneuverability are not up to that of the more car-like minivans.

They simply won't fit into some garages and a tall step-in height can make entry and exit a chore. Plus, protrusion of the engine cover into the cabin significantly reduces front-seat leg room. Finally, they can be costly; our 7-seat tester listed for $26,328.

But these traditional vans have plenty to offer if you need lots of passenger or cargo room, or if you regularly carry hefty payloads. And Ford's is the best of the bunch.

Clockwise from top left: An Econoline E-150 cargo van. A driver-side air bag is standard on all but the heaviest-duty Club Wagons and Econolines. Cargo room is generous even with seats for seven. Middle captain's chairs are optional.

Ford

Prices

Ford Club Wagon	Retail Price	Dealer Invoice	Fair Price
XL, Base regular length	$18332	*	*
XL, Heavy Duty regular length	19344	*	*
XL, Super length	21467	*	*
XLT, Base regular length	21533	*	*
XLT, Heavy Duty regular length	22467	*	*
XLT, Super length	23147	*	*
Chateau, regular length	24610	*	*
Chateau, Heavy Duty regular length	25062	*	*
Destination charge	575	575	575

Standard Equipment:

XL: 4.9-liter 6-cylinder engine, 4-speed automatic transmission (XL), 3-speed automatic transmission (XLT and Chateau), anti-lock brakes, driver-side air bag (NA Super), power steering, Handling Pkg. (Heavy Duty and Super; includes front stabilizer bar, heavy duty front and rear shock absorbers), 8-passenger seating (front bucket seats, two 3-passenger benches), 12-passenger seating (**Heavy Duty** adds 4-passenger rear bench), 15-passenger seating (**Super** adds one 3-passenger and one 4-passenger rear bench to XL), vinyl upholstery, full length floormat, hinged side cargo door, tinted glass, swing-out side/rear door, rear quarter and left bodyside glass, black dual outside mirrors (right convex), dual covered visor mirrors, AM radio, digital clock, intermittent wipers, Class I Trailer Towing Pkg. (Heavy Duty and Super), front dome and rear cargo lights, engine cover map pocket, 235/75R15XL tires (XL), LT225/75R16E tires (Heavy Duty), LT245/75R16E tires (Super). **XLT** adds: air conditioning (NA Super), power windows and door locks, dual captains chairs, cloth upholstery, upgraded door trim, illuminated entry system, underhood and reading lights, AM/FM radio, rear heater (NA Super), Deluxe Insulation Pkg., full length carpet, chrome bumpers, Class I Trailer Towing Pkg., Handling Pkg., full wheel covers (Base), sport wheel covers (Heavy Duty and Super). **Chateau** adds: power driver's seat, driver and front passenger power lumbar support, high capacity front and rear air conditioning, tilt steering column, cruise control, Light and Convenience Group, power mirrors, lighted visor mirrors, privacy glass, anti-theft alarm, leather-wrapped steering wheel, cassette player, rear remote radio controls and two headphones, color-keyed engine cover console, heavy duty alternator, two-tone rocker panel paint, cast alloy wheels (NA Heavy Duty regular length).

Optional Equipment:

	Retail Price	Dealer Invoice	Fair Price
5.0-liter V-8, Base	716	608	630
Requires 4-speed automatic overdrive transmission.			
5.8-liter V-8	937	796	825
Heavy Duty and Super require 4-speed automatic transmission (std. Base).			
7.5-liter V-8, Heavy Duty and Super	1421	1208	1250
Requires 4-speed transmission.			
7.3-liter diesel V-8, Heavy Duty and Super	3733	3173	3285
Includes dual-element engine heater. Requires 4-speed transmission. Not available Chateau.			
4-speed automatic transmission, Heavy Duty and Super	299	254	263
4-speed automatic overdrive transmission, Base	NC	NC	NC
Requires 5.0-liter V-8 engine.			
Limited-slip rear axle	252	215	222
Optional axle ratio	44	37	39
Air conditioning (front only), XL Base and Heavy Duty	973	827	856
Includes super engine cooling. Requires rear heater, (4.9-liter engine also requires heavy duty alternator).			
Front and rear air conditioning, XL Base and Heavy Duty	1885	1603	1659
XL Super with Pkg. 721	705	599	620
XLT	555	472	488
Includes auxiliary rear heater, Light and Convenience Pkg., heavy duty alternator.			
Auxiliary rear heater, XL Base and Heavy Duty	207	176	182
XLT Pkg. 705A, Base with 4.9- or 5.0-liter engine	$737	$626	$649
with 5.8-liter engine	937	796	825
Heavy Duty (Pkg. 713A)	865	735	761
Power mirrors, engine cover console, privacy glass, AM/FM cassette, cruise control, tilt steering column.			
XL Pkg. 721B, Super	805	684	708
Front air conditioning, cruise control, tilt steering column, rear heater, sport wheel covers.			
XLT Pkg. 722A, Super	938	797	825
Cruise control, tilt steering column, high capacity front and rear air conditioning, rear heater, heavy duty alternator, Light and Convenience Group.			
XL Pkg. 723A, Super	2179	1852	1918
Pkg. 722A plus engine cover console, privacy glass, power mirrors, power driver's seat with power lumbar supports, AM/FM cassette.			
Chateau Pkg. 706A, Base	NC	NC	NC
Heavy Duty (Pkg. 714A)	NC	NC	NC
High capacity front and rear air conditioning, anti-theft system, power driver's seat.			
Deluxe Interior Upgrade Pkg., XL	326	277	287
Full length carpeting, side/rear cargo door trim panels, cloth bucket seats.			
Deluxe Insulation Pkg., XL	37	31	33
Optional Equipment Group 1, (NA Super)	540	459	475
Engine cover console, privacy glass.			
Optional Equipment Group 2, (NA Super)	696	592	612
Power mirrors, AM/FM cassette, cruise control, tilt steeing wheel.			
Optional Equipment Group 3	1268	1078	1116
Front air conditioning, auxiliary heater, sport wheel covers.			
Optional Equipment Group 4	1241	1055	1092
Engine cover console, privacy glass, power mirrors, power driver's seat, AM/FM cassette.			
Trailer Towing Package Class II, III, IV (NA XL)	149	127	131
Super engine cooling, trailer wiring harness, front stabilizer bar, heavy duty front and rear shock absorbers, electric brake controller tap-in capability, Pollack-type trailer plugs and bumper bracket, relay system for backup/B+/running lights, heavy duty alternator.			
Light and Convenience Pkg., XL	150	128	132
Underhood light, illuminated entry, warning chimes.			
Power windows and locks, XL	652	554	574
Includes XLT door trim panels. Models with sliding side cargo door also include memory lock module.			
Cruise control/tilt steering column, XL and XLT	383	326	337
Power mirrors, XLT	160	136	141
Bright swing-out mirrors, XL and XLT	59	50	52
Anti-theft system, XLT Base and Heavy Duty	278	236	245
Requires cruise control, tilt steering column.			
7-passenger with Quad Captain's Chairs and rear seat/bed, XLT Base	998	848	878
XLT Heavy Duty	677	575	596
Requires power driver's seat.			
12-passenger with front bucket seats, XL Super (credit)	(140)	(119)	(119)
Credit for deletion of one 3-bench seat.			
Power driver's seat with power lumbar supports, XLT	388	330	341
Engine cover console	152	130	134
Includes fold-out tray, storage area and cassette rack.			
Privacy glass	388	330	341
Heavy Duty auxiliary battery	134	114	118
Heavy duty 84 amp battery and 60 amp auxiliary battery.			
Heavy Duty alternator	66	56	58
Engine block heater	33	28	29
with 7.5-liter engine	66	56	58
Sliding side cargo door (NA Super)	NC	NC	NC
Replaces hinged cargo door.			
AM/FM radio, XL	143	122	126
AM/FM cassette with four speakers, XL	296	252	260
AM/FM cassette with six speakers, XLT	154	131	136
Premium AM/FM cassette with six speakers, XLT	296	252	260
Includes rear remote radio controls and two headphones.			

Some dealer invoice and fair prices not available at time of publication.

Ford

	Retail Price	Dealer Invoice	Fair Price
Premium AM/FM CD player with			
six speakers, XLT	$591	$502	$520
Chateau	295	251	260
Includes rear remote radio controls and two headphones.			
Chrome rear step bumper (NA XL)	122	104	107
Argent rear step bumper	122	104	107
Black or white painted bumpers	NC	NC	NC
Clearcoat paint	171	145	150
Deluxe two-tone paint, XLT	210	179	185
Wheel covers, XL	99	84	87
Alloy wheels, XLT Base	312	265	275
235/75R15XL whitewall all-season tires, Base (NA XL)	102	87	90
LT245/75R16E all-season, Heavy Duty	139	118	122

Ford Econoline

	Retail Price	Dealer Invoice	Fair Price
E-150	$16348	*	*
E-250	16743	*	*
E-250 Super	17450	*	*
E-250 Heavy Duty	17060	*	*
E-250 Heavy Duty Super	17859	*	*
E-350	17841	*	*
E-350 Super	18810	*	*
Destination charge	575	575	575

Standard Equipment:

4.9-liter 6-cylinder engine, 3-speed automatic transmission, anti-lock rear brakes, driver-side air bag (150 and 250), power steering, hinged side doors, vinyl front bucket seats, tinted glass, dual mirrors, AM radio, digital clock, front dome and rear cargo lights, gray engine cover with map pocket, full-length black floormat, Handling Pkg. (350), intermittent wipers, Class I Towing Pkg. (350), Tires, 150: P215/75R15SL. 250 regular: LT225/75R16D. 250 Heavy Duty: LT225/75R16E. 350: LT245/75R16E. All models include full-size spare.

Optional Equipment:

	Retail	Dealer	Fair
5.0-liter V-8, 150	716	608	630
Requires 4-speed automatic transmission.			
5.8-liter V-8	937	796	825
Requires 4-speed automatic transmission.			
7.5-liter V-8, 350	1421	1208	1250
Requires 4-speed automatic transmission.			
7.3-liter diesel V-8, 350	3500	2975	3080
Includes dual-element engine block heater, color-keyed instrument panel. Requires 4-speed automatic transmission.			
Automatic overdrive transmission, 150 with 5.0-liter engine	299	254	263
Electronic 4-speed automatic transmission	299	254	263
Anti-lock brakes	610	254	537
Limited-slip rear axle	252	215	222
Optional axle ratio	44	37	39
Front air conditioning	973	827	856
Includes super engine cooling. Models with 4.9-liter engine require heavy duty alternator.			
High capacity air conditioning			
with auxiliary rear heater	1861	1582	1638
with XL Pkg.	1735	1475	1527
with Pkgs. that includes air conditioning	762	648	671
Includes auxiliary rear heater, Light and Convenience Pkg., heavy duty alternator.			
Auxiliary rear heater	207	176	182
Anti-theft alarm	254	216	224
Cloth bucket seats	20	17	18
Premium cloth captain's chairs, with XL Pkg.	240	204	211
Requires power driver's seat.			
Power driver's seat, with XL Pkg.	388	330	341
Includes power lumbar support.			
XL Pkg. 741A (150), 751A (250), 756A (250 Heavy Duty), 762A (350)	1383	1175	1217

	Retail Price	Dealer Invoice	Fair Price
Cloth captain's chairs, chrome bumpers and grille, aero headlamps, Deluxe Insulation Pkg., Light and Convenience Group, power windows and door locks, wheel covers, AM/FM radio, carpet, upgraded interior trim, reading and underhood lights, covered visor mirror, passenger-side underseat storage bin, illuminated entry.			
Deluxe Insulation Pkg.	$165	$140	$145
Light and Convenience Group	150	128	132
Courtesy light switches, underhood light, illuminated entry, warning chimes.			
Handling Pkg., 150 and 250	79	67	70
Front stabilizer bar, heavy duty front and rear shock absorbers.			
Heavy Duty Service Pkg., 150 and 250	266	226	234
150 and 250 with air conditioning	165	140	145
350 with 4.9- or 5.8-liter engine	187	159	165
350 with 7.3- or 7.5-liter engine or air conditioning	85	73	75
Super engine cooling, dual horns, Handling Pkg., heavy duty alternator.			
Cruise control and tilt steering column	383	326	337
Power windows and door locks	652	554	574
Bright swing-out mirrors	59	50	52
Power mirrors	160	136	141
Requires rear door glass.			
Heavy duty auxiliary battery	134	114	118
Heavy duty alternator	66	56	58
Chrome bumpers	134	114	118
Chrome rear step bumper	295	251	260
with XL Pkg.	161	137	142
Black or white painted bumpers	NC	NC	NC
Argent rear step bumper	122	104	107
Engine cover console	152	129	134
Includes fold-out tray, storage area, cassette rack.			
Fixed rear door glass	59	50	52
Fixed side and rear cargo door glass	100	85	88
Privacy glass, with swing-out side and rear cargo door windows	270	230	238
with windows all-around	388	330	341
Swing-out side and rear cargo door glass	244	207	215
with display van	296	252	260
Includes right rear quarter window.			
Windows all-around	352	299	310
Includes swing-out side and rear door glass.			
Engine block heater	33	28	29
350 with 7.5-liter engine	66	56	58
Clearcoat paint	171	145	150
Deluxe two-tone paint, with XL Pkg.	210	179	185
Heavy Duty suspension, 150	88	75	77
250	323	275	284
GVWR Payload Pkg. (6500 lbs.), 150	102	87	90
350 regular van	NC	NC	NC
Trailer Towing Pkg. (Class I), 150 and 250	205	174	180
with air conditioning, (credit)	(101)	(86)	(86)
Includes Super engine cooling, trailer wiring harness, Handling Pkg., dual horns.			
Trailer Towing Packages (Class II, III, IV),			
150 and 250	370	314	326
350	165	140	145
150, 250, and 350 with air conditioning (credit)	(101)	(86)	(86)
Trailer Towing Pkg. Class I plus electric brake controller tap-in capability, Pollack-type trailer plugs and bumper bracket, relay system for backup/B+/running lights, heavy duty alternator.			
AM radio delete, (credit)	(61)	(52)	(52)
AM/FM radio	143	122	126
AM/FM cassette	296	252	260
with XL Pkg.	154	131	136
Premium AM/FM cassette, with XL Pkg.	74	63	65
Premium AM/FM CD player, with XL Pkg.	545	463	480
Wheel covers, 150	99	84	87
Sport wheel covers, 250 and 350	99	84	87
Forged alloy wheels	283	240	249
Tires, 150: 235/75R15XL tires	84	72	74

*Some dealer invoice and fair prices not available at time of publication.

Ford

Ford Explorer

RECOMMENDED

Ford Explorer XLT 5-door

America's best-selling sport-utility vehicle gets only minor trim and option-package changes for '94. Mazda sells a version of the 3-door Explorer as the Navajo (see separate report).

Body Styles/Chassis

The 3-door Explorer comes in XL, Sport, and Eddie Bauer price series.

The more popular 5-door is offered in XL, XLT, Eddie Bauer, and Limited series. The Limited is distinguished by a body-color grille and bumpers and by integrated running boards, fog lamps, and its own alloy wheels.

All have a rear liftgate with separate-opening window.

The 5-door's 111.9-inch wheelbase is 9.8 inches longer than the 3-door's and is the longest of any compact sport-utility. The 5-door's body is 10.1 inches longer than the 3-door's.

A 4-wheel anti-lock brake system that operates in both 2- and 4-wheel drive is standard.

Payloads are 750 pounds for 3-doors and 900 for 5-doors.

Powertrains

The only engine is a 160-horsepower 4.0-liter V-6. A 5-speed manual transmission is standard on all models and a 4-speed automatic is optional.

Rear-wheel drive is standard. The optional Touch-Drive on-demand 4WD system available on all models is not for use on dry pavement. It has automatic-locking front hubs and can be shifted between 2WD and 4WD-High on the move with the push of a dashboard button, though Ford recommends stopping and then backing up to disengage 4WD completely. A more basic 4WD system with floor-mounted transfer-case lever and manual front hubs is a credit option.

With the optional Trailer Towing Package, 3-door 2WD models can tow up to 5600 pounds and 4x4s up to 5400 pounds. The limits are 200 pounds less for 5-door models.

Accommodations

Explorers come with front bucket seats and a split fold-down rear bench.

Five-door XL and XLT models offer 6-place seating with automatic transmission via a front bench and column-mounted shift lever. Optional for 6-passenger models is a floor mounted mini console with dual cup holders.

The Limited gets unique interior trim and an overhead console with a compass.

On 3-door models, the front seats have a slide-forward feature to facilitate rear entry/exit.

Evaluation

It's no surprise that Explorer has soared to the top of the sport-utility sales chart. Nothing matches its particular blend of interior volume, family-wagon comfort, and all-terrain capability.

The 5-door, which accounts for 80 percent of Explorer sales, is particularly impressive. Though its ride becomes a bit stiff and bouncy on uneven pavement, overall comfort is high, thanks largely to that rangy wheelbase. Back wheels hardly intrude into doorways, which also frees up three-abreast rear hip room. And rear leg room is adequate even with the front seat well back.

The 3-door, on its shorter wheelbase, has a noticeably choppier ride. It's tighter in the back seat, too, though it's still roomy enough for younger, more active types.

Both body styles have a relatively low step-in height. The split rear seatbacks fold flat in a single motion to create a long load floor. And the full-size spare tire is underneath the

Specifications	3-door wagon	5-door wagon
Wheelbase, in.	102.1	111.9
Overall length, in.	174.5	184.3
Overall width, in.	70.2	70.2
Overall height, in.	67.3	67.2
Turn diameter, ft.	35.6	38.5
Curb weight, lbs.	3844	4053
Fuel capacity, gal.	19.0	19.0

Passenger Area Dimensions		
Seating capacity	4	6
Front head room, in.	39.9	39.9
Rear head room, in.	39.1	39.3
Front leg room, in.	42.4	42.4
Rear leg room, in.	36.6	37.7

Cargo Dimensions and Payloads		
Cargo area length, in.	63.1	72.9
Cargo area width, in.	57.9	57.9
Cargo area width between wheels, in.	41.9	41.9
Cargo area height, in.	37.6	37.6
Cargo vol., cu. ft.	69.4	81.6
Max. payload, lbs.	750	900
Max. trailer weight, lbs.	5600	5400

Engines	ohv V-6
Size, liters/cu. in.	4.0/245
Horsepower @ rpm	160 @ 4400
Torque (lbs./ft.) @ rpm	220 @ 2800
Availability	S

EPA city/highway mpg
5-speed OD manual 17/22
4-speed OD automatic 15/20

Built in Louisville, Ky.

KEY: Dimensions and capacities are supplied by the manufacturers. **Curb Weight:** base models, not including optional equipment. **Max. payload, lbs.** = gross amount; net payload may be lower due to optional equipment. **Engines:** ohv = overhead valve; ohc = overhead cam; **I** = inline cylinders; **V** = cylinders in V configuration; **flat** = horizontally opposed cylinders; **rpm** = revolutions per minute; **OD** = overdrive transmission; **S** = standard; **O** = optional; **NA** = not available.

Ford

rear cargo area on a crank-down cradle, so it doesn't take up any of the load space.

Common to all Explorers are simple and well-arranged controls, clear and complete analog gauges, and good outward vision.

Though Explorer's V-6 has less horsepower than rivals from Jeep and General Motors, it produces good low-end torque and brisk acceleration. The engine can be a touch rough and lethargic starting out and it's not that quiet at any speed, but it's less objectionable than the comparable Chevrolet/GMC 4.3-liter V-6.

Shifts with the automatic are quick and unobtrusive, but the manual transmission is rather high-effort by car standards. Ford has done a decent job in isolating noise, vibration, and harshness from all sources, though wind roar is noticeable at highway speeds.

Tight turns bring out moderate body lean, but Explorer feels quite stable in normal driving both on road and off. It resists gusty crosswinds, and the Touch Drive 4WD system is simple, though neither Jeep nor General Motors models require that you stop and reverse direction to fully disengage 4WD. Fuel economy is mediocre: Our test 4WD 5-door averaged just 13.6 mpg in urban commuting on the way to a 15.9-mpg overall average.

Explorer's toughest challenger is Jeep's Grand Cherokee. Explorer has more combined passenger and cargo room than the Jeep, its prices start lower, and Ford matches its rival's full-time anti-lock brakes. But the Jeep offers a driver-side air bag, more versatile 4WD systems, and a V-8 option. Grand Cherokee is also more car-like than Explorer.

Our advice: Drive both the Explorer and Grand Cherokee before choosing.

door includes rear door windows), 235/75R15 OWL tires. **Limited** adds: air conditioning, power luxury leather bucket seats with 3-position driver's-side memory, matching split/folding rear seat, floor console, color-keyed overhead console with compass, temperature gauge, reading lamps and storage compartment, Electronic Group (remote keyless entry with theft-deterrent system, and electrochromic mirror with autolamp), color-keyed front bumper, front fascia with fog lamps, grille, bodyside moldings, striping, color-keyed leather-wrapped steering wheel, and spoke interior trim, heated mirrors, spoke alloy wheels. 4WD models have Touch Drive part-time 4WD.

Prices

Ford Explorer	Retail Price	Dealer Invoice	Fair Price
XL 3-door wagon, 2WD	$17470	*	*
XL 3-door wagon, 4WD	19220	*	*
Sport 3-door wagon, 2WD	18445	*	*
Sport 3-door wagon, 4WD	20155	*	*
Eddie Bauer 3-door wagon, 2WD	21405	*	*
Eddie Bauer 3-door wagon, 4WD	23105	*	*
XL 5-door wagon, 2WD	18360	*	*
XL 5-door wagon, 4WD	20130	*	*
XLT 5-door wagon, 2WD	20835	*	*
XLT 5-door wagon, 4WD	22635	*	*
Eddie Bauer 5-door wagon, 2WD	23400	20782	21482
Eddie Bauer 5-door wagon, 4WD	25205	22370	23070
Limited 5-door wagon, 2WD	26760	*	*
Limited 5-door wagon, 4WD	28560	*	*
Destination charge	485	485	485

Standard Equipment:

XL: 4.0-liter V-6, 5-speed manual transmission, anti-lock brakes, power steering, knitted vinyl front bucket seats, split folding rear seat, tinted glass, Light Group, intermittent wipers, dual outside mirrors, carpet, load floor tiedown hooks, rear seat heat duct, tachometer, coolant temperature gauge, tachometer, trip odometer, AM/FM radio, digital clock, 225/70R15 all-season tires, full-size spare tire. **Sport** adds: rear quarter and rear window privacy glass, rear wiper/washer, rear defogger, map light, load floor tiedown net, cargo area cover, leather-wrapped steering wheel, lighted visor mirrors, alloy wheels. **XLT** adds: cloth captain's chairs, floor console, power mirrors, upgraded door panels with pockets, power windows and locks, cruise control, tilt steering wheel, privacy glass rear door, rear quarter and liftgate, map pockets, floormats. **Eddie Bauer** adds to Sport: power driver's seat with lumbar support, power passenger seat (5-door), duffle and garment bags, luggage rack, privacy glass on rear quarter and liftgate windows (5-

Top: Explorer's interior is car-like, but no air bag is available. Middle: A 5-door Explorer in Eddie Bauer trim. Above: The top-line Limited model comes only as a 5-door with unique trim and standard alloy wheels.

*Some dealer invoice and fair prices not available at time of publication.

Ford

Optional Equipment:	Retail Price	Dealer Invoice	Fair Price
4-speed automatic transmission	$890	$757	$845
Limited-slip rear axle	255	217	242
Optional axle ratio (upgrade)	45	38	42
Optional axle ratio (upgrade) with trailer tow	360	306	342
Air conditioning	805	684	765
with manual transmission	NC	NC	NC
Preferred Pkg. 931A, Sport 3-door	NC	NC	NC
Air conditioning, Power Equipment Group, cloth captain's chairs with console, 235/75R15 outlined white letter tires.			
Preferred Pkg. 932A, Eddie Bauer 3-door	125	106	119
Air conditioning, premium cassette player, leather seats.			
Preferred Pkg. 941A, XLT with automatic	470	400	447
XLT with 5-speed	25	21	24
Air conditioning, striping, premium cassette player.			
Preferred Pkg. 942A, Eddie Bauer 5-door	276	235	262
Air conditioning, premium cassette player, leather seats.			
Preferred Pkg. 943A, Limited	395	336	375
JBL Audio System with cassette, running boards (5-door), step bars (3-door).			
Electronics Group, XLT and Eddie Bauer 5-doors	485	413	460
Remote keyless entry with theft-deterrent system, electrochromatic mirror with autolamp feature.			
Cloth captain's chairs, XL and Sport	280	238	266
Cloth 60/40 split bench seat, XL 5-door	255	216	242
XLT (credit)	(20)	(17)	(17)
Power cloth sport bucket seats, Sport	1020	867	969
upgrade from captain's chairs	750	637	712
XLT	955	812	907
Power leather sport bucket seats, Sport	1600	1360	1520
upgrade from captain's chairs	1326	1127	1259
XLT	1530	1301	1453
Eddie Bauer	NC	NC	NC
Super engine cooling	55	47	52
Privacy glass	220	187	209
Floor-mounted transfer case w/manual locking hubs, 4WD (credit)	(105)	(89)	(89)
Bodyside molding	120	102	114
Power Equipment Group, XL 3-door	900	765	855
XL 5-door	1235	1050	1173
Power windows, locks and mirrors, rear defogger, rear wiper/washer, upgraded door trim panels.			
Tilt-up sunroof	280	238	266
Cruise control and tilt steering wheel	385	328	365
Sport with manual transmission and Pkg. 931A	NC	NC	NC
Deep dish alloy wheels, XL and Sport	250	212	237
XLT and Eddie Bauer	NC	NC	NC
Trailer Towing Pkg.	105	89	99
Rear defogger and wiper/washer, XL	280	238	266
Premium AM/FM cassette	210	178	199
Sport with manual transmission and Pkg. 931A	NC	NC	NC
Ford JBL Audio System	700	595	665
Upgrade from premium cassette	490	416	465
Ford JBL Audio System with CD player	1000	850	950
Upgrade from premium cassette	790	672	750
Limited	300	255	285
Consolette, XL 5-door and XLT	30	26	28
Running boards, 5-door	395	336	375
Delete for credit, Limited	(395)	(336)	(336)
Step bars, 3-doors	245	208	232
Engine block heater	35	30	33
Deluxe tape stripe, 5-doors	55	47	52
Special Appearance Pkg.	285	243	270
Fog lamps, black bodyside molding, tape stripes.			
Deluxe 2-tone paint	120	102	114
Fog lamps, XL and Sport	185	158	175
235/75R15 outline white letter all-terrain tires	230	196	218
Floormats	45	38	42

Ford F-Series

✓ **BEST BUY**

Ford F-150 XLT regular-cab

Ford's full-size pickup gets a driver-side air bag and other safety features as its major changes this year. The air bag is standard on F-Series pickups with a gross vehicle weight rating (GVWR) of less than 8500 pounds. GVWR is the sum of the curb weight of the vehicle and the weight it can carry.

Other new safety features include guard beams for the side doors, a center high-mounted stoplamp, and, on models with automatic transmission, a shift interlock that requires applying the brakes to shift out of park.

The high-performance Lightning model has been dropped.

As the 1993 model year drew to a close, the F-Series line was slightly ahead of the Chevrolet C/K pickup in sales. Ford's big pickups have been the best-selling vehicle in the United States for 11 consecutive years.

Body Styles/Chassis

Regular- and extended-cab bodies, short- and long-bed cargo boxes, and four wheelbases are offered.

Series designations denote payload categories: F-150 (half-ton); F-250 (three-quarter ton); F-350 (one-ton). There's also an F-250 Heavy Duty model.

Two regular-cab models are offered. The 116.8-inch-wheelbase version has a 6 3/4-foot cargo bed and is available as an F-150 only. The 133-inch wheelbase version has an 8-foot bed and comes in all three payload series.

Two extended-cab, or SuperCab, models are offered: a 138.8-inch wheelbase with a 7-foot bed, and a 155-inch wheelbase with the 8-foot bed. SuperCabs are available in the F-150 and F-250 series and as an F-350 long-bed with dual rear wheels.

Models with slab-sided cargo boxes are called Styleside and come in all series. Those with flare-fendered cargo boxes are called Flareside. Flaresides come only as F-150 short-beds, but with both regular and SuperCab bodies.

Finally, there is a 4-door F-350 Crew Cab with a 168.4-inch wheelbase and 8-foot bed. This model is not covered in our report.

All F-Series trucks are available in both 2- and 4-wheel drive except the F-350 SuperCab, which is 2WD.

The base trim level is called S and is confined to the F-150 series. All other F-Series trucks are available in XL or top-drawer XLT form.

Rear anti-lock brakes are standard on all models.

Ford

A new Chrome Appearance Package is standard on XLT and F-150 XL Flareside models and is optional on XL models. It contains a chrome grille and headlight surround and chrome mirrors.

Regular-cab models come standard with a 3-place bench seat. SuperCabs have a rear bench for 6-passenger capacity. Front captain's chair buckets with a center floor console are optional for SuperCabs, which also can be ordered with folding rear jump seats. SuperCabs have 30 cubic feet of storage space behind the front seat with the rear seat folded.

A new option for XLT models is a front bench split 40/20/40. Its center seatback section folds down to became a full armrest with cupholder and a storage compartment. A compact disc player also is a new LXT option.

Making the driver-side air bag standard on models with GVWRs below 8500 pounds puts the safety device in all F-150 models and in the 2WD F-250 regular cab, long-bed model. All other F-Series models have GVWRs above 8500 pounds.

Maximum F-150 payload is 2305 pounds; for the F-250 it's 4265 (in the Heavy Duty model), and for the F-350, it's 5125.

Powertrains

A 4.9-liter inline-6-cylinder with 145 horsepower is the standard engine in F-150 models and in 2WD regular-cab F-250s.

A 5.0-liter V-8 is optional in those same models. Last year, the 5.0 was rated at 185 horsepower. This year, it's rated at 205 horsepower with manual transmission and 195 with automatic.

A 5.8-liter V-8 is standard on F-350 models, on the 4WD F-250 regular-cab heavy-duty model, and on F-250 SuperCab models. It is optional in F-150 models. This engine is rated at 210 horsepower, 10 more than last year. And torque increases by 25 pounds/feet, to 325.

A 7.5-liter V-8 is standard in the 2WD dual-rear-wheel F-350 SuperCab and optional in the Heavy Duty F-250 and F-350 models. The 7.5 is rated at 245 horsepower, five fewer than last year.

A 7.3-liter diesel V-8 with 185 horsepower is optional in on Heavy-Duty F-250 models and on F-350s.

Also optional in these models is a 7.3-liter turbocharged diesel V-8, but Ford will replace it in the spring with an advanced version. The new 7.3-liter turbodiesel V-8 will be rated at 210 horsepower, 20 more than the current version, and will have 420 pounds/feet of torque, 25 more than the current version.

Transmission choices vary with the engine application.

A 5-speed manual is available with all engines. A 3-speed automatic is offered with all but the 5.0-liter V-8. And a 4-speed overdrive automatic is available with all engines. The 4-speed manual transmission has been discontinued.

Four-wheel drive models have a part-time 4WD system that's not for use on dry pavement. It comes with a floor-mounted transfer-case lever and automatic locking front hubs that allow the driver to engage and disengage 4WD on the fly. However, the vehicle must be backed up at least one rotation of the tires to disengage the auto-locking hubs from their 4WD mode. Manual locking hubs are an option.

Optional on F-150 4x4s is Ford's Touch Drive 4WD. It also is an on-demand system, but it electrically engages 4WD at the push of a dashboard button. The auto-locking front hubs used with Touch Drive do not require that the vehicle be reversed to disengaged from 4WD, though Ford recommends it to reduce mechanical wear.

Maximum trailer weight is 7600 pounds on the F-150 and 12,500 pounds on the others. These weights are achieved by trucks equipped with automatic transmission and with fifth-wheel hitches. Models with other types of hitches or with manual transmission have lower towing ratings. Consult your dealer for details.

Evaluation

Chevy was closer than ever to Ford in their annual battle for pickup-truck sales supremacy. However it ends, the F-Series and Chevy's C/K will remain 1-2 in total vehicle sales, car or truck. Ford and Chevy each sell about 500,000 big pickups per year, with Dodge and GMC accounting for about 100,000 each.

Those numbers testify to the wide appeal of these trucks. About 62 percent of the 1.2 million full-size pickups sold each year are personal-use vehicles, and about half of all sales are in half-ton models.

Both Ford and General Motors have a wide array of models for work and play and offer similar cab and bed styles, as well as comparable payload and towing capabilities.

Both manufacturers have dropped their low-volume "muscle trucks," Ford the Lightning and Chevy the 454 SS. And while the GM models actually are a newer design than the F-Series, Ford fought back with a 1992 sheetmetal facelift and this year adds the driver-side air bag, which the GM models don't offer.

Finally, the new Dodge Ram pickup appears to be off to a fast start. Sales are projected at about 225,000 units for 1994, and while it currently offers only a regular-cab body, it does have some attractive features, including a driver-side air bag on all models, an available V-10 engine, and available 4-wheel anti-lock brakes (Ford and Chevy offer only rear-wheel ABS).

Still, choosing a big pickup is mostly a matter of brand loyalty and the best deal you can make on the combination of features you need.

Though the F-Series base 6-cylinder engine nearly matches the torque output of its 5.0-liter V-8, we still prefer the optional gas V-8 engines.

Our test F-150 XLT with the 5.0 and 4-speed automatic transmission was capable of impressive acceleration and passing ability. In fact, it felt just as responsive as the 5.8-liter V-8 in our test F-150 Flareside. And both returned about the same abysmal fuel economy: around 12.5 mpg in a city/highway mix. The 4-speed automatic in our Flareside, however, suffered slurred, lurching shifts and was slow to come down a gear for passing.

Some of our testers say GM's full-size pickups have a tighter steering feel than F-Series models or the Dodge Ram and require less correcting on the highway. Still, all brands handle capably for big pickups. And when you opt for the sportier, personal-use oriented suspension and tire setups, you'll find good balance and grip in turns with only moderate body lean.

Stopping power felt strong on our F-Series models, but the pedal suffered from too light a feel, an undue amount of travel, and was difficult to modulate.

Driven unloaded over city and suburban streets, the ride of the short-wheelbase 4x4s is harsh. The longer-wheelbase models cope much better with bumps. And though some of these trucks have lots of luxury amenities, none does a very good job of suppressing engine noise or tire rumble, though wind noise is moderate.

Bench seatbacks in the regular-cab Ford and Chevy models are fixed at a nearly vertical position, while the Ram offers a reclining seatback. Ford's steering wheel is close to the chest, and the pedals are close to the chair-height seat cushion. Bucket seats offer more adjustments, but you have

CONSUMER GUIDE®

Ford

to get a Supercab to move any seat back far enough for really generous front leg room. Speaking of Supercabs, their rear seats are a convenience, but have minimal knee and foot space.

Any of these trucks has plenty of head room, and cabins are three-adults wide, though the middle rider straddles the transmission tunnel.

The F-Series' analog instruments are clearly marked, but the rim of tilt the steering wheel slices off much of the tachometer and the coolant and oil temperature gauges. High marks for the convenient placement of the power window/mirror/lock controls on the door panel. And the "overdrive off" button is on the tip of the column shift where it's easy to use and protected from inadvertent activation.

Radio and climate controls are clearly marked and simple to use, but the driver must peer from the road and stretch a bit to reach them. Plus, some of the markings on the main climate dial are blocked from the driver's view by the dial itself. But it's still a better arrangement than the confusing radio and climate controls in the big GM pickups.

A high seating position and large outside mirrors aid F-Series visibility. And we enjoyed the rare convenience of opening wing windows.

A good-sized glove box, door map pockets, and dash and console bins compensate some for virtually no storage space behind the folding seatback on regular-cab Ford (or Chevy) models—a problem the Ram does not have. We don't see the sense of spending the extra money for a Flareside, since its box is narrower by 20 inches overall than the Styleside. But the cargo bed on all F-Series pickups measures nearly 51 inches between the wheels, so you can lay 4-foot-wide cargo flat on the floor.

Nothing substitutes for the room, power, payload capacity, towing ability—even the image—of a big pickup. And competition just about guarantees that you'll find a model that suits you. The F-Series tops our list.

Specifications

	Short bed	Long bed	SuperCab Short bed	SuperCab Long bed
Wheelbase, in.	116.8	133.0	138.8	155.0
Overall length, in.	197.1	213.3	219.1	235.3
Overall width, in.	79.0	79.0[1]	79.0	79.0[1]
Overall height, in.	71.0	71.0	71.9	74.0
Turn diameter, ft.	39.2	43.9	45.7	50.4
Curb weight, lbs.	3886	3982	4186	4316
Fuel capacity, gal.	34.7	37.2	34.7	37.2

1. 95.4 with dual rear wheels.

Passenger Area Dimensions

Seating capacity	3	3	6	6
Front head room, in.	40.3	40.3	40.0	40.0
Rear head room, in.	—	—	39.2	39.2
Front leg room, in.	41.1	41.1	41.1	41.1
Rear leg room, in.	—	—	28.5	28.5

Cargo Dimensions and Payloads

Cargo area length, in.	82.1	98.3	82.1	98.3
Cargo area width, in.	70.0[1]	70.0	70.0[1]	70.0
Cargo area width between wheels, in.	50.8	50.8	50.8	50.8
Cargo area height, in.	19.5	19.5	19.5	19.5
Max. payload, lbs.	2305	5125	1850	4600
Max. trailer weight, lbs.	7600	12,500	7600	12,500

1. 48.7 on Flareside.

Engines

	ohv I-6	ohv V-8	ohv V-8	ohv V-8	Diesel ohv V-8
Size, liters/cu. in.	4.9/300	5.0/302	5.8/351	7.5/460	7.3/444
Horsepower @ rpm	145 @ 3400	205 @ 4000	210 @ 3600	245 @ 4000	185 @ 3000[1]
Torque (lbs./ft.) @ rpm	265 @ 2000	275 @ 3000	325 @ 2800	395 @ 2400	360 @ 1400[2]
Availability	S	O	O	O	O
EPA city/highway mpg					
5-speed OD manual	15/20	15/18	NA	NA	NA
3-speed automatic	NA			NA	NA
4-speed OD automatic	15/20	15/20	13/18	NA	NA

1. Turbodiesel, 210 @ 3000. 2. Turbodiesel, 420 @ 1800.

Built in Kansas City, Mo.; Wayne, Mich.; Norfolk, Va.; and Canada.

KEY: Dimensions and capacities are supplied by the manufacturers. **Curb Weight:** base models, not including optional equipment. **Max. payload, lbs.** = gross weight; net payload may be lower due to optional equipment. **Engines: ohv** = overhead valve; **ohc** = overhead cam; **I** = inline cylinders; **V** = cylinders in V configuration; **flat** = horizontally opposed cylinders; **rpm** = revolutions per minute; **OD** = overdrive transmission; **S** = standard; **O** = optional; **NA** = not available.

Prices

Ford F150

	Retail Price	Dealer Invoice	Fair Price
S 2WD, 117-inch WB	$12348	*	*
S 2WD, 133-inch WB	12894	*	*
S 4WD, 117-inch WB	15807	*	*
S 4WD, 133-inch WB	16135	*	*
S 2WD SuperCab, 139-inch WB	14119	12580	13080
S 2WD SuperCab, 155-inch WB	14353	12786	13286
XL/XLT 2WD, 117-inch WB	13956	12018	12518
XL/XLT 2WD, 133-inch WB	14180	12208	12708
Flareside XL/XLT 2WD, 117-inch WB	14834	12764	13264
XL/XLT 4WD, 117-inch WB	16433	*	*
XL/XLT 4WD, 133-inch WB	16791	*	*
Flareside XL/XLT 4WD, 117-inch WB	17279	*	*
XL/XLT 2WD SuperCab, 139-inch WB	15662	*	*
XL/XLT 2WD SuperCab, 155-inch WB	15905	*	*
Flareside XL/XLT 2WD SuperCab, 139-inch WB	16368	*	*
Flareside XL/XLT 4WD SuperCab, 139-inch WB	18671	*	*
XL/XLT 4WD SuperCab, 139-inch WB	17966	*	*
XL/XLT 4WD SuperCab, 155-inch WB	18107	*	*
Destination charge	600	600	600

Standard Equipment:

4.9-liter 6-cylinder engine, 5-speed manual transmission, anti-lock rear brakes, driver-side air bag, power steering, automatic locking front hubs (4WD), vinyl bench seat, rear jump seats (SuperCab), argent grille, tinted glass, trip odometer, color-keyed floormat, color-keyed cloth headliner (SuperCab), dual black mirrors, vent windows, intermittent wipers, argent steel wheels, bright hubcaps. Tires, 2WD regular cab: P215/75R15SL; others: P235/75R15XL. All models include full-size spare. **XL trim** adds: AM radio, digital clock, chrome front bumper, chrome grille (Flareside), cab steps (Flareside). **XLT trim** adds: AM/FM radio, Light/Convenience Group, bright exterior trim, lower bodyside moldings, cloth headliner, cloth door panel trim with carpeted map pockets, color-keyed full carpeting, cloth bench seat (SuperCab), cloth flight bench seat with power lumber support (regular cab), passenger-side visor mirror, leather-wrapped steering wheel.

Optional Equipment:

5.0-liter V-8 engine	637	542	561

Regular cab requires Optional Payload Pkg. Available only with 4-speed automatic transmission California.

*Some dealer invoice and fair prices not available at time of publication.

Ford

	Retail Price	Dealer Invoice	Fair Price
5.8-liter V-8	$857	$729	$754
Requires 4-speed automatic transmission. Regular cab requires Optional Payload Pkg.			
4-speed ECT automatic transmission	924	786	813
4-speed automatic transmission with overdrive	753	641	663
Requires 5.0-liter engine.			
Touch Drive electric shift, XL 4WD	123	105	108
Requires 5.0- or 5.8-liter engine and 4-speed automatic transmission.			
Manual locking front hubs, 4WD (credit)	(60)	(51)	(51)
Air conditioning	806	686	709
Limited-slip front/rear axle	299	254	263
Limited-slip rear axle	252	214	222
Optional axle ratio	44	37	39
Payload Pkg. 2, 2WD	46	39	40
Payload Pkg. 3, 2WD Flareside	93	79	82
Special Pkg. 498A, S 2WD	356	303	313
S 4WD	250	213	220
Headliner and Insulation Pkg., AM/FM radio, digital clock, argent steel wheels, bright hubcaps, 235/75R15XL tires.			
XLT Pkg. 503A, 2WD with 4.9- or			
5.0-liter engine	2102	1789	1850
2WD with 5.8-liter engine	2202	1874	1938
4WD with 4.9- or 5.0-liter engine	1946	1656	1712
4WD with 5.8-liter engine	2046	1741	1800
Air conditioning, Light and Convenience Group B, cruise control, tilt steering wheel, 235/75R15XL tires, argent steel wheels.			
XLT Pkg. 507A, 2WD with 4.9- or			
5.0-liter engine	2256	1920	1985
2WD with 5.8-liter engine	2856	2430	2513
4WD with 4.9- or 5.0-liter engine	2100	1787	1848
4WD with 5.8-liter engine	2700	2298	2376
Pkg. 503A plus power windows and door locks, cassette player, chrome wheels.			
XLT Pkg. 512A, Flareside	NC	NC	NC
235/75R15XL tires, argent steel wheels.			
Flareside Pkg. 515A, 2WD with 4.9- or			
5.0-liter engine	2013	1711	1771
2WD with 5.9-liter engine	2613	2221	2299
4WD with 4.9- or 5.0-liter engine	1857	1578	1634
4WD with 5.8-liter engine	2457	2088	2162
Air conditioning, power windows and door locks, cassette player, cruise control, tilt steering wheel, Light and Convenience Group, 235/75R15XL tires, chrome wheels,			
Special Pkg. 518A, SuperCab	224	190	197
AM/FM radio, digital clock, argent steel wheels.			
XLT Pkg. 523A, SuperCab with 4.9- or			
5.0-liter engine	2096	1782	1844
SuperCab with 5.8-liter	2196	1867	1932
Air conditioning, Light and Convenience Group B, cruise control, tilt steering wheel, argent steel wheels.			
XLT Pkg. 527A, SuperCab with 4.9- or			
5.0-liter engine	2250	1913	1980
SuperCab with 5.8-liter engine	2850	2423	2508
523A Pkg. plus power windows and door locks, cassette player, chrome wheels.			
XLT Pkg. 535A, SuperCab Flareside			
with 4.9- or 5.0-liter engine	2007	1706	1766
SuperCab Flareside with 5.8-liter	2607	2216	2294
Air conditioning, Light and Convenience Group B, cruise control, tilt steering wheel, power windows and door locks, cassette player, chrome wheels.			
Light and Convenience Group A	202	172	178
Dual lighted visor mirrors, automatic dimming day/night rearview mirror. Requires XLT Pkg.			
Light and Convenience Group B	128	109	113
Underhood and dual beam map/dome lights, headlights-on warning buzzer, door map pockets, passenger-side visor mirror, mini-console (regular cab), Headliner and insulation Pkg. (XL regular cab).			
Heavy duty Front Suspension Pkg., XL			
4WD 133-inch WB	99	84	87
Heavy duty front axle, heavy duty front springs, 3.55 rear axle ratio, heavy duty frame. Requires manual locking hubs.			

	Retail Price	Dealer Invoice	Fair Price
Heavy duty Rear Suspension Pkg., XL	$99	$84	$87
Heavy duty auxiliary rear springs.			
Trailer Towing Pkg., XL	362	308	319
with Off-Road Pkg. (credit)	(120)	(102)	(102)
Super engine cooling, trailer wiring harness, heavy duty turn signal flasher, Handling Pkg., heavy duty battery.			
Camper Pkg., XL	362	308	319
with Off-Road Pkg. (credit)	(120)	(102)	(102)
Super engine cooling, trailer wiring harness, heavy duty turn signal flasher, Handling Pkg., heavy duty battery. 2WD 133-inch WB models require Optional Payload Pkg. 2.			
Handling Pkg.	120	102	106
Front and rear stabilizer bars, heavy duty front springs (2WD), quad front shock absorbers (4WD regular cab).			
Headliner and Insulation Pkg.	76	65	67
Color-keyed cloth headliner, back panel cover, B-pillar, and back panel moldings.			
Chrome Appearance Pkg., XL	180	153	158
Chrome grille and manual remote mirrors.			
Off-Road Pkg., XL 4WD	330	281	290
Skid plates, stabilizer bar, 4x4 off-road decal.			
Security Group	254	216	224
Keyless remote entry system, anti-theft system. Requires XLT Pkg., power windows and door locks.			
Power windows and door locks	367	312	323
Requires XLT Pkg. 503A or 523A.			
Bright low-mount swingaway mirrors,			
S and XL	45	38	40
Power mirrors, XLT	99	84	87
Requires power windows and door locks.			
Cruise control and tilt steering column (NA S)	383	326	337
Tachometer	59	50	52
Knitted vinyl bench seat,			
S and XL	71	60	62
XLT	(98)	(83)	(83)
XLT SuperCab	NC	NC	NC
Cloth and vinyl bench seat, S and XL	100	85	88
SuperCab	NC	NC	NC
Cloth captain's chairs, XL SuperCab	752	640	662
XLT SuperCab	591	502	520
Includes floor console, power lumbar support, cloth rear bench seat.			
Power driver's seat, XLT SuperCab	290	247	255
Requires 40/20/40 split bench seat.			
40/20/40 split bench seat, XLT	523	445	460
XLT SuperCab	621	528	546
Includes power lumbar support.			
Vinyl rear bench seat, XL SuperCab	209	178	184
XLT SuperCab	NC	NC	NC
Vinyl rear jump seats (credit),			
XLT SuperCab	(209)	(177)	(177)
Credit when vinyl rear jump seats are substituted for cloth rear bench seat on XLT.			
Heavy duty battery	56	48	49
Manual locking hubs (credit)	(60)	(51)	(51)
Argent rear step bumper, XL	130	111	114
Chrome rear step bumper	238	202	209
Super engine cooling	101	86	89
Engine block heater	33	28	29
Deluxe two-tone paint, XLT	276	235	243
Lower accent two-tone paint, XL	254	216	224
XLT	183	156	161
Includes wheel opening moldings. SuperCab also includes lower bodyside moldings.			
Sliding rear window	113	96	99
AM radio, S	122	104	107
AM/FM radio, XL	148	126	130
AM/FM cassette	257	218	226
with Pkg. with AM/FM radio	110	94	97
Premium AM/FM cassette			
(upgrade from AM radio)	348	296	306
upgrade from AM/FM radio	200	170	176
upgrade from AM/FM cassette	90	77	79
Includes four speakers and amplifier.			

Ford

Top: F-150 XLT SuperCab long-bed. Above: F-150 XL Flareside. A driver-side air bag is standard in F-150 models and in the F-250 2WD regular-cab long-bed.

	Retail Price	Dealer Invoice	Fair Price
Premium AM/FM CD player			
(upgrade from AM radio)	$630	$536	$554
upgrade from AM/FM radio	483	411	425
upgrade from AM/FM cassette	373	317	328
Includes four speakers and amplifier.			
Radio delete (credit)	(61)	(52)	(52)
Argent styled wheels	205	174	180
credit for Pkg. with chrome styled wheels	(177)	(150)	(150)
Forged alloy wheels	382	325	336
Pkg. with argent styled steel wheels	177	150	156
Pkg. with chrome styled wheels	NC	NC	NC
Chrome styled wheels (NA S)	382	325	336
Pkg. with argent styled steel wheels	177	150	156
Tires, 2WD regular cab: 235/75R15XL tires	156	133	137
235/75R15XL whitewall	258	219	227
Pkg. with 235/57R15XL tires (credit)	(156)	(133)	(133)
235/75R15XL outline white letter tires	282	240	248
all-terrain tires	412	350	363
Pkg. with 235/75R15XL tires (credit)	(156)	(133)	(133)
Tires, 4WD: 235/75R15XL whitewall tires	102	87	90
235/75R15XL outline white letter tires	126	107	111
all-terrain tires	256	218	225
235/75R15XL all-terrain tires	55	47	48
265/75R15XL outline white letter all-terrain tires	595	506	524

Ford F-250

	Retail Price	Dealer Invoice	Fair Price
XL 2WD regular cab, 133-inch WB	$14802	*	*
Destination charge	600	600	600

Standard Equipment:
4.9-liter 6-cylinder engine, 5-speed manual transmission, anti-lock rear brakes, driver-side air bag, power steering, vinyl bench seat, voltmeter, oil pressure and temperature gauges, trip odometer, chrome front bumper, argent grille, AM radio, digital clock, tinted glass, color-keyed floormat, black manual mirrors, vent windows, dual fuel tanks, heavy duty shock absorbers, argent steel wheels, bright hubcaps, LT215/85R16D tires.

Optional Equipment:

5.0-liter V-8 engine	637	541	573
5.8-liter V-8 engine	857	729	771
Requires automatic transmission.			
4-speed ECT automatic transmission	924	786	832
Air conditioning	806	685	709
Limited-slip rear axle	252	215	222
Optional axle ratio	44	37	39
XLT Pkg. 543A	2351	1998	2116

Air conditioning, power windows and door locks, Light and Convenience Group, cruise control, tilt steering column, AM/FM cassette, Headliner and Insulation Pkg., sport wheel covers, cloth flight bench seat with power lumbar supports, XLT trim (includes front bumper rub strips, chrome grille, bright headlight/parking light bezels and wheel opening moldings, black lower bodyside moldings, brushed aluminum tailgate trim, black steel wheels, color-keyed carpeting, door map pockets, leather-wrapped steering wheel, passenger-side visor mirror).

Light and Convenience Group A	202	172	178

Dual lighted visor mirrors, automatic dimming day/night rearview mirror. Requires XLT Pkg.

Light and Convenience Group B	128	109	113

Underhood and dual beam map/dome lights, headlights-on warning buzzer, door map pockets, passenger-side visor mirror, mini-console, Headliner and Insulation Pkg.

Heavy Duty Rear Suspension Pkg.	129	110	114
Heavy duty auxiliary rear springs.			
Trailer Towing Pkg.	362	308	319

Super engine cooling, trailer wiring harness, heavy duty turn signal flasher, Handling Pkg., heavy duty battery.

Camper Pkg.	362	308	319

Super engine cooling, trailer wiring harness, heavy duty turn signal flasher, Handling Pkg., heavy duty battery.

Handling Pkg.	120	102	106
Front and rear stabilizer bars, heavy duty front springs.			
Headliner and Insulation Pkg.	76	65	67

Color-keyed cloth headliner, back panel cover, B-pillar, and back panel moldings.

Chrome Appearance Pkg.	180	153	158
Chrome grille and manual remote mirrors.			
Security Group, XLT	254	216	224
Keyless remote entry system, anti-theft system.			
Bright low-mount swingaway mirrors	45	38	40
Power mirrors, XLT	99	84	87
Cruise control and tilt steering column	383	326	337
Tachometer	59	50	52
Knitted vinyl bench seat	71	60	62
Cloth and vinyl bench seat	100	85	88
40/20/40 split bench seat, XLT	523	445	460
Includes power lumbar support.			
Heavy duty battery	56	48	49
Single fuel tank (credit)	(116)	(98)	(98)
Argent rear step bumper	130	111	114
Chrome rear step bumper	238	202	209
Super engine cooling	101	86	89
Engine block heater	33	28	29
Deluxe two-tone paint, XLT	276	235	243
Sliding rear window	113	96	99
AM/FM radio	148	126	130
AM/FM cassette	257	218	226
with XLT Pkg.	110	94	97

Some dealer invoice and fair prices not available at time of publication.

	Retail Price	Dealer Invoice	Fair Price
Premium AM/FM cassette			
(upgrade from AM radio)	$348	$296	$306
upgrade from AM/FM radio	200	170	176
upgrade from AM/FM cassette	90	77	79
Includes four speakers and amplifier.			
Premium AM/FM CD player			
(upgrade from AM radio)	630	536	554
upgrade from AM/FM radio	483	411	425
upgrade from AM/FM cassette	373	317	328
Includes four speakers and amplifier.			
Radio delete (credit)	(61)	(52)	(52)
Sport wheel covers	83	71	73
LT235/85R16E tires	175	149	154
spare tire	267	227	235
LT235/85R16E all-terrain tires	249	212	219

Ford F-250 Heavy Duty

	Retail Price	Dealer Invoice	Fair Price
XL 2WD regular cab, 133-inch WB	$15369	*	*
XL 4WD regular cab, 133-inch WB	18846	*	*
S 2WD SuperCab, 155-inch WB	16597	14734	15234
XL 2WD SuperCab, 155-inch WB	17900	*	*
XL 4WD SuperCab, 155-inch WB	20352	*	*
Destination charge	600	600	600

Standard Equipment:

4.9-liter 6-cylinder engine (2WD regular cab), 5.8-liter V-8 engine (others), 5-speed heavy duty manual transmission, anti-lock rear brakes, driver-side air bag, power steering, automatic locking front hubs (4WD), chrome front bumper (XL), argent bumper (S), voltmeter, oil pressure and temperature gauges, trip odometer, vinyl bench seat, rear jump seat (SuperCab), argent grille, AM radio (XL), digital clock (XL), tinted glass, color-keyed headliner (SuperCab), color-keyed floormat, black manual mirrors, seatback trim panel (SuperCab), intermittent wipers, vent windows, heavy duty shock absorbers, heavy duty alternator (NA 2WD regular cab), dual fuel tanks, argent steel wheels, bright hubcaps, LT235/85R16E tires.

Optional Equipment:

4.9-liter engine, 2WD SuperCab (credit)	(857)	(729)	(729)
5.8-liter V-8, 2WD regular cab	857	728	754
7.5-liter V-8, 2WD regular cab	1341	1140	1180
SuperCab, 4WD regular cab	484	411	426
7.3-liter diesel V-8, 2WD regular cab	3072	2611	2703
SuperCab, 4WD regular cab	2215	1883	1949
7.3-liter turbo diesel V-8, 2WD regular cab	4637	3941	4081
SuperCabs, 4WD regular cab	3779	3212	3326
3-speed automatic transmission	696	592	612
Includes auxiliary transmission oil cooler.			
4-speed automatic transmission	924	785	813
Air conditioning	806	685	709
Limited-slip rear axle	252	215	222
Optional axle ratio	44	37	39
Manual locking hubs (credit)	(60)	(51)	(51)
XLT Pkg. 603A	2351	1998	2116
XLT Pkg. 613A, XL SuperCab	2501	2126	2251
Air conditioning, power windows and door locks, Light and Convenience Group, cruise control, tilt steering column, AM/FM cassette, Headliner and Insulation Pkg., sport wheel covers, cloth flight bench seat with power lumbar supports, cloth rear bench seat (SuperCab), XLT trim (includes front bumper rub strips, chrome grille, bright headlight/parking light bezels and wheel opening moldings, black lower bodyside moldings, brushed aluminum tailgate trim, black steel wheels, color-keyed carpeting, door map pockets, leather-wrapped steering wheel, passenger-side visor mirror).			
Light and Convenience Group A	202	172	178
Dual lighted visor mirrors, automatic dimming day/night rearview mirror. Requires XLT Pkg.			
Light and Convenience Group B	128	109	113
Underhood and dual beam map/dome lights, headlights-on warning buzzer, door map pockets, passenger-side visor mirror, mini-console, Headliner and Insulation Pkg.			

	Retail Price	Dealer Invoice	Fair Price
Heavy Duty Front Suspension Pkg., 4WD	$71	$60	$62
Heavy duty front axle and front springs, 4.10 rear axle ratio.			
Heavy Duty Rear Suspension Pkg.	129	110	114
Heavy duty rear auxiliary rear springs.			
Trailer Towing Pkg.	362	308	319
with Off-Road Pkg. (credit)	(120)	(102)	(102)
with 7.3-liter engine (credit)	(56)	(48)	(48)
with 7.3-liter turbo diesel engine (credit)	(157)	(134)	(134)
with super engine cooling (credit)	(101)	(86)	(86)
Super engine cooling, trailer wiring harness, heavy duty turn signal flasher, Handling Pkg., heavy duty battery.			
Camper Pkg.	362	308	319
with Off-Road Pkg. (credit)	(120)	(102)	(102)
with 7.3-liter engine (credit)	(56)	(48)	(48)
with 7.3-liter turbo diesel engine (credit)	(157)	(134)	(134)
with super engine cooling (credit)	(101)	(86)	(86)
Super engine cooling, trailer wiring harness, heavy duty turn signal flasher, Handling Pkg., heavy duty battery.			
Handling Pkg.	120	102	106
Front and rear stabilizer bars, heavy duty front springs.			
Headliner and Insulation Pkg., regular cab	76	65	67
Color-keyed cloth headliner, back panel cover, B-pillar, and back panel moldings.			
Chrome Appearance Pkg., XL	180	153	158
Chrome grille and manual remote mirrors.			
Security Group, XLT	254	216	224
Keyless remote entry system, anti-theft system.			
Off-Road Pkg., XL 4WD	302	257	266
with 7.3-liter engine	215	183	189
Skid plates, stabilizer bar, 4x4 off-road decal.			
Bright low-mount swingaway mirrors	45	38	40
Bright swing-out mirrors, XL	54	46	48
Power mirrors, XLT	99	84	87
Cruise control and tilt steering column	383	326	337
Tachometer	59	50	52
Knitted vinyl bench seat, XL	71	60	62
XLT	(98)	(83)	(83)
XLT SuperCab	NC	NC	NC
Cloth and vinyl bench seat, XL	100	85	88
SuperCab	NC	NC	NC
Cloth and vinyl bench seat	100	85	88
SuperCab	NC	NC	NC
Cloth captain's chairs, XL SuperCab	752	640	662
XLT SuperCab	591	502	520
Includes floor console, power lumbar support, cloth rear bench seat.			
Power driver's seat, XLT SuperCab	290	247	255
Requires 40/20/40 split bench seat.			
40/20/40 split bench seat, XLT	523	445	460
XLT SuperCab	621	528	546
Includes power lumbar support.			
Vinyl rear bench seat, XL SuperCab	209	178	184
XLT SuperCab	NC	NC	NC
Vinyl rear jump seats (credit), XLT SuperCab	(209)	(177)	(177)
Credit when vinyl rear jump seats are substituted for cloth rear bench seat on XLT.			
Heavy duty battery	56	48	49
Auxiliary fuel tap	30	26	26
Argent rear step bumper	130	111	114
Chrome rear step bumper	238	202	209
Super engine cooling	101	86	89
Engine block heater	33	28	29
Dual element engine block heater, 7.5-liter engine	66	56	58
Roof clearance lights	52	44	46
Deluxe two-tone paint, XLT	276	235	243
Sliding rear window	113	96	99
AM radio, S	122	104	107
AM/FM radio	148	126	130
AM/FM cassette	257	218	226
with XLT Pkg.	110	94	97
Premium AM/FM cassette (upgrade from AM radio)	348	296	306

Some dealer invoice and fair prices not available at time of publication.

Ford

	Retail Price	Dealer Invoice	Fair Price
upgrade from AM/FM radio	$200	$170	$176
upgrade from AM/FM cassette	90	77	79
Includes four speakers and amplifier.			
Premium AM/FM CD player			
(upgrade from AM radio)	630	536	554
upgrade from AM/FM radio	483	411	425
upgrade from AM/FM cassette	373	317	328
Includes four speakers and amplifier.			
Sliding rear window	113	96	102
Tires: LT235/85R16E rear all-terrain tires, 2WD	56	48	50
All-terrain tires, 4WD	111	94	100
Spare tire and wheel	267	227	240
All-terrain	295	251	266
Spare rear wheel	134	114	121

Ford F-350

	Retail Price	Dealer Invoice	Fair Price
F-350 XL 2WD regular cab, 133-inch WB	$17639	*	*
F-350 XL 4WD regular cab, 133-inch WB	19336	*	*
F-350 XL 2WD SuperCab, 155-inch WB	19732	*	*
Destination charge	600	600	600

2WD models have dual rear wheels.

Standard Equipment:
5.8-liter V-8 engine (regular cab), 7.5-liter engine V-8 (SuperCab), heavy duty 5-speed manual transmission, anti-lock rear brakes, power steering, automatic locking front hubs (4WD), vinyl bench seat, rear jump seat (SuperCab), roof clearance lights (2WD), voltmeter, oil pressure and temperature gauge, trip odometer, intermittent wipers, chrome bumpers, argent grille, AM radio, digital clock, tinted glass, color-keyed headliner (SuperCab), color-keyed floormat, black manual mirrors, seatback trim panel (SuperCab), vent windows, LT215/85R16D tires (2WD), LT235/75R16E tires (4WD), argent wheels (2WD).

Optional Equipment:

7.5-liter V-8 engine, regular cab	484	411	426
7.3-liter diesel V-8 engine, regular cab	2215	1883	1949
SuperCab	1730	1471	1522
7.3-liter turbo diesel V-8 engine, regular cab	3779	3212	3326
SuperCab	3295	2801	2900
Includes heavy duty cooling, tachometer.			
3-speed automatic transmission, regular cab	696	592	612
4-speed automatic	924	785	813
Manual locking front hubs, 4WD (credit)	(60)	(51)	(51)
Air conditioning	806	685	709
Manual locking hubs (credit)	(60)	(51)	(51)
Limited-slip rear axle	252	214	222
Optional axle ratio	44	37	39
XLT Pkg. 651A, 2WD regular cab	2268	1928	1996
XLT Pkg. 642A, 4WD regular cab	2351	1998	2069
XLT Pkg. 618A, 2WD SuperCab	2418	2055	2128

Air conditioning, power windows and door locks, Light and Convenience Group, cruise control, tilt steering column, AM/FM cassette, Headliner and Insulation Pkg. (regular cab), sport wheel covers, cloth flight bench seat with power lumbar supports, cloth rear bench seat (SuperCab), XLT trim (includes front bumper rub strips, chrome grille, bright headlight/parking light bezels and wheel opening moldings, black lower bodyside moldings, brushed aluminum tailgate trim, black steel wheels, color-keyed carpeting, door map pockets, leather-wrapped steering wheel, passenger-side visor mirror).

Light and Convenience Group A	202	172	178

Dual lighted visor mirrors, automatic dimming day/night rearview mirror. Requires XLT Pkg.

Light and Convenience Group B	128	109	113

Underhood and dual beam map/dome lights, headlights-on warning buzzer, door map pockets, passenger-side visor mirror, mini-console, Headliner and Insulation Pkg. (regular cab).

Heavy Duty Front Suspension Pkg.,			
4WD regular cab	27	23	24

Heavy duty front springs. Requires manual locking front hubs.

	Retail Price	Dealer Invoice	Fair Price
Trailer Towing/Camper Pkg.	$362	$308	$319
with Off-Road Pkg. (credit)	(120)	(102)	(102)
with 7.3-liter diesel engine (credit)	(56)	(48)	(48)
with 7.3-liter turbo diesel engine (credit)	(157)	(134)	(134)
with super engine cooling (credit)	(101)	(86)	(86)
Super engine cooling, trailer wiring harness, heavy duty turn signal flasher, Handling Pkg., heavy duty battery.			
Handling Pkg.	120	102	106
Front and rear stabilizer bars, heavy duty front springs.			
Headliner and Insulation Pkg., regular cab	76	65	67
Color-keyed cloth headliner, back panel cover, B-pillar, and back panel moldings.			
Chrome Appearance Pkg., XL	180	153	158
Chrome grille and manual remote mirrors.			
Security Group, XLT	254	216	224
Keyless remote entry system, anti-theft system.			
Off-Road Pkg., XL 4WD	259	220	228
with 7.3-liter engine	171	145	150
Skid plates, stabilizer bar, 4x4 off-road decal.			
Bright low-mount swingaway mirrors	45	38	40
Bright swing-out mirrors, XL	54	46	48
Power mirrors, XLT 4WD	99	84	87
Cruise control and tilt steering column	383	326	337
Tachometer	59	50	52
Knitted vinyl bench seat, XL	71	60	62
XLT	(98)	(83)	(83)
XLT SuperCab	NC	NC	NC
Cloth and vinyl bench seat, XL	100	85	88
SuperCab	NC	NC	NC
Cloth and vinyl bench seat	100	85	88
SuperCab	NC	NC	NC
Cloth captain's chairs, XL SuperCab	752	640	662
XLT SuperCab	591	502	520
Includes floor console, power lumbar support, cloth rear bench seat.			
Power driver's seat, XLT SuperCab	290	247	255
Requires 40/20/40 split bench seat.			
40/20/40 split bench seat, XLT	523	445	460
XLT SuperCab	621	528	546
Includes power lumbar support.			
Vinyl rear bench seat, XL SuperCab	209	178	184
XLT SuperCab	NC	NC	NC
Vinyl rear jump seats (credit), XLT SuperCab	(209)	(177)	(177)
Credit when vinyl rear jump seats are substituted for cloth rear bench seat on XLT.			
Heavy duty battery	56	48	49
Single fuel tank (credit), 4WD	(116)	(98)	(98)
Auxiliary fuel tap	30	26	26
Chrome rear step bumper	238	202	209
Super engine cooling	101	86	89
Engine block heater	33	28	29
Dual element engine block heater,			
7.5-liter engine	66	56	58
Roof clearance lights, 4WD	52	44	46
Deluxe two-tone paint, XLT 4WD	276	235	243
XLT 2WD	166	141	146
XLT 4WD includes wheel opening moldings.			
Sliding rear window	113	96	99
AM/FM radio	148	126	130
AM/FM cassette	257	218	226
with XLT Pkg.	110	94	97
Premium AM/FM cassette			
(upgrade from AM radio)	348	296	306
upgrade from AM/FM radio	200	170	176
upgrade from AM/FM cassette	90	77	79
Includes four speakers and amplifier.			
Premium AM/FM CD player			
(upgrade from AM radio)	630	536	554
upgrade from AM/FM radio	483	411	425
upgrade from AM/FM cassette	373	317	328
Includes four speakers and amplifier.			
Radio delete (credit)	(61)	(52)	(52)
Sport wheel covers	83	71	75
Tires: LT235/85R16E all-terrain tires, 4WD	111	94	98

Some dealer invoice and fair prices not available at time of publication.

Ford Ranger

RECOMMENDED

Ford Ranger Splash SuperCab

America's best-selling compact pickup introduced the first flare-fender cargo box in the class last year and expands on that theme for 1994. Called the Splash, the flare-fender model adds an extended-cab body style to go along with its regular-cab version.

Side door guard beams also are new for all models of the Ranger, which got new exterior sheetmetal and a new interior design last year.

Mazda for 1994 shelves its Japanese-built compact pickups in favor of rebadged and slightly restyled versions of the Ranger. However, a flare-fender model is not offered in Mazda's line of B-Series pickups, which are covered in a separate report.

Body Styles/Chassis

Ranger continues in regular- and extended-cab SuperCab form with both slab-side and flareside cargo boxes.

Three sizes are offered: a 108-inch-wheelbase regular-cab with a 6-foot cargo bed; a 114-inch regular-cab with a 7-foot bed; and 125-inch-wheelbase SuperCab with a 6-foot bed. Regular-cab Splash models come with the short-bed only.

Side door guard beams join the center high-mounted stoplamp, which was added for 1993. Cargo tie-down hooks will be added to all models later in the year as a new standard feature.

Slab-side cargo box Rangers come in XL, XLT, and STX trim. There's also an XL Sport package for regular-cab models that includes exterior tape stripes and other dress-up items. Splash models incorporate many XLT-level features.

All models can be ordered in either 2- or 4-wheel drive. Four-wheel drive Rangers are distinguished from 2WD models by a unique front valance panel, fender flares, and standard 15-inch tires instead of 14-inch.

Splash models have a cargo box styled after that on Ford's full-size F-Series Flareside pickups. A body-color grille and bumpers, a lowered sport suspension, and chrome or alloy wheels are standard on Splash models.

On all Rangers, rear anti-lock brakes are standard and work only in 2WD.

A 3-place bench seat is standard in regular-cab XL models. A 60/40 split bench with center storage armrest is optional on XL and STX models and standard on all other Rangers.

STX models come with front captain's chairs and a floor console. Bucket seats are optional on XLT, STX, and Splash models.

SuperCab Rangers are available with a pair of jump seats that fold out from the corners of the rear-cabin area. That rear-cabin area has 22.2 cubic feet of storage space, or 18.1 with the jump seats.

Maximum payload is 1650 pounds on 2WD models and 1550 on 4x4s and SuperCabs.

Powertrains

A 98-horsepower 2.3-liter 4-cylinder is the base engine.

A 140-horsepower 3.0-liter V-6 is standard on STX models and on all 4WD models except the XL and XLT, where it's optional. The 3.0 also is optional on the remaining 2WD models.

A 160-horsepower 4.0-liter V-6 is optional on all models.

All engines are available with a 5-speed manual or 4-speed overdrive automatic transmission, though the 4-cylinder engine is not offered with automatic on 4WD models.

Standard on 4x4s is Ford's Touch Drive on-demand 4WD, which is not for use on dry pavement. It has automatic-locking front hubs and allows shifting on the fly between 2WD and 4WD High with the press of a dashboard button. Available as a credit option is a 4WD system that uses manual locking front hubs with a floor-mounted transfer-case lever. With either system, Ford recommends that the vehicle be stopped and reversed for a short distance to fully disengage 4WD.

Maximum towing capacity is 6000 pounds on 2WD regular-cab models and 5900 on 2WD SuperCabs. It's slightly less on 4x4 models.

Evaluation

Last year's restyle gave Ranger a longer, lower nose. New flush-mounted glass and "limousine-style" doors that extend further into the roof added to the new look. The dashboard was little changed, but door panels and seat trim were revised.

Overall, Ford sought a more car-like look and feel for Ranger, and that's what it got. Some rugged truck character was lost, but we view the changes as improvements, particularly for the vast majority of owners who use Ranger as an around-town hoofer instead of a heavy-duty hauler.

That same advance holds true for General Motors' redesign of its 1994 Chevrolet S10 Pickup and GMC Sonoma. The GM trucks now rival Ranger for overall refinement and ergonomics, and with comparable powertrains, payloads, and towing ratings, most shoppers' buying decision probably will come down to brand loyalty and the kind of deal they can make.

No other compact pickup offers a flareside model like the Splash, and Ford builds on that exclusivity by added the SuperCab Splash for 1994. But the GM models do have an available 195-horsepower V-6 engine and so have bragging rights for all-out muscle. Note, however, that no compact pickup offers a driver-side air bag, though the Dodge Dakota, which is marketed as a "mid-size" pickup, does have that safety feature for 1994.

All these domestic pickups, as well as the Mazda B-Series, which now shares Ranger's design and powertrains, have more hauling and towing ability than Japanese rivals.

Still, a Ranger with the 4-cylinder engine and 5-speed manual has adequate performance if you use your compact

Ford

pickup as a second car, but the 2.3-liter labors under a heavy load or with automatic transmission.

The 4.0 V-6 uses only slightly more fuel than the 3.0 V-6, but it doesn't add much to the sticker price and gives Ranger low-speed power unmatched by the imports. The 4.0, which is shared with the Ford Explorer sport-utility, is sometimes coarse and noisy, and it seems run out of breath at higher engine speeds—but high-end horsepower is not as useful as low-end torque in a pickup.

Ranger has excellent ride and handling qualities for a truck. The suspension absorbs most big bumps without jarring and is stable in turns. Steering feedback and response is top-notch, and Ranger overall has a notably solid feel.

Touch Drive's convenient dash button and automatic locking hubs are features many imports lack. But GM's compact pickups have an edge here because they don't require that you stop and reverse to fully disengaged 4WD.

Ranger's regular-cab interior doesn't have as much room behind the seat as does the new GM design. And with a steering wheel that protrudes too far, there's no surplus of room for larger drivers—but that's true of most compact pickups.

Power window and lock buttons are within easy reach. Gauges are large and readable. Climate and audio controls sit high in the dash, but it's an awkward reach around the steering wheel to get to them and the small radio buttons are hard to hit even when traveling on glass-smooth pavement.

Ranger has some tough competition in the new GM trucks, so put brand loyalty aside and shop them both.

Specifications

	Short bed	Long bed	SuperCab
Wheelbase, in.	108.0	114.0	125.0
Overall length, in.	180.0	193.0	198.2
Overall width, in.	69.4	69.4	69.4
Overall height, in.	64.0	64.0	64.1
Turn diameter, ft.	36.5	38.3	41.6
Curb weight, lbs.	2918	2955	3208
Fuel capacity, gal.	16.3	16.3	20.0

Passenger Area Dimensions

Seating capacity	3	3	5
Front head room, in.	39.1	39.1	39.4
Rear head room, in.	—	—	NA
Front leg room, in.	42.4	42.4	43.4
Rear leg room, in.	—	—	NA

Cargo Dimensions and Payloads

Cargo area length, in.	72.2	84.2	72.2
Cargo area width, in.	51.2[1]	51.2	51.2[1]
Cargo area width between wheels, in.	40.4	40.4	40.4
Cargo area height, in.	16.5	16.5	16.5
Max. payload, lbs.	1650	1650	1550
Max. trailer weight, lbs.	6000	6000	5900

1. 46.5 in., Ranger Splash.

Engines

	ohv I-4	ohv V-6	ohv V-6
Size, liters/cu. in.	2.3/140	3.0/182	4.0/245
Horsepower @ rpm	98 @ 4600	140 @ 4800	160 @ 4000
Torque (lbs./ft.) @ rpm	130 @ 2600	160 @ 3000	225 @ 2500
Availability	S	O[1]	O

EPA city/highway mpg

5-speed OD manual	22/27	19/25	18/24
4-speed OD automatic	21/24	18/23	16/21

1. Standard on STX, 4WD SuperCab, and 4WD Splash.

Built in Louisville, Ky., St. Paul, Minn., and Edison, N.J.

KEY: Dimensions and capacities are supplied by the manufacturers. **Curb Weight:** base models, not including optional equipment. **Max. payload, lbs.** = gross amount; net payload may be lower due to optional equipment. **Engines:** ohv = overhead valve; ohc = overhead cam; **I** = inline cylinders; **V** = cylinders in V configuration; **flat** = horizontally opposed cylinders; **rpm** = revolutions per minute; **OD** = overdrive transmission; **S** = standard; **O** = optional; **NA** = not available.

Prices

Ford Ranger

	Retail Price	Dealer Invoice	Fair Price
XL 2WD regular cab, 108-inch WB	$9449	*	*
XL 2WD regular cab, 114-inch WB	9825	*	*
XLT 2WD regular cab, 108-inch WB	11171	*	*
XLT 2WD regular cab, 114-inch WB	11721	*	*
STX 2WD regular cab, 108-inch WB	12220	*	*
STX 2WD regular cab, 114-inch WB	12772	*	*
XL 4WD regular cab, 108-inch WB	13918	*	*
XL 4WD regular cab, 114-inch WB	14253	*	*
XLT 4WD regular cab, 108-inch WB	15486	*	*
XLT 4WD regular cab, 114-inch WB	16085	*	*
STX 4WD regular cab, 108-inch WB	16382	*	*
STX 4WD regular cab, 114-inch WB	16981	*	*
XL 2WD SuperCab, 125-inch WB	11892	*	*
XL 4WD SuperCab, 125-inch WB	15525	*	*
XLT 2WD SuperCab, 125-inch WB	12388	*	*
XLT 4WD SuperCab, 125-inch WB	16828	*	*
STX 2WD SuperCab, 125-inch WB	13388	*	*
STX 4WD SuperCab, 125-inch WB	17507	*	*
Splash 2WD regular cab, 108-inch WB	12454	*	*
Splash 4WD regular cab, 108-inch WB	17413	*	*
Splash 2WD SuperCab, 125-inch WB	14014	*	*
Splash 4WD SuperCab, 125-inch WB	18328	*	*
Destination charge	460	460	460

Standard Equipment:

XL: 2.3-liter 4-cylinder engine, 3.0-liter V-6 engine (SuperCab 4WD), 5-speed manual transmission, anti-lock rear brakes, power steering (ex. regular cab 2WD), vinyl bench seat (regular cab), 60/40 cloth split bench seat with storage armrest (SuperCab), coolant temperature and oil pressure gauges, trip odometer, tachometer (4WD), grey painted bumpers, tinted glass, passenger-side visor mirror (SuperCab), front black spoiler, black vinyl floormat, black outside mirrors, intermittent wipers, heavy duty battery (SuperCab), heavy duty gas shock absorbers (4WD), automatic locking front hubs (4WD), high capacity fuel tank (SuperCab), rear mud flaps (2WD), front and rear mud flaps (4WD), 195/70R14SL tires (2WD), 215/75R15 tires (4WD), argent styled steel wheels, grey hub covers. **XLT** adds: cloth 60/40 split front cloth bench seat with storage armrest, cloth door trim panels, floor consolette, carpeting, AM/FM radio, digital clock, Light Group, door map pockets, passenger-side visor mirror, cargo area cover (SuperCab), cloth headliner, front chrome bumpers, chrome rear step bumper, chrome grille (4WD), cargo box light, striping, full-face steel wheels. **STX** adds: 3.0-liter V-6 engine, power steering, tachometer, dual cloth captains chairs with full floor console, leather-wrapped steering wheel, Handling Pkg. (2WD), grey painted front bumper, rear step bumper, and grille, 225/70R14SL outline white letter tires (2WD), 215/75R15SL all-terrain tires (4WD). **Splash** adds to XL: 3.0-liter V-6 engine (4WD), power steering, 60/40 cloth bench seat with storage armrest, floor consolette, carpeting, AM/FM radio, digital clock, color-keyed bumpers, grille, and power mirrors, passenger-side visor mirror, front and rear stabilizer bars, cloth headliner and door trim panels, door map pockets, tachometer (SuperCab), front and rear mud Light Group, cargo box light, cargo area cover (4WD), 235/60R16 tires (2WD), 235/75R15SL outline white letter all-terrain tires (4WD), chrome wheels (2WD), deep-dish alloy wheels (4WD).

*Some dealer invoice and fair prices not available at time of publication.

Ford

Optional Equipment:

	Retail Price	Dealer Invoice	Fair Price
3.0-liter V-6, 2WD XL, XLT and Splash	$489	$416	$430
4WD XL and XLT regular cab	605	514	532
4WD includes skid plates. Regular cab 2WD requires power steering.			
4.0-liter V-6, 2WD XL, XLT and Splash	668	568	588
4WD XL and XLT regular cab	784	667	690
STX models and SuperCab 4WD	179	152	158
4WD includes skid plates. Requires tachometer. Regular cab 2WD also requires power steering.			
4-speed automatic transmission	990	842	871
Regular cab 2WD requires power steering.			
Limited-slip rear axle	252	215	222
Requires V-6 engine.			
Manual locking front hubs, 4WD (credit)	(104)	(88)	(88)
Power steering, 2WD XL and XLT regular cab	274	233	241
Air conditioning	780	663	686
Regular cab 2WD requires power steering.			
XL Sport Pkg. 862A, XL regular cab 2WD	625	532	550
4WD	529	450	466
AM/FM cassette, limited service spare tire (2WD), sport tape stripe, 215/70R14 tires (2WD), deep dish alloy wheels.			
XLT Special Value Pkg. 864A, 2WD			
regular cab 5-speed	169	144	149
2WD regular cab with 4-speed automatic	552	469	486
4WD regular cab with 5-speed	812	690	715
4WD regular cab with automatic	811	689	714
3.0-liter engine (4WD), power steering (2WD), AM/FM cassette, chrome rear step bumper (2WD), accent tape stripe, rear sliding window, 225/70R14 outline white letter tires (2WD), 235/75R15 outline white letter all-terrain tires (4WD).			
STX Pkg. 865A, 2WD regular cab			
with 5-speed	138	117	121
2WD regular cab with 4-speed automatic	388	330	341
4WD regular cab with 5-speed	341	290	300
4WD regular cab with 4-speed automatic	591	502	520
AM/FM cassette stereo, cloth sport bucket seats with floor console, fog lamps (4WD), deep dish alloy wheels (2WD), sport alloy wheels (4WD), 235/75R15 outline white letter all-terrain tires (4WD).			
XLT Special Value Pkg. 853A, 2WD			
SuperCab with 5-speed	471	400	414
2WD SuperCab with 4-speed automatic	682	580	600
4WD SuperCab with 5-speed	433	368	381
4WD SuperCab with 4-speed automatic	667	567	587
AM/FM cassette stereo, rear jump seat, sliding rear window, chrome rear step bumper (2WD), tape stripe, 225/70R14 outline white letter tires (2WD), 235/70R15 outline white letter all-terrain tires (4WD).			
STX Pkg. 854A, 2WD SuperCab with 5-speed	459	390	404
2WD SuperCab with 4-speed automatic	709	603	624
4WD SuperCab with 5-speed	662	563	583
4WD SuperCab with 4-speed automatic	912	775	803
AM/FM cassette, cruise control, tilt steering column, cloth sport bucket seats with floor console, rear jump seat, fog lamps (4WD), 235/75R15 tires, deep dish alloy wheels (2WD), sport alloy wheels (4WD).			
Splash Pkg. 866A, regular cab	NC	NC	NC
AM/FM cassette, sliding rear window.			
Splash Pkg. 855A, SuperCab	NC	NC	NC
AM/FM cassette, sliding rear window, rear jump seat.			
Performance Pkg., 4WD SuperCab and 114-inch WB XLT and STX	541	460	476
4.0-liter engine, limited-slip rear axle, 265/75R15SL outline white letter all-terrain tires.			
Comfort Cab Pkg., XL SuperCab	NC	NC	NC
Color-keyed carpeting, 60/40 cloth split bench seat, upgraded door trim panels, full face steel wheels, 215/70R14 tires.			
Optional Payload Pkg. 2	59	50	52
2WD requires P215 tires and Handling Pkg. XLT also requires power steering.			
Handling Pkg., 2WD regular cab with			
2.3-liter engine and manual steering	116	99	102
2WD regualr cab with 2.3-liter and power steering	78	66	69
2WD regular cab with 3.0-liter engine	40	34	35

Top: Ranger has a well-designed interior. Bucket seats are optional. Middle: SuperCab models can be fitted with rear jump seats. Above: An XLT SuperCab.

Ford

	Retail Price	Dealer Invoice	Fair Price
SuperCab 2WD	NC	NC	NC

Includes front and rear stabilizer bars (std. SuperCab and regular cab with power steering), heavy duty front and rear shock absorbers (2WD only). 2WD requires P215 tires.

Power Window and Lock Group	$379	$322	$334

Requires power mirrors. Not available XL.

Power mirrors, XLT and STX	140	119	123
Cruise control and tilt steering column	395	336	348

Not available XL and with 2.3-liter engine and automatic transmission. Requires 3.73 rear axle with 2.3-liter engine and 5-speed. Requires power steering.

60/40 cloth split bench seat, XL regular cab	256	218	225
STX (credit)	(312)	(265)	(265)
XL SuperCab	NC	NC	NC

Credit when 60/40 cloth seats are substituted for std. cloth captains chairs on STX models.

Cloth sport bucket seats with floor console, XLT and Splash	361	307	318
STX base	49	42	43
STX with option pkg.	NC	NC	NC
Cloth captains chairs with floor console, XL and XLT SuperCab	312	265	275
Vinyl rear jump seats	226	192	199
Vinyl 60/40 split bench seat, XLT and Splash SuperCab	NC	NC	NC
Floor consolette, XL and STX	30	26	26

STX requires 60/40 split bench seat.

Chrome rear step bumper, XLT 2WD	99	84	87
Super engine cooling	55	47	48
High-capacity fuel tank	24	20	21

Not available with 108-inch wheel base.

Tachometer	55	47	48
Fog lights	185	157	163

4WD only. Not available with 2.3-liter engine, 235 or 265 tires.

Heavy duty battery	54	46	48
Engine block heater	30	26	26
Bodyside moldings, XLT and STX	121	103	106
Clearcoat paint, XL	84	71	74
Deluxe two-tone paint, XLT	277	235	244
XLT with option pkg.	234	199	206
Sliding rear window	113	96	99
Pivoting quarter windows, SuperCab	49	42	43
AM/FM radio, XL	177	150	156
XLT and Splash with option pkg. (credit)	(138)	(117)	(117)
AM/FM cassette, XL	315	268	277
XLT, STX and Splash	138	117	121
Premium AM/FM cassette, XLT, STX and Splash	212	180	187
XLT, STX and Splash with option pkg.	74	63	65

Requires cruise control and tilt steering column.

Premium AM/FM CD player, XLT, STX and Splash	507	431	446
with option pkgs.	370	315	326
Sport striping	100	85	88
delete from Sport Pkg., STX or Splash (credit)	(65)	(55)	(55)
Full face steel wheels, XL	101	86	89
Alloy wheels, XL	352	299	310
XL with Comfort Cab Pkg., XLT with 4-speed automatic, and STX	251	213	221
Tires: 215/70R14 tires, 2WD	96	82	84
225/70R14 outline white letter tires, 2WD	239	203	210
XL with 862A Sport Pkg. and Comfort Cab Pkg.	143	122	126
215/75R15 outline white letter all-terrain tires, 4WD	232	197	204
235/75R15 outline white letter all-terrain tires, 4WD	300	255	264
265/75R15 outline white letter all-terrain tires, 4WD	410	349	361
STX	178	151	157
XLT and STX with option pkg.	110	94	97

1995 Ford Windstar

1995 Ford Windstar

Windstar, Ford's first homegrown front-wheel-drive minivan goes on sale in March as an early 1995 model. It has a V-6 engine and dual air bags, seats seven, and targets the Dodge Grand Caravan in specifications, equipment, and price.

Windstar will be offered in passenger and cargo versions. It has some chassis components in common with the Ford Taurus, but Ford says its platform is not shared with any other Ford product. The company says Windstar meets all 1998 passenger-car safety standards.

Sales of the Windstar will overlap those of Ford's Aerostar minivan for about six months. The truck-based rear- and 4-wheel-drive Aerostar is to be retired at the end of the 1994 model year.

Body Styles/Chassis

Windstar comes in a single body length with a sliding right-side door and a one-piece rear liftgate without a separate-opening window.

The wheelbase of the new Ford is the longest of any minivan, at 120.7 inches. That's 1.4 inches longer than the wheelbase of the Grand Caravan—the stretched version of the best-selling Dodge minivan. Windstar's wheelbase is also 2 inches longer than the stretched version of the Aerostar, and 8.5 inches longer overall than the Nissan-developed front-drive minivan sold as the Nissan Quest and Mercury Villager.

At 201 inches, Windstar's body is 8.2 inches longer than the Grand Caravan's and about 10 longer than the Villager and the stretched Aerostar.

Compared to the Grand Caravan, virtually all of Windstar's additional body length is accounted for by the Ford's longer nose and bumpers. Thus, passenger-area dimensions for the Windstar and Grand Caravan are quite similar. Cargo volume for passenger models is similar as well: With all rear seats removed, Ford lists 144 cubic feet of cargo space, Dodge lists 141.3.

Windstar has a center high-mounted stoplamp and side door guard beams, as currently required by law. And Ford says it also meets 1995 federal roof-crush standards.

A 4-wheel anti-lock system on front-disc/rear-drum brakes is standard. The standard tires are size 205/70R15, with 215/70R15s on alloy wheels optional.

Ford

Passenger models will be offered in base GL and upper-level LX trim. The cargo van will come in a single trim level without rear or side glass. Windstar has an all-metal body, unlike the plastic-composite skin of General Motors' front-drive minivans.

Windstar's maximum payload rating is 1250 pounds, 750 less than Grand Caravan's.

Specifications

	4-door van
Wheelbase, in.	120.7
Overall length, in.	201.0
Overall width, in.	75.0
Overall height, in.	68.0
Turn diameter, ft.	40.7
Curb weight, lbs.	3800
Fuel capacity, gal.	20.0[1]

1. 25.0 gals. optional.

Passenger Area Dimensions

Seating capacity	7
Front head room, in.	39.3
Rear head room, in.	38.9
Front leg room, in.	40.7
Rear leg room, in.	39.2

Available Seating

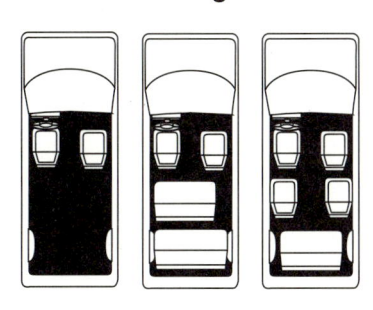

Cargo Dimensions and Payloads

Cargo area length, in.	93.0
Cargo area width, in.	60.3
Cargo area width between wheels, in.	48.5
Cargo area height, in.	49.2
Cargo vol., cu. ft.	144.0
Max. payload, lbs.	1250
Max. trailer weight, lbs.	2000

Engines

	ohv V-6
Size, liters/cu. in.	3.8/232
Horsepower @ rpm	155 @ 4000
Torque (lbs./ft.) @ rpm	220 @ 3000
Availability	S

EPA city/highway mpg

4-speed OD automatic	NA

Built in Canada.

KEY: Dimensions and capacities are supplied by the manufacturers. **Curb Weight:** base models, not including optional equipment. **Max. payload, lbs.** = gross amount; net payload may be lower due to optional equipment. **Engines: ohv** = overhead valve; **ohc** = overhead cam; **I** = inline cylinders; **V** = cylinders in V configuration; **flat** = horizontally opposed cylinders; **rpm** = revolutions per minute; **OD** = overdrive transmission; **S** = standard; **O** = optional; **NA** = not available.

Standard equipment, options, and prices unavailable at time of publication.

Powertrains

All Windstar models will be introduced with a 3.8-liter V-6 engine. It's the same basic V-6 used in the Taurus and Lincoln Continental, though in Windstar it is rated at 155 horsepower, closer to the 160 of the Lincoln than the 140 of the Taurus.

A 4-speed electronically controlled automatic is the sole transmission.

In the autumn of 1994, coinciding with the start of the official 1995 model year, a 147-horsepower 3.0-liter V-6 will become the standard engine for the Windstar GL. It also will use the 4-speed automatic. The 3.8-liter V-6 will remain standard on the LX.

Ford says it has no plans to offer a 4-wheel-drive version of the Windstar, though an optional traction-control system will eventually be available.

Standard towing capacity is 2000 pounds. A 3500-pound trailering package, matching that of the Grand Caravan, is to join Windstar's options list in the fall of 1994. The rear-drive Aerostar has a towing capacity of 4900 pounds.

Accommodations

Two front bucket seats, a 2-person middle bench seat, and a 3-place rear bench are standard on passenger models. Cargo vans come with two front buckets.

Optional in place of the middle bench are two middle bucket seats. Also optional are two child seats that fold out from the backrest of the middle bench. Similar to those in the Aerostar, the integrated child seats have 5-point safety harnesses and are designed for youngsters weighing between 20 and 60 pounds.

The standard analog gauges include a tachometer. The optional electronic instrumentation uses a digital speedometer and analog-style displays for other functions.

A center floor console, a compact disc player, and power swing-out rear quarter windows are among other options, as is a rear air-conditioning system that has roof-mounted vents. Ford says it has no plans to offer a power sliding door like the one optional on GM's Chevrolet Lumina Minivan, Pontiac Trans Sport, and Oldsmobile Silhouette.

Evaluation

We had not test driven a Windstar at presstime and so cannot comment on its performance. Based on a thorough examination of a production-ready model, however, we have the following observations.

Windstar's overall design seems as car-like as any minivan's, with particular credit due its low floor and wide doors, which allow passengers to step in and out with less effort than in any rival. However, getting into or out of Windstar's rearmost seat requires occupants to negotiate past a shoulder belt that's mounted on the roof and intended for use by the middle seat's right-side passenger.

Head and leg room in the front seats is excellent. Head room diminished noticeably in the rear seats of the LX model we examined. The rear cushions were quite high off the floor and the overhead air-conditioning ducts took up room within the headliner.

The rear seats remove without tools, though Ford admits they are quite heavy. The rearmost bench slides fore and aft on a 7-inch track to enlarge rear cargo space slightly or to provide a bit more leg room, and its seatback folds. But the seat itself does not tumble forward. Cargo room with all seats in place is comparable to that of the Grand Caravan, though the slope of Windstar's hatch is

CONSUMER GUIDE® 87

Ford • Geo

greater than that of the Grand Caravan, so load space above the beltline isn't as spacious in the Ford.

The dashboard uses a two-tier design similar to that in the Lincoln Mark VIII. All gauges are unobstructed and the radio and climate controls are close by on a center section of the dashboard that is canted toward the driver. A simple dash knob controls the headlamps and a steering-column stalk governs the front wipers.

Two cup holders pull out from the dash, and there are several molded-in beverage holders for the rear-seat positions. The front doors contain map pockets and the dashboard has a glove box and a pull-out bin near the floor. The optional center console is peppered with more bins and cubbies, but it obstructs movement from the front seats to the rear of the vehicle.

No sunroof is planned, but Windstar does offer convenient driver-operated power rear quarter windows that hinge open a few inches for added ventilation.

Ford had not announced prices at presstime but said Windstar would be priced to match the Grand Caravan, which would suggest a base price of about $18,000-$19,000 for the GL model and around $22,000-$23,000 for the LX. Ford said it expects to sell about 225,000 Windstars annually, with GL models accounting for 65 percent of the total.

Windstar has standard dual air bags. The minivan's overall size is similar to that of the Dodge Grand Caravan.

Geo Tracker

Geo Tracker convertible

Geo's pint-sized sport-utility vehicle gets a handful of equipment changes for 1994 and California models get their own engine.

Tracker is built in Canada from a Suzuki design and is sold by Chevrolet dealers with Geo-brand outlets. Suzuki markets its own version as the Sidekick (see separate report), but substitutes a 5-door model for Geo's 3-door hardtop.

Body Styles/Chassis

Tracker comes as a 2-door convertible or as a 3-door hardtop. The lineup consists of a base-level 2-wheel drive convertible, 4WD convertible, and 4WD hardtop. The 4WD models also are offered in upscale LSi guise.

Convertibles have a swing-out tailgate, hardtops a full-height rear door. Rear anti-lock brakes are standard on all, but they do not function in 4WD.

On the safety front, Tracker now comes with a center high-mounted stoplamp. The 4WD models now have all-season 205/75R15 tires as standard equipment instead of on/off-road tires of the same size. The optional aluminum wheels are of a new design.

Maximum payload capacity, 898 pounds, is found on the 2WD convertible.

Powertrains

All Trackers have a 1.6-liter 4-cylinder engine. Models sold in all states except California and New York are rated at 80 horsepower. California and New York models now use a version with four valves per cylinder rated at 95 horsepower. The 16-valve version is the same engine Suzuki uses in its 5-door Sidekick.

Both Tracker engines come standard with a 5-speed manual transmission, with a 3-speed automatic optional.

Tracker's 4WD is an on-demand, part-time system (not for use on dry pavement) with a floor-mounted transfer-case lever. Base-model 4x4s have manual-locking front hubs; LSi versions add automatic-locking hubs. On both versions, the vehicle must be stopped to engage the hubs and backed up to disengage them. Once the automatic hubs are locked, you can shift from 2WD to 4WD High at any speed so long as the front wheels are pointed straight ahead. Geo warns against running in 2WD with the manual hubs locked.

Maximum trailer towing capacity is 1000 pounds.

Geo

Accommodations

All Trackers come with seats for four except the base convertible, where the folding 2-place rear bench is optional. High-back reclining front buckets are standard on base models. LSi versions get low-back seats with adjustable "see-through" head restraints.

Changes for '94 include new interior fabrics, the addition of two cup holders and storage space in a new center console, and a compact disc/cassette player audio system as a new option.

Evaluation

Tracker is more modern and refined than the paramilitary Jeep Wrangler, but we still don't recommend the Geo—or any of its ilk—if you do much highway driving or long-distance commuting. They're better viewed as urban runabouts or low-cost off-road vehicles. Sure, they represent a cheap way to get into 4WD, but you pay the price in inhospitable road manners.

With manual transmission, Tracker has adequate power, but with automatic, staying abreast of any but the slowest traffic requires you to regularly floor the throttle. Tracker is pretty thrifty for a sport-utility, however: We averaged 24 mpg with a 4WD ragtop and 28.6 mpg with a 2WD version.

The 2WD model has a softer suspension than the 4WD models, so potholes aren't as jarring, but Tracker's ride is still quite choppy. In turns, lots of body lean brought on by the tall, narrow body encourages low speeds.

Braking is okay, with acceptably short stopping distances. But models we tested showed a tendency to sudden wheel-locking that can be a real problem in panic situations, let alone on wet surfaces.

Instrumentation is clear, and controls fall readily to hand. Larger drivers are squeezed by a shortage of rearward seat travel and tight shoulder room on the left. Cargo space behind the rear seat is minuscule, though it's ample with the seat folded forward.

One example of the compromise demanded by vehicles like this is that you have to unsnap the rear curtain on the convertible Tracker to open the tailgate. And noise levels from engine, road, and wind are very high on all models.

Tracker convertibles handily outsell the hardtop, but the convertible's roof is one of its least endearing features: flimsy yet over-complicated, with numerous snaps and zippers, plug-in rear top bows that bend too easily, and plastic windows prone to early yellowing.

If you're determined to spend your money on this sort of vehicle, we suggest you also look at Isuzu's Amigo. It's larger and costlier than Tracker, but since it's based on a pickup truck, it feels more substantial.

Specifications

	2-door wagon
Wheelbase, in.	86.6
Overall length, in.	142.5
Overall width, in.	64.2
Overall height, in.	65.6
Turn diameter, ft.	32.2
Curb weight, lbs.	2365
Fuel capacity, gal.	11.1

Passenger Area Dimensions

Seating capacity	4
Front head room, in.	39.5
Rear head room, in.	38.3
Front leg room, in.	42.1
Rear leg room, in.	31.6

Cargo Dimensions and Payloads

Cargo area length, in.	31.0
Cargo area width, in.	50.2
Cargo area width between wheels, in.	41.2
Cargo area height, in.	39.8
Cargo vol., cu. ft.	8.9
Max. payload, lbs.	898
Max. trailer weight, lbs.	1000

Engines

	ohc I-4	ohc I-4
Size, liters/cu. in.	1.6/97	1.6/97
Horsepower @ rpm	80 @ 5400	95 @ 5600
Torque (lbs./ft.) @ rpm	94 @ 3000	98 @ 4000
Availability	S	S[1]

EPA city/highway mpg

5-speed OD manual	25/27	24/26
3-speed automatic	23/24	23/24

1. California and New York vehicles.

Built in Canada.

KEY: Dimensions and capacities are supplied by the manufacturers. **Curb Weight:** base models, not including optional equipment. **Max. payload, lbs.** = gross amount; net payload may be lower due to optional equipment. **Engines: ohv** = overhead valve; **ohc** = overhead cam; **I** = inline cylinders; **V** = cylinders in V configuration; **flat** = horizontally opposed cylinders; **rpm** = revolutions per minute; **OD** = overdrive transmission; **S** = standard; **O** = optional; **NA** = not available.

Prices

Geo Tracker	Retail Price	Dealer Invoice	Fair Price
2-door convertible, 2WD	$11015	*	*
3-door wagon, 4WD	12445	*	*
LSi 3-door wagon, 4WD	13915	*	*
2-door convertible, 4WD	12285	*	*
LSi 2-door convertible, 4WD	13650	*	*
Destination charge	300	300	300

Standard Equipment:

1.6-liter 4-cylinder engine, 5-speed manual transmission, anti-lock rear brakes, rear defogger (wagon only), cloth/vinyl reclining front bucket seats, folding rear bench seat (4WD), center console with storage tray and cup holders, tachometer (4WD), trip odometer, dual mirrors, intermittent wipers, full-size lockable spare tire, spare tire cover, front and rear tow hooks, 195/75R15 tires, (205/75R15 tires 4WD). **LSi** adds: automatic locking front hubs, power steering, AM/FM radio, floormats, tinted glass, upgraded cloth/vinyl upholstery and door trim, adjustable rear bucket seats, rear wiper/washer (wagon only), bodyside moldings, styled steel wheels.

Optional Equipment:

3-speed automatic transmission	595	530	538
Air conditioning	745	663	674
Tilt steering wheel	115	102	104
UL1 AM/FM radio	306	272	277
Includes seek and scan, digital clock, and four speakers.			
UL0 AM/FM cassette player	501	446	453
LSi	195	174	176
Includes seek and scan, theft deterrent, tone select, digital clock, and four speakers.			
UP0 AM/FM radio with CD and cassette player, LSi	897	798	812
LSi	591	526	535
Includes seek and scan, theft deterrent, tone select, digital clock, and four speakers.			

*Some dealer invoice and fair prices not available at time of publication.

Geo • GMC

	Retail Price	Dealer Invoice	Fair Price
Convertible 2WD Preferred Group 2	$581	$517	$526
UL1 AM/FM radio, power steering.			
With UL0 AM/FM cassette, add	195	174	176
With UP0 AM/FM radio, CD, and cassette player, add	591	526	535
Base and convertible 4WD Preferred Equipment Group 2	581	517	526
UL1 AM/FM radio, power steering.			
With UL0 AM/FM cassette, add	195	174	176
With UP0 AM/FM radio, CD, and cassette player, add	591	526	535
Rear seat, 2WD	445	396	403
Transfer case shield, 4WD	75	67	68
Alloy wheels	335	298	303
Floormats, base	28	25	25
Bodyside moldings, base wagon	59	53	53
Convertibles	85	76	77

Top: Tracker's dashboard is convenient, but the driving position is cramped. Above: A Tracker 3-door LSi hardtop.

GMC Jimmy

GMC Jimmy SLT 5-door

GMC's compact sport-utility vehicle will be redesigned as an early 1995 model by next summer, so the addition of side door guard beams and a center high-mounted stoplamp are among the few changes to the '94 version. GMC, however, has discontinued the high-performance Typhoon variant of the Jimmy, which had a turbocharged engine and permanently engaged 4-wheel drive.

Jimmy is mechanically identical to the Chevrolet S10 Blazer and similar to the Oldsmobile Bravada (see separate reports), but Jimmy's base prices are slightly higher than S10's to reflect some standard equipment differences, such as its FM radio. Option-package names differ, but their prices are the same as the S10's.

Body Styles/Chassis

Jimmy comes as a 3-door wagon and as a 5-door variant with a 6.5-inch longer wheelbase and body. The fold-down tailgate is topped with a separate swing-up window.

Four-wheel anti-lock brakes that work in both 2- and 4-wheel drive are standard on all models.

Three-door models are available in entry-level SL trim, and both body styles can be ordered in SLS, SLE, and SLT guise.

Maximum payload is 1164 pounds on 3-door Jimmys and 1453 on 5-doors.

Powertrains

A 4.3-liter V-6 is Jimmy's only engine. It's rated at 165 horsepower when mated to the standard 5-speed manual transmission. An "enhanced" variant of the 4.3 with 200 horsepower comes only in a package that includes a 4-speed electronic automatic.

Jimmy's available 4WD system is General Motors' Insta-Trac, an on-demand, a part-time setup not for use on dry pavement. It has automatic locking front hubs and full shift-on-the-fly. An electronic transfer case activated by a dashboard switch is standard. A floor-mounted transfer-case operated by a lever is a credit option. (On Chevy's S10 Blazer, the floor-mounted lever is standard and the electronic transfer case is optional.)

Maximum towing capacity is 5500 pounds on both 3- and 5-door Jimmys.

90 CONSUMER GUIDE®

GMC

Accommodations

A 3-place front bench seat is now standard on 5-door Jimmys. Front bucket seats are optional on the 5-door models and standard on the 3-door models.

Five-door models come standard with a 3-place folding rear bench seat; a 2-place folding rear bench seat is optional on 3-doors.

Evaluation

Now that it's lost the Typhoon, which was a unique piece in the sport-utility field, Jimmy is again a spitting image of the S10 Blazer, so it has the same plus and minus points.

Jimmy doesn't match the more modern Ford Explorer and Jeep Grand Cherokee in key areas such as overall room and ride quality. One key reason is that the basic design for the GM compact sport-utilities dates to the 1983 model year, while the Explorer was introduced for 1991 and the Grand Cherokee for 1992.

The Jeep is the only one of this group with a standard driver-side air bag, and the only one to offer a V-8 engine or permanently engaged 4WD. (The 1995 Jimmy is to get a driver-side air bag, and the current Oldsmobile Bravada, a luxury version of the 5-door S10/Jimmy, comes with permanent 4WD.)

Jimmy's attributes include 4-wheel anti-lock brakes, a convenient 4WD system with full shift-on-the-fly, and strong engines. In addition, GMC dealers should be discounting heavily because of the stiff competition from Ford and Jeep.

Specifications

	3-door wagon	5-door wagon
Wheelbase, in.	100.5	107.0
Overall length, in.	170.3	176.8
Overall width, in.	65.4	65.4
Overall height, in.	64.3	64.3
Turn diameter, ft.	34.6	35.4
Curb weight, lbs.	3536	3776
Fuel capacity, gal.	20.0	20.0

Passenger Area Dimensions

Seating capacity	4	6
Front head room, in.	39.1	39.1
Rear head room, in.	38.7	38.8
Front leg room, in.	42.5	42.5
Rear leg room, in.	35.5	36.5

Cargo Dimensions and Payloads

Cargo area length, in.	68.6	76.1
Cargo area width, in.	50.0	52.5
Cargo area width between wheels, in.	38.4	38.4
Cargo area height, in.	39.1	39.1
Cargo vol., cu. ft.	67.3	74.3
Max. payload, lbs.	1164	1453
Max. trailer weight, lbs.	5500	5500

Engines

	ohv V-6	ohv V-6
Size, liters/cu. in.	4.3/262	4.3/262
Horsepower @ rpm	165 @ 4000	200 @ 4500
Torque (lbs./ft.) @ rpm	235 @ 2400	260 @ 3600
Availability	S	O

EPA city/highway mpg

5-speed OD manual	16/21	
4-speed OD automatic		16/21

Built in Pontiac, Mich. and Moraine, Ohio.

KEY: Dimensions and capacities are supplied by the manufacturers. **Curb Weight:** base models, not including optional equipment. **Max. payload, lbs.** = gross amount; net payload may be lower due to optional equipment. **Engines: ohv** = overhead valve; **ohc** = overhead cam; **I** = inline cylinders; **V** = cylinders in V configuration; **flat** = horizontally opposed cylinders; **rpm** = revolutions per minute; **OD** = overdrive transmission; **S** = standard; **O** = optional; **NA** = not available.

Prices

GMC Jimmy	Retail Price	Dealer Invoice	Fair Price
3-door wagon, 2WD	$15639	$14153	$14353
3-door wagon, 4WD	17558	15890	16090
5-door wagon, 2WD	16941	15332	15782
5-door wagon, 4WD	19298	17465	17915
Destination charge	475	475	475

Standard Equipment:

3-door: 4.3-liter V-6 engine, 5-speed manual transmission, part-time 4WD with electronic transfer case (4WD), 4-wheel anti-lock brakes, power steering, solar-control tinted glass, coolant temperature and oil pressure gauges, voltmeter, trip odometer, AM/FM radio, dual outside mirrors, front highback reclining buckets seats, door map pockets, 205/75R15 tires, full-size spare tire, front tow hooks, wheel trim rings (4WD). **5-door** adds: cloth 60/40 reclining split bench seat with folding center armrest, folding rear 3-passenger bench seat (4WD), mirrors, illuminated entry, reading lights, lighted visor mirrors, seat back convenience net, cupholders, floormats, bodyside moldings, wheel trim rings.

Option Pkgs., 3-door:

SL Pkg. 2	684	588	609

AM/FM cassette, cruise control, tilt steering wheel, folding rear 3-passenger bench seat, deep-tinted glass with light-tinted rear window, luggage carrier.

SLS Pkg. 2, 2WD	1310	1127	1166
4WD	1278	1099	1137

SL Pkg. 2 contents plus SLS Sport.

Decor Pkg. SLE Pkg. 2	1412	1214	1257

SL Pkg. 2 contents plus SLE Comfort Decor Pkg.

SLS Pkg. 3	2708	2329	2410

SLS Sport Decor Pkg. plus air conditioning, AM/FM cassette, cruise control, tilt steering wheel, power door locks and windows, rear wiper/washer, alloy wheels, folding rear 3-passenger bench seat, deep-tinted glass, luggage carrier.

SLE Pkg 3	2662	2289	2369

SLE Comfort Decor Pkg. plus air conditioning, AM/FM cassette, cruise control, tilt steering wheel, power door locks and windows, rear wiper/washer, alloy wheels, folding rear 3-passenger bench seat, deep-tinted glass, luggage carrier.

GMC Jimmy 3-door

GMC

	Retail Price	Dealer Invoice	Fair Price
SLT Pkg. 4, 2WD	$4216	$3626	$3752
4WD	4441	3819	3952

SLT Touring Decor Pkg. plus air conditioning, cruise control, tilt steering wheel, AM/FM cassette with equalizer, power mirrors, rear defogger, power tailgate release, rear wiper/washer, deep-tinted glass, luggage carrier.

Option Pkgs., 5-door:

	Retail Price	Dealer Invoice	Fair Price
SLE Pkg. 2, 2WD	410	353	365
4WD (credit)	(25)	(22)	(22)

Cruise control, tilt steering wheel, AM/FM cassette, folding rear 3-passenger bench seat (std. 4WD), deep-tinted glass with light-tinted rear window, luggage carrier.

SLE Pkg. 3, 2WD	2194	1887	1953
4WD	1791	1540	1594

SLE Pkg. 2 plus air conditioning, power door locks and windows, rear wiper/washer, rear defogger, power tailgate release, cloth reclining bucket seat and floor console (60/40 split bench seat may be substituted at no additional cost), alloy wheels.

SLS Pkg. 3, 2WD	2248	1933	2001
4WD	1845	1587	1642

SLS Pkg. 2 plus air conditioning, power door locks and windows, rear wiper/washer, rear defogger, power tailgate release, cloth reclining bucket seat and floor console (60/40 split bench seat may be substituted at no additional cost), alloy wheels.

SLT Pkg. 4, 2WD	3735	3212	3324
4WD	3557	3059	3166

SLT Touring Decor Pkg. plus air conditioning, cruise control, tilt steering wheel, AM/FM cassette with equalizer, power mirrors, rear defogger, power tailgate release, rear wiper/washer, deep-tinted glass, luggage carrier.

Individual Options:

	Retail Price	Dealer Invoice	Fair Price
Enhanced Powertrain Pkg.	1160	998	1032

Includes high output 4.3-liter V-6, 4-speed automatic transmission, extra capacity cooling.

Optional axle ratio	(NC)	(NC)	(NC)
Locking differential	252	217	224
Manual transfer case, 4WD (credit)	(123)	(106)	(106)

Replaces standard electronic push button shift with manual floor mounted shift.

SLE Comfort Decor Pkg. (std. 5-door), 3-door 2WD	900	774	801
4WD	868	746	773

Reclining bucket seats, cloth upholstery, upgraded door trim, chrome grille, bodyside and wheel opening moldings, floor console, illuminated entry, lighted visor mirrors, reading lights, floormats, rally wheels (2WD), wheel trim rings (4WD).

SLS Sport Decor Pkg., 3-door	1202	1034	1070

Reclining bucket seats, floor console, leather-wrapped steering wheel, illuminated entry, lighted visor mirrors, reading lights, convenience net (2-door), body-color bumpers and grille, upgraded door trim, bodyside and wheel opening moldings, floormats, alloy wheels.

SLS Sport Decor Pkg. 5-door 2WD	302	260	269
5-door 2WD with bucket seats	513	441	457
5-door 4WD	334	287	297
5-door 4WD with bucket seats	545	469	485

Leather-wrapped steering wheel, body-color bumpers, grille, and wheel opening moldings, alloy wheels.

SLT Touring Decor Pkg., 3-door 2WD	3325	2860	2959
3-door 4WD	3550	3053	3160
5-door 2WD	2844	2446	2531
5-door 4WD	2666	2293	2373

Reclining leather buckets seat with driver- and passenger-side lumbar adjustment, 6-way power driver's seat, folding rear 3-passenger bench seat, floor and overhead consoles, power windows and door locks, remote keyless entry system, illuminated entry, reading lights, lighted visor mirrors, leather-wrapped steering wheel, body-color bumpers, bodyside and wheel opening moldings, upgraded door trim, conventional 2-tone paint, convenience net (3-door), floormats, 205/75R15 all-season tires, alloy wheels. 4WD adds: Bilstein shocks, 235/75R15 all-season tires.

Air conditioning	780	671	694
Folding rear seat, 3-door	409	352	364
Cloth folding rear seat, 3-door and 5-door 2WD	$435	$374	$387
Cloth bucket seats, 3-door	76	65	68
5-door	211	181	188
6-way power driver's seat and driver/passenger power lumbar support	290	249	258

Requires SLE or SLS Decor Pkgs., power windows and locks, reclining bucket seats.

Floor console	145	125	129

Requires reclining bucket seats.

Overhead console	83	71	74

Includes reading lights and storage compartments. Requires SLE or SLS decor Pkgs., bucket seats.

Heavy duty battery	56	48	50
Spare wheel and tire carrier	159	137	142
Cold Climate Pkg., 3-door SLE, SLS or SLT 3-door,	179	154	159
5-door	109	94	97
Convenience Pkg. ZQ3	383	329	341

Cruise control, tilt steering wheel.

Convenience Pkg. ZM8	197	169	175

Remote tailgate release, rear defogger.

Convenience Pkg. ZQ2, 3-door	367	316	327
5-door	542	466	482

Power windows and locks.

Deep-tinted glass	225	194	200
with light-tinted rear window	144	124	128

Requires Convenience Pkg. ZM8.

Air deflector with fog lamps, 2WD	115	99	102
Rear wiper/washer	125	108	111

Requires ZM8 Convenience Pkg.

Sliding side window (2WD only)	257	221	229
Electronic instrumentation	195	168	174
Remote keyless entry	135	116	120

Requires ZQ2 and ZM8 Convenience Pkgs., bucket seats, floor console.

Luggage carrier	126	108	112
Power mirrors	83	71	74
Wheel opening moldings	43	37	38
Special 2-tone paint	172	148	153
Conventional 2-tone paint (NA SL or SLS decor)	172	148	153
AM/FM cassette	122	105	109
AM/FM cassette with equalizer	272	234	242
AM/FM with CD player	406	349	361
AM/FM radio delete (credit)	(226)	(194)	(194)
AM radio (credit)	(131)	(113)	(113)

Credit when AM radio is substituted for standard AM/FM radio.

Shield Pkg., 4WD (NA SLT Decor Pkg.)	75	65	67
Heavy duty shock absorbers (NA SLT Decor Pkg.)	40	34	36
Heavy duty front springs, 4WD	63	54	56
Softride Suspension, 5-door	235	202	209
with 235/75R15 WL tires	358	308	319
Off-Road Suspension Pkg., 3-door, 4WD	122	105	109

Bilstein gas shock absorbers, larger torsion bar, jounce bumpers, stabilizer bar, larger body mounted tow hooks. NA SLT.

Heavy duty trailering equipment	345	297	307
with high output 4.3-liter V-6 engine	210	181	187
Light duty trailering equipment	300	258	267
with high output 4.3-liter V-6 engine	109	94	97
205/75R15 on/off-road WL tires	170	146	151
205/75R15 all-season WL tires	121	104	108
235/75R15 all-season tires	153	132	136
235/75R15 all-season WL tires, 4WD	286	246	255
with SLT	133	114	118
235/75R15 on/off-road WL tires, 4WD	335	288	298

WL denotes white letter; OWL denotes outline white letter.

Alloy wheels	340	292	303
with SLE	284	244	253
Wheel trim rings, 3-door	60	52	53
Rally wheels, 2WD	92	79	82
Body striping	55	47	49

GMC Rally/Vandura

GMC Rally STX

Topping the changes to GMC's full-size passenger van is a driver-side air bag as standard on all models with a gross vehicle weight rating (GVWR) below 8500 pounds. All models also get side guard beams in the front doors and a center high-mounted stoplamp in the roof.

Chevrolet dealers sell similar models under the Sportvan and Van labels (see separate report).

Body Styles/Chassis

The passenger version is again called the Rally and the cargo model is the Vandura.

GMC, like Chevrolet, offers its big vans in three wheelbases and body lengths, though both divisions no longer offer their passenger models in the shortest wheelbase or body length.

Thus, the Vandura starts off with a 110-inch wheelbase and a 180.1-inch-long body. Rally models no longer are offered in this size.

Both Rally and Vandura come in a 125-inch wheelbase with a 204.1-inch body, and in a 146-inch wheelbase with a 223.2-inch body.

Series numbers correspond to general payload categories: 1500 (half-ton); 2500 (three-quarter ton); and 3500 (one-ton). In addition, there is a Heavy Duty 3500 with a gross vehicle weight of 8600 pounds.

The 110-inch wheelbase model comes in the 1500 series only. The 125-inch wheelbase version comes in all three weight classes. The extended-length model is a 3500 only.

All have dual swing-out rear doors and a choice of a single sliding side door or dual swing-open side doors. Passenger models have windows all around; cargo models come without side or rear glass, though a variety of window options is offered. All glass comes with Solar-Ray tinting.

Four-wheel anti-lock brakes (ABS) are standard on all models.

Maximum payload for Rally models is 2142 on the 2500 and 3951 on the 3500. The slightly higher payloads listed in the specification chart are for Vandura cargo models.

Powertrains

Engine choices mirror those of the Chevrolet vans.

A 155-horsepower 4.3-liter V-6 is standard on all models except the Rally 3500 and the long-wheelbase Vandura 3500.

A 170-horsepower 5.0-liter V-8 is optional on Rally 2500s and on Vandura 1500 and 2500 models.

Specifications	5-door van	5-door van	5-door van
Wheelbase, in.	110.0	125.0	146.0
Overall length, in.	180.1	204.1	223.2
Overall width, in.	79.1	79.5	79.5
Overall height, in.	79.4	79.5	82.3
Turn diameter, ft.	41.3	46.0	54.0
Curb weight, lbs.	3938	4093	4979
Fuel capacity, gal.	22.0	33.0	33.0

Passenger Area Dimensions

Seating capacity	2	12	15
Front head room, in.	40.8	40.8	40.8
Rear head room, in.	40.9	40.9	40.9
Front leg room, in.	39.5	39.5	39.5
Rear leg room, in.	37.2	37.2	37.2

Available Seating

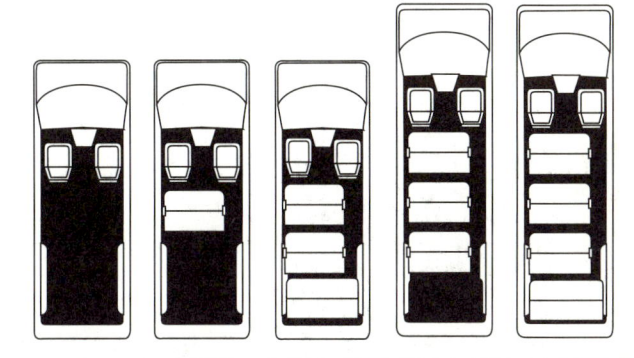

Cargo Dimensions and Payloads

Cargo area length, in.	102.5	126.3	147.5
Cargo area width, in.	70.8	70.8	70.8
Cargo area width between wheels, in.	53.5	53.5	53.5
Cargo area height, in.	49.2	49.2	49.2
Cargo vol., cu. ft.	207.0	260.0	306.0
Max. payload, lbs.	2142	4182	4288
Max. trailer weight, lbs.	6000	10,000	10,000

Engines	ohv V-6	ohv V-8	ohv V-8	ohv V-8	Diesel ohv V-8
Size, liters/cu. in.	4.3/262	5.0/305	5.7/350	7.4/454	6.5/400
Horsepower @ rpm	155 @ 4000	170 @ 4000	195 @ 4000	230 @ 3600	155 @ 3600
Torque (lbs./ft.) @ rpm	230 @ 2000	265 @ 2400	290 @ 2400	385 @ 1600	275 @ 1700
Availability	S	O	O	O[1]	O
EPA city/highway mpg 4-speed OD automatic	15/18	13/18	13/17	NA	16/20

1. Standard, 3500 model.

Built in Flint, Mich.

KEY: Dimensions and capacities are supplied by the manufacturers. **Curb Weight:** base models, not including optional equipment. **Max. payload, lbs.** = gross amount; net payload may be lower due to optional equipment. **Engines: ohv** = overhead valve; **ohc** = overhead cam; **I** = inline cylinders; **V** = cylinders in V configuration; **flat** = horizontally opposed cylinders; **rpm** = revolutions per minute; **OD** = overdrive transmission; **S** = standard; **O** = optional; **NA** = not available.

GMC

A 195-horsepower 5.7-liter V-8 is standard on both Rally 3500s and on long-wheelbase Vandura 3500s. The 5.7 is optional the Rally 2500 and on Vandura 2500s and 3500s with the 125-inch wheelbase. (Chevrolet lists this same engine at 200 horsepower.)

A 230-horsepower 7.4-liter V-8 is optional on 3500-series versions of both the Rally and Vandura.

A 155-horsepower 6.5-liter diesel V-8 also is optional on all Rally models and on all Vandura except the 1500. This is a naturally aspirated engine that replaces a 145-horsepower 6.2-liter turbocharged diesel V-8 in the engine lineup.

A 4-speed overdrive automatic is the only transmission. It has electronic shift controls and can be locked in second gear for better traction in start-ups on slippery surfaces. An interlock prevents shifting from park without the brake pedal applied.

Towing ceilings are 6000 pounds for 1500s; 7000 pounds for 2500s; and 10,000 pounds for 3500s.

Accommodations

Rallys come in base or STX decor; cargo vans are offered in a single trim level.

On 124-inch wheelbase Rallys, seats for 8 are standard, with optional seating for up to 12. Twelve-person seating is standard on the extended Rally 3500, which can be outfitted to accommodate up to 15 passengers.

Cargo models come with a driver's seat standard; an auxiliary front seat is optional.

The air bag is installed on models with GVWRs below 8500 pounds, which means the safety device is in all Rally and Vandura models except the diesel-engine 3500s and the 146-inch wheelbase models.

See the report on the Chevrolet Sportvan and Van for our evaluation of the GMC Rally and Vandura.

Prices

GMC Rally 2500	Retail Price	Dealer Invoice	Fair Price
125-inch wheelbase	$19086	$16700	$17100
Destination charge	580	580	580

Standard Equipment:

4.3-liter V-6 engine, 4-speed automatic transmission, anti-lock brakes, driver-side air bag, power steering, vinyl front bucket seats, 3-passenger middle bench seat, 60/40 swing-out side doors (sliding side door may be substituted at no charge), intermittent wipers, Solar-Ray glass, swing-out front quarter and rear door windows, chrome bumpers, trip odometer, dual stainless steel outside mirrors, black rubber floor mat, AM/FM radio, digital clock, front stabilizer bar, 225/75R15 tires.

Optional Equipment:

5.0-liter V-8 engine	575	495	512
5.7-liter V-8 engine	865	744	770
6.5-liter diesel V-8 engine	2870	2468	2554
Optional axle ratio	44	38	39
Locking differential	252	217	224
Front air conditioning	975	839	868
Front & rear air conditioning	1574	1354	1401
Rear heater	205	176	182
STX Decor Pkg.	838	721	746

Black bodyside moldings, chrome wheel openings, interior trim moldings, deluxe front appearance, carpeting, floormats, front seat storage compartments, spare tire cover, passenger-side visor mirror, vinyl or cloth upholstery.

Marketing Option Pkg. 2	1083	931	964
with STX Decor Pkg.	1921	1652	1710

Front air conditioning, cruise control, tilt steering column.

	Retail Price	Dealer Invoice	Fair Price
Marketing Option Pkg. 3	$1704	$1465	$1517

Pkg. 2 plus STX Decor Pkg., cassette player, deep-tinted glass, auxiliary lighting.

Marketing Option Pkg. 4	2496	2147	2221

Pkg. 3 plus power mirrors, power antenna, remote keyless entry system, power windows and door locks.

Cold Climate Pkg.	48	41	43

Engine block heater.

ZQ2 Convenience Group	434	373	386

Power windows and door locks.

ZQ3 Convenience Group	383	329	341

Cruise control and tilt steering column.

6875 lbs. GVWR, with 5.7-liter engine	319	274	284
with 6.5-liter diesel	NC	NC	NC
Heavy Duty Trailering Special Equipment	508	437	452
with 6.5-liter diesel engine	310	267	276

Trailer hitch, 7-wire harness.

Light Duty Trailering Special Equipment	132	114	117

Trailer hitch, 5-wire harness.

Rear defogger	95	82	85

Includes fixed rear door glass.

Heavy duty cooling system	198	170	176

Engine oil cooler, transmission oil cooler, heavy duty radiator.

Power locks	223	192	198
Power mirrors	98	84	87

Requires ZQ2 Convenience Pkg.

Power antenna	85	73	76
Deep-tinted Solar-Ray glass	380	327	338
Auxiliary lighting	156	134	139

Reading, stepwell and underhood lights, front and rear dome lights.

Lighted visor mirrors	75	65	67

Requires STX Decor Pkg.

Two-tone paint	269	231	239
with STX Decor Pkg.	137	118	122

Includes bodyside moldings.

AM/FM cassette	122	105	109
AM/FM cassette with equalizer	272	234	242
AM/FM CD player	396	341	352
AM radio (credit)	(141)	(121)	(121)

Credit when AM radio is substituted for std. AM/FM radio.

Radio delete (credit)	(236)	(203)	(203)
Remote keyless entry system	175	151	156

Includes headlamp delay. Requires ZQ2 Convenience Pkg. and auxiliary lighting.

Cloth reclining front seats	402	346	358

Requires STX Decor Pkg.

Rear seat delete (credit)	(371)	(319)	(319)
Leather-wrapped steering wheel	60	52	53
Rally wheels	121	104	108
Alloy wheels	331	285	295
225/75R15 spare tire	137	118	122
225/75R15 white wall tires, each axle	36	31	32
spare tire	155	133	138
225/75R15 white letter tires, each axle	50	43	45
spare tire	161	138	143
235/75R15 tires, each axle	NC	NC	NC
spare tire	151	130	134

GMC Rally 3500	Retail Price	Dealer Invoice	Fair Price
Base, 125-inch wheelbase	$20370	$17824	18174
Extended, 146-inch wheelbase	21526	18835	19185
Destination charge	580	580	580

Standard Equipment:

5.7-liter V-8 engine, 4-speed heavy duty automatic transmission, anti-lock brakes, driver-side air bag, power steering, vinyl front bucket seats, 3-passenger middle bench seat, 4-passenger rear bench seat (extended), 60/40 swing-out side doors (sliding side door may be substituted at no charge), intermittent wipers, Solar-Ray glass, swing-out front quarter and rear door windows, chrome bumpers, trip odometer, dual stainless steel outside mir-

GMC

rors, black rubber floor mat, AM/FM radio, digital clock, front stabilizer bar, LT225/75R16D tires (base), LT225/75R16E tires (extended).

Optional Equipment:

	Retail Price	Dealer Invoice	Fair Price
7.4-liter V-8 engine	$605	$520	$538
6.5-liter diesel V-8 engine	1655	1423	1473
Optional axle ratio	44	38	39
Locking differential	252	217	224
Front air conditioning	975	839	868
Front & rear air conditioning	1574	1354	1401
Rear heater	205	176	182
STX Decor Pkg.	838	721	746

Black bodyside moldings, chrome wheel openings, interior trim moldings, deluxe front appearance, carpeting, floormats, front seat storage compartments, spare tire cover, passenger-side visor mirror, vinyl or cloth upholstery.

Marketing Option Pkg. 2	1083	931	964
with STX Decor Pkg.	1921	1652	1710

Front air conditioning, cruise control, tilt steering column.

Marketing Option Pkg. 3	1704	1465	1517

Pkg. 2 plus STX Decor Pkg., cassette player, deep-tinted glass, auxiliary lighting.

Marketing Option Pkg. 4	2496	2147	2221

Pkg. 3 plus power mirrors, power antenna, remote keyless entry system, power windows and door locks.

Cold Climate Pkg.	48	41	43

Engine block heater.

ZQ2 Convenience Group	434	373	386

Power windows and door locks.

ZQ3 Convenience Group	383	329	341

Cruise control and tilt steering column.

8600 lbs. GVWR, base	251	216	223
9200 lbs. GVWR, base	371	319	330
extended	240	206	214
Heavy Duty Trailering Special Equipment	508	437	452
with 7.4-liter or 6.2-liter diesel engine	310	267	276

Trailer hitch, 7-wire harness.

Light Duty Trailering Special Equipment	132	114	117

Trailer hitch, 5-wire harness.

Rear defogger	95	82	85

Includes fixed rear door glass.

Heavy duty cooling system	198	170	176

Engine oil cooler, transmission oil cooler, heavy duty radiator.

Power locks	223	192	198
Power mirrors	98	84	87

Requires ZQ2 Convenience Pkg.

Power antenna	85	73	76
Deep-tinted Solar-Ray glass	380	327	338
Auxiliary lighting	156	134	139

Reading, stepwell and underhood lights, front and rear dome lights.

Lighted visor mirrors	75	65	67

Requires STX Decor Pkg.

Two-tone paint	269	231	239
with STX Decor Pkg.	137	118	122

Includes bodyside moldings.

AM/FM cassette	122	105	109
AM/FM cassette with equalizer	272	234	242
AM/FM CD player	396	341	352
Radio delete (credit)	(236)	(203)	(203)
Remote keyless entry system	175	151	156

Includes headlamp delay. Requires ZQ2 Convenience Pkg. and auxiliary lighting.

Cloth reclining front seats	402	346	358

Requires STX Decor Pkg.

15-passenger seating, extended	371	319	330

Includes additional 4-passenger bench seat.

8-passenger seating (rear seat delete for credit)	(371)	(319)	(319)
Leather-wrapped steering wheel	60	52	53
Bright full wheel covers	42	36	37
LT225/75R16D spare tire, base	249	214	222
LT225/75R16E tires, each axle	34	29	30
spare tire	224	193	199

GMC Vandura G1500

	Retail Price	Dealer Invoice	Fair Price
110-inch wheelbase	$16006	$14005	$14355
125-inch wheelbase	16190	14166	14516
Destination charge	580	580	580

Standard Equipment:

4.3-liter V-6 engine, 4-speed automatic transmission, anti-lock brakes, driver-side air bag, power steering, vinyl bucket driver's seat, trip odometer, storage box, Solar-Ray glass, intermittent wipers, dual stainless steel outside mirrors, AM radio, digital clock, 60/40 hinged swingout side doors (sliding side door may be substituted at no charge), painted bumpers, 215/75R15 tires.

Optional Equipment:

5.0-liter V-8 engine	575	495	512
Front air conditioning	975	839	868
Front and rear air conditioning	1574	1354	1401
with RV Conversion Group	599	515	533
Rear heater	205	176	182
Optional axle ratio	NC	NC	NC
Locking differential	252	217	224
Marketing Option Pkg. 2	1162	999	1034

Front air conditioning, auxiliary front seat.

Marketing Option Pkg. 3	1308	1125	1164

Pkg. 2 plus Fixed Glass Pkg., AM/FM radio.

RV Conversion Group, (NA 110-inch wheelbase)	2672	2298	2378

Air conditioning, stainless steel mirrors, deluxe front appearance pkg., chrome bumpers, power windows and door locks, cruise control, tilt steering column, AM/FM cassette, 33-gallon fuel tank, heavy duty rear springs, fixed rear door glass, stepwell and underhood lights, override switch, driver- and passenger-side front seat riser track and seat belts, temporary driver's seat. Deletes headliner, interior paint, dome light, and front floormats.

RV Conversion/Marketing Option Pkg. 1,	1462	1257	1301

RV Conversion Group, Fixed Glass Pkg., rub strip delete.

RV Conversion/Marketing Option Pkg. 2,	2125	1828	1891

Pkg. 1 plus swingout Glass Pkg., heavy duty cooling system, visor mirrors, power mirrors, leather-wrapped steering wheel, 215/75R15 whitewall tires, rally wheels.

RV Conversion/Marketing Option Pkg. 3, 125-inch	2250	1935	2003

Pkg. 2 plus AM/FM cassette player with equalizer, power antenna, deep tinted glass.

Deluxe front appearance pkg.	142	122	126

Dark argent grille with bright trim, rectangular headlamps.

Chrome bumpers	76	65	68
Cold Climate Pkg.	48	41	43

Engine block heater.

ZQ2 Convenience Group	434	373	386

Power windows and locks.

ZQ3 Convenience Group	383	329	341

Cruise control and tilt steering wheel.

Remote keyless entry	175	151	156

Includes headlamp delay. Requires auxiliary lighting and ZQ2 Convenience Pkg.

Power door locks	223	192	198
Power mirrors	98	84	87

Requires ZQ2 Convenience Group, swingout Glass Pkg. or Fixed Glass Pkg.

Lighted visor mirrors	75	65	67

Requires RV Conversion Pkg.

Swingout Glass Pkg. I	226	194	201
with RV Conversion Group	176	151	157

Swingout glass for rear and side doors.

Swingout Glass Pkg. II	278	239	247
with RV Conversion Group	248	213	221

Swingout glass for rear and side doors, fixed right body glass.

Fixed Glass Pkg. I	90	77	80
with RV Conversion Group	40	34	36

Fixed rear and side door glass.

GMC

	Retail Price	Dealer Invoice	Fair Price
Fixed Glass Pkg. II	$142	$122	$126
with RV Conversion Group	92	79	82
Fixed rear and side door glass, fixed right body glass.			
Fixed full body glass (six windows)	234	201	208
with RV Conversion Group	184	158	164
Requires Swingout Glass Pkg.			
Swingout full body glass	370	318	329
with RV Conversion Group	320	275	285
Deep tinted glass, RV Conversion Group.			
with fixed or swingout full body glass	380	327	338
with Pkg. II fixed or swingout glass	225	194	200
with Pkg. I fixed or swingout glass	140	120	125
with fixed rear door glass	50	43	45
with swingout rear door glass	109	94	97
Rear defogger	154	132	137
Requires Fixed Glass Pkg. II, fixed rear door glass or fixed full body glass.			
Heavy duty cooling system	198	170	176
Engine and transmission oil coolers, heavy duty radiator.			
Auxiliary lighting	156	134	139
Front and rear dome/reading lights, underhood light.			
Leather-wrapped steering wheel	60	52	53
Carpet	157	135	140
Requires auxiliary front seat.			
Front passenger seat	187	161	166
Temporary driver's seat (credit)	(93)	(80)	(80)
Highback bucket seats	276	237	246
Requires RV Conversion Group.			
Highback bucket driver's seat	NC	NC	NC
AM/FM radio	96	83	85
AM/FM cassette	218	187	194
AM/FM cassette with equalizer	368	316	328
with RV Conversion Group	150	129	134
AM/FM CD player	299	257	266
Requires RV Conversion Group.			
Radio delete (credit)	(95)	(82)	(82)
Power antenna	85	73	76
Trailering Special Equipment	132	114	117
Bumper-mounted trailer hitch, wiring harness, heavy duty flasher.			
33-gallon fuel tank (NA 110-inch wheel base)	96	83	85
Rally wheels	121	104	108
Alloy wheels	331	285	295
215/75R15 whitewall tires, each axle	30	26	27
spare tire	15	13	13
215/75R15 outline white letter tires, each axle	44	38	39
spare tire	22	19	20

GMC Vandura G2500

	Retail Price	Dealer Invoice	Fair Price
110-inch wheelbase	$15975	$13978	$14378
125-inch wheelbase	16180	14158	14508
Destination charge	580	580	580

Standard Equipment:

4.3-liter V-6 engine, 4-speed automatic transmission, anti-lock brakes, driver-side air bag, power steering, vinyl bucket driver's seat, trip odometer, storage box, Solar-Ray glass, intermittent wipers, dual stainless steel outside mirrors, AM radio, digital clock, 60/40 hinged swing-out side doors (sliding side door may be substituted at no charge), painted bumpers, 225/75R15 tires.

Optional Equipment:

	Retail	Dealer	Fair
5.0-liter V-8 engine	575	495	512
5.7-liter V-8 engine (NA 110-inch wheelbase)	865	744	770
6.5-liter diesel V-8 engine (NA 110-inch wheelbase)	2870	2468	2554
Front air conditioning	975	839	868
Front and rear air conditioning	1574	1354	1401
with RV Conversion Group	599	515	533
Rear heater	205	176	182
Optional axle ratio	NC	NC	NC
Locking differential	$252	$217	$224
Marketing Option Pkg. 2	1162	999	1034
Front air conditioning, auxiliary front seat.			
Marketing Option Pkg. 3	1308	1125	1164
Pkg. 2 plus Fixed Glass Pkg., AM/FM radio.			
RV Conversion Group, 110-inch wheelbase and 125-inch with diesel engine	2576	2215	2293
125-inch wheelbase	2672	2298	2378
Air conditioning, stainless steel mirrors, deluxe front appearance pkg., chrome bumpers, power windows and door locks, cruise control, tilt steering column, AM/FM cassette, 33-gallon fuel tank, heavy duty rear springs, fixed rear door glass, stepwell and underhood lights, override switch, driver- and passenger-side front seat riser track and seat belts, temporary driver's seat. Deletes headliner, interior paint, dome light, and front floormats.			
RV Conversion/Marketing Option Pkg. 1,			
110-inch wheelbase	1366	1175	1216
125-inch wheelbase	1462	1257	1301
125-inch wheelbase with diesel engine	1366	1175	1216
RV Conversion Group, Fixed Glass Pkg., rub strip delete.			
RV Conversion/Marketing Option Pkg. 2,			
110-inch wheelbase	2181	1876	1941
125-inch wheelbase	2277	1958	2027
125-inch wheelbase with diesel engine	1907	1640	1697
Pkg. 1 plus Swingout Glass Pkg., heavy duty cooling system, visor mirrors, power mirrors, leather-wrapped steering wheel, 235/75R15 whitewall tires, rally wheels.			
RV Conversion/Marketing Option Pkg. 3,			
125-inch wheelbase	2735	2352	2434
Pkg. 2 plus AM/FM cassette player with equalizer, power antenna, deep tinted glass.			
Deluxe front appearance pkg.	142	122	126
Dark argent grille with bright trim, rectangular headlamps.			
Chrome bumpers	76	65	68
Cold Climate Pkg.	48	41	43
Engine block heater.			
ZQ2 Convenience Group	434	373	386
Power windows and locks.			
ZQ3 Convenience Group	383	329	341
Cruise control and tilt steering wheel.			
Remote keyless entry	175	151	156
Includes headlamp delay. Requires auxiliary lighting and ZQ2 Convenience Pkg.			
Power door locks	223	192	198
Power mirrors	98	84	87
Requires ZQ2 Convenience Group, Swingout Glass Pkg. or Fixed Glass Pkg.			
Lighted visor mirrors	75	65	67
Requires RV Conversion Pkg.			
Swingout Glass Pkg. I	226	194	201
with RV Conversion Group	176	151	157
Swingout glass for rear and side doors.			
Swingout Glass Pkg. II	278	239	247
with RV Conversion Group	248	213	221
Swingout glass for rear and side doors, fixed right body glass.			
Fixed Glass Pkg. I	90	77	80
with RV Conversion Group	40	34	36
Fixed rear and side door glass.			
Fixed Glass Pkg. II	142	122	126
with RV Conversion Group	92	79	82
Fixed rear and side door glass, fixed right body glass.			
Fixed full body glass (six windows)	234	201	208
with RV Conversion Group	184	158	164
Requires Swingout Glass Pkg.			
Swingout full body glass	370	318	329
with RV Conversion Group	320	275	285
Rear defogger	154	132	137
Requires Fixed Glass Pkg. II, fixed rear door glass or fixed full body glass.			
Heavy duty cooling system	198	170	176
Engine and transmission oil coolers, heavy duty radiator.			

GMC

	Retail Price	Dealer Invoice	Fair Price
6875 lbs. GVWR, 125-inch wheelbase			
with 5.7-liter engine	$319	$274	$284
with 6.5-liter diesel engine	NC	NC	NC
Auxiliary lighting	156	134	139
Front and rear dome/reading lights, underhood light.			
Leather-wrapped steering wheel	60	52	53
Carpet	157	135	140
Requires auxiliary front seat.			
Front passenger seat	187	161	166
Highback bucket seats	276	237	246
Requires RV Conversion Group.			
AM/FM radio	96	83	85
AM/FM cassette	218	187	194
AM/FM cassette with equalizer	368	316	328
with RV Conversion Group	150	129	134
AM/FM CD player	299	257	266
Requires RV Conversion Group.			
Power antenna	85	73	76
Trailering Special Equipment	132	114	117
Bumper-mounted trailer hitch, wiring harness, heavy duty flasher.			
33-gallon fuel tank (NA 110-inch wheel base)	96	83	85
Rally wheels	121	104	108
Alloy wheels	331	285	295
225/75R15 spare tire	137	118	122
225/75R15 whitewall tires, each axle	36	31	32
spare tire	155	133	138
225/75R15 white letter tires, each axle	50	43	45
spare tire	161	138	143
235/75R15, each axle	NC	NC	NC
spare tire	151	NC	NC
235/75R15 whitewall tires, each axle	36	31	32
spare tire	169	145	150

GMC Vandura G3500

	Retail Price	Dealer Invoice	Fair Price
Base 125-inch wheelbase	$16239	$14209	$14609
Extended 146-inch wheelbase	18359	16064	16414
Destination charge	580	580	580

Standard Equipment:
4.3-liter V-6 engine (Base), 5.7-liter V-8 engine (Extended), 4-speed automatic transmission (heavy duty Extended), anti-lock brakes, driver-side air bag, power steering, vinyl bucket driver's seat, trip odometer, storage box, Solar-Ray glass, intermittent wipers, dual stainless steel outside mirrors, AM radio, digital clock, 60/40 hinged swing-out side doors (sliding side door may be substituted at no charge), painted bumpers, 33-gallon fuel tank (Extended), LT225/75R16D tires (Base), LT225/75R16E (Extended).

Optional Equipment:

	Retail Price	Dealer Invoice	Fair Price
4.3-liter V-6 engine, Base	NC	NC	NC
with 8600 lbs. GVWR, (credit)	(865)	(744)	(770)
5.7-liter V-8 engine	NC	NC	NC
7.4-liter V-8 engine	605	520	538
6.5-liter turbo diesel V-8 engine	1655	1423	1473
Front air conditioning	975	839	868
Front and rear air conditioning	1574	1354	1401
with RV Conversion Group	599	515	533
Rear heater	205	176	182
Optional axle ratio	NC	NC	NC
Locking differential	252	217	224
Marketing Option Pkg. 2	1162	999	1034
Front air conditioning, auxiliary front seat.			
Marketing Option Pkg. 3	1308	1125	1164
Pkg. 2 plus Fixed Glass Pkg., AM/FM radio.			
RV Conversion Group, Base	2672	2298	2378
Extended	2576	2215	2293
Air conditioning, stainless steel mirrors, deluxe front appearance pkg., chrome bumpers, power windows and door locks, cruise control, tilt steering column, AM/FM cassette, 33-gallon fuel tank, heavy duty rear springs, fixed rear door glass, stepwell and underhood lights, override switch, driver- and passenger-side front seat riser track and seat belts, temporary driver's seat. Deletes headliner, interior paint, dome light, and front floormats.			
RV Conversion/Marketing Option Pkg. 1, Base	$1462	$1257	$1301
Extended	1366	1175	1216
RV Conversion Group, Fixed Glass Pkg., rub strip delete.			
RV Conversion/Marketing Option Pkg. 2, Base	2023	1740	1800
with 6.5-liter turbo diesel engine	1955	1681	1740
Extended	2057	1769	1831
with 6.5-liter turbo diesel engine	1859	1599	1655
Pkg. 1 plus Swingout Glass Pkg., heavy duty cooling system, visor mirrors, power mirrors, leather-wrapped steering wheel, 235/75R15 whitewall tires, rally wheels.			
RV Conversion/Marketing Option Pkg. 3, Base	2148	1847	1912
with 6.5-liter turbo diesel engine	2080	1789	1851
Extended	2182	1877	1942
with 6.5-liter turbo diesel engine	1984	1706	1766
Pkg. 2 plus AM/FM cassette player with equalizer, power antenna, deep tinted glass.			
Deluxe front appearance pkg.	142	122	126
Dark argent grille with bright trim, rectangular headlamps.			
Chrome bumpers	76	65	68
Cold Climate Pkg.	48	41	43
Engine block heater.			
ZQ2 Convenience Group	434	373	386
Power windows and locks.			
ZQ3 Convenience Group	383	329	341
Cruise control and tilt steering wheel.			
Remote keyless entry	175	151	156
Includes headlamp delay. Requires auxiliary lighting and ZQ2 Convenience Pkg.			
Power door locks	223	192	198
Power mirrors	98	84	87
Requires ZQ2 Convenience Group, Swingout Glass Pkg. or Fixed Glass Pkg.			
Lighted visor mirrors	75	65	67
Requires RV Conversion Pkg.			
Swingout Glass Pkg. I	226	194	201
with RV Conversion Group	176	151	157
Swingout glass for rear and side doors.			
Swingout Glass Pkg. II	278	239	247
with RV Conversion Group	248	213	221
Swingout glass for rear and side doors, fixed right body glass.			
Fixed Glass Pkg. I	90	77	80
with RV Conversion Group	40	34	36
Fixed rear and side door glass.			
Fixed Glass Pkg. II	142	122	126
with RV Conversion Group	92	79	82
Fixed rear and side door glass, fixed right body glass.			
Fixed full body glass (six windows)	234	201	208
with RV Conversion Group	184	158	164
Requires Swingout Glass Pkg.			
Swingout full body glass	370	318	329
with RV Conversion Group	320	275	285
Deep tinted glass, RV Conversion Group			
with fixed or swingout full body glass	380	327	338
with Pkg. II fixed or swingout glass	225	194	200
with Pkg. I fixed or swingout glass	140	120	125
with fixed rear door glass	50	43	45
with swingout rear door glass	109	94	97
Rear defogger	154	132	137
Requires Fixed Glass Pkg. II, fixed rear door glass or fixed full body glass.			
Heavy duty cooling system	198	170	176
Engine and transmission oil coolers, heavy duty radiator.			
7400 lbs. GVWR, with 5.7-liter engine	837	720	745
8600 lbs. GVWR	1032	888	918
9200 lbs. GVWR, Base	1272	1094	1132
Extended	240	206	214
NA 4.3-liter engine.			
Auxiliary lighting	156	134	139
Front and rear dome/reading lights, underhood light.			
Leather-wrapped steering wheel	60	52	53
Carpet	157	135	140
Requires auxiliary front seat.			

GMC

	Retail Price	Dealer Invoice	Fair Price
Front passenger seat	$187	$161	$166
Temporary driver's seat (credit)	(93)	(80)	(80)
Highback bucket seats	276	237	246
Requires RV Conversion Group.			
Highback bucket driver's seat	NC	NC	NC
AM/FM radio	96	83	85
AM/FM cassette	218	187	194
AM/FM cassette with equalizer	368	316	328
with RV Conversion Group	150	129	134
AM/FM CD player	299	257	266
Requires RV Conversion Group.			
Radio delete (credit)	(95)	(82)	(82)
Power antenna	85	73	76
Heavy Duty Trailering Special Equipment	310	267	276
with 6.5-liter diesel engine	508	437	452
Trailer hitch, 7-wire harness, heavy duty flasher.			
Light Duty Trailering Special Equipment	132	114	117
Trailer hitch, 5-wire harness, heavy duty flasher.			
33-gallon fuel tank (NA 110-inch wheel base)	96	83	85
Bright wheel covers	42	36	37
LT225/75R16D spare	207	178	184
LT225/75R16ED tires, each axle	34	29	30
spare tire	224	193	199

GMC Safari

GMC Safari SLE extended-length 4WD

Like its corporate twin, the Chevrolet Astro, GMC's Safari minivan gets a driver-side air bag as standard equipment after introducing it as an option last spring.

Other new safety features include stronger side guard door beams and a high-mounted rear stoplamp. Air conditioners now use CFC-free refrigerant. Safari and Astro differ only in minor appearance features and in the names of their trim levels.

Body Styles/Chassis

Passenger and cargo versions are offered, with all models riding a 111-inch wheelbase. Regular- and extended-length bodies are available, the latter adding 10 extra inches behind the rear wheels for an additional 18.6 cubic feet of storage space. Passenger Safaris come in base, SLX, SLE, and SLT trim.

A sliding side door and dual swing-out rear doors are standard. Optional "Dutch" rear doors have a one-piece glass liftgate above side-hinged split panel doors. The Dutch doors come with an electric liftgate release and a rear wiper/washer.

Four-wheel anti-lock brakes (ABS) are standard on all models. Maximum payload is 1740 pounds on regular-length models and 1914 on extended versions.

Powertrains

A 4.3-liter V-6 is the only engine. Standard in 2WD Astros is a version with 165 horsepower. Standard on 4WD models

Specifications

	4-door van	4-door van
Wheelbase, in.	111.0	111.0
Overall length, in.	176.8	186.8
Overall width, in.	77.0	77.0
Overall height, in.	76.4	76.4
Turn diameter, ft.	39.5	39.5
Curb weight, lbs.	3960	4036
Fuel capacity, gal.	27.0	27.0

Passenger Area Dimensions

Seating capacity	8	8
Front head room, in.	39.2	39.2
Rear head room, in.	37.9	37.9
Front leg room, in.	41.6	41.6
Rear leg room, in.	36.5	36.5

Available Seating

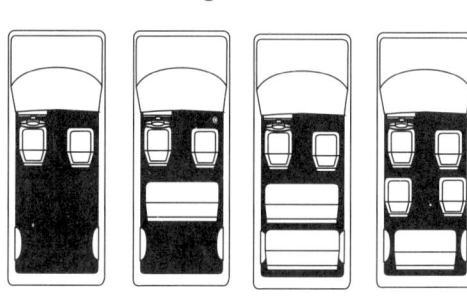

Cargo Dimensions and Payloads

Cargo area length, in.	88.9	98.9
Cargo area width, in.	57.0	57.0
Cargo area width between wheels, in.	51.6	51.6
Cargo area height, in.	44.7	44.7
Cargo vol., cu. ft.	151.8	170.4
Max. payload, lbs.	1740	1914
Max. trailer weight, lbs.	5500	5500

Engines

	ohv V-6	ohv V-6
Size, liters/cu. in.	4.3/262	4.3/262
Horsepower @ rpm	165 @ 4000	200 @ 4500
Torque (lbs./ft.) @ rpm	235 @ 2000	260 @ 3600
Availability	S	O[1]

EPA city/highway mpg

4-speed OD automatic	16/21	15/20

1. Std., 4WD models.

Built in Baltimore, Md.

KEY: Dimensions and capacities are supplied by the manufacturers. **Curb Weight:** base models, not including optional equipment. **Max. payload, lbs.** = gross amount; net payload may be lower due to optional equipment. **Engines:** ohv = overhead valve; ohc = overhead cam; **I** = inline cylinders; **V** = cylinders in V configuration; **flat** = horizontally opposed cylinders; **rpm** = revolutions per minute; **OD** = overdrive transmission; **S** = standard; **O** = optional; **NA** = not available.

and optional on 2WDs is an "enhanced" version with 200 horsepower.

A 4-speed electronic overdrive automatic is the only transmission. A second-gear start feature is included to improve traction on slippery surfaces

Available on all Safaris is a permanently engaged 4WD system that normally splits engine power 65-percent rear wheels/35-percent front. It automatically transfers more power to the axle with the best grip when there's wheel slip.

Properly equipped, Safari can tow up to 5500 pounds.

Accommodations

Passenger models have standard seating for five; 7- and 8-passenger arrangements are optional. Middle and rear bench seats on passenger models can be removed. Cargo models come with two front bucket seats.

For 1994, the carpeting is treated with Scotchgard-brand fabric protection. There also are new graphics for the analog gauges, and all windows have solar-control tinted glass.

See the Chevrolet Astro report for an evaluation of the Safari.

Prices

GMC Safari Passenger Van	Retail Price	Dealer Invoice	Fair Price
2WD	$16746	$15155	$15405
AWD	19075	17263	17513
2WD Extended	17048	15428	15678
AWD Extended	19377	17536	17786
Destination charge	545	545	545

Additional "value-priced" models may also be available in California.

Standard Equipment:

4.3-liter V-6 engine (high output V-6, AWD), 4-speed automatic transmission, 4-wheel anti-lock brakes, driver-side air bag, power steering, trip odometer, solar-control tinted glass, intermittent wipers, AM/FM radio, digital clock, highback bucket seats, 3-passenger bench seat, color-keyed carpeting, door map pockets, dual outside mirrors, passenger-side visor mirror, remote fuel door release, 205/75R15 tires (base 2WD), 215/75R15, others. AWD models have permanent 4-wheel drive. **California model** adds: air conditioning, cruise control, tilt steering wheel, cassette player, SLX Appearance Pkg., eight passenger seating with reclining bucket seats, deep-tinted glass.

Optional Equipment:

	Retail Price	Dealer Invoice	Fair Price
4.3-liter high-output V-6, 2WD	500	430	445

Includes engine oil cooler, heavy duty radiator, transmission oil cooler.

GMC

	Retail Price	Dealer Invoice	Fair Price
Front air conditioning	$845	$727	$752
Front and rear air conditioning	1368	1176	1218
with Pkg. 2, 3, 4	523	450	465
SLE Decor Pkg.	1086	934	967

Front air dam with fog lamps, auxiliary lighting, color-keyed front and rear bumpers, floormats, deluxe black grille with argent headlights, lighted visor mirror, rally wheels, black body side and wheel opening moldings, swing-out rear door glass, seatback map pockets, upgraded door trim.

SLT Decor Pkg.	2896	2491	2577

SLE Pkg. plus leather-wrapped steering wheel, deep-tinted glass, complete body glass, cloth upholstery, storage bag, striping, special reclining wide front and split rear bench seat backs, wide body side molding.

SLX Appearance Pkg.	465	400	414

Color-keyed bumpers and rubber floormats, black grille with argent headlights, wide bodyside molding, rally wheels.

1SB Option Pkg. 2, SLX	682	587	607
SLE	1768	1520	1574

Front air conditioning, below-eye-line mirrors, reclining seats with armrests, cassette player, cruise control, tilt steering wheel, complete body glass.

1SC Option Pkg. 3, SLX	1219	1048	1085
SLE	2178	1873	1938
SLT	3586	3084	3192

1SB plus luggage rack, roof console, auxiliary lighting, power windows and locks.

1SD Option Pkg. 4, SLE	2899	2493	2580
SLT	4307	3704	3833

1SC plus front and rear air conditioning, power mirrors, remote cassette player with equalizer, stowage compartment, alloy wheels.

Rear heater	205	176	182
Locking differential	252	217	224
7-passenger seating	1043	897	928
w/SLE Decor Pkg.	955	821	850
w/SLT Decor Pkg.	852	733	758
8-passenger seating	395	340	352
w/SLT	877	754	781
Reclining seats w/armrests	245	211	218
6-way power driver's seat	240	206	214
Rear door liftgate	364	313	324

Includes rear wiper/washer and electric release.

Deluxe chrome bumpers, CS	128	110	114
w/SLE and SLT Decor Pkg. or SLX Appearance Pkg.	76	65	68
Luggage rack	126	108	112
Cold Climate Pkg.	46	40	41
Rear defogger	154	132	137

Requires rear door liftgate.

Roof console	83	71	74
w/SLE and SLT Decor Pkgs.	50	43	45
Underseat storage tray	30	26	27
ZQ2 Convenience Pkg.	434	373	386

Power windows and locks.

Left: Available Dutch doors replace dual side-hinged doors. Above: Four captain's-chair setup is optional.

GMC

	Retail Price	Dealer Invoice	Fair Price
ZQ3 Convenience Pkg.	$383	$329	$341
Cruise control, tilt steering wheel.			
Power locks	223	192	198
Heavy-duty cooling system	198	170	176
Complete body glass	157	135	140
Deep-tinted glass	161	138	143
w/complete body glass	290	249	258
Electronic instrumentation	195	168	174
Auxiliary lighting	127	109	113
w/roof console	94	81	84
Deluxe outside mirrors	52	45	46
Power mirrors	150	129	134
Deluxe 2-tone paint	476	409	424
w/SLE Decor Pkg. or SLX Appearance Pkg.	251	216	223
2-tone paint	329	283	293
w/SLE and SLT Decor Pkgs. or SLX Appearance Pkg.	104	89	93
Radio delete (credit)	(246)	(212)	(212)
AM radio (credit)	(151)	(130)	(130)
Credit when AM radio replaces standard AM/FM radio. Not available with option pkgs.			
AM/FM cassette	122	105	109
AM/FM cassette w/equalizer	272	234	242
AM/FM CD player	406	349	361
Leather-wrapped steering wheel	54	46	48
Luggage rack	126	108	112
205/75R15 whitewall tires, base 2WD	72	62	64
205/75R15 white letter tires, base 2WD	96	83	85
215/75R15 whitewall tires	60	52	53
215/75R15 white letter tires	88	76	78
Trailering Special Equipment, heavy duty	507	436	451
w/high-output V-6	309	266	275
Alloy wheels	340	292	303
w/SLE, SLT Decor Pkg. or SLX Appearance Pkg.	248	213	221
Rally wheels	92	79	82

GMC Safari Cargo Van

	Retail Price	Dealer Invoice	Fair Price
Base 2WD	$15661	$14173	$14423
Base 4WD	17980	16272	16522
Extended 2WD	16134	14601	14851
Extended 4WD	18453	16700	16950
Destination charge	545	545	545

Standard Equipment:

4.3-liter V-6 engine (2WD), 4.3-liter V-6 engine (4WD), 4-speed automatic transmission, anti-lock brakes, driver-side air bag, power steering, vinyl highback bucket driver's seat, remote fuel door release, tinted glass, dual black outside mirrors, color-keyed bumpers, black grille, black air dam, front stabilizer bar, storage box, AM radio, digital clock, trip odometer, intermittent wipers, 205/75R15 tires (215/75R15, 4WD and Extended).

Optional Equipment:

4.3-liter V-6 engine	500	430	445
Air conditioning	845	727	752
Rear heater	205	176	182
Optional axle ratio	NC	NC	NC
Locking differential	252	217	224
Marketing Option Pkg. 2	932	802	829
Air conditioning, rear panel doors.			
Marketing Option Pkg. 3	1080	929	961
Pkg. 2 plus dual black mirrors, AM/FM radio.			
RV Conversion Group, Base	1760	1514	1566
Extended	1690	1453	1504
Air conditioning, dual black mirrors, AM/FM radio, cruise control, tilt steering wheel. Base also includes heavy duty rear springs. Deletes driver's seat, dome light and floormat.			
Marketing Option Pkg. 4, Base	686	590	611
Extended	616	530	548
RV Conversion Group, power locks and windows, rally wheels.			
Marketing Option Pkg. 5, Base	$1223	$1052	$1088
Extended	1153	992	1026
Pkg.4 plus deluxe bumpers and grille, sliding side and rear door windows, deep tinted glass, cassette player, power mirrors.			
Marketing Option Pkg. 6, Base	1731	1489	1541
Extended	1661	1428	1478
Pkg. 5 plus, air dam with fog lights, electronic instrumentation, AM/FM cassette with equalizer, alloy wheels.			
6-way power driver's seat	240	206	214
Requires RV Conversion Group.			
Front passenger seat	214	184	190
Seatback recliner and armrests	245	211	218
Cloth seat trim	NC	NC	NC
Temporary driver's seat	NC	NC	NC
Requires RV Conversion Group.			
Chrome bumpers	128	110	114
Requires RV Conversion Group.			
Color-keyed bumpers with rub strips	52	45	46
Rear defogger	154	132	137
Requires dutch doors.			
Air dam with fog lights	115	99	102
Requires RV Conversion Group.			
Dutch doors	364	313	324
Includes rear wiper/washer power release. Replaces standard swing-out rear doors. Requires RV Conversion Group.			
Cold Climate Pkg.	46	40	41
Engine block heater, coolant protection.			
Roof console	83	71	74
Includes map and reading lights, two storage compartments. Requires auxiliary lighting or RV Conversion Group.			
Auxiliary lighting	127	109	113
with roof console	94	81	84
Front and rear dome lights, reading lights, courtesy light switches on all doors, glove box light, stepwell lights.			
ZQ2 Convenience Group	434	373	386
Power windows and locks.			
ZQ3 Convenience Group	383	329	341
Cruise control and tilt steering wheel.			
Power locks	223	192	198
Heavy duty cooling system	198	170	176
Engine and transmission oil cooler.			
Deep tinted glass	NC	NC	NC
Complete body glass	368	316	328
with deep tinted glass	630	542	561
Rear panel door glass	87	75	77
with deep tinted glass	141	121	125
Side door and rear panel door glass	155	133	138
with deep tinted glass	262	225	233
Swing-out rear/side door glass	136	117	121
Swing-out rear door glass	77	66	69
Deluxe grille	27	23	24
Electronic instrumentation	195	168	174
Heavy duty Trailering Special Equipment	507	436	451
with 4.3-liter engine	309	266	275
Platform trailer hitch, wiring harness, heavy duty cooling system.			
Deluxe black outside mirrors	52	45	46
Power mirrors	150	129	134
with RV Conversion Group	98	84	87
AM/FM radio	96	83	85
AM/FM cassette	218	187	194
with RV Conversion Group	98	84	87
AM/FM cassette with equalizer	218	187	194
Requires RV Conversion Group.			
AM/FM CD player	406	349	361
Requires RV Conversion Group.			
Radio delete (credit)	(95)	(82)	(82)
with RV Conversion Group	(246)	(212)	(212)
Leather-wrapped steering wheel	54	46	48
Luggage rack	126	108	112
Requires front passenger seat.			
Heavy duty rear springs, base	70	60	62
Underseat storage compartment	30	26	27

GMC Sierra

RECOMMENDED

GMC Sierra C1500 regular-cab long-bed

GMC Truck's full-size pickups gain door guard beams and a center high-mounted stoplamp as new standard features. Plus, the grilles are modestly restyled, and leather upholstery and two 6.5-liter diesel V-8 engines join the options list.

Sierra matches the Chevrolet C/K pickups in body styles, powertrains, equipment, and trim levels. The GMC models have slightly higher base prices, however, because Sierra models come standard with an FM radio and digital clock. Option package prices are the same, though the names are different.

Body Styles/Chassis

Series numbers denote payload categories: 1500 (half-ton), 2500 (three-quarter ton), and 3500 (one-ton). All are available with 2-wheel-drive, identified by a "C" prefix, or 4-wheel-drive, indicated by a "K."

Short-bed regular-cabs come in the 1500-series only and have a 117.5-inch wheelbase and 6.5-foot bed.

Long-bed models come in all three series and have a 131.5-inch wheelbase and 8-foot bed.

GMC calls its extended-cab models the Club Coupe. They come in all three series and have either a 141.5-inch wheelbase and a 6.5-foot bed or a 155.5-inch wheelbase and 8-foot bed. (The short-bed Club Coupe is unavailable in the 3500 series.)

Models with flare-fender cargo boxes are called Sportside; those with slab-side boxes are called Wideside. Sportside models come in both regular-cab and Club Coupe form, but only in the 1500-series and only with the short-bed.

Dual-rear-wheels are offered on 2500- and 3500-series models.

The Sierra Crew Cab model has four side doors and comes in the 3500 series only. The Crew Cab is a low-volume model and is not covered in this report.

Sierra's roster begins with the Special model, a work-oriented regular cab 1500-series Wideside available in either 2- or 4-wheel drive.

Above the Special are two main trim levels: SL and SLE. SLE models are distinguished by a unique nose appearance that incorporates composite headlamps.

Available on C/K1500 models in SLE trim is a Sport package that includes GT decals, a grille of yet a third style, a monochrome exterior appearance, and alloy wheels. The new SLT package for Club Coupes includes leather upholstery.

A 3-place front bench seat is standard; front buckets are optional. A 3-place rear bench is standard on Club Coupes.

GMC says rear-seat entry and exit on Club Coupes is improved due to a memory feature for the front seatback. Plus, Club Coupes with uplevel trim are available with a newly optional 6-way power driver's seat.

Models with front bench seats have pull-out dashboard cup holders; a floor console with cup holders comes with the optional custom reclining high-back buckets.

Anti-lock rear brakes, which work in 2WD only, continue as standard on all models.

Maximum payloads ranges from 2240 pounds on the short-bed models to 4782 pounds on the C3500 regular-cab long-bed.

Specifications

	Short bed	Long bed	Club Coupe	Club Coupe
Wheelbase, in.	117.5	131.5	141.5	155.5
Overall length, in.	194.0	212.6	218.0	237.0
Overall width, in.	76.8	76.8	76.8	76.8
Overall height, in.	70.4	70.4	70.4	74.9
Turn diameter, ft.	40.3	44.4	47.1	52.9
Curb weight, lbs.	3809	3860	3967	4116
Fuel capacity, gal.	25.0	34.0	34.0	34.0

Passenger Area Dimensions

Seating capacity	3	3	6	6
Front head room, in.	40.0	40.0	40.0	40.0
Rear head room, in.	—	—	NA	NA
Front leg room, in.	41.7	41.7	41.7	41.7
Rear leg room, in.	—	—	32.1	32.1

Cargo Dimensions and Payloads

Cargo area length, in.	78.7	97.6	78.7	97.6
Cargo area width, in.	64.4[1]	64.4	64.4[1]	64.4
Cargo area width between wheels, in.	49.1	49.1	49.1	49.1
Cargo area height, in.	19.3	19.3	19.3	19.3
Max. payload, lbs.	2240	5033	3030	4782
Max. trailer weight, lbs.	8500	13,500	11,000	13,500

1. 49.1 on Sportside.

Engines	ohv V-6	ohv V-8	ohv V-8	ohv V-8	Diesel ohv V-8
Size, liters/cu. in.	4.3/262	5.0/305	5.7/350	7.4/454	6.5/400
Horsepower @ rpm	165 @ 4000	175 @ 4200	210 @ 4000	230 @ 3600	155 @ 3400[1]
Torque (lbs./ft.) @ rpm	235 @ 2000	265 @ 2800	310 @ 2400	385 @ 1600	255 @ 1900[2]
Availability	S	O	S	O	O

EPA city/highway mpg

5-speed OD manual	17/22	14/19	14/19	NA	19/24
4-speed OD automatic	17/21	14/19	14/18	NA	17/23

1. 6.5-liter turbodiesel, 180 @ 3400. 2. 6.5-liter turbodiesel, 360 @ 1700.

Built in Janesville, Wisc.; Ft. Wayne, Ind.; Pontiac, Mich.; and Canada.

KEY: Dimensions and capacities are supplied by the manufacturers. **Curb Weight:** base models, not including optional equipment. **Max. payload, lbs.** = gross amount; net payload may be lower due to optional equipment. **Engines: ohv** = overhead valve; **ohc** = overhead cam; **I** = inline cylinders; **V** = cylinders in V configuration; **flat** = horizontally opposed cylinders; **rpm** = revolutions per minute; **OD** = overdrive transmission; **S** = standard; **O** = optional; **NA** = not available.

GMC

Powertrains

Most 1500- and 2500-series models come standard with a 165-horsepower 4.3-liter V-6.

Available on C/K2500 models over 8500 pounds gross vehicle weight is a Heavy Duty 4.3 V-6 with slightly less rated power, but other modifications that make it better suited for hard-use heavy-duty applications.

Three gasoline V-8s are available, including a 5.0-liter with 175 horsepower and a 5.7 with 210. A Heavy Duty version of the 5.0 is available in 2500- and 3500-series models.

A 230-horsepower 7.4-liter V-8 is optional in heavy-duty and Club Coupe C/K2500s and in all 3500s.

Gone is last year's 6.2-liter naturally aspirated diesel V-8, which had 140 horsepower, or 150 in heavy-duty form. It is replaced by a naturally aspirated 6.5-liter diesel V-8 rated at 155 horsepower. This engine is optional in all 1500 and 2500 models.

Newly available for all 1500 and 2500 models is a new 180-horsepower turbocharged 6.5-liter diesel V-8. This engine is also available on the comparable Chevy C/K pickups and General Motors says it's the first turbodiesel V-8 ever offered in trucks with gross vehicle weight ratings under 8500 pounds.

Carried over as an option for heavy-duty C/K 2500 models over 8500 pounds GVWR and in C/K 3500 pickups is a turbocharged 6.5-liter diesel V-8 of 190 horsepower.

A 5-speed manual transmission is standard with all gasoline engines and with the naturally aspirated diesel V-8.

A 4-speed overdrive automatic with electronic controls is optional with those engines and is the only transmission available with the turbodiesels.

Sierra's available 4WD is GM's Insta-Trac, an on-demand, part-time system (not for use on dry pavement) with automatic locking front hubs and shift-on-the-fly.

Maximum trailer-towing weight is found on the gasoline-powered V-8 models. On the 1500 series, it's 7500 pounds; it's 12,500 pounds on the 2500; and 13,500 pounds on 3500 models equipped with a fifth wheel kingpin-type hitch.

See our report on the Chevrolet Pickup for an evaluation of the GMC Sierra.

Prices

GMC Sierra C/K 1500

	Retail Price	Dealer Invoice	Fair Price
C Special, long bed	$12624	$11046	$11546
C Special, short bed	12424	11244	11744
C Sportside, short bed	14930	13064	13564
C Wideside short bed	14267	12484	12984
C Wideside long bed	14547	12729	13229
K Special, short bed	15516	14042	14542
K Sportside, short bed	17271	15112	15612
K Wideside short bed	16709	14620	15120
K Wideside long bed	17008	14882	15382
C Club Coupe, short bed	16094	14082	14582
C Club Coupe, long bed	16937	14820	15320
C Sportside Club Coupe, short bed	16506	14443	14943
K Club Coupe, short bed	18419	16113	16613
K Club Coupe, long bed	19193	16790	17290
K Sportside Club Coupe, short bed	18831	16474	16974
Destination charge	600	600	600

C denotes 2WD; K denotes 4WD.

Standard Equipment:

4.3-liter V-6 engine (5.0-liter V-8 engine, C/K Club Coupe long bed), 5-speed manual transmission, anti-lock rear brakes, power steering, fold-down 3-passenger vinyl bench seat (regular cab), 60/40 split fold-down 3-passenger vinyl bench seat (Club Coupe), fold-down rear seat (Club Coupe), solar-control glass, intermittent wipers, dual outside mirrors, cloth headliner (Club Coupe), AM/FM radio (except Special), under dash cup holders, coolant temperature and oil pressure gauges, voltmeter, trip odometer, front tow hooks (4WD), full-size spare tire (except Special). Tires, C regular cab: 225/75R15; C Club Coupe: 235/75R15; K regular cab: LT225/75R16; K Club Coupe: LT245/75R16.

Optional Equipment:

	Retail Price	Dealer Invoice	Fair Price
5.0-liter V-8 (std. Club Coupe long bed)	$575	$495	$512
5.7-liter V-8	865	744	770
with Club Coupe long bed	290	249	258
6.5-liter V-8 diesel	2870	2468	2554
with Club Coupe long bed	2295	1973	2043

Includes heavy duty chassis, 235/75R15 tires (regular cab).

6.5-liter V-8 turbo diesel	3670	3156	3266
with Club Coupe long bed	3095	2661	2755

Includes heavy duty chassis, 235/75R15 tires (regular cab).

Alternative fuel conversion, 2WD regular cab long bed, and 4WD regular cab, long bed	125	108	111

Requires 5.7-liter engine and 4-speed automatic transmission.

4-speed automatic transmission	930	800	828
Heavy duty 5-speed manual transmission	98	84	87
diesel models	NC	NC	NC
Air conditioning	805	692	716
SLE Decor Pkg.	798	686	710

Deluxe front appearance pkg., wheel trim rings, sport steering wheel, chrome front bumper with rub strip, bright bodyside and wheel opening moldings, door map pockets, carpeting, behind seat storage tray, passenger-side visor mirror, floormats (regular cab), front and rear floormats (Club Coupe), swingout rear quarter windows (Club Coupe).

Sport Pkg., 2WD	474	408	422
short bed and 2WD with Sport Handling Pkg.	185	159	165
4WD	654	562	582
2WD Club Coupe	404	347	360
4WD Club Coupe	511	439	455

Color-keyed bumpers, GT sport decals, fog lights (2WD), alloy wheels. Requires SLE Decor Pkg.

Special Pkg. 2, 2WD	162	139	144
4WD	223	192	198

Painted rear step bumper, AM radio, wheel trim rings and hubcaps, 225/75R15 tires (2WD), LT225/75R16C tires (4WD).

SL Pkg. 2	405	348	360
Automatic transmission credit	(890)	(765)	(765)
Air conditioning, SLE Pkg. 3	1092	939	972
Automatic transmission credit	(500)	(430)	(430)

SLE Decor Pkg., air conditioning, stainless steel mirrors, auxiliary lighting.

SLE Pkg. 4	1714	1474	1525
Automatic transmission credit	(500)	(430)	(430)

Pkg. 4 plus cruise control, tilt steering wheel, power window and door locks, AM/FM cassette player.

SLE Sport Pkg. 1, 2WD	872	750	776
4WD	1047	900	932
2WD Club Coupe	802	690	714
4WD Club Coupe	907	780	807

SLE Decor Pkg., Sport Pkg.

SLE Sport Pkg. 2, 2WD	1976	1699	1759
4WD	2151	1850	1914
2WD Club Coupe	1906	1639	1696
4WD Club Coupe	2011	1729	1790

SLE Sport Pkg. 1 plus air conditioning, cruise control, tilt steering wheel, auxiliary, AM/FM cassette player.

SLT Pkg. 1, 2WD and 4WD Club Coupe	4744	4080	4222

SLT Leather Pkg. (leather upholstery, leather-wrapped steering wheel, electrochromatic inside rearview mirror with compass, overhead console, instrument panel mounted cup holders, black below eyeline outside mirrors, lighted visor mirrors, accent striping), air conditioning, cruise control, tilt steering wheel, power windows and door locks, AM/FM cassette with equalizer, tachometer, reclining highback bucket seats, 6-way power driver's seat, chrome rear step bumper, front bumper guards, bedliner, alloy wheels.

GMC

	Retail Price	Dealer Invoice	Fair Price
Optional axle ratio	NC	NC	NC
Locking differential	$252	$217	$224
Cold-Climate Pkg.	33	28	29
Engine block heater, added insulation.			
Appearance Pkg.	191	164	170
Color-keyed grille, composite halogen headlights, dual horns.			
Convenience Group ZQ2	367	316	327
Power windows and locks.			
Convenience Group ZQ3	383	329	341
Cruise control and tilt steering column.			
Off-Road Chassis Pkg., 4WD	270	232	240
Bilstein gas shocks absorbers, skid plate.			
Sport Handling Pkg.	1065	916	948
with SLE Decor Pkg.	974	838	867
Bilstein gas shock absorbers, chrome wheels, 275/60R15 tires.			
Heavy Duty Trailering Special Equipment	250	215	223
with Snow Plow Prep Pkg., Off-Road Chassis Pkg. or Sport Handling Pkg.	210	297	187
Trailer hitch, wiring harness.			
Snow Plow Prep Pkg.	158	136	141
with Off-Road Chassis Pkg.	55	47	49
Bedliner	225	194	200
Chrome rear step bumper	229	197	204
Front bumper rub strip	26	22	23
Painted rear step bumper	130	112	116
Front bumper guards	32	28	28
Heavy duty chassis, 4WD Club Coupe	230	198	205
Engine oil cooler	135	116	120
Heavy duty engine and transmission oil coolers	198	170	176
Requires gasoline engine and automatic transmission.			
Rear defogger, Club Coupe	154	132	137
Requires SLE Decor Pkg.			
Tachometer	59	51	53
Dome and reading lights	33	28	29
Roof marker lights	52	45	46
Auxiliary lighting	94	81	84
Dome and reading lights, glovebox light, underhood light.			
Stainless steel mirrors	45	39	40
Camper-type mirrors	53	46	47
Bright bodyside moldings, Wideside	107	92	95
Sportside or with Sport Handling Pkg.	76	65	68
Conventional 2-tone paint	132	114	117
Deluxe 2-tone paint	243	209	216
AM radio (credit)	(170)	(146)	(146)
Radio delete	(287)	(245)	(245)
AM radio, Special	162	139	144
AM/FM radio, Special	332	286	295
AM/FM cassette	122	105	109
Special	454	390	404
AM/FM cassette with equalizer	272	234	242
Not available Special.			
Power driver's seat, Club Coupe	240	206	214
Requires SLE Decor Pkg., 60/40 split bench seat or front highback reclining buckets seats.			
60/40 split bench seat	174	150	155
Front reclining highback bucket seats	490	421	436
Club Coupe	291	250	259
Includes center console and inboard armrests.			
Front reclining lowback bucket seats	289	249	257
Club Coupe	115	99	102
Includes center console.			
Rear seat delete, Club Coupe (credit)	(395)	(340)	(340)
Heavy duty shock absorbers	40	34	36
Skid plate, 4WD	95	82	85
Front tow hooks (std. 4WD)	38	33	34
Heavy duty front torsion bars, 4WD	63	54	56
Deep tinted glass, Club Coupe	150	129	134
with SLE Decor Pkg.	107	92	95
with sliding rear window	115	99	102
with SLE Decor Pkg. and sliding rear window or rear defogger	72	62	64
Sliding rear window	113	97	101

Top: A Sierra K1500 Club Coupe with the Sportside cargo box and optional GT trim. Middle: Club Coupes come with a rear bench seat. Above: Standard front bench has 3-across seating.

	Retail Price	Dealer Invoice	Fair Price
Swing-out rear quarter window, Club Coupe	$43	$37	$38
Auxiliary battery	134	115	119
Bright wheel covers	42	36	37
Rally wheel trim	60	52	53
Cast alloy wheels	310	267	276
with SLE Decor Pkg.	250	215	223
Chrome wheels, 2WD	299	257	266
with SLE Decor Pkg.	257	221	229
Side-mounted spare tire carrier	NC	NC	NC
Tires: 225/75R15 white letter, each axle	50	35	45
Spare	25	22	22
Spare, Special	185	159	165
225/75R15 spare, Special	160	138	142
235/75R15, each axle	28	24	25
Spare	14	12	12
Spare, Special	174	150	155
LT225/75R16C spare, 4WD Special	221	190	197

CONSUMER GUIDE®

GMC

	Retail Price	Dealer Invoice	Fair Price
LT225/75R16C on/off road, each axle 4WD	$22	$19	$20
Spare	11	9	10
Spare, 4WD Special	232	200	206
235/75R15 whitewall, each axle	64	55	57
with diesel engine or Club Coupe	36	31	32
Spare	32	28	28
with diesel engine or Club Coupe	18	15	16
Spare, Special	192	165	171
235/75R15 white letter, each axle	78	67	69
with diesel engine or Club Coupe	50	43	45
Spare	39	34	35
with diesel engine or Club Coupe	25	22	22
Spare, Special	199	171	177
LT225/75R16C on/off road outline white letter, each axle 4WD	72	62	64
Spare	36	31	32
Spare, Special	257	221	229
LT265/75R16C, each axle 4WD	134	115	119
Spare	67	58	60
Club Coupe	76	65	68
Spare	38	33	34
LT265/75R16C outline white letter, each axle 4WD	184	158	164
Spare	92	79	82

GMC Sierra C/K 2500

	Retail Price	Dealer Invoice	Fair Price
C Wideside regular cab long bed	$15154	$13260	$13760
C Wideside regular cab long bed, Heavy Duty	16823	14720	15220
K Wideside regular cab long bed	17183	15035	15535
K Wideside regular cab long bed, Heavy Duty	19275	16866	17366
C Club Coupe short bed	17882	15647	16147
C Club Coupe long bed	18570	16249	16749
K Club Coupe short bed	19699	17234	17734
K Club Coupe long bed	21042	18412	18912
Destination charge	600	600	600

C denotes 2WD; K denotes 4WD.

Standard Equipment:

4.3-liter V-6 engine (regular cab), 5.0-liter V-8 engine (Club Coupe short bed), 5.7-liter V-8 engine (Heavy Duty and Club Coupe long bed), 5-speed manual transmission (heavy duty on Heavy Duty models and Club Coupe long bed), anti-lock rear brakes, power steering, fold-down cloth or vinyl bench seat (regular cab), 60/40 split fold-down cloth or vinyl bench seat (Club Coupe), fold-down rear bench seat (Club Coupe), chromed front bumper, solar-control glass, dual outside mirrors, AM/FM radio, digital clock, trip odometer, front stabilizer bar, cloth headliner (Club Coupe), floormat, front tow hooks (4WD), painted silver wheels, intermittent wipers, LT225/75R16D tires (regular cab and Club Coupe short bed), LT245/75R16C (4WD Club Coupe short bed), LT245/75R16E (Heavy Duty and Club Coupe long bed).

Optional Equipment:

	Retail	Dealer	Fair
5.0-liter V-8 engine	575	495	512
5.7-liter V-8 engine	865	744	770
Club Coupe	290	249	258
7.4-liter V-8 engine, Heavy Duty and Club Coupe long bed	1315	1131	1170
6.5-liter diesel V-8 engine	2870	2468	2554
Club Coupe short bed	2295	1974	2043
6.5-liter turbo diesel V-8 engine	3670	3156	3266
Club Coupe short bed	3095	2662	2755
Heavy Duty and Club Coupe long bed	2825	2430	2514
4-speed automatic transmission	930	800	828
Heavy duty 5-speed manual transmission	98	84	87
diesel models	NC	NC	NC
Air conditioning	805	692	716
Optional axle ratio	NC	NC	NC
Locking differential	252	217	224
SLE Decor Pkg.	$798	$686	$710

Deluxe front appearance pkg., wheel trim rings, sport steering wheel, chrome front bumper with rub strip, bright bodyside and wheel opening moldings, door map pockets, carpeting, behind seat storage tray, passenger-side visor mirror, floormats (regular cab), front and rear floormats (Club Coupe), swingout rear quarter windows (Club Coupe).

SL Pkg. 2	405	348	360

Air conditioning.

SLE Pkg. 3, regular cab	1242	1068	1105
Club Coupe	1142	982	1016

SLE Decor Pkg., air conditioning, stainless steel mirrors, auxiliary lighting.

SLE Pkg. 4	2014	1732	1792
Club Coupe	1914	1646	1703

Pkg. 4 plus cruise control, tilt steering wheel, power window and door locks, AM/FM cassette player.

Camper Equipment	233	200	207
with diesel engine	99	85	88

Camper style stainless steel mirrors, camper wiring harness. Gas models include heavy duty battery.

Cold-Climate Pkg.	33	28	29

Engine block heater, added insulation.

Appearance Pkg.	191	164	170

Color-keyed grille, composite halogen headlights, dual horns.

Convenience Group ZQ2	367	316	327

Power windows and locks.

Convenience Group ZQ3	383	329	341

Cruise control and tilt steering column.

Heavy Duty Trailering Special Equipment	210	181	187

Trailer hitch, wiring harness.

Snow Plow Prep Pkg.	118	101	105
Bedliner	225	194	200
Chrome rear step bumper	229	197	204
Painted rear step bumper	130	112	116
Front bumper guards	32	28	28
Engine oil cooler	135	116	120
Heavy duty engine and transmission oil coolers	198	170	176

Requires gasoline engine and automatic transmission.

Rear defogger, Club Coupe	154	132	137

Requires SLE Decor Pkg.

Tachometer	59	51	53
Dome and reading lights	33	28	29
Roof marker lights	52	45	46
Auxiliary lighting	94	81	84

Dome and reading lights, glovebox light, underhood light.

Stainless steel mirrors	45	39	40
Camper-type mirrors	53	46	47
Bright bodyside moldings	107	92	95
4WD Heavy Duty and 4WD Club Coupe long bed	76	65	68
Conventional 2-tone paint	132	114	117
Deluxe 2-tone paint	243	209	216
AM radio (credit)	(170)	(146)	(146)
Radio delete	(287)	(245)	(245)
AM/FM cassette	122	105	109
AM/FM cassette with equalizer	272	234	242
Power driver's seat, Club Coupe	240	206	214

Requires SLE Decor Pkg., 60/40 split bench seat or front highback reclining buckets seats.

60/40 split bench seat	174	150	155
Front reclining highback bucket seats	490	421	436
Club Coupe	291	250	259

Includes center console and inboard armrests.

Front reclining lowback bucket seats	289	249	257
Club Coupe	115	99	102

Includes center console.

Rear seat delete, Club Coupe (credit)	(395)	(340)	(340)
Skid plate, 4WD	95	82	85
Front tow hooks (std. 4WD)	38	33	34
Heavy duty front torsion bars, 4WD	63	54	56
Deep tinted glass, Club Coupe	150	129	134
with SLE Decor Pkg.	107	92	95

GMC

	Retail Price	Dealer Invoice	Fair Price
Sliding rear window	$113	$97	$101
Swing-out rear quarter window, Club Coupe	43	37	38
Auxiliary battery	134	115	119
Bright wheel covers	42	36	37
Rally wheel trim	60	52	53
Side-mounted spare tire carrier	NC	NC	NC
Tires: LT225/75R16D spare tire	289	249	257
LT225/75R16D on/off road tires, each axle	22	19	20
spare	300	258	267
LT245/75R16C on/off road, each axle 4WD Club Coupe	23	19	20
spare	312	268	278
LT245/75R16C on/off road outline white letter, each axle 4WD Club Coupe	72	62	64
spare	337	290	300
LT245/75R16E, each axle	92	79	82
spare	335	288	298
LT245/75R16E on/off road tires, each axle	114	98	101
Heavy Duty	22	19	20
spare (all models)	346	298	308

GMC Sierra C/K 3500

	Retail Price	Dealer Invoice	Fair Price
C Wideside regular cab	$16820	$14718	$15218
K Wideside regular cab	19431	17002	17502
C Club Coupe	20064	17556	18056
K Club Coupe	22462	19654	20154
Destination charge	600	600	600

C denotes 2WD; K denotes 4WD. All 3500s are long bed.

Standard Equipment:
5.7-liter V-8 engine, heavy duty 5-speed manual transmission, anti-lock rear brakes, power steering, engine oil cooler, cloth or vinyl fold-down bench seat, 60/40 cloth or vinyl split folding bench seat (Club Coupe), folding rear bench seat (Club Coupe), chrome front bumper, solar-control glass, dual outside mirrors, AM/FM radio digital clock, trip odometer, front tow hooks (4WD), black rubber floormat, front stabilizer bar, cloth headliner (Club Coupe), painted silver wheels, intermittent wipers, LT245/75R16E tires; LT225/75R16C front and 245/75R16E rear tires (2WD Club Coupe), LT245/75R16D (4WD Club Coupe). Club Coupes have dual rear wheels.

Optional Equipment:

	Retail	Dealer	Fair
7.4-liter V-8 engine	470	404	418
6.5-liter turbo diesel engine	2825	2430	2514
4-speed automatic transmission	930	800	828
Air conditioning	805	692	716
Optional axle ratio	NC	NC	NC
Locking differential	252	217	224
SLE Decor Pkg.	798	686	710

Deluxe Front Appearance Pkg., wheel trim rings, sport steering wheel, chrome front bumper with rub strip, bright bodyside and wheel opening moldings, door map pockets, carpeting, behind seat storage tray, passenger-side visor mirror, floormats (regular cab), front and rear floormats (Club Coupe), swingout rear quarter windows (Club Coupe).

SL Pkg. 2	405	348	360

Air conditioning.

SLE Pkg. 3, regular cab	1342	1154	1194
Club Coupe	1142	982	1016

SLE Decor Pkg., air conditioning, stainless steel mirrors, auxiliary lighting.

SLE Pkg. 4	2014	1732	1792
Club Coupe	1914	1646	1703

Pkg. 4 plus cruise control, tilt steering wheel, power window and door locks, AM/FM cassette player.

Camper Equipment	233	200	207
with diesel engine	99	85	88

Camper style stainless steel mirrors, camper wiring harness. Gas models include heavy duty battery.

Cold-Climate Pkg.	33	28	29

Engine block heater, added insulation.

	Retail Price	Dealer Invoice	Fair Price
Appearance Pkg.	$191	$164	$170
Color-keyed grille, composite halogen headlights, dual horns.			
Convenience Group ZQ2	367	316	327
Power windows and locks.			
Convenience Group ZQ3	383	329	341
Cruise control and tilt steering column.			
Heavy Duty Trailering Special Equipment	210	181	187
Trailer hitch, wiring harness.			
Snow Plow Prep Pkg.	118	101	105
Bedliner	225	194	200
Chrome rear step bumper	229	197	204
Painted rear step bumper	130	112	116
Front bumper guards	32	28	28
Rear defogger, Club Coupe	154	132	137
Requires SLE Decor Pkg.			
Tachometer	59	51	53
Dome and reading lights	33	28	29
Roof marker lights	52	45	46
Auxiliary lighting	94	81	84
Dome and reading lights, glovebox light, underhood light.			
Stainless steel mirrors	45	39	40
Camper-type mirrors	53	46	47
Bright bodyside moldings, 2WD regular cab	107	92	95
4WD regular cab	76	65	68
Conventional 2-tone paint	132	114	117
Deluxe 2-tone paint	243	209	216
AM radio (credit)	(170)	(146)	(146)
Radio delete	(287)	(245)	(245)
AM/FM cassette	122	105	109
AM/FM cassette with equalizer	272	234	242
Power driver's seat, Club Coupe	240	206	214
Requires SLE Decor Pkg., 60/40 split bench seat or front highback reclining buckets seats.			
60/40 split bench seat	174	150	155
Front reclining highback bucket seats	490	421	436
Club Coupe	291	250	259
Includes center console and inboard armrests.			
Front reclining lowback bucket seats	289	249	257
Club Coupe	115	99	102
Includes center console.			
Rear seat delete, Club Coupe (credit)	(395)	(340)	(340)
Skid plate, 4WD	95	82	85
Front tow hooks (std. 4WD)	38	33	34
Heavy duty front torsion bars, 4WD	63	54	56
Deep tinted glass, Club Coupe	150	129	134
with SLE Decor Pkg.	107	92	95
with sliding rear window	115	99	102
with SLE Decor Pkg. and sliding rear window or rear defogger	72	62	64
Sliding rear window	113	97	101
Swing-out rear quarter window, Club Coupe	43	37	38
Auxiliary battery	134	115	119
Bright wheel covers	42	36	37
Rally wheel trim	60	52	53
Side-mounted spare tire carrier	NC	NC	NC
Dual rear wheels, regular cab	955	821	850
Tires: LT225/75R16C tires (front), 2WD regular cab (credit)	(104)	(88)	(88)
2WD Club Coupe	NC	NC	NC
LT225/75R16D tires (front), regular cab (credit)	(70)	(58)	(58)
rear	428	368	381
spare	300	258	267
LT225/75R16D on/off road tires (front), regular cab (credit)	(48)	(40)	(40)
front Club Coupe	22	19	20
dual rear, regular cab	472	406	420
dual rear, Club Coupe	44	38	39
spare	311	267	277
LT245/75R116E spare tire, regular cab	335	288	298
LT245/75R16E on/off road tires, 4WD regular cab each axle	22	19	20
spare	346	298	308

GMC

GMC Sonoma

RECOMMENDED

GMC Sonoma Club Coupe SLS

GMC's compact pickup has been redesigned for 1994 with new styling, more powerful engines, and available 4-wheel anti-lock brakes. Sonoma is again available with rear- or 4-wheel drive, regular or extended cabs, and 4-cylinder or V-6 power.

The Chevrolet S10 Pickup is built from the same design as Sonoma and also has been redesigned (see separate report).

Body Styles/Chassis

The 1994 Sonoma uses a modified version of the previous-generation platform, so wheelbases are unchanged at 108.3 inches for the regular-cab short-bed, 117.9 for the regular-cab long-bed, and 122.9 for the extended-cab.

However, overall lengths increase by about 10 inches for all three body styles: the regular-cab long- and short-bed, and the extended-cab short-bed, which GMC calls the Club Coupe. Length of the standard cargo bed remains at six feet. Long-bed models retain a 7.5-foot box.

A center high-mounted stoplamp and side door guard beams are newly standard.

Rear anti-lock brakes are standard on 4-cylinder Sonomas. V-6 models have 4-wheel anti-lock brakes that work in both rear- and 4WD. Last year, rear anti-lock brakes were standard and worked only in 2WD.

Exterior width of the cab increases by one inch, but GMC says shoulder room increases by three inches due to revised door panels.

A 3-place bench seat is standard on regular-cab models. Club Coupes add two rear jump seats. Front buckets are optional on both. The dashboard has been redesigned, a new center console contains two cup holders, and two auxiliary 12-volt power outlets are available.

The base trim level is called the SL and is available on regular-cab models with either bed length. The SLS trim level is available on regular-cab short-bed models and on Club Coupes. In addition, a regular-cab long-bed model is offered in SLE trim.

Like the Chevy S10, the new Sonoma is available in special off-road 4WD regular-cab short-bed form with a 4-inch-wider track, a 3-inch higher stance, an off-road suspension/tire package, wheel flares, and underbody shields. Sonoma calls this the Highrider package, Chevy calls it the ZR2 package.

GMC does not offer a specific package to match the S10's 2WD regular-cab Super Sport, though Sonoma's SLS trim does include such Super Sport features as a body-colored grille.

Payload ceilings are 1703 pounds for the regular-cab short-bed, 1743 for the regular-cab long-bed, and 1519 for the extended-cab model.

Powertrains

As on the S10, Sonoma's base engine is a new 118-horsepower 2.2-liter 4-cylinder. It's available with either a 5-speed manual or a 4-speed automatic transmission with electronic shift controls. The 2.2 replaces a 105-horsepower 2.5-liter four.

Again standard on 4WD models is a 165-horsepower 4.3-liter V-6. It's available with either transmission.

Optional on all models a 195-horsepower "enhanced" version of the 4.3-liter V-6. On the Sonoma, this "enhanced" V-6 is available only with manual transmission n the Highrider truck and only with automatic on all others. On the

Specifications	Short bed	Long bed	Club Coupe
Wheelbase, in.	108.3	117.9	122.9
Overall length, in.	188.8	204.7	203.4
Overall width, in.	67.9	67.9	67.9
Overall height, in.	60.5	60.5	60.5
Turn diameter, ft.	36.9	39.9	41.6
Curb weight, lbs.	2897	3157	3081
Fuel capacity, gal.	20.0	20.0	20.0

Passenger Area Dimensions

Seating capacity	3	3	5
Front head room, in.	39.5	39.5	39.5
Rear head room, in.	—	—	NA
Front leg room, in.	42.4	42.4	42.4
Rear leg room, in.	—	—	NA

Cargo Dimensions and Payloads

Cargo area length, in.	72.6	88.6	72.6
Cargo area width, in.	56.5	56.5	56.5
Cargo area width between wheels, in.	39.5	39.5	39.5
Cargo area height, in.	16.8	16.8	16.8
Max. payload, lbs.	1703	1743	1519
Max. trailer weight, lbs.	6000	6000	6000

Engines	ohv I-4	ohv V-6	ohv V-6
Size, liters/cu. in.	2.2/134	4.3/262	4.3/262
Horsepower @ rpm	118 @ 5200	165 @ 4000	195 @ 4500
Torque (lbs./ft.) @ rpm	130 @ 2800	235 @ 2400	260 @ 3600
Availability	S	O[1]	O

EPA city/highway mpg

5-speed OD manual	23/28	18/23	18/25
4-speed OD automatic	19/25	18/23	17/24

1. Standard on 4WD models.

Built in Shreveport, La., and Linden, N.J.

KEY: Dimensions and capacities are supplied by the manufacturers. **Curb Weight:** base models, not including optional equipment. **Max. payload, lbs.** = gross amount; net payload may be lower due to optional equipment. **Engines: ohv** = overhead valve; **ohc** = overhead cam; **l** = inline cylinders; **V** = cylinders in V configuration; **flat** = horizontally opposed cylinders; **rpm** = revolutions per minute; **OD** = overdrive transmission; **S** = standard; **O** = optional; **NA** = not available.

S10, it can be mated to the 5-speed manual only when ordered in the ZR2 package.

Sonoma 4x4s use GM's Insta-Trac on-demand, part-time 4WD system that's not for use on dry pavement. It has automatic locking front hubs and shift-on-the-fly between 2WD and 4WD High.

Optional on 4WD SLS and SLE Sonomas is an electronic-shift transfer case. Instead of a floor-mounted transfer-case lever, this option allows shifting into and out of 4WD and between 4WD High and 4WD Low with the push of a dashboard button.

SL models can tow up to 2000 pounds. A heavy-duty towing package, which requires the 165-horsepower 4.3 V-6, allows 2WD models to tow up to 6000 pounds and enables 4x4s to pull up to 5500 pounds.

See our report on the Chevrolet S10 for an evaluation of the Sonoma.

Prices

GMC Sonoma

	Retail Price	Dealer Invoice	Fair Price
2WD SL regular cab, short bed	$9806	$9267	$9567
2WD SLS regular cab, short bed	11138	10080	10380
2WD SL regular cab, long bed	10106	9550	9850
2WD SLE regular cab, long bed	11680	10570	10870
4WD SL regular cab, short bed	14306	13519	13819
4WD SLS regular cab, short bed	15638	14152	14452
4WD SL regular cab, long bed	14606	13803	14103
4WD SLE regular cab, long bed	16180	14643	14943
2WD SLS Club Coupe extended cab, short bed	12113	10962	11262
4WD SLS Club Coupe extended cab, short bed	16613	15035	15335
Destination charge	470	470	470

Additional "value-priced" models may also be available in California.

Standard Equipment:

SL: 2.2-liter 4-cylinder engine (2WD), 4.3-liter V-6 engine (4WD), 5-speed manual transmission, anti-lock rear braking system (4-wheel anti-lock on 4WD), power steering, vinyl or cloth fold-down bench seat, rear jump seats (Club Cab), solar-control tinted glass, manual outside mirrors, intermittent wipers, oil pressure and coolant temperature gauges, voltmeter, trip odometer, AM/FM radio, right visor mirror, 205/75R15 tires (2WD), 235/75R15 tires (4WD), full-size spare tire. **SLS** adds: cloth reclining bucket seats, floor console, carpeting, illuminated entry system, reading lights, lighted visor mirrors, floormats, body-color bumpers, striping, heavy duty suspension (Club Coupe), rally wheels. **SLE** adds to SLS: 60/40 reclining split bench seat, conventional two-tone paint, gray bumpers and moldings.

Optional Equipment:

4.3-liter V-6, 2WD	850	731	757
Includes 4-wheel anti-lock brakes.			
4.3-liter HP V-6, 2WD	1409	1212	1254
4WD	559	481	498
Includes engine oil cooler, heavy duty radiator and transmission oil cooler, tachometer, 4-wheel anti-lock brakes.			
4-speed automatic transmission	927	797	825
Locking differential	252	217	224
Electronic shift transfer case, 4WD SLS or SLE	123	106	109
Air conditioning	805	692	716
SLS Sport Decor, 2WD regular cab with short bed	NC	NC	NC
4WD regular cab with short bed	NC	NC	NC
See standard equipment list for package content.			
SLE Comfort Decor, 2WD or 4WD regular cab with long bed	NC	NC	NC
2WD or 4WD regular cab with short bed, 2WD or 4WD Club Coupe	267	230	238
See standard equipment list for package content.			

GMC

	Retail Price	Dealer Invoice	Fair Price
SL Pkg. 1SB (credit)	(281)	(242)	(242)
Deletes radio and rear bumper.			
SLS Pkg. 1SC	NC	NC	NC
SLS trim may be upgraded to SLE trim.			
SLS/SLE Pkg. 1SC w/Bonus Value Pkg.	NC	NC	NC
SLS Pkg. 1SC plus alloy wheels.			
SLS Pkg. 1SD	$122	$105	$109
SLS trim may be upgraded to SLE trim; adds cassette player.			
SLS/SLE Pkg. 1SD w/Bonus Value Pkg.	122	105	109
SLS Pkg. 1SD plus alloy wheels.			
Heavy Duty Trailering Equipment with V-6 and automatic transmission	408	351	363
with V-6 and manual transmission	345	297	307
with HP V-6	210	181	187
Heavy Duty Suspension Pkg.			
2WD regular cab with short bed	64	55	57
4WD regular cab	217	187	193
Includes heavy duty rear springs, front and rear shocks.			
Sport Suspension Pkg. 2WD SLS or SLE regular cab with short bed	316	272	281
2WD SLE regular cab with long bed	252	217	224
Includes heavy duty rear springs, heavy duty front and rear shocks, 215/65R15 white letter tires.			
Highrider Suspension Pkg., 4WD SLS regular cab with short bed	1685	1449	1500
Wheel opening flares, Bilstein shocks, heavy duty springs, Shield Pkg., 31x10.5R15 on-off road tires.			
Off-Road Suspension Pkg. 4WD regular cab with short bed	481	414	428
4WD regular cab with long bed	417	359	371
4WD Club Coupe	328	282	292
Bilstein gas shocks, upsized torsion bar, jounce bumpers, stabilizer bar, heavy duty springs, 235/75R15 on-off road white letter tires.			
Underbody Shield Pkg., 4WD	126	108	112
5-lead wiring harness	41	35	36
Heavy duty cooling, 4.3-liter V-6 with 5-speed	135	116	120
4.3-liter V-6 with automatic	198	170	176
Includes engine oil cooler, transmission oil cooler (with automatic).			
Heavy duty battery	56	48	50
Cold Climate Pkg.	109	94	97
Engine block heater, heavy duty battery.			
Convenience Pkg. ZQ6	475	409	423
Power windows and locks, power mirrors. Requires SLS or SLE Decor.			
Convenience Pkg. ZQ3	383	329	341
Tilt steering wheel, cruise control.			
Carpeting and floormats, SL	75	65	67
Rubber floorcovering, SLS, SLE (credit)	(20)	(17)	(17)
AM/FM cassette	122	105	109
AM/FM cassette with equalizer	272	234	242
AM/FM CD player	406	349	361
Radio delete, SL (credit)	(226)	(194)	(194)
60/40 reclining split bench seat, 2WD or 4WD SLS regular cab with short bed (credit)	(181)	(156)	(156)
2WD or 4WD Club Coupe (credit)	(156)	(134)	(134)
Cloth reclining front bucket seats with console, 2WD or 4WD regular cab	181	156	161
2WD or 4WD SLE Club Coupe	156	134	139
Leather-wrapped steering wheel, SLS, SLE	54	46	48
Tachometer, w/4.3-liter HP V-6	59	51	53
Below-eye-line mirrors, SL	52	45	46
Sliding rear window	113	97	101
Air deflector and fog lamps, 2WD or 4WD SLE	115	99	102
Rear bumper delete, SL (credit)	(55)	(47)	(47)
Special two-tone paint, SLS	297	255	264
Striping, SL	55	47	49
205/75R15 white letter tires	121	104	108
205/75R15 on-off road white letter tires	170	146	151
235/75R15 on-off road white letter tires	182	157	162
235/75R15 tires	NC	NC	NC
31x10.5R15 on-off road tires	NC	NC	NC
Four alloy wheels, 2WD SLS or SLE	248	213	221
4WD SLS or SLE	280	241	249

GMC Suburban

GMC Suburban C2500

This big sport-utility gets side door guard beams, a center high-mounted stoplamp, a new grille, and an optional 6.5-liter turbocharged diesel V-8 for 1994.

Suburban, a 4-door wagon based on the full-size General Motors pickup truck, is sold in nearly identical form by Chevrolet dealers (see separate report).

Body Styles/Chassis

Suburban comes with four side doors and two swing-open rear doors. A tailgate with a top-hinged rear window is a no-cost option.

Rear-drive Suburbans carry the "C" designation, 4-wheel-drive models use a "K" designation. The 1500-series Suburbans have a half-ton payload rating and the 2500 series a three-quarter-ton rating.

Suburban's grille has been slightly revised for 1994 and a new body-color grille surround teamed with composite headlamps is available.

Anti-lock brakes that work on all four wheels in both 2WD and 4WD are standard on all models.

Maximum payload, 3430 pounds, is found on the C2500.

Powertrains

Standard on all models is a 5.7-liter V-8. It's rated at 210 horsepower in 1500-series models and at 190 horsepower in the 2500s.

A 230-horsepower 7.4-liter V-8 is optional on 2500-series Suburbans.

A 6.5-liter turbocharged diesel V-8 rated at 190 horsepower is a new option for 2500-series Suburbans. It is the first diesel offered since Suburban was redesigned on the C/K pickup platform for the 1992 model year.

A 4-speed overdrive automatic is the only transmission. It has electronic shift controls and a second-gear-start feature for increased traction on slippery surfaces.

Suburban 4x4s use GM's Insta-Trac 4WD system, which allows shifting in and out of 4WD High at any speed. It comes with automatic locking front hubs, but is a part-time system and is not for use on dry pavement.

Maximum towing capacity is 6500 pounds on the 1500-series and 10,000 pounds on the 2500s.

Accommodations

The GMC Suburban comes in a base trim level, with SLE again the label for the uplevel option packages.

A 3-place front bench is standard in base models. SLE models add a 3-place split/folding middle bench, which is optional on base Suburbans. Also optional on both models are front bucket seats and a removable 3-place third seat.

See the Chevrolet Suburban report for an evaluation of the GMC Suburban.

Specifications

	4-door wagon
Wheelbase, in.	131.5
Overall length, in.	219.5
Overall width, in.	76.4
Overall height, in.	68.8
Turn diameter, ft.	45.8
Curb weight, lbs.	4657
Fuel capacity, gal.	42.0

Passenger Area Dimensions

Seating capacity	9
Front head room, in.	39.9
Rear head room, in.	38.8
Front leg room, in.	41.7
Rear leg room, in.	36.3

Cargo Dimensions and Payloads

Cargo area length, in.	99.6
Cargo area width, in.	64.0
Cargo area width between wheels, in.	48.5
Cargo area height, in.	40.8
Cargo vol., cu. ft.	149.5
Max. payload, lbs.	3430
Max. trailer weight, lbs.	10,000

Engines

	ohv V-8	ohv V-8	Turbodiesel ohv V-8
Size, liters/cu. in.	5.7/350	7.4/454	6.5/400
Horsepower @ rpm	210 @ 4000[1]	230 @ 3600	190 @ 3400
Torque (lbs./ft.) @ rpm	300 @ 2800	385 @ 1600	385 @ 1700
Availability	S	O[2]	O[2]

EPA city/highway mpg

4-speed OD automatic	13/17	NA	15/19

1. 190 horsepower in 2500 series. 2. 2500 series.

Built in Janesville, Wisc.

KEY: Dimensions and capacities are supplied by the manufacturers. **Curb Weight:** base models, not including optional equipment. **Max. payload, lbs.** = gross amount; net payload may be lower due to optional equipment. **Engines: ohv** = overhead valve; **ohc** = overhead cam; **I** = inline cylinders; **V** = cylinders in V configuration; **flat** = horizontally opposed cylinders; **rpm** = revolutions per minute; **OD** = overdrive transmission; **S** = standard; **O** = optional; **NA** = not available.

Prices

GMC Suburban

	Retail Price	Dealer Invoice	Fair Price
C1500 4-door wagon	$20476	$17917	$18917
K1500 4-door wagon	22727	19886	20886
C2500 4-door wagon	21704	18991	19991
K2500 4-door wagon	23923	20933	21933
Destination charge	640	640	640

C denotes 2WD; K denotes 4WD.

Standard Equipment:

5.7-liter V-8 engine, 4-speed automatic transmission (heavy duty on 2500), anti-lock brakes, power steering, vinyl front bench seat, dual outside mirrors, intermittent wipers, coolant temperature and oil pressure gauges, volt-

GMC

meter, trip odometer, solar-control tinted glass, AM/FM radio, digital clock, front stabilizer bar, front tow hooks (4WD), chrome bumpers, black front air dam (1500), wheel flares (2500), 235/75R15XL tires (C1500), LT225/75R16D tires (K1500), LT245/85R16E tires (2500).

Optional Equipment:

	Retail Price	Dealer Invoice	Fair Price
7.4-liter V-8 engine, 2500	$605	$520	$538
6.5-liter turbo diesel V-8 engine, 2500	2825	2430	2514
Front air conditioning	845	727	752
Front and rear air conditioning	1295	1114	1153
with Group 2	450	387	401
Optional axle ratio	NC	NC	NC
Locking differential	252	217	224
Tailgate body (replaces swing-out rear doors)	NC	NC	NC
SLE Decor Group	1926	1656	1714
Deluxe moldings, cloth upholstery, added insulation, carpet, floormats, front end appearance pkg., auxiliary lighting, upgraded door panel trim, door map pockets, 60/40 split folding center seat, bright wheel covers, deluxe bumpers with bumper guards, sport steering wheel, lighted visor mirrors.			
SLE Pkg. 2	3980	3423	3542
SLE Decor Pkg., air conditioning, tilt steering column, cruise control, power windows and door locks, power mirrors, 60/40 split folding center seat, cassette player.			
SLE Pkg. 3	5313	4569	4729
Pkg. 2 plus front and rear air conditioning, deep-tinted glass, rear seat.			
Cold Climate Pkg.	33	28	29
Engine block heater.			
Convenience Pkg. I	606	521	539
with tailgate body	542	466	482
Power windows and locks. Requires SLE Decor Pkg.			
Convenience Pkg. ZQ3	383	329	341
Cruise control and tilt steering column.			
Appearance Pkg.	191	164	170
Color-keyed grille, composite halogen headlights, dual horns.			
Trailer Towing Pkg.	210	181	187
Platform hitch, wiring harness, heavy duty flasher.			
Engine and transmission oil cooling	198	170	176
with Trailer Towing Pkg.	NC	NC	NC
Skid Plate Pkg.	225	194	200
Differential, transfer case, fuel tank, and engine shields.			
Rear Window Equipment Pkg.	279	240	248
Rear window wiper/washer, rear defogger. Requires tailgate body.			
Rear defogger	154	132	137
Rear defogger and wiper/washer	279	240	248
Rear wiper/washer	125	108	111
Requires tailgate body.			
Deep-tinted glass	305	262	271
Rear heater	205	176	182
Roof marker lamps	52	45	46
Camper style mirrors	53	46	47
Power mirrors, 1500	98	84	87
Requires power windows and door locks.			
Conventional 2-tone paint	180	155	160
Deluxe 2-tone paint	290	249	258
AM/FM cassette	122	105	109
AM/FM cassette with equalizer	272	234	242
Premium speakers	85	73	76
AM radio credit	(170)	(146)	(146)
Radio delete (credit)	(287)	(247)	(247)
60/40 cloth center seat	585	503	521
Center and rear seats	1095	942	975
with SLE Decor Pkg.	578	497	514
Custom cloth reclining 60/40 split front seat	174	150	155
Requires SLE Decor Pkg.			
Custom cloth reclining bucket seats	540	464	481
Requires SLE Decor Pkg.			
Custom cloth bench seat	NC	NC	NC
Power driver's seat	240	206	214
Leather reclining 60/40 split bench seat	1015	873	903
with center and rear seats	1380	1187	1228
Heavy duty front torsion bars, 4WD	63	54	56
Tow hooks (std. 4WD)	38	33	34

Top: Front bucket seats with center console are optional. Middle: Even with three rows of seats, Suburban has plenty of cargo room. Above: Rear side-hinged doors are standard.

	Retail Price	Dealer Invoice	Fair Price
Roof rack	$126	$108	$112
Tachometer	59	51	53
Wheel flares molding, 1500	180	155	160
Bright wheel trim rings	60	52	53
with SLE Decor Pkg.	18	15	16
Alloy wheels, 1500	310	267	276
with SLE Decor Pkg.	268	230	239
Tires, C1500 235/75R15XLS whitewall	95	82	85
Tires, K1500 LT225/75R16D on/off road, each axle	55	47	49
LT245/75R16C, each axle	59	47	53
LT245/75R16C on/off road, each axle	116	95	103
LT245/75R16C on/off road white letter, each axle	241	207	214
LT245/75R16E, each axle	230	194	205
Tires, 2500 LT245/75R16E on/off-road black letter, each axle	55	47	49
Spare tire and wheel delete, 2500 (credit)	(283)	(243)	(243)

CONSUMER GUIDE®

GMC

GMC Yukon

RECOMMENDED

GMC Yukon SLE

Yukon, GMC's version of the full-size sport-utility vehicle sold by Chevrolet as the Blazer, gets new standard safety features and a turbocharged diesel V-8 as a new option. In addition, the optional air conditioning now uses CFC-free refrigerant. The Blazer also gets those changes this year (see separate report).

Body Styles/Chassis

Yukon comes only as a 3-door wagon and like the Blazer, is built from the same design as General Motors' big C/K pickups. These sport-utility wagons have a full-length metal roof with a tailgate and top-hinged window.

New safety features include side door guard beams and a center high-mounted stoplamp located in the roof.

Anti-lock brakes that work on all four wheels in both 2- and 4-wheel drive are standard.

Yukon comes in a single price series, but there are SL and SLE Decor packages with fancier exterior and interior trim. There also is a Sport Package that includes sportier exterior trim and "Yukon GT" identification. A new grille gives the Yukon a slightly different appearance at the front. Models with one of the decor packages also get new dual composite headlamps. Maximum payload is 1540 pounds.

Powertrains

A 210-horsepower 5.7-liter gasoline V-8 returns as the standard engine.

The new optional engine is Yukon's first turbocharged diesel. It's a 6.5-liter V-8 and is rated at 180 horsepower.

The gas engine is available with a standard 5-speed manual transmission or optional 4-speed electronic automatic. The diesel comes only with a heavy-duty 4-speed automatic.

All Yukons have GM's Insta-Trac 4WD, a part-time system that's not for use on dry pavement. It has automatic locking front hubs and allows shifting between 2WD and 4WD High at any speed.

Towing capacity is 6500 pounds with the optional trailering package.

Accommodations

A pair of low-back front bucket seats is standard. A 3-place 40/60 split front bench and high-back buckets are optional with the SLE package. A folding 3-place rear bench is standard.

For an evaluation of the Yukon, see the Chevrolet Blazer report.

Specifications

	3-door wagon
Wheelbase, in.	111.5
Overall length, in.	187.7
Overall width, in.	76.4
Overall height, in.	71.0
Turn diameter, ft.	41.5
Curb weight, lbs.	4606
Fuel capacity, gal.	30.0

Passenger Area Dimensions

Seating capacity	6
Front head room, in.	40.2
Rear head room, in.	38.0
Front leg room, in.	41.7
Rear leg room, in.	37.6

Cargo Dimensions and Payloads

Cargo area length, in.	73.2
Cargo area width, in.	NA
Cargo area width between wheels, in.	48.5
Cargo area height, in.	41.7
Cargo vol., cu. ft.	102.8
Max. payload, lbs.	1517
Max. trailer weight, lbs.	700

Cargo Dimensions and Payload

Cargo area length, in.	73.2
Cargo area width, in.	NA
Cargo area width between wheels, in.	48.5
Cargo area height, in.	41.7
Cargo vol., cu. ft.	102.8
Max. payload, lbs.	1517
Max. trailer weight, lbs.	7000

Engines

	ohv V-8	Turbodiesel ohv V-8
Size, liters/cu. in.	5.7/350	6.5/395
Horsepower @ rpm	210 @ 4000	180 @ 3400
Torque (lbs./ft.) @ rpm	300 @ 2800	360 @ 1700
Availability	S	O

EPA city/highway mpg

5-speed OD manual	12/16	
4-speed OD automatic	12/16	15/19

Built in Janesville, Wisc.

KEY: Dimensions and capacities are supplied by the manufacturers. **Curb Weight:** base models, not including optional equipment. **Max. payload, lbs.** = gross amount; net payload may be lower due to optional equipment. **Engines: ohv** = overhead valve; **ohc** = overhead cam; **I** = inline cylinders; **V** = cylinders in V configuration; **flat** = horizontally opposed cylinders; **rpm** = revolutions per minute; **OD** = overdrive transmission; **S** = standard; **O** = optional; **NA** = not available.

Prices

GMC Yukon	Retail Price	Dealer Invoice	Fair Price
SL 4WD 3-door wagon	$21396	$18721	$19522
Destination charge	600	600	600

Standard Equipment:

5.7-liter V-8 engine, 5-speed manual transmission, automatic locking front hubs, part-time 4-wheel drive with 2-speed transfer case, 4-wheel anti-lock

GMC • Honda

brakes, power steering, vinyl front bucket seats, 3-passenger rear bench seat, solar-control glass, AM/FM radio, trip odometer, voltmeter, oil pressure and engine temperature gauges, dual outside mirrors, intermittent wipers, front tow hooks, front stabilizer bar, chrome bumpers, painted argent grille, heavy duty battery, black bodyside moldings, bright wheel opening moldings, LT245/75R16C tires.

Optional Equipment:

	Retail Price	Dealer Invoice	Fair Price
6.5-liter turbodiesel engine	$2825	$2430	$2514
4-speed automatic transmission	930	800	828
Air conditioning	845	727	752
Optional axle ratio	NC	NC	NC
Locking differential	252	217	224
SLE Decor Pkg.	927	797	825

Deluxe front appearance pkg., carpet, auxiliary lighting, cargo net, floormats, sport steering wheel, front and rear map lights, door map pockets, cloth upholstery, lighted visor mirrors.

Sport Pkg.	569	489	506

Color-keyed bumpers with rub strips, wheel flares, black mirrors, sport decals, alloy wheels. Requires SLE Decor Pkg.

SLE Pkg. 2	1977	1700	1760

SLE Decor Pkg., air conditioning, tilt steering wheel, cruise control, AM/FM cassette player.

SLE Pkg. 3	2457	2113	2187

SLE Group 2 plus power mirrors, power windows and door locks, deep-tinted glass, alloy wheels.

Sport Pkg. 4	2726	2344	2426

SLE Group 3 plus Sport Pkg.

Heavy Duty Trailering Special Equipment	210	181	187

Includes trailer hitch and platform, wiring harness, engine and transmission oil cooler, heavy duty radiator. Requires automatic transmission.

Skid Plate Pkg.	225	194	200

Differential, transfer case, fuel tank, and engine shields.

Appearance Pkg.	191	164	170

Includes chrome grille, composite halogen headlights, dual horns.

Cold Climate Pkg.	33	28	29

Includes engine block heater.

Off-Road Chassis Pkg.	400	344	356

Includes Skid Plate Pkg. Requires 265/75R16 tires.

Convenience Pkg. I	367	316	327

Power front windows, power locks. Requires SLE Decor Pkg.

Convenience Pkg. II	383	329	341

Cruise control and tilt steering wheel.

Defroster Pkg.	279	240	248

Rear window wiper/washer, rear defogger.

Tachometer	59	51	53
Engine oil cooler	135	116	120
Engine oil and transmission cooler	198	170	176
Deep-tinted glass	215	185	191
Power driver's seat	240	206	214
Cloth reclining highback front bucket seats	341	293	303

Includes floor and roof consoles. Requires SLE Decor Pkg.

Cloth reclining 60/40 split bench seat	NC	NC	NC

Requires SLE Decor Pkg.

Power mirrors, painted	98	84	87
Camper style stainless steel mirrors	53	46	47
AM/FM cassette	122	105	109
AM/FM cassette with equalizer	272	234	242
AM radio credit	(170)	(146)	(146)
Radio delete (credit)	(287)	(247)	(247)
Heavy duty front torsion bars	63	54	56
Conventional 2-tone paint	180	155	160
Deluxe 2-tone paint	290	249	258
Roof carrier	126	108	112
Rear wiper/washer	125	108	111
Wheel flare moldings	180	155	160
Wheel trim rings	60	52	53
Alloy wheels	310	267	276
with SLE Decor Pkg.	250	215	223
Tires: LT245/75R16C	57	49	51
LT245/75R16C white outline letter	182	157	162
LT265/75R16C	191	164	170
LT265/75R16C white outline letter	315	271	280

Honda Passport

Honda Passport EX

Passport went on sale in mid-December as Honda's belated entry in the lucrative sport-utility market, where it's been conspicuously absent among major Japanese nameplates.

The Passport is based on the design and mechanical features of the Isuzu Rodeo. The two vehicles are built in the same Indiana plant. Passport differs from Rodeo in styling details, colors, equipment packaging, and slightly higher prices.

Production constraints limit Honda to 20,000 Passports for 1994, but the firm says it's in the sport-utility market to stay and one company official says Honda is already working with Isuzu on the next-generation Passport/Rodeo design, which should appear in about two years.

Body Styles/Chassis

Like Rodeo, Passport comes in a single 5-door wagon body style with a glass hatch above a side-hinged tailgate.

But where Isuzu offers two trim levels, Honda has three, starting with a price-leader DX model sold only with a 4-cylinder engine, 5-speed manual transmission, and 2-wheel drive. One step up are Passport V-6 LX models with 2- or 4-wheel-drive and manual or automatic transmission. Topping the line is a 4WD-only V-6 EX.

Also like Rodeo, all Passports have standard rear anti-lock brakes (ABS) operable in 2WD only. (Honda says 4-wheel discs and ABS are in the works for 1995.) The one major option is a $600 package for the LX and EX that replaces the standard 15-inch wheels and tires with 16-inch tires and chrome wheels.

Not surprisingly, Passport's maximum payloads are nearly the same as Rodeo's: 955 pounds for 4x4s, 1015 for 4x2s.

Powertrains

Passport's 4-cylinder engine is the familiar 2.6-liter single-cam Isuzu unit with 120 horsepower. The V-6 in the Passport LX and EX is the same single-cam 3.2-liter offered in Rodeo and Isuzu's Trooper S.

Like Rodeo's, Passport's automatic transmission features electronic shift control with "Power" and "Normal" modes, plus a "Winter" mode that starts you off in third gear to minimize wheel slip in slippery conditions.

CONSUMER GUIDE® 111

Honda

Passport 4x4s inherit Rodeo's part-time 4WD drive system (not for use on dry pavement) with a 2-speed transfer case and standard auto-lock front hubs. But where Isuzu says 4WD-High can be engaged "on-the-fly" at up to 5 mph, Honda recommends a complete stop. Like Rodeo, going from 4-High to 2WD requires stopping and then backing up about three feet to fully disengage the front hubs.

Towing capacities duplicate Rodeo's: 2000 pounds for the base DX and 4500 for other models.

Accommodations

Again like Rodeo, the base Passport has a front bench seat and seats six. Other models carry five via twin front buckets. All Passports have a three-person rear bench with fold-down seatback, split 60/40 on EX.

As on all 1994 Rodeos, a swing-out exterior spare-tire carrier is standard across-the-board. No air bag is offered.

Evaluation

As you might guess, Honda's "badge-engineered" Rodeo has the same pluses and minuses as Isuzu's version.

Specifications

	Regular cab
Wheelbase, in.	108.7
Overall length, in.	176.5
Overall width, in.	66.5
Overall height, in.	66.5
Turn diameter, ft.	37.7
Curb weight, lbs.	3545
Fuel capacity, gal.	21.9

Passenger Area Dimensions

Seating capacity	6
Front head room, in.	38.0
Rear head room, in.	38.0
Front leg room, in.	42.5
Rear leg room, in.	36.0

Cargo Dimensions and Payloads

Cargo area length, in.	67.3
Cargo area width, in.	55.0
Cargo area width between wheels, in.	40.0
Cargo area height, in.	74.9
Max. payload, lbs.	1015
Max. trailer weight, lbs.	4500

Engines

	ohc I-4	ohc V-6
Size, liters/cu. in.	2.6/156	3.2/193
Horsepower @ rpm	120 @ 4600	175 @ 5200
Torque (lbs./ft.) @ rpm	150 @ 2600	188 @ 4000
Availability	S[1]	S

EPA city/highway mpg

5-speed OD manual	16/20	16/19
4-speed OD automatic		15/18

1. Passport DX.

Built in Lafayette, Ind.

KEY: Dimensions and capacities are supplied by the manufacturers. **Curb Weight:** base models, not including optional equipment. **Max. payload, lbs.** = gross amount; net payload may be lower due to optional equipment. **Engines: ohv** = overhead valve; **ohc** = overhead cam; **I** = inline cylinders; **V** = cylinders in V configuration; **flat** = horizontally opposed cylinders; **rpm** = revolutions per minute; **OD** = overdrive transmission; **S** = standard; **O** = optional; **NA** = not available.

Passport shares its design with the Isuzu Rodeo, including the dashboard. A 5-door body style is the only one offered. Cargo room is so-so for the class, though a folding rear seatback, split 60/40 on EX model, increases luggage space.

As with the Rodeo, the smooth and quiet V-6 engine is preferable to the 4-cylinder. The six doesn't have the low-speed muscle of the 6-cylinder engines in rivals from Jeep, Ford, and General Motors, but it does furnish sufficient acceleration even with automatic transmission.

We've had little seat time with the 4-cylinder engine, but experience with it in the related Amigo suggests it won't have the muscle to move the bigger, heavier Passport/Rodeo with any gusto on or off the road.

Though Rodeo itself is little changed for 1994, Honda

convinced Isuzu to tighten up the steering, which now has less on-center play and far better feel. The results are easier course corrections in gusty winds on the highway and more positive steering control when you're crawling along unbeaten paths.

Serious off-roaders might not mind the part-time 4WD, but we think the lack of true shift-on-the-fly capability is a big drawback for all-around use, especially since so many competitors offer it. Honda knows this too, and is working with Isuzu to come up with a more convenient 4WD system in time for model-year '96, by which time driver- and passenger-side air bags should be available, too.

That apart, you'll like Passport if you like the Rodeo. Both are solidly built, easy to drive in the daily grind, quiet at most speeds (though wind noise is noticed on the highway), easy-riding, comfortable, and reasonably roomy. Faults include a lofty interior step-up, so-so cargo space for the class, overly complex multi-button lighting and wiper controls, and a radio/tape player mounted too low for easy adjustments while driving.

So why choose Passport over Rodeo? No reason, really, but Honda is hoping that its superior brand image, different price/equipment mixes, and maybe better treatment by its dealers will convince people otherwise. For our money, a better overall value would be the roomier, more powerful Ford Explorer or the Jeep Grand Cherokee, which has superior 4WD systems and a driver-side air bag.

Prices

Honda Passport	Retail Price	Dealer Invoice	Fair Price
DX 2WD 5-door wagon, 5-speed	$15660	—	—
LX 2WD 5-door wagon, 5-speed	18870	—	—
LX 2WD 5-door wagon, automatic	19770	—	—
LX 4WD 5-door wagon, 5-speed	21350	—	—
LX 4WD 5-door wagon with 16-inch Wheel Pkg., 5-speed	21950	—	—
LX 4WD 5-door wagon, automatic	22450	—	—
LX 4WD 5-door wagon with 16-inch Wheel Pkg., automatic	23050	—	—
EX 4WD 5-door wagon, 5-speed	23900	—	—
EX 4WD 5-door wagon, automatic	25000	—	—
EX 4WD 5-door wagon with 16-inch Wheel Pkg., 5-speed	24500	—	—
EX 4WD 5-door wagon with 16-inch Wheel Pkg., automatic	25600	—	—
Destination charge	350	350	350

Dealer invoice and fair price not available at time of publication.

Standard Equipment:

DX: 2.6-liter 4-cylinder engine, 5-speed manual transmission, anti-lock rear brakes, variable-assist power steering, front bench seat with folding center armrest, folding rear seatback, tinted glass, rear defogger, cargo area light, fuel tank skid plate, full-size spare tire, outside mounted spare tire carrier, 225/75R15 mud and snow tires, styled steel wheels. **LX 2WD** adds: 3.2-liter V-6 engine, 5-speed manual or 4-speed automatic transmission, 4-wheel disc brakes, cruise control, power windows and door locks, reclining front bucket seats, center storage console, tilt steering column, remote tailgate release, tachometer, upgraded door trim panels, door courtesy lights, AM/FM cassette player. **LX 4WD** adds to LX 2WD: part-time 4-wheel drive, automatic locking front hubs, air conditioning, 2-speed transfer case, transfer case skid plate, alloy wheels. **EX** adds to LX 4WD: removable tilt-up moonroof, heated power mirrors, 60/40 split folding rear bench seat, rear chrome bumpers, rear privacy glass, rear wiper/washer, leather-wrapped steering wheel, intermittent wipers, cargo net, passenger-side visor mirror, map lights. 16-inch Wheel Pkg. adds: limited-slip differential, flared wheel opening moldings, splash guards, 245/70R16 tires, 16-inch alloy wheels.

Options are available as dealer-installed accessories.

Isuzu Amigo

Isuzu Amigo S

Isuzu's open-air compact sport-utility vehicle loses its base engine and automatic transmission, but gains some new standard features for 1994, including power steering.

Isuzu has stopped producing cars. This Japanese company now builds only sport-utility vehicles and pickup trucks. General Motors owns an equity interest in Isuzu and the two companies have shared vehicles in the past.

Body Styles/Chassis

Amigo is basically a shortened Isuzu pickup truck with a side-hinged tailgate. In place of the pickup box is an open seating/cargo area covered by a removable canvas top. The roof above the front seats is solid and can be optionally fitted with a tilt/take-out moonroof, making Amigo a semi-convertible.

Models labeled S and XS are offered and both rear- and 4-wheel drive form.

All Amigos have 4-wheel disc brakes with rear-wheel anti-lock control. The anti-lock system works only in 2-wheel drive.

A high-mounted rear stoplamp is a new safety feature. Vent windows are dropped, and a spare tire cover is standard on all models.

Also, 16-inch wheels and tires are now standard, replacing 15s on S models and 31x10.5R tires on the 4WD XS.

Maximum payloads are 710 pounds for 2WD models and 885 pounds for the 4x4s.

Powertrains

Gone is the 96-horsepower 2.3-liter 4-cylinder engine used in last year's entry-level S model.

All Amigos now use a 2.6-liter 4-cylinder that's unchanged from last year at 120 horsepower. A 5-speed manual now is the only transmission. Gone is the 4-speed automatic that had been optional for 2.6-liter 2WD models.

Amigo's part-time on-demand 4WD is not for use on dry pavement. It has manual front hubs that can be locked only from outside the vehicle when it is stopped. With the hubs engaged, you can shift between 2WD and 4WD High at speeds below about 5 mph.

Maximum towing capacity is 2000 pounds.

Isuzu

Accommodations

All Amigos have front bucket seats and a 2-place rear bench that folds for extra cargo room and is removable via a wrench.

For '94, all models come standard with power steering, power door mirrors, and a center floor console. Also, location of the emergency-brake lever changes from beneath the dashboard to the floor.

Evaluation

Because it's derived from a pickup truck, Amigo feels more substantial than other mini-4x4s. The penalty is relatively high curb weights of 3390 pounds on 2WD models and 3495 on 4x4s.

That heft overburdened the 2.3-liter engine, so dropping it was a wise move. But even a 2.6-liter 4WD model with manual transmission needed a plodding 15.5 seconds to get to 60 mph in our tests. And it returned a disappointing 14.4 mpg, though admittedly in hard city and suburban driving.

At least shifting the 5-speed allows you to keep the well-mannered engine in the meaty part of its powerband, so around-town acceleration isn't really as bad as the 0-60-mph time might suggest. The automatic afforded no such luxury, so its demise is unmourned, as well.

Amigo's 91.7-inch wheelbase falls between the Geo Tracker/Suzuki Sidekick's 86.6 inches and the Jeep Wrangler's 93.4. But with standard 245/70R16 tires, Amigo's 58-inch track (the distance between wheels on the same axle) is three inches wider than Tracker/Sidekick's and an inch broader than the base Wrangler's.

That width contributes to relatively predictable handling, though as with any of these rigs, you must respect the short wheelbase and high center of gravity by not trying to take corners as you would in a sports sedan. Also, Amigo's relatively wide body hampers maneuvering in tight places despite a fairly compact turning circle.

Amigo has a more compliant ride than its class rivals: firm but not rocky. Hard braking produces no unwanted rear-wheel lock-up, though stopping distances are average.

Isuzu's 4WD is far less convenient than the shift-on-the-fly systems of costlier sport-utility wagons and the rival Jeep Wrangler. (The Geo Tracker/Suzuki Sidekick don't have shift-on-the-fly, either.)

The final advantage of Amigo's width is a more spacious interior than in Wrangler or Tracker/Sidekick. Amigo's reclining front seats slide forward when tipped, though they don't slide quite far enough to make getting to the rear seat really easy. That rear bench is narrow, hard, and bolt-upright. And all the painted metal in back is likely to get scratched quite easily.

Amigo shares its dashboard with Isuzu's pickups and its 5-door Rodeo sport-utility. It's flawed only by a radio mounted too low and by too many switches for lights and wipers. Wide side pillars impede vision over the shoulder; the tailgate-mounted spare tire does the same astern.

The canvas half-top is held by an overabundance of fasteners, but it's still more straightforward than most competitors' affairs. It seals pretty well too, and the rear rolls up for extra ventilation, but we found that the plastic windows can mist up quickly, and the top support bar further clutters driver vision.

Specifications

	2-door wagon
Wheelbase, in.	91.7
Overall length, in.	168.1
Overall width, in.	70.1
Overall height, in.	69.9
Turn diameter, ft.	33.5
Curb weight, lbs.	3615
Fuel capacity, gal.	21.9

Passenger Area Dimensions

Seating capacity	4
Front head room, in.	38.0
Rear head room, in.	32.0
Front leg room, in.	42.5
Rear leg room, in.	19.5

Cargo Dimensions and Payloads

Cargo area length, in.	51.4
Cargo area width, in.	NA
Cargo area width between wheels, in.	40.5
Cargo area height, in.	37.9
Cargo vol., cu. ft.	51.0
Max. payload, lbs.	885
Max. trailer weight, lbs.	2000

Engines

	ohc I-4
Size, liters/cu. in.	2.6/156
Horsepower @ rpm	120 @ 4600
Torque (lbs./ft.) @ rpm	150 @ 2600
Availability	S

EPA city/highway mpg

5-speed OD manual	17/20

Built in Japan.

KEY: Dimensions and capacities are supplied by the manufacturers. **Curb Weight:** base models, not including optional equipment. **Max. payload, lbs.** = gross amount; net payload may be lower due to optional equipment. **Engines: ohv** = overhead valve; **ohc** = overhead cam; **I** = inline cylinders; **V** = cylinders in V configuration; **flat** = horizontally opposed cylinders; **rpm** = revolutions per minute; **OD** = overdrive transmission; **S** = standard; **O** = optional; **NA** = not available.

Prices

Isuzu Amigo

	Retail Price	Dealer Invoice	Fair Price
S 2WD	$14849	$13067	$13567
XS 2WD	15499	13639	14139
S 4WD	16799	14783	15283
XS 4WD	17199	15135	15635
Destination charge	350	350	350

Standard Equipment:

S: 2.6-liter 4-cylinder engine, 5-speed manual transmission, 4-wheel disc brakes with rear anti-lock control, speed sensitive power steering, cloth reclining front bucket seats, rear bench seat, center storage console with cup holders, carpet, power mirrors, trip odometer, coolant temperature gauge, tinted glass, fuel tank skid plate (2WD), transfer case, radiator, and oil pan skid plates (4WD), day/night mirror, floormats, 245/70R16 outline white letter mud and snow tires, full size spare, spare tire cover. **XS** adds: upgraded door trim, bright power mirrors with defogger, bright exterior trim, tilt steering column, tachometer, voltmeter, oil pressure gauge, intermittent wipers, alloy wheels (4WD).

Optional Equipment:

Air conditioning	830	706	768
Sunroof	300	256	278
AM/FM cassette with two speakers	405	284	345
Pull-out AM/FM cassette with four speakers	520	376	448

Isuzu Pickup

Isuzu Pickup regular-cab long-bed

This compact pickup gains a high-mounted stoplamp and loses its vent windows for 1994. Power steering is now standard on models with the larger of the two available engines, and the outside rearview mirrors are restyled.

Body Styles/Chassis

Isuzu offers three pickup body styles.

The regular-cab short-bed has a 105.6-inch wheelbase and a 6-foot cargo bed. It's available in 2- or 4-wheel drive.

The regular-cab long-bed has a 119.2-inch wheelbase and a 7.5-foot cargo bed. It's available in 2WD only.

The Spacecab has the same wheelbase and overall length as the long-bed model, but uses a 6-foot bed and is available in 2WD only.

All models are offered in a single trim level.

Regular cabs have a 3-place bench seat. Spacecabs have front buckets, two forward-facing rear jump seats, and a rear-cab cargo cover.

Rear anti-lock brakes that work in 2WD only are standard. Four-wheel-drive models come standard with 4-wheel disc brakes in place of the others' front-disc/rear-drum setup.

Maximum payloads are 1470 pounds on the 2WD short-bed, 1345 pounds on the 4WD short-bed, 1360 on the long-bed, and 1190 on the Spacecab.

Powertrains

A 2.3-liter 4-cylinder is the base engine on 2WD regular-cab short- and long-bed models. It's rated at 96-horsepower with a 2-barrel carburetor; models sold in California have fuel injection and are rated at 100 horsepower.

A 2.6-liter fuel-injected 4-cylinder rated at 120 horsepower is available on 2WD and 4WD short-bed models and is the only engine on the Spacecab.

A 3.1-liter V-6 built by General Motors and also rated at 120 horsepower is available on the 4WD regular-cab short-bed.

The Spacecab is available only with a 4-speed automatic transmission. All other Isuzu pickups come only with a 5-speed manual.

Four-wheel-drive models have an on-demand, part-time 4WD system that is not for use on dry pavement. Manual locking front hubs are standard. Lacking shift-on-the-fly, you have to stop the vehicle to engage 4WD, and back up a few feet to release the front hubs upon disengaging 4WD.

The towing limit for all models is 2000 pounds for trailers with their own brakes, 1000 pounds for trailers without.

Evaluation

Isuzu's limited U.S. dealer network means there may not be a factory-authorized outlet near you. And without a 4WD extended-cab model or wide availability of automatic transmission, the model lineup is very constricted.

If you can find an Isuzu dealer, however, this pickup is worth considering. It's a solidly built rig and Isuzu dealers, hungry for market share, are likely to offer more sizeable discounts than most other Japanese dealers.

Our most recent test model was a short-bed 4x4 with the V-6 and 5-speed. Acceleration was adequate, but not in a league with a 4.0-liter Ford Ranger or 4.3-liter Chevrolet S10 pickup. Actually, while the GM-built 3.1-liter V-6 is slightly smoother than the gruff Isuzu 2.6 four, it isn't that much faster. Still, we'd like to see the six made available with 2WD or with an extended-cab body.

We averaged a mediocre 16.2 mpg with the V-6, compared to 18.5 with the 5-speed 4WD 2.6-liter 4-cylinder model. The base 2.3 is acceptable for the lightest-duty chores.

Specifications

	Short bed	Long bed	Spacecab
Wheelbase, in.	105.6	119.2	119.2
Overall length, in.	177.3	193.8	193.8
Overall width, in.	66.6	66.6	66.6
Overall height, in.	62.3	62.3	62.6
Turn diameter, ft.	35.4	39.4	39.4
Curb weight, lbs.	2830	2940	3110
Fuel capacity, gal.	14.0	19.8	19.8

Passenger Area Dimensions

Seating capacity	3	3	4
Front head room, in.	38.2	38.2	38.2
Rear head room, in.	—	—	NA
Front leg room, in.	42.5	42.5	42.5
Rear leg room, in.	—	—	NA

Cargo Dimensions and Payloads

Cargo area length, in.	74.0	90.4	72.7
Cargo area width, in.	57.9	57.9	57.9
Cargo area width between wheels, in.	42.0	42.0	42.0
Cargo area height, in.	16.2	16.2	16.2
Max. payload, lbs.	1470	1360	1190
Max. trailer weight, lbs.	2000	2000	2000

Engines

	ohc I-4	ohc I-4	ohv V-6
Size, liters/cu. in.	2.3/138	2.6/156	3.1/191
Horsepower @ rpm	96 @ 4600	120 @ 4600	120 @ 4400
Torque (lbs./ft.) @ rpm	123 @ 2600	150 @ 2600	165 @ 2800
Availability	S	S[1]	O[2]
EPA city/highway mpg			
5-speed OD manual	22/24	19/23	15/19
4-speed OD automatic		20/24	

1. Std., 4WD models and Spacecab.   2. 4WD Regular Cab short-bed.

Built in Lafayette, Ind., and Japan.

KEY: Dimensions and capacities are supplied by the manufacturers. **Curb Weight:** base models, not including optional equipment. **Max. payload, lbs.** = gross amount; net payload may be lower due to optional equipment. **Engines: ohv** = overhead valve; **ohc** = overhead cam; **I** = inline cylinders; **V** = cylinders in V configuration; **flat** = horizontally opposed cylinders; **rpm** = revolutions per minute; **OD** = overdrive transmission; **S** = standard; **O** = optional; **NA** = not available.

Isuzu

Continued lack of automatic-locking hubs and shift-on-the-fly keeps Isuzu's pickups a huge step behind most of the competition in 4WD convenience.

The 4x4s' all-disc brake system is unusual for this class, however. Pedal action is hard, but stopping distances short and we saw no rear lockup even with an empty cargo bed.

The ride is truck-like and is especially choppy on the short-bed 4x4. Noise levels are average. Payloads are a little light for this class, but towing limits are paltry.

Interior trim is attractive, and Spacecabs come with jump seats and a nifty roller-blind cargo cover. Ergonomics, cab comfort, and driver vision are on par with the field, though the lights and wipers are governed by a multitude of small buttons rather than the more-convenient stalk controls. Otherwise, this could be most any Japanese pickup.

Prices

Isuzu Pickup	Retail Price	Dealer Invoice	Low Price
S 2WD 2.3 standard bed, 5-speed	$9399	$8506	$8706
S 2WD 2.3 long bed, 5-speed	10809	9620	9820
S 2WD 2.6 standard bed, 5-speed	11999	10679	10879
S 2WD 2.6 Spacecab, automatic	12709	11311	11511
S 4WD 2.6 standard bed, 5-speed	13519	11897	12097
S 4WD 3.1 standard bed, 5-speed	14379	12654	12854
Destination charge	350	350	350

Standard Equipment:

S 2.3: 2.3-liter 4-cylinder engine, 5-speed manual transmission, anti-lock rear brakes, cloth bench seat with folding armrest, dual mirrors, tinted glass, carpeting, day/night mirror, trip odometer, coolant temperature gauge, 195/75R14 tires. **S 2.6/3.1** adds: 2.6-liter 4-cylinder engine or 3.1-liter V-6 engine, 5-speed manual transmission, power steering, carpeted floormats. **4WD models** add: 4-wheel disc brakes, tachometer, oil pressure gauge, voltmeter, coolant temperature guage, trip odometer, skid plates, 225/75R15 tires with full size spare and bright hub caps. **Spacecab** adds: 4-speed automatic transmission, reclining front bucket seats, rear jump seats, retractable cargo cover.

Optional Equipment:

Air conditioning (NA 2WD 2.6 models)	830	706	741
Power steering, 2.3 models	325	276	290
10.5 Tire and Wheel Pkg., 4WD	1145	974	1023
31x10.5R off-road tires on alloy wheels, fender flares, mud flaps.			
Bright Pkg., 2WD	525	447	469
Bright bumpers, grille, mirrors and handles, trim rings.			
Bright Pkg., 4WD	1670	1421	1492
Bright bumpers, grille, mirrors, handles and wheel opening moldings. Includes 10.5 Tire and Wheel Pkg.			
AM/FM cassette	405	284	298
Brush/Grille guard, 4WD	305	216	227

A 4-cylinder is standard in regular-cab long-bed models.

Isuzu Rodeo

Isuzu Rodeo LS

This compact sport-utility wagon gets some minor equipment revisions, but the big news is that re-trimmed Rodeos will become Honda's first sport-utility offerings.

Rodeo is built in Indiana at a plant Isuzu shares with Subaru. The plant also will produce the Honda Passport, which goes on sale in early 1994 (see separate report).

Body Styles/Chassis

Rodeo, like the Amigo, is based on Isuzu's pickup truck, but Rodeo is a 5-door wagon with a one-piece tailgate whose rear window opens independently.

Base S and top-rung LS models are offered, both with 2- or 4-wheel drive. The slow-selling LS 2WD model with manual transmission has been dropped. For appearance sake, 4x2s have the same ride height as 4x4s regardless of wheel/tire package.

V-6 Rodeos come with 4-wheel disc brakes, rare for this class. Anti-lock rear brakes are standard and on 4x4 models they work in 2WD only.

For '94, power steering is standard instead of optional on the base 4-cylinder S model, while air conditioning is a new standard feature on LS models. Front vent windows have been dropped, and a rear wiper/washer and an outside spare tire carrier are now standard on all V-6 models, not just 4x4s.

Maximum payloads are 930 pounds on 4WDs, 1015 on 4x2s.

Powertrains

A 120-horsepower 2.6-liter 4-cylinder is again standard on 2WD S models. A 175-horsepower 3.2-liter V-6 is available in the 2WD S and is standard in all other Rodeos.

A 5-speed manual is standard with both engines. Optional only with the V-6 is a 4-speed overdrive automatic with electronic shift control, power and economy settings, and a separate winter mode for third-gear starts to minimize tire slippage on slippery surfaces.

Rodeo's part-time, on-demand 4WD is not for use on dry pavement. It has a floor-mounted transfer-case lever and automatic-locking front hubs. The system has limited shift-on-the-fly capability: 4WD High can be engaged at speeds up to 5 mph, but the vehicle must be stopped and reversed to return to 2WD.

Towing capacity is 2000 pounds with the 4-cylinder engine, 4500 pounds with the V-6.

CONSUMER GUIDE®

Isuzu

Accommodations

Reclining bucket seats are standard except on the 2WD S, where a bench provides what Isuzu terms "occasional seating for three." All models have a fold-down 3-place rear bench, which is split 50/50 on the LS.

Evaluation

Among Rodeo's strong points is an absorbent suspension that provides a comfortable ride and stands up to off-road work. There's also ample head room and leg room front and rear, though the rear doors open only about 70 degrees and are tough to negotiate while stepping up into the interior. The rear seat folds flat to create a wide cargo floor that's 67 inches long. A full-size spare is mounted inside on the 4-cylinder model and it takes up a big chunk of cargo space.

Isuzu's V-6 doesn't have the low-speed muscle of the larger Ford and Jeep sixes, but it works well with the automatic transmission, which changes gears smoothly and downshifts promptly for passing. Though engine noise is moderate, road noise is prominent enough to interfere with normal conversation at highway speeds.

One of Rodeo's biggest drawbacks to those in the snow-belt is its rather primitive 4WD system. Many competitors offer full-time 4WD that can be left engaged on dry pavement, which Rodeo's cannot. Even more have "shift-on-the-fly" units, while Rodeo—even with its automatic-locking hubs—must be nearly stopped before engaging 4WD, then stopped and backed up to disengage it.

The rear ABS is another halfway measure, particularly in a "family" 4x4. Stopping distances were acceptable, but our 4x2 test vehicle tended to lock its front brakes in hard stops. This, plus experience with other like-equipped trucks, makes us doubt the effectiveness of anti-lock control for the rear brakes alone. Though it may help with heavy loads in back, the forward weight transfer that occurs in hard braking

Specifications

	5-door wagon
Wheelbase, in.	108.7
Overall length, in.	176.5
Overall width, in.	66.5
Overall height, in.	65.4
Turn diameter, ft.	37.7
Curb weight, lbs.	3545[1]
Fuel capacity, gal.	21.9

1. 3995 lbs., 4WD.

Passenger Area Dimensions

Seating capacity	6
Front head room, in.	38.2
Rear head room, in.	37.8
Front leg room, in.	42.5
Rear leg room, in.	36.1

Cargo Dimensions and Payloads

Cargo area length, in.	67.3
Cargo area width, in.	55.0
Cargo area width between wheels, in.	40.0
Cargo area height, in.	37.0
Cargo vol., cu. ft.	74.9
Max. payload, lbs.	1015
Max. trailer weight, lbs.	4500

Engines

	ohc I-4	ohc V-6
Size, liters/cu. in.	2.6/156	3.2/193
Horsepower @ rpm	120 @ 4600	175 @ 5200
Torque (lbs./ft.) @ rpm	150 @ 2600	188 @ 4000
Availability	S[1]	S
EPA city/highway mpg		
5-speed OD manual	16/20	16/19
4-speed OD automatic		15/18

1. 2WD S model.

Built in Lafayette, Ind.

KEY: Dimensions and capacities are supplied by the manufacturers. **Curb Weight:** base models, not including optional equipment. **Max. payload, lbs.** = gross amount; net payload may be lower due to optional equipment. **Engines: ohv** = overhead valve; **ohc** = overhead cam; **I** = inline cylinders; **V** = cylinders in V configuration; **flat** = horizontally opposed cylinders; **rpm** = revolutions per minute; **OD** = overdrive transmission; **S** = standard; **O** = optional; **NA** = not available.

Top: Rodeo's radio is mounted too low for easy adjustment. Middle: Inside-mount spare tire eats into cargo space. Above: Outside spare and rear wiper are newly standard for V-6 Rodeos.

CONSUMER GUIDE®

Isuzu

demands skid resistance at the front wheels to maintain vital steering control, especially with light loads. And what is the wisdom of disabling ABS in 4WD?

Handling is about par for the class, but there's good feedback through the nicely weighted variable-assist power steering. Hard cornering causes no frightful lean angles or alarming tippyness.

Our test drivers' only other complaints were a radio mounted too low for easy adjustment while driving, and multi-button wiper and lighting controls that flank the gauge cluster but would be handier as steering-column stalks.

At the beginning of the '93 model year, we rated Rodeo as a good value in the sport-utility market despite its primitive 4WD system and rear-only anti-lock brakes. But prices skyrocketed during the year and went up again for the little-changed '94s. Compared to this time last year, list price for the base 2WD S model is about $1300 higher, while the top-line LS 4WD V-6 rose a whopping $2800. At their current prices, we no longer feel the Rodeo is such a good value.

Prices

Isuzu Rodeo	Retail Price	Dealer Invoice	Fair Price
S 4-cylinder 2WD 5-door wagon, 5-speed	$14969	$13472	$13972
S V-6 2WD 5-door wagon, 5-speed	17499	15311	15811
S V-6 2WD 5-door wagon, automatic	18399	16099	16599
LS V-6 2WD 5-door wagon, automatic	22729	19887	20387
S V-6 4WD 5-door wagon, 5-speed	19249	16746	17246
S V-6 4WD 5-door wagon, automatic	20349	17703	18203
LS V-6 4WD 5-door wagon, 5-speed	23799	20705	21205
LS V-6 4WD 5-door wagon, automatic	24899	21662	22162
Destination charge	375	375	375

Standard Equipment:

S: 2.6-liter 4-cylinder engine, 5-speed manual transmission, anti-lock rear brakes, power steering, cloth front bench seat with folding armrest, folding rear seat, rear defogger, tinted glass, day/night mirror, cargo rope hooks, carpet, 225/75R15 all-terrain tires, styled steel wheels with bright center caps. **S V-6** adds: 3.2-liter V-6, 5-speed manual or 4-speed automatic transmission, 4-wheel disc brakes, reclining front bucket seats, center console, tachometer, oil pressure and coolant temperature guages, voltmeter, intermittent rear wiper/washer, carpeted floormats, outside spare tire, wheel trim rings. **LS** adds: air conditioning, tilt steering column, split folding rear seat, power windows and doors, cruise control, cassette player, velour upholstery, map and courtesy lights, intermittent wipers, right visor mirror, leather-wrapped steering wheel, bright exterior trim, roof rack, privacy rear quarter and rear side glass, cargo net, alloy wheels. **4WD** adds: part-time 4WD automatic locking hubs, tow hooks, skid plates, 245/70R16 tires, alloy wheels.

Optional Equipment:

Air conditioning, S	850	722	786
Preferred Equipment Pkg., S V-6	1990	1690	1840
Air conditioning, power windows and locks, cruise control, intermittent rear wiper/washer, roof rack, 4-speaker cassette player, cargo net.			
Alloy Wheel Pkg., S 4WD	990	847	919
16-inch alloy wheels, 245/70R16 tires, limited-slip differential.			
Limited-slip differential, LS 4WD	260	210	235
Sunroof, LS	300	255	278
Rear wiper/washer, S 4-cylinder	185	158	172
Outside spare tire carrier, S 4-cylinder	275	234	255
Brush/grille guard	305	216	261
AM/FM cassette, S	585	410	498
CD player, LS	550	385	468
Aero roof rack, S	195	137	166
Carpeted floormats (std. V-6)	55	39	47

Isuzu Trooper

Isuzu Trooper LS

Wider availability of a 4-wheel anti-lock brake system (ABS) is the major change for Isuzu's high-line sport-utility vehicle.

Body Styles/Chassis

Trooper S and LS models have four side doors and unique 70/30 split rear doors.

The RS model has two side doors and is 17 inches shorter than the 4-door in wheelbase and overall length. For 1994, the RS has new 16-inch alloy wheels as standard equipment.

Last year, rear-wheel ABS was standard on all models and 4-wheel ABS was optional only on the most-expensive model, the LS. This year, 4-wheel ABS is standard on the LS and optional on S and RS. Rear-wheel ABS remains standard on S and RS.

Towing capacity is 5000 pounds for both body styles.

Powertrains

All Troopers have an Isuzu-designed-and-built 3.2-liter V-6 with 4 valves per cylinder. The S model uses a single-cam version rated at 175 horsepower while LS and RS have a dual-cam unit with 190 horsepower.

With both engines, a 5-speed manual transmission is standard and a 4-speed overdrive automatic is optional. The automatic features Normal and Power shift programs, the latter engaged by a console-mounted button. A second similar button activates a Winter mode that locks out first gear to minimize wheel slip in slick conditions.

Standard is part-time 4-wheel drive that's not for use on dry pavement. It has a floor-mounted transfer-case lever and lacks true shift-on-the-fly capability. Though 4-wheel High can be engaged on-the-move at speeds up to 5 mph, returning to 2WD requires stopping and backing up a few feet.

Maximum recommended payloads are 1290 pounds for the S and RS, 1245 for the LS.

Accommodations

All Troopers seat five on front bucket seats and a 3-person rear bench that double folds for maximum cargo space. Standard on the LS is a 70/30 split rear seat.

Isuzu

For '94, leather upholstery (in gray only) is a new option for the LS and is accompanied by heated front seats with power adjustments. Also, a gear position-indicator is added to the instrument cluster for models with automatic transmission.

Evaluation

The 2-door RS is a puzzler: smaller than the 4-door yet more expensive than the S. Most other Japanese companies have dropped their 2-door sport-utility models because of slow sales and a 25-percent import tariff that makes them uncompetitive. The 4-door, however, is mostly on target.

Routine acceleration with either version of the 3.2 V-6 is adequate (11.7 seconds to 60 mph in our LS test vehicle), but speed tails off on steep uphill grades, forcing the automatic transmission to move down a gear—sometimes two. That can also mean busy hunting between gears and lots of torque-converter locking and unlocking. Happily, the automatic's shifts are mostly smooth and always prompt. We were less pleased with fuel economy. Our test LS averaged just 15.8 mpg even with a lot of highway driving, where our best was 17.4.

The engines are well muffled, but wind noise is on the high side.

Trooper's power steering is a little vague on-center but communicates well otherwise. And it works nicely with the suspension, which delivers a firm yet pleasantly supple on-road ride and takes off-road humps and gulleys comfortably in stride. Fast highway cornering induces mild body lean but little tippyness. Braking is good, though pedal action is a trifle touchy. Our LS's 4-wheel ABS did its job, kicking in momentarily when we encountered some iced-over mountain snow patches.

The 4-door Trooper is one of the roomiest sport-utility vehicles. It boasts loads of head clearance front and rear, plus enough rear seat width for three adults to fit without squeezing each other. The rear seat is split 70/30 on the LS and double-folds for maximum cargo space.

Isuzu's trademark 70/30 rear cargo door (something like an upright refrigerator/freezer) opens onto a tall, long cargo

Specifications	2-door wagon	4-door wagon
Wheelbase, in.	91.7	108.7
Overall length, in.	166.5	183.5
Overall width, in.	68.7	68.7
Overall height, in.	72.8	72.8
Turn diameter, ft.	32.8	38.1
Curb weight, lbs.	4060	4210
Fuel capacity, gal.	22.5	22.5

Passenger Area Dimensions		
Seating capacity	5	5
Front head room, in.	39.8	39.8
Rear head room, in.	39.8	39.8
Front leg room, in.	40.8	40.8
Rear leg room, in.	32.2	39.1

Cargo Dimensions and Payloads		
Cargo area length, in.	43.3	60.8
Cargo area width, in.	53.5	53.5
Cargo area width between wheels, in.	40.0	40.0
Cargo area height, in.	41.5	41.5
Cargo vol., cu. ft.	68.3	90.0
Max. payload, lbs.	1290	1290
Max. trailer weight, lbs.	5000	5000

Engines	ohc V-6	dohc V-6
Size, liters/cu. in.	3.2/193	3.2/193
Horsepower @ rpm	175 @ 5200	190 @ 5600
Torque (lbs./ft.) @ rpm	188 @ 4000	195 @ 3800
Availability	S[1]	S[2]

EPA city/highway mpg		
5-speed OD manual	16/18	15/17
4-speed OD automatic	15/18	15/18

1. S 4-door. 2. LS, RS

Built in Japan.

KEY: Dimensions and capacities are supplied by the manufacturers. **Curb Weight:** base models, not including optional equipment. **Max. payload, lbs.** = gross amount; net payload may be lower due to optional equipment. **Engines: ohv** = overhead valve; **ohc** = overhead cam; **I** = inline cylinders; **V** = cylinders in V configuration; **flat** = horizontally opposed cylinders; **rpm** = revolutions per minute; **OD** = overdrive transmission; **S** = standard; **O** = optional; **NA** = not available.

Top: Trooper has a roomy cabin and fine ergonomics. Above: Side-hinged back doors open in a unique 70/30 split. An RS model with two side doors also is offered.

Isuzu • Jeep

deck. We haven't yet tested the shorter RS, but its smaller size naturally will cut down on cargo space and rear-seat leg room.

Trooper 4-doors are an attractive choice among upper-end sport-utilities. High refinement and a roomy interior are their greatest strengths, though we also like their ride, on-road agility, and general user-friendly nature.

Offsetting all their good dynamic qualities, Troopers remain at competitive disadvantage in lacking true shift-on-the-fly capability. Though they come with auto-lock front hubs, that's no substitute for the greater convenience of Ford's Touch Drive and similar systems. Plus, base prices increase a healthy $1500 on S models, $1850 on LS models, and $1650 on the RS from this time last year.

Prices

Isuzu Trooper	Retail Price	Dealer Invoice	Fair Price
S 4-door 4WD wagon, 5-speed	$21250	$18381	$18881
S 4-door 4WD wagon, automatic	22400	19376	19876
LS 4-door 4WD wagon, 5-speed	26850	22822	23322
LS 4-door 4WD wagon, automatic	28000	23800	24300
RS 2-door 4WD wagon, 5-speed	24000	21120	21620
RS 2-door 4WD wagon, automatic	25150	22132	22632
Destination charge	400	400	400

Standard Equipment:

S: 3.2-liter V-6 engine, 5-speed manual transmission, power steering, 4-wheel disc brakes, anti-lock rear brakes, part-time 4WD system with automatic locking front hubs, cloth reclining front bucket seats, folding rear seat, full door trim, AM/FM cassette, center console, dual outside mirrors, rear defogger, tilt steering column, intermittent wipers, rear wiper/washer, skid plates, tachometer, voltmeter, oil pressure gauge, visor mirrors, tinted glass, rear step pad, rear air deflector, 245/70R16 tires, wheel trim rings. **LS** adds: 3.2-liter DOHC engine, 4-wheel anti-lock brakes, limited-slip differential, air conditioning, power windows and locks, cruise control, multi-adjustable driver's seat, split folding rear seat, bright exterior trim, color-keyed bumpers, variable intermittent wipers, headlamp wiper/washer, leather-wrapped steering wheel, heated power mirrors, privacy glass, premium cassette system with six speakers, power antenna, anti-theft alarm, visor mirrors, fog lamps, cargo floor rails, retractable cargo cover, cargo net, alloy wheels. **RS** deletes 4-wheel anti-lock brakes, bright exterior trim and adds: anti-lock rear brakes, sport cloth interior, one-piece folding and reclining rear seat, flip-out quarter windows, color-keyed grille, 2-tone paint, gas shocks.

Optional Equipment:

4-wheel anti-lock brakes, S and RS	1100	880	990
Limited slip-differential, S	260	210	235
Requires Preferred Equipment Pkg.			
Air conditioning, S	900	720	810
Preferred Equipment Pkg., S	1880	1600	1740
Air conditioning, power windows and locks, 6-speaker radio, split-folding rear seat, power mirrors, cruise control, retractable cargo cover, cargo net.			
Appearance Pkg., S	750	600	675
Alloy wheels with locks, bright radiator grille and mirrors, color-keyed bumpers. Requires Preferred Equipment Pkg.			
Power sunroof, LS	1100	1915	2083
Heated leather power seats, LS 2250			
Split folding rear seat, S	250	200	225
CD player, S with Preferred Equipment Pkg., RS and LS	550	385	468
2-tone paint, LS	280	225	253
Retractable cargo cover, S	120	84	102
Cargo net, S	30	21	26

Jeep Cherokee

RECOMMENDED

Jeep Cherokee Country 5-door 4WD

Cherokee returns for its 11th season with side door guard beams and a center high-mounted stoplamp as new standard safety features. Both are now federally required on truck-based vehicles such as Cherokee. Also, an automatic transmission is offered with the 4-cylinder engine for the first time.

With the arrival of the larger Grand Cherokee for 1993, this line of sport-utility vehicles was downgraded in price and equipment.

Body Styles/Chassis

Cherokee continues in 3- and 5-door body styles. Both have a one-piece rear liftgate and each is offered with 2- or 4-wheel drive.

The base model is called SE this year and it joins the mid-level Sport and top-shelf Country models. All are available in either body style.

Anti-lock brakes (ABS) that work in both 2WD and 4WD are optional on models equipped with the 6-cylinder engine (see below).

Maximum payload for any Cherokee is 1150 pounds.

Powertrains

A 130-horsepower 2.5-liter 4-cylinder is standard on the Cherokee SE. A 190-horsepower 4.0-liter inline-6 is optional on the SE and standard on Sport and Country.

A 5-speed manual transmission is standard with both engines and a 4-speed overdrive automatic is optional with the six. A 3-speed automatic is newly optional with the 4-cylinder engine.

Two 4WD systems are available. Command-Trac, a part-time system for use only on slick surfaces, is standard on 4WD models. Selec-Trac, a full-time system that can be used on smooth, dry pavement, is optional on Sport and Country models with the automatic transmission.

Maximum trailer weight is 5000 pounds with the 6-cylinder engine, automatic transmission, and optional trailer towing package.

Accommodations

All Cherokees have two front bucket seats and a 3-place rear bench with a one-piece folding backrest.

Country interiors are distinguished by plastic woodgrain trim.

120   CONSUMER GUIDE®

Jeep

Evaluation

Introduced as a 1984 model, Cherokee shows its age, though it's still among the best choices in a compact 4x4.

It has convenient 4WD systems, commendable off-road capabilities, and civilized on-road manners. It isn't as roomy as a Grand Cherokee or Ford Explorer, but Cherokee will carry four adults in comfort.

Luggage space is ample when you lower the rear seat-back, but the cargo bay isn't that tall, and while its floor is flat, it's also rather far off the ground, despite Cherokee's slightly lower-than-average ride-height. A split-fold backrest would be nice for versatility, but you can't get one even as an option. We'd also appreciate less wind and engine noise.

Most Cherokees are ordered with the strong 6-cylinder engine, which allows you to scoot off the line and pass other vehicles quickly with either transmission. Six-cylinder

Among direct competitors, only the Grand Cherokee offers a driver-side air bag. Even without one, Cherokee is ahead of some newer rivals in features, and a better value to boot.

Specifications

	3-door wagon	5-door wagon
Wheelbase, in.	101.4	101.4
Overall length, in.	168.8	168.8
Overall width, in.	67.7	67.7
Overall height, in.	63.9	63.9
Turn diameter, ft.	35.9	35.9
Curb weight, lbs.	3042	3090
Fuel capacity, gal.	20.0	20.0

Passenger Area Dimensions

Seating capacity	5	5
Front head room, in.	38.3	38.3
Rear head room, in.	38.0	38.0
Front leg room, in.	41.0	41.0
Rear leg room, in.	35.3	35.3

Cargo Dimensions and Payloads

Cargo area length, in.	58.0	58.0
Cargo area width, in.	49.0	49.0
Cargo area width between wheels, in.	42.5	42.5
Cargo area height, in.	36.0	36.0
Cargo vol., cu. ft.	71.8	71.8
Max. payload, lbs.	1150	1150
Max. trailer weight, lbs.	5000	5000

Engines

	ohv I-4	ohv I-6
Size, liters/cu. in.	2.5/150	4.0/242
Horsepower @ rpm	130 @ 5250	190 @ 4750
Torque (lbs./ft.) @ rpm	149 @ 3000	225 @ 4000
Availability	S	S[1]

EPA city/highway mpg

5-speed OD manual	19/22	17/21
3-speed automatic	NA	
4-speed OD automatic		15/19

1. Optional, Cherokee SE.

Built in Toledo, Ohio.

KEY: Dimensions and capacities are supplied by the manufacturers. **Curb Weight:** base models, not including optional equipment. **Max. payload, lbs.** = gross amount; net payload may be lower due to optional equipment. **Engines: ohv** = overhead valve; **ohc** = overhead cam; **I** = inline cylinders; **V** = cylinders in V configuration; **flat** = horizontally opposed cylinders; **rpm** = revolutions per minute; **OD** = overdrive transmission; **S** = standard; **O** = optional; **NA** = not available.

CONSUMER GUIDE®

Prices

Jeep Cherokee

	Retail Price	Dealer Invoice	Fair Price
SE 3-door 2WD	$13077	$12355	$12555
SE 3-door 4WD	14562	13721	13921
SE 5-door 2WD	14087	13289	13739
SE 5-door 4WD	15572	14661	15111
Sport 3-door 2WD	15234	13861	14061
Sport 3-door 4WD	16719	15183	15383
Sport 5-door 2WD	16244	14765	15215
Sport 5-door 4WD	17729	16092	16542
Country 3-door 2WD	16871	15301	15551
Country 3-door 4WD	18356	16623	16873
Country 5-door 2WD	17881	16205	16655
Country 5-door 4WD	19366	17532	17982
Destination charge	495	495	495

Standard Equipment:

SE: 2.5-liter 4-cylinder engine, 5-speed manual transmission, power steering, vinyl front bucket seats, front armrest, folding rear seat, mini console, AM/FM radio with two speakers, tinted glass, dual remote mirrors, 215/75R15 tires; 4WD system is Command-Trac part-time. **Sport** adds: 4.0-liter 6-cylinder engine, cloth reclining front bucket seats, tachometer, trip odometer, oil pressure and coolant temperature gauges, voltmeter, intermittent wipers, Sport Decor Group, spare tire cover, cargo tiedown hooks, 2-tone paint, 225/75R15 outlined white letter all-terrain tires. **Country** adds: front console with armrest and storage, rear seat heater ducts, AM/FM stereo with four speakers, Light Group, leather-wrapped steering wheel, roof rack, rear wiper/washer, dual remote break-away mirrors, Country Decor Group, Extra-Quiet Insulation Pkg., front floormats, bodyside cladding, 225/70R15 tires, lattice-design alloy wheels.

Optional Equipment:

Pkg. 23B/25B/26B, SE	492	418	431

Cloth reclining bucket seats, floor console with armrest, Visibility Group. Pkg. 25B requires 4.0-liter V-6. Pkg. 26B requies 4.0-liter V-6 and automatic transmission.

Pkg. 26E, Sport	897	762	785

Adds 4-speed automatic transmission.

Pkg. 25E/26E, Sport	1169	994	1023

Air conditioning, floor console with armrest, roof rack, leather-wrapped tilt steering wheel, rear wiper/washer, floormats. Pkg. 26E requires automatic transmission.

Pkg. 25H/26H, Country	824	700	721

Air conditioning, cruise control, cassette player with four speakers, tilt steering wheel. Pkg. 26H requires automatic transmission.

4.0-liter 6-cylinder engine	612	520	536
4-speed automatic transmission	897	762	785
Selec-Trac full-time 4WD, Sport, Country	394	335	345

Requires automatic transmission.

Trac-Lok rear differential	285	242	249

Requires conventional spare tire.

Jeep Cherokee Sport 3-door 4WD

Jeep

	Retail Price	Dealer Invoice	Fair Price
Anti-lock brakes	$599	$509	$524
Requires 4.0-liter engine.			
Heavy Duty Alternator/Battery Group	135	115	118
with rear defogger	63	54	55
Air conditioning	836	711	732
Includes Heavy Duty Alternator/Battery Group.			
Rear defogger	161	137	141
Requires air conditioning or Heavy Duty Alternator/Battery Group.			
Visibility Group, SE	208	177	182
Intermittent wipers, rear wiper/washer.			
Fog lamps, Sport, Country	110	94	96
Requires air conditioning or Heavy Duty Alternator/Battery Group.			
Rear wiper/washer, Sport	147	125	129
Deep-tinted glass, Sport and Country 3-doors ..	305	259	267
Sport and Country 5-doors	144	122	126
Front vent windows	91	77	80
Power Windows and Door Locks Group,			
Sport and Country 3-doors	437	371	382
Sport and Country 5-doors	582	495	509
Power windows and locks, remote keyless entry.			
Dual remote break-away mirrors, SE, Sport	22	19	20
Power mirrors, Country	100	85	88
Requires Power Windows and Door Locks Group.			
Tilt steering wheel	132	112	116
SE requires Visibility Group.			
Cruise control	230	196	201
SE requires Visibility Group.			
Leather-wrapped steering wheel, SE, Sport	48	41	42
Cassette player with four speakers, SE, Sport ...	291	247	255
Country	201	171	176
Premium speakers (six), Country	128	109	112
Requires Power Windows and Door Locks Group.			
Fabric seats, SE	137	116	120
SE w/Pkgs. 23B, 25B, 26B	NC	NC	NC
Power driver's seat, Country	296	252	259
Leather seats, Country 5-door	831	706	727
Floor console with armrest, SE, Sport	147	125	129
Overhead console, Sport, Country	203	173	178
Includes compass and thermometer, reading lights. Requires Power Windows and Door Locks Group.			
Cargo area cover	72	61	63
Roof rack, SE, Sport	139	118	122
Light Group, SE, Sport	195	166	171
Headlamp-off delay system, lighted visor mirrors, misc. lights.			
Bright Group, Country	202	172	177
Bright dual power remote mirrors, front and rear bumpers, grille and headlamp bezels, door handles and escutcheons, windshield and drip rail moldings. Requires Power Windows and Door Locks Group.			
Trailer Tow Group	358	304	313
4WD models with Off-Road Suspension	242	206	212
Requires 4.0-liter engine, automatic transmission, Heavy Duty Alternator/ Battery Group, conventional spare tire.			
Off-Road Suspension (4WD only), SE	761	647	666
Sport	448	381	392
Country	360	306	315
Requires Heavy Duty Alternator/Battery Group, dual remote break-away mirrors (SE and Sport).			
Skid Plates Group, 4WD models	144	122	126
225/75R15 outlined white letter tires (four), SE	313	266	274
spare 225/75R15 tire (required), SE	116	99	102
Conventional (215/75R15) spare tire, SE	71	60	62
Conventional (225/75R15 outlined white letter)			
spare tire, Sport	116	99	102
Conventional (225/70R15) spare tire, Country ..	140	119	123
10-hole alloy wheels, SE	435	370	381
Sport	332	282	291
Country	87	74	76
Requires conventional spare tire.			
Matching fifth alloy wheel, Sport	26	22	23
Country	87	74	76
Requires conventional spare tire.			
Front floormats, SE, Sport	20	17	18
Engine block heater (Alaska only)	31	26	27

Jeep Grand Cherokee

✓ BEST BUY

Jeep Grand Cherokee Limited

This 5-door wagon was the first sport-utility vehicle with a driver-side air bag when it was introduced as an early 1993 model, and side door guard beams are among the additions for its second season.

Body Styles/Chassis

Grand Cherokee comes in a single 5-door body with a one-piece rear liftgate.

The base model has been renamed SE. Returning are the Laredo, which is the most popular model, and the top-line Limited. Discontinued is the Grand Wagoneer model, which included imitation wood exterior trim.

Four-wheel anti-lock brakes that work in both 2WD and 4WD are standard, as is a center high-mounted stoplamp and a rear wiper/washer.

For '94, the Limited gains rear disc brakes as a new standard feature. And Jeep says a power sunroof is to be added to the options list later in the model year.

Maximum payload is 1150 pounds for all models.

Powertrains

A 190-horsepower 4.0-liter 6-cylinder engine is standard on all models and a 220-horsepower V-8 is optional on all.

The 6-cylinder comes with either a 5-speed manual or 4-speed automatic transmission, and the V-8 only with automatic.

The SE and Laredo are offered with 2- or 4-wheel drive; the Limited comes with 4WD.

Three 4WD systems are available: Command-Trac, a part-time setup for use only on slippery surfaces; Selec-Trac, which can be used on all surfaces; and Quadra-Trac, a permanently engaged 4WD system. Command-Trac is standard on SE and Laredo 4x4 models. Select-Trac is optional on all models with the 6-cylinder engine. Quadra-Trac is standard on the Limited, optional on the others, and is included in the V-8-engine option package.

Trailer capacity with the optional tow group is 5000 pounds. The V-8 increases that to 6500 pounds.

Accommodations

Front buckets and a 60/40 split folding rear bench are standard on all models. Rear seatbacks fold flat and the lower

Jeep

cushions remove to free up storage space in the wells behind the front seats.

Jeep says an integrated child safety seat will be added to the options list later in the model year.

Evaluation

Ford's Explorer remains the best-selling sport-utility vehicle, but Grand Cherokee is an impressive rival with some features Explorer lacks. Among them are the driver-side air bag, permanent 4WD, and a V-8 engine.

Both ride and handle well for 4x4s, but the Jeep has a more car-like manner overall. The Jeep's ride is also slightly softer, though don't order Grand Cherokee's optional Up-Country suspension unless you actually do a lot of off-road driving. It enhances off-road control, but makes the on-road ride stiff and jittery.

The 6-cylinder engines in both the Explorer and Grand Cherokee furnish good acceleration. In an even mix of city and expressway driving, a test of a 6-cylinder Grand Cherokee netted an average of 16.5 mpg; not great, but better than the 13.3 we averaged with a V-8.

The 6-cylinder has a loud roar and a raspy exhaust in acceleration, and the V-8 an even louder roar. Both engines are much quieter when cruising. The V-8 does enhance low-speed acceleration, but its biggest benefit is in its 6500-pound towing capacity, 1100 pounds more than either the 6-cylinder Grand Cherokee or the Explorer.

Jeep also offers an unprecedented array of 4WD systems. Both of its on-demand setups have shift-on-the-fly, as does Explorer's, but Select-Trac can be used on dry pavement—a feature the Ford lacks. Neither does Explorer have a permanent 4WD system to match Jeep's Quadra-Trac. Both brands have full-time ABS, but only Grand Cherokee and the Mitsubishi Montero have an air bag in the compact 4x4 segment.

Jeep's steering wheel has a standard tilt feature, but is still too close to the driver's chest for some tastes. Grand Cherokee's front seats lack lumbar adjustments, and some drivers may find them too softly padded for long-distance comfort.

The rather short rear seat cushion eases entry and exit, but sacrifices some thigh support. The back seat does hold three adults because the rear wheel wells are aft of the rear seatbacks. Head and leg room are generous all around. Noise from wind and tires is not intrusive.

Clear analog gauges and a simple control layout lend the dashboard a sport-sedan ambience. Switches and dials move with a sophisticated feel, and the automatic climate system allows several combinations of manual and automatic settings. However, the dashboard, center console, and much of the door panels are covered in hard plastic with molded-in grain. Grand Cherokee's upscale audience deserves richer-feeling padded surfaces.

Grand Cherokee has more ground clearance than Explorer, and the Jeep's unibody construction gives it a roughly one-inch lower sill than the body-on-frame Ford, so getting in and out isn't much different than with an automobile. The lip of the cargo floor is lower, too, and while Grand Cherokee's liftgate has a handy molded-in grab handle for easy closing, it lacks the separate-opening window of most rivals.

With the seatbacks up, there's not much more luggage room than in a mid-size car—unless you allow the load to eat into rear visibility. Here, Explorer, with its spare tire stowed below the body, has an advantage over the Jeep and its mandatory inside tire mount.

Overall, its air bag, sophisticated ABS, superior 4WD systems, and fine suspension give Grand Cherokee a unique array of features in this class. Explorer fights back with a more spacious interior, a proven track record, and some less-expensive 2WD and 4WD models.

Specifications

	5-door wagon
Wheelbase, in.	105.9
Overall length, in.	179.0
Overall width, in.	70.9
Overall height, in.	64.8
Turn diameter, ft.	36.6
Curb weight, lbs.	3674
Fuel capacity, gal.	23.0

Passenger Area Dimensions

Seating capacity	5
Front head room, in.	38.9
Rear head room, in.	39.1
Front leg room, in.	40.8
Rear leg room, in.	35.7

Cargo Dimensions and Payloads

Cargo area length, in.	67.0
Cargo area width, in.	56.0
Cargo area width between wheels, in.	43.1
Cargo area height, in.	39.5
Cargo vol., cu. ft.	79.6
Max. payload, lbs.	1150
Max. trailer weight, lbs.	6500

Engines

	ohv I-6	ohv V-8
Size, liters/cu. in.	4.0/242	5.2/318
Horsepower @ rpm	190 @ 4750	220 @ 4800
Torque (lbs./ft.) @ rpm	225 @ 4000	285 @ 3600
Availability	S	O

EPA city/highway mpg

5-speed OD manual	16/20	
4-speed OD automatic	15/20	14/18

Built in Detroit, Mich.

KEY: Dimensions and capacities are supplied by the manufacturers. **Curb Weight:** base models, not including optional equipment. **Max. payload, lbs.** = gross amount; net payload may be lower due to optional equipment. **Engines:** ohv = overhead valve; ohc = overhead cam; I = inline cylinders; V = cylinders in V configuration; flat = horizontally opposed cylinders; rpm = revolutions per minute; OD = overdrive transmission; S = standard; O = optional; NA = not available.

Prices

Jeep Grand Cherokee

	Retail Price	Dealer Invoice	Fair Price
SE 5-door 2WD	$21156	$19242	$19942
SE 5-door 4WD	22096	20109	20809
Laredo 5-door 2WD	22192	20123	20823
Laredo 5-door 4WD	23132	21659	22359
Limited 5-door 4WD	29618	26728	27628
Destination charge	495	495	495

Standard Equipment:

SE: 4.0-liter 6-cylinder engine, 5-speed manual transmission (4WD) or 4-speed automatic transmission (2WD), driver-side air bag, anti-lock brakes, power steering, cloth reclining front bucket seats, split folding rear seat, air conditioning, leather-wrapped tilt steering wheel, cruise control, tachometer, voltage and temperature gauges, console with armrest and cupholders, AM/FM cassette, tinted glass, rear defogger, intermittent rear wiper/washer,

Jeep

Top: A driver-side air bag is standard on all Grand Cherokees. Middle: Split rear seatback folds, but spare tire eats up cargo space. Above: Grand Cherokee Laredo.

dual outside mirrors, remote fuel door release, trip odometer, map lights, roof rack, striping, 215/75R15 tires, wheel covers. 4WD system is Command-Trac part-time. **Laredo** adds: power windows and locks, power mirrors, remote keyless entry system, lighted visor mirrors, extra sound insulation, floormats, cargo area tie-down hooks and skid strips, cargo area cover and net, 225/75R15 outlined white letter tires, alloy wheels. **Limited** adds: 4-speed automatic transmission, 4-wheel disc brakes, automatic temperature control, leather power front seats, automatic day/night rearview mirror, automatic headlamp system, illuminated entry system, anti-theft alarm, overhead console with compass and temperature display, trip com-

puter, heated power mirrors, fog lamps, deep tinted side and rear glass, 6-speaker AM/FM cassette with equalizer and amplifier, power antenna, 225/70R15 outlined white letter tires, alloy wheels, full-size spare tire. 4WD system is Quadra-Trac permanent 4WD.

Optional Equipment:

	Retail Price	Dealer Invoice	Fair Price
Pkg. 26F, Laredo 2WD	$3020	$2567	$2869
Pkg. 26F/28F, Laredo 4WD	3464	2944	3291

Luxury Group, Security Group, overhead console, deep-tinted glass, cassette system with equalizer and six speakers. Pkg. 26F (4WD) requires automatic transmission. Pkg. 28F requires 5.2-liter V-8 engine, automatic transmission.

5.2-liter V-8 engine, 4WD SE and Laredo	1176	1000	1117
Laredo w/Pkg. 28F and Limited	732	622	695

Requires automatic transmission (std. Limited).

4-speed automatic transmission, SE, Laredo	897	762	852
Selec-Trac full-time 4WD, SE, Laredo	394	335	374
Limited	NC	NC	NC

Requires automatic transmission. Not available with 5.2-liter V-8.

Quadra-Track permanent 4WD, SE, Laredo	444	377	422

Requires automatic transmission.

Trac-Lok rear differential	285	242	271

Requires automatic transmission.

Power Group, SE	616	524	585

Power windows and locks, remote keyless entry.

Luxury Group, Laredo 4WD	593	504	563
4WD with automatic transmission, 2WD	688	585	654

Power front seats, automatic day/night rearview mirror, automatic headlamp system.

Protection Group, SE	146	124	139

Cargo area cover and net, floormats.

Security Group, SE, Laredo	226	192	215

Theft security system, illuminated entry system. Requires Power Group.

Trailer Tow Prep Group	100	85	95

Requires automatic transmission.

Trailer Tow Group III	358	304	340

Requires automatic transmission.

Trailer Tow Group IV	242	206	230

Requires automatic transmission and 5.2-liter V-8.

Fog lamps, 2WD SE and Laredo	110	94	105
Fog Lamp/Skid Plate Group (4WD), SE, Laredo	254	216	241
w/Up Country Suspension Group	110	94	105
Limited with 4.0-liter engine	144	122	137
Up Country Suspension Group, SE 4WD	720	612	684
Laredo 4WD	504	428	479
Limited	349	297	332

Skid Plate Group, tow hooks, high-pressure gas shocks, 245/70R15 outlined white letter all-terrain tires, conventional spare tire, matching fifth wheel.

Overhead console, Laredo	232	197	220

Includes compass, thermometer, and trip computer.

Leather seats, Laredo	576	490	547

Requires Luxury Group.

Luxury leather seats, Limited	300	255	285
Power mirrors, SE	95	81	90
Heated power mirrors, SE	140	119	133
Laredo	45	38	43
Deep tinted glass, SE, Laredo	226	192	215
AM/FM cassette with equalizer, SE, Laredo	617	524	586

Includes amplifier, power antenna.

AM/FM with CD and equalizer, SE, Laredo	787	669	748
Laredo w/Pkg. 26F, 28F, Limited	170	145	162

Includes six speakers, amplifier, power antenna.

	656	558	623
Conventional spare tire, SE	130	111	124
Laredo, Limited	160	136	152
225/75R15 outlined white letter tires, SE	246	209	234
225/75R15 outlined white letter all-terrain tires, SE	313	266	297
Laredo	67	57	64
Limited	NC	NC	NC
Engine block heater	31	26	29

Jeep Wrangler

Jeep Wrangler S

Automatic transmission is now available with the 4-cylinder engine on Jeep's smallest sport-utility vehicle.

Body Styles/Chassis

A removable vinyl top, half-height metal doors, right-hinged tailgate, and swing-away spare-tire carrier are standard. A metal hardtop with glass windows is a line-wide option. The hardtop is bolted on before delivery to the customer. Wranglers ordered with it do not come with a soft top.

With either top, Wrangler gets a standard roll bar (Jeep calls it a sportbar) that extends to the rear of the cargo area to anchor the 3-point rear safety belts.

The lineup consists of S and SE models, with SE taking the place of last year's "base" trim. Sahara and Renegade option packages return, the last bringing wraparound plastic fenders with integral running boards and front fog lamps.

A new Sport option package includes body-colored fender flares and bodyside steps among its features. Anti-lock brakes (ABS) are optional only with the 6-cylinder engine (see below) and work in both 2- and 4-wheel drive.

A center high-mounted stoplamp is a new standard feature and is affixed to a gooseneck bracket on the tailgate.

Due later in the model year is a new folding soft top with hardtop-style full metal doors instead of half doors. Like the standard folding top, it has plastic, zip-out side curtains instead of glass windows. Jeep says the new top is easier to raise and lower. Also due later is the Add-a-Trunk, an optional steel storage container that bolts in behind the back seat. Its hinged lid can be opened when the tailgate is locked.

Maximum payload is 800 pounds for all models.

Powertrains

A 123-horsepower 2.5-liter 4-cylinder engine is standard on the S model. A 180-horsepower 4.0-liter in-line 6-cylinder is standard on the SE, which is the only model that can get the Sahara and Renegade packages.

A 5-speed manual transmission is standard with both engines. A 3-speed automatic had been optional only with the six; now it is offered with the 4-cylinder, as well.

All models have a part-time on-demand 4WD system with full shift-on-the-fly capability. It is not intended for dry-pavement use.

Maximum trailering weight is 2000 pounds.

Accommodations

All Wranglers come with front bucket seats. A 2-place fold-and-tumble rear seat is standard on all except the S model, where it's optional.

Evaluation

Wrangler's direct competitors are Suzuki's Samurai and Sidekick, and the Geo Tracker, which Suzuki builds for General Motors. The Isuzu Amigo also might be considered.

Sidekick and Tracker are newer designs than Wrangler. They're somewhat more refined, and boast friendlier ergonomics. But no rival offers 4-wheel ABS, and all have 4-cylinder engines that can't match Jeep's muscular 4.0 six. Neither can they duplicate Wrangler's classic image. That image dictates some compromises on the road, however, where Wranglers spend most of their time.

One compromise is a stiff suspension that produces a karate-chop ride on all but glass-smooth surfaces. The poor ride is aggravated by the short wheelbase. A second compromise involves Wrangler's compact size and narrow stance. These combine for great maneuverability, but also demand conservative cornering speeds. Turning too quickly

Specifications

	2-door w/soft top
Wheelbase, in.	93.4
Overall length, in.	151.9
Overall width, in.	66.0
Overall height, in.	71.9
Turn diameter, ft.	32.9
Curb weight, lbs.	2943
Fuel capacity, gal.	15.0[1]

1. 20.0 gal. on Sahara and Renegade.

Passenger Area Dimensions

Seating capacity	4
Front head room, in.	41.4
Rear head room, in.	40.3
Front leg room, in.	39.4
Rear leg room, in.	35.0

Cargo Dimensions and Payloads

Cargo area length, in.	39.0	39.0
Cargo area width, in.	58.0	58.0
Cargo area width between wheels, in.	34.5	34.5
Cargo area height, in.	47.0	47.0
Max. payload, lbs.	800	800
Max. trailer weight, lbs.	2000	2000

Engines

	ohv I-4	ohv I-6
Size, liters/cu. in.	2.5/150	4.0/242
Horsepower @ rpm	123 @ 5250	180 @ 4750
Torque (lbs./ft.) @ rpm	139 @ 3250	220 @ 4000
Availability	S	S[1]

EPA city/highway mpg

5-speed OD manual	19/20	16/18
3-speed automatic	17/18	15/17

1. SE model.

Built in Toledo, Ohio.

KEY: Dimensions and capacities are supplied by the manufacturers. **Curb Weight:** base models, not including optional equipment. **Max. payload, lbs.** = gross amount; net payload may be lower due to optional equipment. **Engines: ohv** = overhead valve; **ohc** = overhead cam; **I** = inline cylinders; **V** = cylinders in V configuration; **flat** = horizontally opposed cylinders; **rpm** = revolutions per minute; **OD** = overdrive transmission; **S** = standard; **O** = optional; **NA** = not available.

Jeep

generates alarming body roll, the result of a high center of gravity that also makes for poor straight-line stability in crosswinds.

The base S model, which comes only with the 4-cylinder engine, accounts for 40-percent of Wrangler sales, so many buyers evidently are content with its modest acceleration and lower cost. The 4.0 six is indeed much quicker—about 10 seconds 0-60 mph with automatic transmission—but it's almost overkill in a vehicle like this. And now it's no longer your only choice if you must have automatic.

Fuel economy is surprisingly poor. In daily driving, you'll be lucky to average 18 mpg with the 4-cylinder and 15 mpg with the six. On the upside is Jeep's convenient shift-on-the-fly 4WD, a Wrangler exclusive among mini-4x4s.

You don't expect soft-top sport-utility vehicles to be quiet, and Wrangler is not. You'll be assaulted by road noise and wind buffeting—top up or down. The hardtop is quieter, but still drums, and robs Wrangler of one of its chief assets: open-air sportiness. Ample head room at all points lets tall people sit upright, but there's not much rear leg room, and a high step-up hampers entry/exit despite the cutaway door openings.

Gauges are strung clear across the dash, so some aren't easy to read, and an overly long steering column puts the wheel close to the chest (the optional tilt column doesn't help much). Just as bad, there's scant cargo space behind the back seat, which must be folded up to accommodate even medium-size loads.

Chrysler hasn't tampered with Wrangler's rugged, para-military personality since acquiring Jeep in the American Motors takeover of 1987. That's good. But we can't recommend any of these small 4x4s as daily transportation. If you're hooked, then be prepared for big compromises compared to passenger cars.

Prices

Jeep Wrangler	Retail Price	Dealer Invoice	Fair Price
S soft top	$11390	$10988	$11288
SE soft top	14454	13115	13415
Destination charge	495	495	495

Standard Equipment:

S: 2.5-liter PFI 4-cylinder engine, 5-speed manual transmission, vinyl front bucket seats, tachometer, coolant temperature and oil pressure gauges, voltmeter, trip odometer, tinted windshield, fuel tank skid plate, swingaway outside spare tire carrier, 205/75R15 tires. **SE** adds: 4.0-liter engine, reclining front seats, fold-and-tumble rear seat, right outside mirror, AM/FM radio, 215/75R15 all-terrain tires, 6-spoke steel wheels.

Optional Equipment:

	Retail Price	Dealer Invoice	Fair Price
Pkg. 22A, S	624	530	543

Adds automatic transmission. Requires tilt steering wheel.

Pkg. 23B/22B, S	1030	876	896

Power steering, vinyl reclining front bucket seats, rear seat, right outside mirror, carpeting, rear bumperettes. Pkg. 22B requires automatic transmission and tilt steering wheel.

Pkg. 24C, SE	624	530	543

Adds automatic transmission. Requires tilt steering wheel.

Pkg. 25D/24D, SE	973	827	847

Power steering, tilt steering wheel, Convenience Group, carpeting, 20-gallon fuel tank, conventional spare tire. Pkg. 24 D requires automatic transmission.

Sport Pkg. 25F/24F, SE	1640	1394	1427

Sport Pkg. (Convenience Group, power steering, tilt steering wheel, Sound Bar, sport striping, body-color fender flares and bodyside steps, carpeting, 215/75R15 outlined white letter all-terrain tires, full face steel wheels). Pkg. 24F requires automatic transmission.

	Retail Price	Dealer Invoice	Fair Price
Sahara Pkg. 25H/24H, SE	$2423	$2060	$2108

Sahara Decor Group (black exterior trim, tilt steering wheel, fog lights, vinyl spare tire cover, exterior graphics, color-keyed fender flares and bodyside steps, cloth upholstery, map pockets, leather-wrapped steering wheel, carpeting, front floormats, Convenience Group, power steering, 20-gallon fuel tank, off road gas shocks, full face steel wheels), AM/FM cassette, Sound Bar, conventional spare tire. Pkg. 24H requires automatic transmission.

Renegade Pkg. 25K/24K, SE	4252	3614	3699

Renegade Decor Group (Sahara Pkg. plus: unique lower body panels and fascias, color-keyed bumpers with steps, bodyside steps, unique exterior graphics, five 29-9.5R15LT outlined white letter all-terrain tires, alloy wheels). Pkg. 24K requires automatic transmission.

3-speed automatic transmission	624	530	543

Requires tilt steering wheel.

Anti-lock brakes, SE	599	509	521
Trac-Lok rear differential, SE	278	236	242

Requires conventional spare tire and 215 or 225 tires.

Air conditioning, SE	878	746	764

Requires 4.0-liter engine, power steering, carpeting. Includes Heavy Duty Alternator/Battery Group.

Power steering	300	255	261
Vinyl reclining front seats, S	75	64	65

Requires rear seat and carpeting.

Cloth reclining front bucket seats with reclining rear seat, SE	107	91	93
Rear seat, S	455	387	396

Requires carpeting and reclining front seats.

Add-A-Trunk lockable storage	125	106	109

Requires carpeting.

Carpeting	137	116	119

Requires reclining front seats and rear seat.

Hardtop	755	642	657
SE with Sahara or Renegade Pkg.	923	785	803

Includes dual outside mirrors, rear wiper/washer, tinted glass (deep-tinted on Sahara and Renegade), full doors with vent windows.

Bright Exterior Group, SE	197	167	171

Includes bright bumpers, grille overlay, and headlamp bezels.

Bodyside steps, SE	73	62	64
Convenience Group	233	198	203
SE with tilt steering column	170	145	148

Intermittent wipers, center console with cup holders, misc. lights, glove box lock.

Heavy Duty Alternator/Battery Group	135	115	117
Right outside mirror, S	27	23	23
Rear defogger for hardtop	164	139	143
Off-Road Pkg., SE	129	110	112

Heavy duty shock absorbers, draw bar, tow hooks.

Sound bar with 2 rear speakers, SE	204	173	177
AM/FM radio with 2 speakers, S	270	230	235
AM/FM cassette with 2 speakers, S	534	454	465
S with Sound Group, SE	264	224	230
Sound Group, S	494	420	430

AM/FM stereo, Sound Bar, sport bar padding.

Tilt steering wheel	193	164	168
Leather-wrapped steering wheel, SE	48	41	42
Five 215/75R15 outlined white letter all-terrain tires (and wheels), S	272	231	237
SE	228	194	198
SE w/Pkgs. 25D, 24D, 25F, 24F, Sahara Pkg.	117	99	102

Requires 15 x 7 wheels.

Five 225/75R15 outlined white letter all-terrain tires (and wheels), S	463	394	403
SE	419	356	365
SE w/Pkgs. 25D, 24D, Renegade Pkg.	308	262	268
SE w/Pkgs. 25F, 24F	191	162	166

Requires 15 x 7 wheels.

Conventional spare tire	111	94	97
Five 15 x 7 styled steel wheels, S	NC	NC	NC

Requires 215 or 225 tires and conventional spare tire.

Four 15 x 7 full face steel wheels, SE	102	87	89

	Retail Price	Dealer Invoice	Fair Price
Five 15 x 7 full face steel wheels, SE	$128	$109	$111
Requires conventional spare tire.			
15 x 7 alloy wheels, S, SE	339	288	295
SE w/Pkg. 25F, 24F	211	179	184
Requires conventional spare and 215 or 225 tires.			
Five 15 x 7 five-spoke alloy wheels,			
SE w/Sahara Pkg.	237	201	206
Rear bumperettes, S	36	31	31
20-gallon fuel tank	62	53	54
Engine block heater (Alaska only)	31	26	27

1995 Kia Sportage

1995 Kia Sportage

South Korea's first entry in the sport-utility market segment arrives in the fall of 1994 as a 1995 model. Called Sportage (SPORT-ij), it's a compact 5-door wagon from Kia, South Korea's second largest auto company after Hyundai.

Kia, which builds the new Ford Aspire minicar, entered the U.S. market under its own name this winter with the Sephia subcompact sedan, a 1994 model for sale in 11 Western states.

Sportage will lead Kia's push into the Southwest and Southeast regions during calendar 1994, when the company hopes to add 150 dealers. Kia's long-range plans call for 300 dealers nationwide by the end of 1995.

Sportage went on sale this fall in Korea. U.S. prices haven't been set, but a Kia spokesman said the target for a base price is around $15,000.

Body Styles/Chassis

Sportage debuts with only a 5-door body style, though Kia says a 3-door version also is planned during the 1995 model year.

Sportage's 104.3-inch wheelbase is the same as the Nissan Pathfinder, the top-selling imported sport-utility wagon. At 159.7 inches, Kia's body is about 12 inches shorter and one inch wider than the Nissan's. Sportage's estimated curb weight of 3000 pounds is about 900 less than Pathfinder's curb weight.

By comparison, the 5-door Explorer—the most popular sport-utility vehicle in America—has a 111.9-inch wheelbase, weighs nearly 4000 pounds, and is 184.3 inches long.

Rear anti-lock brakes will be standard.

Powertrains

Full specifications weren't available for this issue, but the Sportage engine will be a dual-cam camshaft 2.0-liter 4-cylinder with 16 valves and 140 horsepower.

Kia said both a 4-speed manual and a 4-speed automatic transmission would be available.

Standard equipment will include an on-demand, part-time 4-wheel-drive system (for use only on slick surfaces) and anti-lock rear brakes.

Accommodations

Sportage will seat five, with front bucket seats and a folding 3-place rear bench seat.

We have not driven the Sportage, so we can't evaluate its performance.

Specifications	5-door wagon
Wheelbase, in.	104.3
Overall length, in.	159.7
Overall width, in.	67.3
Overall height, in.	65.1
Turn diameter, ft.	NA
Curb weight, lbs.	3000
Fuel capacity, gal.	15.1

Passenger Area Dimensions

Seating capacity	5
Front head room, in.	NA
Rear head room, in.	NA
Front leg room, in.	NA
Rear leg room, in.	NA

Cargo Dimensions and Payloads

Cargo area length, in.	NA
Cargo area width, in.	NA
Cargo area width between wheels, in.	NA
Cargo area height, in.	NA
Cargo vol., cu. ft.	NA
Max. payload, lbs.	NA
Max. trailer weight, lbs.	NA

Engines	dohc I-4
Size, liters/cu. in.	2.0/120
Horsepower @ rpm	140 @ 6000
Torque (lbs./ft.) @ rpm	127 @ 5000
Availability	S

EPA city/highway mpg

5-speed OD manual	NA
4-speed OD automatic	NA

Built in South Korea.

KEY: Dimensions and capacities are supplied by the manufacturers. **Curb Weight:** base models, not including optional equipment. **Max. payload, lbs.** = gross amount; net payload may be lower due to optional equipment. **Engines: ohv** = overhead valve; **ohc** = overhead cam; **I** = inline cylinders; **V** = cylinders in V configuration; **flat** = horizontally opposed cylinders; **rpm** = revolutions per minute; **OD** = overdrive transmission; **S** = standard; **O** = optional. **NA** = not available.

Standard Equipment, options, and prices unavailable at time of publication.

Land Rover

Land Rover/Range Rover

Range Rover County

Range Rover changed its corporate name to Land Rover North America for 1993, and for '94 introduces its second U.S. product under that badge, the Land Rover Defender 90.

Continuing under the Range Rover banner are two 5-door wagons: the Range Rover County and Range Rover County LWB, the latter's suffix identifying it as the long-wheelbase model.

Not carried over is the Land Rover Defender 110 model, a 9-seat descendant of the slab-sided utilitarian Land Rover. It was offered in a limited U.S. run of 500 units for 1993.

Body Styles/Chassis

First, the Range Rovers. Both are 5-door wagons with a bottom-hinged tailgate and separate, top-hinged rear window. And both have aluminum body panels over a steel chassis.

Range Rover County has a 100-inch wheelbase and 175-inch overall length. County LWB stretches the wheelbase to 108 inches and overall length to 183.

The County comes in a single trim level. The LWB is available with three extra-cost paint and trim options.

For '94, the County gains the electronic air suspension introduced last year with the LWB. It can raise or lower the vehicle over a range of 5.1 inches. "Normal" ride height is maintained in routine driving and when towing. "Low profile" is automatically engaged cruising above 50 mph, dropping ¾ of an inch for what Land Rover says is better aerodynamics and improved fuel economy.

When parked, the driver may select "access" height to lower the vehicle 2.4 inches for easier entry and exit. "High profile" raises it 1.6 inches so the County or LWB can wade in water 22 inches deep. If the vehicle is hung on an off-road obstacle, the "extended profile" setting allows a suspended wheel to reach down 2.8 inches to gain traction.

Slotted as the British luxury 4x4-maker's entry-level model, the new Land Rover Defender 90 is the only convertible V-8-powered sport-utility vehicle available in the U.S.

It is seven inches shorter in wheelbase and 14.5 inches shorter overall than the regular County. It comes from the factory with only a tonneau cover to protect the interior. A removable full fabric top with plastic side and rear windows is optional and a "bikini" half-top is available from the dealer.

All Land Rover and Range Rovers come with 4-wheel disc brakes. An anti-lock system is standard on the Range Rover models, but is unavailable on the 90.

The maximum payload rating is 1618 pounds on the County and 1445 pounds on the Ranger Rover County LWB, and 2443 on the Defender 90.

Powertrains

A 182-horsepower 3.9-liter V-8 is common to both the Land Rover Defender 90 and the Ranger Rover County. The 90, however, comes only with a 5-speed manual transmission and the County and LWB only with a 4-speed automatic.

The Range Rover County LWB returns with a 4.2-liter version of this V-8 rated at 200 horsepower.

Permanently engaged 4-wheel drive is standard on all these vehicles. It is fitted with a 2-speed gear-driven transfer case with a manually locking center differential activated by a floor-mounted lever.

The County model can tow trailers up to 5500 pounds when the transfer case is in its High position and 7700 pounds when the transfer case is in the Low setting. The

Specifications

	2-door conv.	5-door wagon	LWB 5-door wagon
Wheelbase, in.	92.9	100.0	108.0
Overall length, in.	160.5	175.0	183.0
Overall width, in.	70.5	71.4	71.4
Overall height, in.	80.2	70.8	72.2
Turn diameter, ft.	40.0	39.4	44.8
Curb weight, lbs.	3560	4401	4574
Fuel capacity, gal.	15.6	21.6	21.6

Passenger Area Dimensions

Seating capacity	4	5	5
Front head room, in.	57.0	38.4	38.4
Rear head room, in.	NA	37.3	37.3
Front leg room, in.	NA	41.0	41.0
Rear leg room, in.	NA	32.7	39.7

Cargo Dimensions and Payloads

Cargo area length, in.	NA	72.0	NA
Cargo area width, in.	55.1	51.7	51.7
Cargo area width between wheels, in.	36.4	NA	NA
Cargo area height, in.	57.0	40.0	40.0
Cargo vol., cu. ft.	NA	82.8	76.3
Max. payload, lbs.	2443	1618	1445
Max. trailer weight, lbs.	3500	7700	7700

Engines

	ohv V-8	ohv V-8
Size, liters/cu. in.	3.9/241	4.2/261
Horsepower	182 @	200 @
@ rpm	4750	4850
Torque (lbs./ft.)	232 @	251 @
@ rpm	3100	3250
Availability	S	S[1]

EPA city/highway mpg

5-speed OD manual	12/15	13/16
4-speed OD automatic		13/16

1. County LWB.

Built in England.

KEY: Dimensions and capacities are supplied by the manufacturers. **Curb Weight:** base models, not including optional equipment. **Max. payload, lbs.** = gross amount; net payload may be lower due to optional equipment. **Engines: ohv** = overhead valve; **ohc** = overhead cam; **I** = inline cylinders; **V** = cylinders in V configuration; **flat** = horizontally opposed cylinders; **rpm** = revolutions per minute; **OD** = overdrive transmission; **S** = standard; **O** = optional; **NA** = not available.

Land Rover

LWB's ratings are 6500 pounds and 7700, respectively. Maximum trailer weight for the Defender 90 is 3500 pounds.

Accommodations

Both Range Rover models come with two front bucket seats and a 3-person rear bench split 70/30. With the rear seat folded, the LWB has 76.3 cubic feet of luggage space, compared to 70.6 for the regular County. However, the rear seat of the regular County can be removed, providing 82.8 cubic feet of space.

The Defender 90 comes with just two front bucket seats. Items such as a 2-place folding rear seat, air conditioning, and full carpeting are extra-cost accessories.

Evaluation

We haven't driven a Defender 90, but at $28,000 without such features as a roof or a rear seat, it's more of a lifestyle accessory for high rollers than a great sport-utility value.

Both Range Rover models offer loads of luxury, snob appeal, and extraordinary abilities. But it's difficult to justify prices this high when a Jeep Grand Cherokee Limited or Toyota Land Cruiser offers most all of their key qualities for much less. The County LWB's extra wheelbase provides an additional seven inches of rear leg room compared to the regular County, which has just adequate back-seat knee space. The versatile air suspension not only allows an amazing range of ride heights, but Land Rover claims it provides even softer passage over bumps. Suspension control is already one of Range Rover's best features. Even the regular-length County model's ride is surprisingly supple over bad pavement and well controlled at speed despite the short wheelbase.

Other tangible assets include proven, permanent 4WD and lots of luxury features. Acceleration is spirited given these vehicles' hefty curb weights, though don't expect to average more than 11-14 mpg with either rig.

Both Range Rovers exhibit pronounced body roll in turns, aggravated by the relatively soft, long-travel suspension that combines with the boxy shape to make them quite sensitive to strong crosswinds. Hang on, though, and they cling to the road quite well. And the standard anti-lock brakes feel strong and stop with good directional stability.

But the elderly, little-changed design shows up in areas like confusing minor controls, the lack of a tilt steering wheel even as an option, the absence of a driver-side air bag, mediocre noise suppression from all sources, and a cargo floor that's fairly high off the ground and not that long or wide. The aluminum body panels save weight and are impervious to rust, but may be prone to easy denting and are expensive to fix.

Prices

Land Rover Defender 90	Retail Price	Dealer Invoice	Fair Price
Defender 90	$27900	$25100	—
Destination charge	595	595	595

Fair price not available at time of publication.

Standard Equipment:

3.9-liter V-8, 5-speed manual transmission, permanent 4WD, power 4-wheel disc brakes, power steering, reclining cloth front bucket seats, tachometer, front brush guard, rear step bumper, center console, dual outside mirrors, AM/FM cassette, front and rear anti-sway bars, swing-away rear-mounted outside spare tire, roof rack system, front and rear mud flaps, side runners, rear lamp guards, 8000-pound Warn winch system, front and rear rubber floormats, rear seat auxiliary heater, Class III towing hitch receiver, intermittent wipers, cloth convertible top, 265/75R16 tires, styled steel wheels.

Optional Equipment:	Retail Price	Dealer Invoice	Fair Price
Premium Soft Top Pkg.	$1975	$1680	—
Soft top, side door windows, full safari cage.			
Air conditioning	1800	1530	—
5-spoke alloy wheels	900	750	—

Range Rover	Retail Price	Dealer Invoice	Fair Price
County 5-door 4WD wagon	$46900	—	—
County LWB 5-door 4WD wagon	50200	—	—
Destination charge	625	625	625

Dealer invoice and fair price not available at time of publication.

Standard Equipment:

3.9-liter V-8, 4-speed automatic transmission, permanent 4-wheel drive, electronic traction control, anti-lock 4-wheel disc brakes, power steering, air conditioning, electronically controled air suspension, 8-way power heated front seats, leather seats, 60/40 folding rear seat, power windows with front auto-down feature, power locks, cruise control, heated power mirrors, heated windshield, automatic day/night rearview mirror, power sunroof, AM/FM/cassette/CD with 6-disc changer and diversity antenna, intermittent wipers, rear wiper/washer, walnut trim, leather-wrapped steering wheel, keyless entry system, alarm system, rear defogger, remote fuel door release, tinted glass, map lights, headlamp washers, fog lights, automatic load-leveling suspension, trailer hitch, trailer wiring harness, 205R16 tires, alloy wheels. **LWB** adds: 4.2-liter V-8, dual memory presets for power front seats.

Optional Equipment:

Beluga black paint		300	— —
Montpellier Sable Edition (MSE),			
County LWB		750	— —
Montpellier Red exterior paint and black sable leather interior treatment.			
Light Stone Edition (LSE),			
County LWB		750	— —
Brooklands Green or Cornish Cream exterior paint and Light Stone Conolly leather interior treatment.			
Black Sable Edition (BSE),			
County LWB		1050	— —
Beluga black exterior paint and black sable leather interior upholstery and trim.			

New to the U.S. for 1994 is the Land Rover Defender 90. It's a 4WD V-8 convertible and lists for $27,900.

Mazda

Mazda B-Series Pickup

RECOMMENDED

Mazda B3000 regular-cab long-bed

Mazda shelves its imported compact pickup and rebadges a Ford Ranger to create the 1994 B-Series line.

Mazda's models are built alongside Ranger at a Ford plant in New Jersey. That enables the Japanese company to avoid the 25-percent federal tariff on imported trucks. Ford owns an equity interest in Mazda and the two companies share other vehicles and components.

Body Styles/Chassis

The B-Series matches the Ranger in dimensions, though unlike the Ford, it does not offer a flare-fender cargo box.

The Mazda lineup consists of a regular cab with a 108-inch wheelbase and a 6-foot cargo bed; a regular cab with a 114-inch wheelbase and a 7-foot bed; and a 125-inch wheelbase extended cab (called Cab Plus) with the 6-foot bed.

Though Mazda had to maintain key structural and design elements of the Ranger, the B-Series truck has its own hood, grille, front fenders, rear-quarter panels, and tail-lamps—changes that increase its overall length by several inches compared to the Ford. The Mazda shares Ranger's tire sizes, but gets its own wheel styles.

Mazda's previous Japanese-designed-and-built compact pickups did not feature a long-bed model. There's little size difference between the previous and current regular-cab models, though today's B-Series Cab Plus is 7.6 inches longer in wheelbase and 3.9 inches longer overall than its predecessor.

Base, SE, and LS trim levels are offered. The B-Series shares Ranger's interior design, with the only differences being seat fabrics, the name on the steering wheel, and some dashboard appliques.

A 3-place front-bench seat is standard on base models, SE versions come with two front buckets, and a 60/40 reclining split front bench with a fold-down armrest is standard on LE models and on base Cab Plus models.

A pair of fold-down rear jump seats are standard on Cab Plus SE and LE models, but are unavailable on the base-level Cab Plus.

Rear anti-lock brakes are standard on all B-Series models.

Maximum payload is 1650 pounds on 2WD models and 1550 on 4x4s and the Cab Plus.

Powertrains

The B-Series uses the Ranger's engines, transmissions, and 4-wheel drive systems.

Engine size is the basis for the model names.

The B2300 has a 2.3-liter 4-cylinder engine with 98 horsepower.

The B3000 has a 3.0-liter V-6 with 140 horsepower.

The B4000 has a 4.0-liter V-6 with 160 horsepower.

The previous Mazda pickup was available only with 4-cylinder engines.

On all models, a 5-speed manual transmission is standard and a 4-speed automatic is optional.

The 4x4s use Ford's Touch Drive 4WD system, which is for use only on slick surfaces. It has automatic-locking front hubs and allows shift-on-the-fly between 2WD and 4WD High with a dashboard button. The vehicle must be stopped and backed up a few feet to fully disengage 4WD.

Maximum towing capacity is 6000 pounds on 2WD regular-cab models and 5900 on 2WD Cab Plus models. It's slightly less on 4x4 models.

Evaluation

Like Ranger, the new B-Series is a highly competent compact pickup with fine assembly quality and competitive prices.

Specifications

	Short bed	Long bed	Cab Plus
Wheelbase, in.	108.0	114.0	125.1
Overall length, in.	184.5	197.5	202.7
Overall width, in.	69.4	69.4	69.4
Overall height, in.	64.0	64.0	64.1
Turn diameter, ft.	36.5	38.3	41.6
Curb weight, lbs.	2918	2955	3208
Fuel capacity, gal.	16.3	19.6	19.6

Passenger Area Dimensions

Seating capacity	3	3	5
Front head room, in.	39.1	39.1	39.4
Rear head room, in.	—	—	NA
Front leg room, in.	42.4	42.4	43.4
Rear leg room, in.	—	—	NA

Cargo Dimensions and Payloads

Cargo area length, in.	72.2	84.2	72.2
Cargo area width, in.	51.2	51.2	51.2
Cargo area width between wheels, in.	40.4	40.4	40.4
Cargo area height, in.	16.5	16.5	16.5
Max. payload, lbs.	1650	1650	1550
Max. trailer weight, lbs.	6000	6000	5900

Engines

	ohv I-4	ohv V-6	ohv V-6
Size, liters/cu. in.	2.3/140	3.0/182	4.0/245
Horsepower @ rpm	98 @ 4600	140 @ 4800	160 @ 4000
Torque (lbs./ft.) @ rpm	130 @ 2600	160 @ 3000	225 @ 2500
Availability	S	O	O

EPA city/highway mpg

5-speed OD manual	22/26	19/24	18/24
4-speed OD automatic	21/24	19/24	17/23

Built in Edison, N.J.

KEY: Dimensions and capacities are supplied by the manufacturers. **Curb Weight:** base models, not including optional equipment. **Max. payload, lbs.** = gross amount; net payload may be lower due to optional equipment. **Engines: ohv** = overhead valve; **ohc** = overhead cam; **I** = inline cylinders; **V** = cylinders in V configuration; **flat** = horizontally opposed cylinders; **rpm** = revolutions per minute; **OD** = overdrive transmission; **S** = standard; **O** = optional; **NA** = not available.

Mazda

Mazda says the most popular B-Series model will be the regular-cab 2WD B3000. Such a truck would have more usable power than a B2300 model, though we prefer the 4.0-liter engine for its extra muscle.

Ride quality is good on all models, though the off-pavement setups make for a stiff ride on 4x4s. Road manners are good, as well, and you won't be assaulted by undue tire, engine, or wind noise.

Since they are functionally the same, choosing between a Ranger or B-Series is mostly a matter of styling taste and which dealer offers the best deal. Ford, of course has more dealerships, so it has an edge in convenience. But Mazda's factory warranty includes 3-year/50,000-mile bumper-to-bumper coverage to Ford's 3/36,000.

Even though it's a domestically built and engineered truck, Mazda says it expects most B-Series customers to be import-pickup owners. And in comparison to Toyota and Nissan compact pickups, the B-Series does look good. Its payload ratings are competitive and it has a higher towing capacity, plus no import rival offers an engine as strong as the 4.0-liter V-6.

The biggest competitive threat is probably the new Chevrolet S10 pickup and its GMC Sonoma cousin. Redesigned for 1994, they feature refinement and dynamic qualities to rival the Ranger/B-Series, but have a roomier regular-cab body and a 4WD system that doesn't require that you stop and reverse to fully disengage 4WD.

It's this sort of competition that should work to your advantage if you're willing to shop around for the best deal.

Prices

Mazda Pickups	Retail Price	Dealer Invoice	Fair Price
B2300 Base 2WD regular cab, 5-speed	$9390	$8652	$8852
B2300 Base 2WD regular cab, automatic	10830	9979	10279
B2300 SE 2WD regular cab, 5-speed	11210	9875	10175
B2300 Base 2WD Cab Plus, 5-speed	12020	10588	11088
B3000 SE 2WD regular cab, 5-speed	11680	10289	10589
B3000 SE 2WD regular cab, automatic	12995	11447	11747
B3000 SE 2WD regular cab long bed, 5-speed	12325	10857	11157
B3000 SE 2WD regular cab long bed, automatic	13895	12240	12540
B3000 SE 2WD Cab Plus, 5-speed	13170	11601	12101
B3000 SE 2WD Cab Plus, automatic	14625	12883	13383
B3000 Base 4WD regular cab, 5-speed	14435	13300	13600
B3000 Base 4WD Cab Plus, 5-speed	15495	13650	14150
B4000 SE 2WD regular cab long bed, 5-speed	12500	11011	11311
B4000 LE 2WD Cab Plus, automatic	15355	13526	14026
B4000 SE 4WD regular cab, 5-speed	16425	14469	14769
B4000 SE 4WD Cab Plus, 5-speed	17295	15235	15735
B4000 LE 4WD Cab Plus, automatic	19500	17177	17677
Destination charge	460	460	460

Prices are for vehicles distributed by Mazda Motor of America, Inc. Prices may be higher in areas served by independent distributors.

Standard Equipment:

Base: 2.3-liter 4-cylinder engine, 5-speed manual or 4-speed automatic transmission, rear anti-lock brakes, power steering (Cab Plus), vinyl 3-passenger bench seat (regular cab), 60/40 vinyl split bench seat (Cab Plus), AM/FM radio, trip odometer, tinted glass, black rear step bumper, heavy duty battery (Cab Plus), dual outside mirrors, floor consolette (Cab Plus), rear mud guards, 195/70R14 tires, full size spare tire. **SE** adds: 3.0-liter V-6 engine (B3000), 4.0-liter V-6 engine (B4000), power steering, cloth reclining bucket seats (2WD), cloth reclining sport bucket seats with adjustable thigh and lumbar support (4WD), folding rear jump seats (Cab Plus), deluxe floor console, AM/FM cassette player, digital clock, manual remote mirrors, automatic locking hubs (4WD), upgraded door trim panels, door map pock-

The new B-Series borrows its interior, basic design, and powertrains from the Ford Ranger, though Mazda adds some of its own exterior panels. Above: A B4000 Cab Plus 4WD.

ets, carpet, fender flares (4WD), front mud guards (4WD), tachometer, heavy duty shock absorbers (long bed and 4WD), skid plates (4WD), front and rear stabilizer bars (long bed and 4WD), leather-wrapped steering wheel, flip-open rear quarter windows (Cab Plus), sliding rear window (4WD), 225/70R14 tires (2WD), 235/75R15 all-terrain tires (4WD), styled steel wheels. **LE** adds to SE: cruise control, power mirrors and door locks, power sliding rear window, tilt steering column, 60/40 split reclining bench seat with center folding armrest, premium AM/FM cassette player, bright exterior accents.

Optional Equipment:	Retail Price	Dealer Invoice	Fair Price
Air conditioning	$800	$656	$686
Power steering, B2300 regular cab, 5-speed	275	226	236
Alloy Wheel Pkg., 4WD Cab Plus	610	500	523
Alloy wheels, 265/75R15 all-terrain tires, performance axle.			
LE Upgrade Pkg., LE 4WD Cab Plus	610	500	523
with Alloy Wheel Pkg.	360	295	308
Sport bucket seats, performance axle.			
Performance Pkg., 2WD long bed	250	150	157
Performance axle.			
Performance Pkg., 2WD Cab Plus	350	287	300
Performance axle, rear stabilizer bar, heavy duty shock absorbers. Not available B2300.			
SE Upgrade Pkg., SE 2WD long bed	680	558	583
SE 2WD Cab Plus	730	599	626
Power windows, door locks and mirrors, sliding rear window, sport bucket seats, cargo cover (Cab Plus).			
SE Upgrade Pkg., SE 4WD	770	631	659
SE 4WD Cab Plus	820	672	702
SE 4WD Cab Plus with Alloy Wheel Pkg.	570	467	488
Power windows, door locks and mirrors, performance axle, cargo cover (Cab Plus).			
Value Plus Pkg., Base Cab Plus 2WD	NC	NC	NC
Upgraded cloth upholstery, 60/40 split bench seat, folding center armrest, upgraded door trim panels, door map pockets, 215/70R14 tires, styled steel wheels.			
AM/FM radio, B2300 base 5-speed	175	144	150
CD player, LE	295	242	253
Bed liner	250	205	214
Alloy wheels (NA Base)	250	205	214

Mazda

Mazda MPV

Mazda MPV

Mazda's minivan, the MPV (Multi-Purpose Vehicle), gained a driver-side air bag during the 1993 model year and gets additional safety features for '94.

Body Styles/Chassis

MPV is offered in a single body size with two conventional front doors and a one-piece rear liftgate. It deviates from the minivan norm with a swing-open hinged right-rear door instead of the typical sliding side door.

A single trim level is offered, but there are several optional equipment packages.

For '94, a center high-mounted brake light and side-door impact beams join the list of standard equipment. Four-wheel disc brakes also are new—the rear brakes previously were drums—but the standard anti-lock system continues to operate only on the rear brakes.

In other changes, the standard tire size increases from 205/70R14 to 195/75R15, and alloy wheels are no longer part of option package B.

Payload limits range from 1000 to 1400 pounds depending on the number of seats.

Powertrains

MPV offers rear-wheel drive or on-demand, full-time 4-wheel drive.

Rear-drive MPVs come standard with a 121-horsepower 2.6-liter 4-cylinder engine.

Standard on the 4WD model and available on 2WD models is a 155-horsepower 3.0-liter V-6. Both engines have 3 valves per cylinder: 2 intake and one exhaust.

A 4-speed overdrive automatic is the only transmission. V-6s team with an electronically controlled automatic. On 2WD models, it has "Power" and "Economy" shift programs and a "Hold" feature that's activated by a switch on the steering-column selector and permits locking in any of the three lower gears for full manual shifting, or extra traction on hills and slippery surfaces.

MPV's 4WD system can be used on dry pavement but is not intended for off-road use. It is engaged by pushing a button on the transmission shift lever and can be shifted between 2WD and 4WD at speeds up to 65 mph. A center differential can be locked by a dashboard button for maximum traction.

Standard towing capacities are 2300 pounds with 4-cylinder engine and 2600 with V-6; an extra-cost V-6 trailering package increases the limit to 4500 pounds on rear-drive models, 4200 pounds on the 4WD model.

Accommodations

All MPVs have standard reclining front bucket seats. Two-wheel-drive 4-cylinder models come with one 3-place mid-

Specifications

	4-door van
Wheelbase, in.	110.4
Overall length, in.	175.8
Overall width, in.	71.9
Overall height, in.	68.1
Turn diameter, ft.	36.1
Curb weight, lbs.	3595[1]
Fuel capacity, gal.	15.9[2]

1. 4040 lbs, 4WD. 2. 19.6 gal., V-6; 19.8 gal., 4WD.

Passenger Area Dimensions

Seating capacity	8
Front head room, in.	40.0
Rear head room, in.	39.0
Front leg room, in.	40.6
Rear leg room, in.	34.8

Available Seating

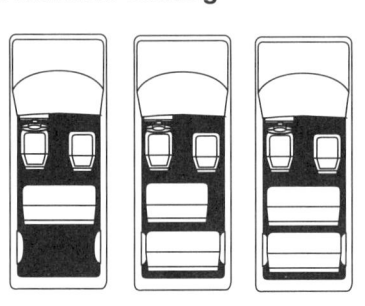

Cargo Dimensions and Payloads

Cargo area length, in.	79.4
Cargo area width, in.	57.5
Cargo area width between wheels, in.	NA
Cargo area height, in.	48.7
Cargo vol., cu. ft.	110.0
Max. payload, lbs.	1400
Max. trailer weight, lbs.	4500

Engines

	ohc I-4	ohc V-6
Size, liters/cu. in.	2.6/159	3.0/180
Horsepower @ rpm	121 @ 4600	155 @ 5000
Torque (lbs./ft.) @ rpm	149 @ 3500	169 @ 4000
Availability	S	O[1]

EPA city/highway mpg

4-speed OD automatic	18/24	16/22

1. Standard on 4WD models.

Built in Japan.

KEY: Dimensions and capacities are supplied by the manufacturers. **Curb Weight:** base models, not including optional equipment. **Max. payload, lbs.** = gross amount; net payload may be lower due to optional equipment. **Engines: ohv** = overhead valve; **ohc** = overhead cam; **I** = inline cylinders; **V** = cylinders in V configuration; **flat** = horizontally opposed cylinders; **rpm** = revolutions per minute; **OD** = overdrive transmission; **S** = standard; **O** = optional; **NA** = not available.

Mazda

dle bench for 5-passenger seating or a 2-place middle bench and a 3-place rear bench for 7-passenger capacity.

All models with the V-6 or 4WD have the 7-seat setup. Optional for 2WD V-6 models only is a Touring Package that includes a 3-place middle bench for 8-passenger seating.

Center bench seats have reclining backrests and fore/aft adjustment and can be removed with quick-release clamps. Third seats are bolted in, but can be removed with hand tools; they also double-fold forward for additional cargo space, and their backrests can be laid down to form a mini-bed when the center seatbacks are fully flat too.

Cargo space with all seats folded is 37.5 cubic feet and with all rear seats removed it's 110 cubic feet.

Evaluation

Though it lacks some of the features and roominess of class leaders like the Dodge Caravan/Plymouth Voyager and Mercury Villager/Nissan Quest, MPV is worthy of consideration.

It has a flexible passenger package, well-designed dashboard, and a pleasant, car-like driving feel.

The 4-cylinder and 4WD models have subpar acceleration because they weigh too much for the available engine torque (4WD adds about 450 pounds to the curb weight). The heavy 4WD model also guzzles lots of gas (14.2 mpg in our test) and has a rather truck-like ride.

However, 4WD is conveniently engaged by a switch on the transmission shift lever and provides better grip in rain and snow than the standard rear-wheel drive.

The V-6 has adequate pickup, but falls far short of the power provided by the 3.8-liter V-6s available in the Chrysler products and in the Pontiac Trans Sport, Chevrolet Lumina Minivan, or Oldsmobile Silhouette.

Braking power feels adequate with the standard rear anti-lock brakes, but for this type of family wagon, we think the MPV ought to have a 4-wheel anti-lock system—as do rivals from Toyota, Chrysler, Ford, and General Motors. And minivans from Chrysler, Toyota, and the new Ford Windstar also have dual air bags.

MPV's chassis copes well with big bumps and dips, though some choppiness is evident on freeways. Noise levels, though not outstandingly low even for a minivan, are acceptable.

Two drawbacks to MPV's interior are modest cargo space behind the rear seat on 7- and 8-passenger models, and a rear seat that's bolted in so it can't be easily removed. The middle bench has quick-release latches, but it's a back-breaker for one person to haul out the side door.

The MPV is high priced compared to Chrysler's minivans when similarly equipped. You should be able to get a discount from a Mazda dealer, but the same is true of Dodge and Plymouth dealers.

Prices

Mazda MPV

	Retail Price	Dealer Invoice	Fair Price
4-door van, 5-passenger, 2.6	$18195	$16212	$16712
4-door van, 7-passenger, 2.6	19595	17460	17960
4-door van, 7-passenger, 3.0	20395	18172	18672
4WD van, 7-passenger, 3.0	23395	20845	21345
Destination charge	445	445	445

Prices are for vehicles distributed by Mazda Motor of America, Inc. Prices may be higher in areas served by independent distributors.

A driver-side air bag was made standard during the 1993 model year and continues into 1994 on all MPVs.

Standard Equipment:

5-passenger: 2.6-liter 4-cylinder engine, 4-speed automatic transmission, anti-lock rear brakes, driver-side air bag, power steering, cloth reclining front bucket seats, removable reclining 3-passenger bench seat, remote mirrors, tachometer, coolant temperature gauge, trip odometer, intermittent wipers, rear defogger and wiper/washer, tinted glass, door pockets, remote fuel door release, tilt steering column, AM/FM cassette w/four speakers, digital clock, wheel covers, 195/75R15 tires. **7-passenger:** 2.6-liter 4-cylinder or 3.0-liter V-6, removable reclining 2-passenger middle and flip-fold 3-passenger rear bench seats, AM/FM cassette with six speakers, power mirrors. 4WD has on-demand 4WD, 215/65R15 tires, alloy wheels.

Optional Equipment:

	Retail Price	Dealer Invoice	Fair Price
Single air conditioning	$860	$705	$792
Dual air conditioning	1500	1230	1382
Requires V-6 engine and Pkg. A, B, C, or D.			
Touring Pkg.1, V-6 2WD	570	490	537
8-passenger seating, 3-passenger middle seat with fold-down armrests, cup holders, and outboard armrests. Requires Option Pkg. B or D.			
Cold Pkg.	300	258	283
Heavy duty battery, larger windshield washer solvent reservoir, rear heater.			
Option Pkg. A, 2WD	1050	872	973
Power windows and locks, cruise control, bronze-tinted windshield, rear privacy glass.			
Option Pkg. B, 2WD V-6	1350	1121	1251
Pkg. A plus keyless entry system, body-color grille, rear license plate illumination bar.			
Option Pkg. C, 4WD	1350	1121	1251
Pkg. A plus keyless entry system, body-color grille, rear license plate illumination bar.			
Luxury Pkg. (Option Pkg. D), 2WD V-6	3995	3316	3702
4WD	3550	2947	3290
Pkg. B (2WD), Pkg. C (4WD), leather upholstery, leather-wrapped steering wheel, color-keyed bodyside moldings, 2-tone paint, lace alloy wheels; requires dual air conditioning, Towing Pkg. and moonroof.			
CD player, 2WD V-6, 4WD	700	560	638
Requires Pkg. D.			
Power moonroof, 2WD V6, 4WD	1000	820	922
Requires Pkg. B, C, or D.			
2-tone paint	300	246	276
Towing Pkg., 2WD V-6	500	430	471
4WD	400	344	377
Transmission oil cooler, automatic load leveling, heavy duty cooling fan (2WD), conventional spare (2WD). 2WD requires Alloy wheel Pkg. or Pkg. D; 4WD requires Pkg. C or D.			
Alloy wheel Pkg., 2WD V-6	450	374	417
215/65R15 tires, alloy wheels. Requires Pkg. B.			
Floormats, 5-passenger	65	47	57
7-passenger	90	65	78
8-passenger	95	69	83

CONSUMER GUIDE® 133

Mazda

Mazda Navajo

Mazda Navajo LX 4WD

Restyled alloy wheels are the only change to this clone of the 3-door Ford Explorer. Mazda, which is partly owned by Ford, buys the Explorers from Ford and puts on its own grille and some minor exterior trim. The two companies share some other vehicles and components, as well.

Body Styles/Chassis

Navajo comes only as a 3-door wagon with a swing-up tailgate and separate-opening top-hinged window. (Explorer comes in 3- and 5-door body styles, the latter accounting for more than 90 percent of Explorer's sales.)

Navajo is offered in base DX and upscale LX price levels, both available with 2-wheel drive or 4-wheel drive. The DX is equipped much like the mid-range 3-door Explorer Sport; Navajo LX borrows features from the 5-door Explorer's upper-level XLT and Eddie Bauer trim levels.

Navajo also shares with Explorer all-wheel anti-lock brakes that operate in 4WD as well as 2WD. Navajo also inherits other Explorer safety features, such as a center high-mount stoplamp. Neither has an air bag.

The 750-pound maximum payload rating also mimics Explorer.

Powertrains

Navajo uses Explorer's 160-horsepower 4.0-liter V-6. Standard is a 5-speed manual transmission with 4-speed automatic optional on the LX model only.

Navajo 4x4s employ Explorer's electronic Touch Drive part-time 4WD system with full shift-on-the-fly capability (via a dash button and auto-lock front hubs). It's not intended for dry-pavement use and the vehicle must be stopped and reversed to fully disengage the 4WD mechanism.

Standard Navajos have a 3800-pound towing maximum. An optional trailering package available only with automatic transmission lifts it to 5000 pounds with 4WD and 5400 with 2WD.

Accommodations

Here, too, Navajo trods the 3-door Explorer path, with twin reclining front buckets and a 2-place rear bench with flop-down 50/50 seatback.

The grouping of standard and optional equipment is somewhat different than on the Ford versions.

Evaluation

Since Mazda can't afford to develop its own sport-utility vehicle, it buys the Explorer and rebadges it. Mazda would love to get a version of the 5-door, but Ford jealously keeps the 5-door for itself because it's been a gold mine for the company as the best-selling vehicle in its class.

Since Navajo is the same vehicle as the 3-door Explorer, there's no practical advantage to buying either, though Mazda's 3-year/50,000-mile warranty has an edge over Ford's 3/36,000 coverage.

Navajo's 3-door configuration makes getting into and out of the rear seat relatively difficult, this despite a lift-forward front passenger's seat. And against the longer 5-door Explorer, it suffers a choppier ride.

Then again, the Mazda fares no worse than rival 3-doors in either of these respects and four adults ride with plenty of head and leg room in car-like surroundings. Cargo volume

Specifications

	3-door wagon
Wheelbase, in.	102.1
Overall length, in.	175.3
Overall width, in.	70.2
Overall height, in.	68.1
Turn diameter, ft.	35.6
Curb weight, lbs.	3785
Fuel capacity, gal.	19.3

Passenger Area Dimensions

Seating capacity	4
Front head room, in.	39.9
Rear head room, in.	39.1
Front leg room, in.	42.4
Rear leg room, in.	36.6

Cargo Dimensions and Payloads

Cargo area length, in.	59.5
Cargo area width, in.	57.9
Cargo area width between wheels, in.	41.9
Cargo area height, in.	36.0
Cargo vol., cu. ft.	69.5
Max. payload, lbs.	750
Max. trailer weight, lbs.	5400

Engines

	ohv V-6
Size, liters/cu. in.	4.0/245
Horsepower @ rpm	160 @ 4500
Torque (lbs./ft.) @ rpm	220 @ 2500
Availability	S

EPA city/highway mpg

5-speed OD manual	17/22
4-speed OD automatic	15/20

Built in Louisville, Ky.

KEY: Dimensions and capacities are supplied by the manufacturers. **Curb Weight:** base models, not including optional equipment. **Max. payload, lbs.** = gross amount; net payload may be lower due to optional equipment. **Engines: ohv** = overhead valve; **ohc** = overhead cam; **I** = inline cylinders; **V** = cylinders in V configuration; **flat** = horizontally opposed cylinders; **rpm** = revolutions per minute; **OD** = overdrive transmission; **S** = standard; **O** = optional; **NA** = not available.

is excellent, helped by a design that puts the full-size spare in a crank-down cradle beneath the rear cargo deck.

With curb weights ranging from 3785 pounds to 4101 pounds, fuel economy is just as mediocre in the 3-door version of this vehicle as it is in the heavier 5-door. We averaged just 16 mpg in a 4WD Navajo with the automatic, virtually the same as we averaged in a 5-door Explorer.

Though the V-6 strains against this heft with a full load and up hills, ample low- and mid-range torque gives satisfying acceleration around town and on the highway. Aiding the cause is a smooth-shifting 4-speed automatic that promptly drops to a lower gear when asked. The 5-speed has slightly notchy action, but isn't tiresome.

The Touch Drive 4x4 couldn't be easier to use, though it's a nuisance to stop and then back up a bit to fully disengage the 4WD hardware, as the owner's manual advises.

Relatively low demand for 3-door sport-utility vehicles has resulted in big discounts on the Navajo and 3-door Explorer. If you're interested, also look at the Jeep Cherokee 3-door, which offers similar features and good value.

Prices

Mazda Navajo	Retail Price	Dealer Invoice	Fair Price
DX 3-door 2WD wagon	$17775	$15658	$15958
LX 3-door 2WD wagon	18995	16733	17033
DX 3-door 4WD wagon	19565	17234	17524
LX 3-door 4WD wagon	20785	18309	18609
Destination charge	490	490	490

Prices are for vehicles distributed by Mazda Motor of America, Inc. Prices may be higher in areas served by independent distributors.

Standard Equipment:
DX: 4.0-liter V-6 engine, 5-speed manual transmission, anti-lock brakes, power steering, cloth reclining front bucket seats, split folding rear seat, intermittent wipers, tinted glass, AM/FM radio, skid plates, 225/70R15 tires. **LX** adds: power windows and locks, cassette player, rear window privacy glass, leather-wrapped steering wheel, power mirrors, lighted visor mirrors, upgraded door trim, retractable cargo cover, cargo net, alloy wheels. 4WD models add part-time 4WD with electronic transfer case.

Optional Equipment:
4-speed automatic transmission (NA DX)	890	757	803
DX Special Equipment Pkg., 5-speed	295	251	266

Air conditioning, cassette player, console with armrest and cup holders, bodyside moldings.

LX Premium Pkg., 5-speed	495	421	447
with automatic	1095	931	988

Air conditioning, premium cassette player, removable glass moonroof, cruise control, tilt steering wheel, sport front seats with power lumbar and adjustable side bolsters, rear defogger and wiper/washer, console with armrest and cup holders, roof rack, floormats, 235/75R15 all-terrain tires.

LX Leather Pkg.	3995	3396	3605

Includes LX Premium Pkg. plus leather upholstery, automatic transmission, Towing Pkg., power driver's seat.

Towing Pkg., LX	350	298	316

Performance axle, heavy duty cooling system, heavy duty flasher, trailer wiring harness, limited-slip differential. Requires automatic transmission.

CD player, LX	300	255	271

Mazda • Mercury

Mercury Villager

RECOMMENDED

Mercury Villager LS

Mercury's minivan gets a driver-side air bag and a luxury special-edition version for its second model year.

Villager shares its front-drive platform and most interior and mechanical features with the Nissan Quest. They differ slightly in grille and tail appearance.

These front-drive minivans are the product of a joint effort by Ford Motor Company and Nissan. Villager and Quest were designed at Nissan's California styling studios and are built at a Ford plant in Ohio.

The 1994 Villagers were officially introduced in late November, so unlike the Quest, Mercury says there are no early 1994 models without the air bag.

Body Styles/Chassis
Villager is offered in a single body size with a sliding curb-side door and a rear liftgate that can be equipped with a window that opens separately.

GS and LS models are joined by a top-line Nautica edition that features a 2-tone blue-and-white paint scheme, white alloy wheels, and blue leather upholstery.

Villager has Mercury's trademark full-width illuminated grille treatment and different taillamps to differentiate it from the Quest. Also, 4-wheel anti-lock brakes are standard on all Villager models, but optional on the base Quest.

Maximum cargo volume is 126.4 cubic feet, about the same as the regular-length Chrysler minivans. Payload is 1290 pounds.

Powertrains
All Villagers have a Nissan-made 3.0-liter V-6 engine rated at 150 horsepower and a 4-speed overdrive automatic transmission with column shift.

An optional trailering package increases the towing limit from 2000 pounds to 3500.

Accommodations
Seats for seven are standard on all Villagers this year; last year, the GS came with seats for five. The GS and LS have a removable 2-place middle bench seat and a 3-place rear bench. Optional on the LS and standard on the Nautica are removable middle captains chairs.

Mercury

Villager shares with Quest a unique seating feature by which the 3-place bench can slide along a track in the floor. The seat can be located at the rear of the vehicle to open the middle for cargo room. Or it can slide to the middle to open up the rear area. Outboard shoulder belts are provided for either position. The seat also can tip and fold to maximize cargo space. The second- and third-row seats also recline or fold flat and have molded-in cupholders in their backs.

Specifications

	4-door wagon
Wheelbase, in.	112.2
Overall length, in.	189.9
Overall width, in.	73.7
Overall height, in.	67.6
Turn diameter, ft.	39.9
Curb weight, lbs.	3990
Fuel capacity, gal.	20.0

Passenger Area Dimensions

Seating capacity	7
Front head room, in.	39.4
Rear head room, in.	39.7
Front leg room, in.	39.9
Rear leg room, in.	34.8

Available Seating

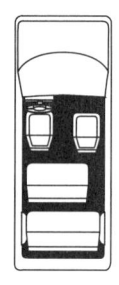

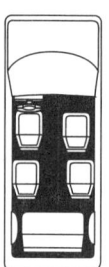

Cargo Dimensions and Payloads

Cargo area length, in.	84.6
Cargo area width, in.	48.6
Cargo area width between wheels, in.	48.1
Cargo area height, in.	114.8
Cargo vol., cu. ft.	126.4
Max. payload, lbs.	1290
Max. trailer weight, lbs.	3500

Engines

	ohc V-6
Size, liters/cu. in.	3.0/181
Horsepower @ rpm	151 @ 4800
Torque (lbs./ft.) @ rpm	174 @ 4400
Availability	S

EPA city/highway mpg

4-speed OD automatic	17/23

Built in Avon Lake, Ohio.

KEY: Dimensions and capacities are supplied by the manufacturers. **Curb Weight:** base models, not including optional equipment. **Max. payload, lbs.** = gross amount; net payload may be lower due to optional equipment. **Engines: ohv** = overhead valve; **ohc** = overhead cam; **I** = inline cylinders; **V** = cylinders in V configuration; **flat** = horizontally opposed cylinders; **rpm** = revolutions per minute; **OD** = overdrive transmission; **S** = standard; **O** = optional; **NA** = not available.

Villager meets passenger car safety standards with such features as a high-mounted rear stoplamp and side-guard door beams.

Villager and Quest met all passenger-car safety standards upon their introduction, but used motorized shoulder belts and manual lap belts for the front seats. This safety-belt system is retained for 1994, despite the addition of the driver-side air bag.

Evaluation

In overall performance and driving feel, Villager and Quest rank among the best minivans. These are luxury-oriented people movers that stress car-like comfort over towing and heavy-duty work.

The 3.0-liter engine can't match the muscle of the 3.8-liter V-6s in front-drive minivans from General Motors and Chrysler Corporation. Acceleration is adequate, but there's not enough power to easily merge into highway traffic with a full load of passengers and cargo, so you have to allow extra room.

Our staff test-drove a Villager LS more than 10,000 miles. We averaged 22-23 mpg in highway cruising—which is better than most other minivans—but dropped to as low as 15 mpg in city traffic.

Body lean is noticeable in turns, but the tires grip securely and understeer (resistance to turning) is moderate. A wide turning circle makes Villager harder to maneuver in tight spots than most cars.

The suspension is firm enough to minimize bouncing on wavy roads, but at times our test model just banged over bumps instead of soaking them up. The rear wheels especially seemed to lack resilience.

Head room and leg room are ample for the front seats, and adequate for the middle and rear seats. Despite Villager's high profile, there's hardly any step up into the interior.

Villager is nearly a foot longer than the standard-length Dodge Caravan. Overall length is very similar to that of the stretched-body Chrysler minivans and to that of Ford's new Windstar.

Unike Windstar or the extended-body Chrysler products, Villager has only a small cargo area at the rear when all seats are in their regular positions. It's a chore to remove the cumbersome middle bench or buckets, but once done, you can slide the rear seat forward for ample cargo room. In addition, both the rear and middle seats recline and fold flat for use as tables.

The optional electronic instrument cluster includes a large digital speedometer and a bar graph tachometer that's shaped like a hockey stick. The digital speedometer is easy to read; the tachometer is difficult to read and of little value. The stereo is mounted low on the dashboard and has small controls that are hard to find without a long look away from the road.

Wind noise is prominent at highway speeds. And our long-term test Villager developed several squeaks and rattles and the 4-speed automatic transmission had to be serviced to reduce vibration when it shifted into second gear.

Overall, however, the air bag, standard anti-lock brakes, and refined overall design make Villager an attractive upscale minivan choice.

Prices

Mercury Villager	Retail Price	Dealer Invoice	Fair Price
GS 4-door van	$18375	$16355	$17575
LS 4-door van	23155	20562	22355

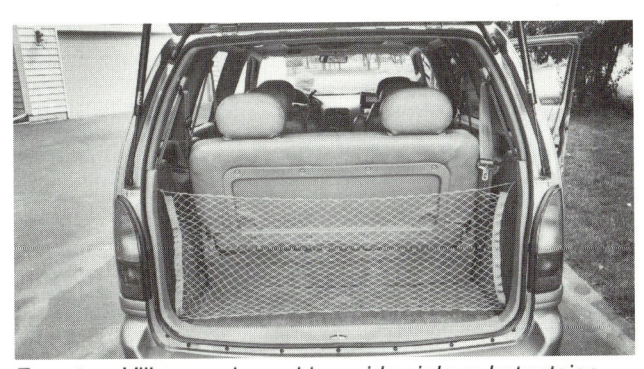

From top: Villager gains a driver-side air bag, but retains motorized front shoulder belts. Rearmost bench seat slides fore and aft on tracks. Middle seats are removable. Cargo space is tight with all 7 seats in place.

Mercury

	Retail Price	Dealer Invoice	Fair Price
Nautica 4-door van	$24635	$21864	$23835
Destination charge	540	540	540

Standard Equipment:

GS: 3.0-liter V-6 engine, 4-speed automatic transmission, driver-side air bag, anti-lock brakes, power steering, cloth reclining front bucket seats, 3-passenger bench seat, cloth upholstery, AM/FM cassette player, tachometer, coolant temperature gauge, trip odometer, dual outside mirrors, visor mirrors, tinted glass, variable-intermittent wipers, rear wiper/washer, remote fuel door release, black bodyside moldings, color-keyed bumpers, cornering lamps, front door map pockets, floormats, 205/75R15 all-season tires, wheel covers. **LS** adds: front air conditioning, 2-passenger middle and 3-passenger rear bench seats, tilt steering column, cruise control, power windows and locks, Light Group, privacy glass, rear defogger, lighted visor mirrors, luggage rack, lighted visor mirrors, leather-wrapped steering wheel, seatback map pockets, rear cargo net, lockable underseat storage bin, 2-tone paint, color-keyed bodyside molding, striping. **Nautica** adds to LS: two middle bucket seats, leather upholstery, unique exterior paint, yellow striping, white alloy wheels, duffle bag.

Optional Equipment:

Front air conditioning, GS	855	727	787
Auxiliary rear air conditioning with rear heater, GS	465	395	428
Preferred Equipment Pkg. 691A, GS	1505	1279	1385
Front Air conditioning, 7-passenger seating, power windows and door locks, tilt steering column, cruise control, rear defogger, power mirrors.			
Preferred Equipment Pkg. 692A, GS	2310	1964	2125
Pkg. 691A plus power driver's seat, player, luggage rack, underseat storage bin, alloy wheels.			
Preferred Equipment Pkg. 695A, LS	345	294	317
Power driver's seat, rear air conditioning with rear heater, premium AM/FM cassette player, flip open liftgate window, alloy wheels.			
Preferred Equipment Pkg. 696A, LS	1750	1489	1610
Pkg. 695A plus power passenger seat, quad bucket seats, keyless entry system, headlamp delay system, electronic instrumentation.			
Preferred Euipment Pkg. 697A, Nautica	1750	1489	1610
Power driver's seat, power passenger seat, rear air conditioning with rear heater, premium AM/FM cassette player, flip open liftgate window, keyless entry system, headlamp delay system, electronic instrumentation, locking alloy wheels..			
Light Group, GS	155	132	143
Trailer Towing Pkg.	250	213	230
Power windows and locks, GS	530	451	488
Power mirrors, GS	100	85	92
Power moonroof, LS and Nautica	776	659	714
7-passenger seating, GS	330	281	304
Quad captains chairs, LS	600	510	552
8-way power driver's seat	395	336	363
Leather upholstery, LS	865	735	796
Requires quad captains chairs, power driver and passenger seats.			
Electronic instrumentation, LS	244	207	224
Keyless entry and headlamp delay systems, LS	300	255	276
Tilt steering column and cruise control, GS	370	314	340
Rear defogger, GS	170	144	156
Flip open liftgate window	90	77	83
Premium AM/FM cassette player, LS	330	281	304
Premium AM/FM cassette and CD player, GS with Pkg. 629A	660	561	607
LS with Pkg. 695A or 696A, and Nautica with Pkg. 697A	330	281	304
Supersound AM/FM cassette and CD player, LS and Nautica	900	765	828
Includes rear radio controls with front seat lockout, dual mini headphone jacks, cassette/CD storage console, power diversity antenna, subwoofer speaker.			
Luggage rack, GS	145	123	133
Underseat storage bin, GS	35	30	32
Monotone paint, LS	NC	NC	NC
Bodyside striping, GS	45	38	41
Locking alloy wheels	380	323	350

CONSUMER GUIDE® 137

Mitsubishi Expo

Mitsubishi Expo

The addition of a driver-side air bag makes news for Mitsubishi's "sport wagons," which come in two sizes.

Mitsubishi calls the 7-seat model the Expo and its shorter 5-seat version the Expo LRV. Chrysler sells slightly different versions of the Expo LRV as the Plymouth Colt Vista and Eagle Summit Wagon (see separate reports).

Body Styles/Chassis

The LRV, for Light Recreational Vehicle, spans a 99.2-inch wheelbase and is 168.5 inches long overall.

Regular Expos add about 8 inches to wheelbase and 9 inches to overall length.

All models have two conventional front passenger doors and a one-piece liftgate.

LRVs come with a minivan-style sliding right-rear door running in a unique hidden track, making for a 4-door body type. Expos have a conventional side-hinged rear door on each side, making them 5-door models.

For '94, Expo loses its uplevel SP models, but base Expos gain some of their features as standard. Expos again offer a choice of front-wheel drive or on the Expo AWD, permanently engaged all-wheel drive.

The LRV comes in front-drive base and Sport models. The LRV AWD model is no longer available.

Expos are built by Mitsubishi in Japan and are classified under U.S. regulations as automobiles, not passenger vans. As such they carry all required auto safety equipment.

Anti-lock brakes with rear discs instead of drums are optional for all but base LRV models. Regular Expos gain newly optional alloy wheels.

Mitsubishi doesn't quote payload ratings for Expos.

Powertrains

A 113-horsepower 1.8-liter 4-cylinder engine comes in the base LRV.

All other Expos and LRVs use a 136-horsepower 2.4-liter 4-cylinder.

With either engine, a 5-speed manual transmission is standard and a 4-speed automatic is optional.

The Expo AWD has a permanently engaged all-wheel-drive system that normally divides engine torque 50/50 front/rear. When wheel slip is detected, electronic controls automatically reapportion torque to the axle with the best traction. The AWD is not intended for off-road use and adds nothing to ride height.

Maximum trailering weights are 2000 pounds for front-drive models and 2500 for the Expo AWD. All models are limited to 1000 pounds for trailers without brakes.

Accommodations

All models have front bucket seats. The 5-seat LRV comes with a removable 3-person fold-up back seat that's split

Specifications

	4-door wagon	5-door wagon
Wheelbase, in.	99.2	107.1
Overall length, in.	168.5	177.4
Overall width, in.	66.7	66.7
Overall height, in.	62.1	62.6
Turn diameter, ft.	33.5	36.8
Curb weight, lbs.	2745	3020
Fuel capacity, gal.	14.5	15.8

Passenger Area Dimensions

Seating capacity	5	7
Front head room, in.	40.0	39.3
Rear head room, in.	38.6	39.3
Front leg room, in.	40.8	40.5
Rear leg room, in.	36.1	36.9

Available Seating

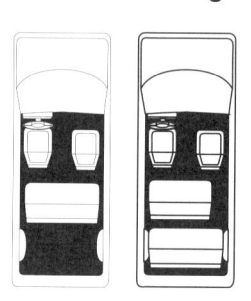

Cargo Dimensions and Payloads

Cargo area length, in.	67.8	71.9
Cargo area width, in.	41.3	41.3
Cargo area width between wheels, in.	39.0	39.0
Cargo area height, in.	43.4	35.8
Cargo vol., cu. ft.	67.8	75.0
Max. payload, lbs.	NA	NA
Max. trailer weight, lbs.	2000	2500

Engines

	ohc I-4	ohc I-4
Size, liters/cu. in.	1.8/112	2.4/143
Horsepower @ rpm	113 @ 6000	136 @ 5500
Torque (lbs./ft.) @ rpm	116 @ 4500	145 @ 4250
Availability	S[1]	S

EPA city/highway mpg

5-speed OD manual	24/29	22/27
4-speed OD automatic	24/29	20/26

1. LRV.

Built in Japan.

KEY: Dimensions and capacities are supplied by the manufacturers. **Curb Weight:** base models, not including optional equipment. **Max. payload, lbs.** = gross amount; net payload may be lower due to optional equipment. **Engines: ohv** = overhead valve; **ohc** = overhead cam; **I** = inline cylinders; **V** = cylinders in V configuration; **flat** = horizontally opposed cylinders; **rpm** = revolutions per minute; **OD** = overdrive transmission; **S** = standard; **O** = optional; **NA** = not available.

Mitsubishi

50/50. Regular Expos have 50/50 non-removable fold-and-recline second and third seats giving 7-passenger capacity.

The new air bag is housed in a new 4-spoke steering wheel and is accompanied by a manual 3-point driver-side safety belt with height-adjustable shoulder belt. A motorized shoulder belt and manual lap belt are still used on the passenger side to meet federal passive-restraint rules.

The optional air conditioning has non-CFC refrigerant. And LRVs get low-back front bucket seats, with a new driver's height adjustment included on the Sport.

Evaluation

Expo and its Chrysler cousins haven't been hot sellers, probably because they can cost almost much as some base-trim minivans. But Mitsubishi would prefer you think of them as taller, roomier versions of the conventional compact wagon, in which case they make more sense.

Consider an Expo if it's sized right for you—and if you can negotiate a price well below full sticker. The air bag is a laudable improvement, and Mitsubishi is wise to limit the puny 1.8-liter engine to the lighter LRV.

The 2.4-liter four, with its extra low-speed torque, is a far better bet for everyday driving, particularly with automatic and/or a major load. Even then, Expo is no musclebound hauler. We timed the "big" model with automatic at a leisurely 11.7 seconds 0-60 mph; the like-equipped LRV is little, if any, quicker.

Fuel economy, on the other hand, is fine: nearly 25 mpg for the automatic Expo in our hard driving.

Performance aside, all Expos remain pleasant compact wagons with versatile passenger/cargo packages. Cornering ability is modest and noise levels are fairly high, but the ride is comfortably pliant, and maneuverability is great for the urban grind.

Clockwise from top left: The 5-seat Expo LRV is shorter than the 7-seat Expo models. Expo and Expo LRVs gain a driver-side air bag for 1994. The LRV's rear seat folds and is removable. The Expo's rear seats also fold, but are not removable.

Mitsubishi

Expos put their drivers in a high, somewhat bus-like position. Big windows create panoramic outward vision, but upper-level models clutter it with a forest of rear headrests. Dash design is generally convenient, though the radio is too low for easy use.

Passenger room is plentiful—better for rear-seaters in the long-wheelbase models—and all-round head room is towering. The regular Expo's optional third seat seems meant for two kids, and is hard to reach even though the second seat slides forward to assist. Neither rear seat removes on standard Expos, but the 50/50 split backrests fold forward for cargo-carrying or recline flat for a makeshift bed. Cup holders and cubbyholes abound in both, but there's not much luggage space with all seats up.

Prices

Mitsubishi Expo	Retail Price	Dealer Invoice	Fair Price
LRV base 4-door wagon, 5-speed	$13019	$11716	$12216
LRV base 4-door wagon, automatic	13859	12474	12974
LRV Sport 4-door wagon, 5-speed	16799	14619	15119
LRV Sport 4-door wagon, automatic	17489	15219	15719
Base 5-door wagon, 5-speed	15689	13648	14148
Base 5-door wagon, automatic	16379	14248	14748
Base AWD 5-door wagon, 5-speed	17129	14900	15400
Base AWD 5-door wagon, automatic	17819	15500	16000
Destination charge	445	445	445

Standard Equipment:

LRV base: 1.8-liter 4-cylinder engine, 5-speed manual or 4-speed automatic transmission, driver-side air bag, power steering, tilt steering column, cloth reclining front bucket seats, 50/50 folding rear bench seat, coolant temperature gauge, trip odometer, remote fuel door release, front air dam, color-keyed bumpers and bodyside molding, 2-tone paint, dual outside mirrors, rear window defogger, variable intermittent wipers, wheel covers, 185/75R14 tires. **LRV Sport** adds: 2.4-liter 4-cylinder engine, air conditioning, rear heater ducts, power windows and locks, power mirrors and tailgate lock/release, remote keyless entry, rear intermittent wiper/washer, cruise control, tachometer, digital clock, center armrest, map pockets, cargo cover, AM/FM cassette, 205/70R14 all-season tires, alloy wheels. **Base Expo** adds to base LRV: 2.4-liter 4-cylinder engine, 7-passenger seating with split folding middle and rear reclining bench seats, power mirrors, power tailgate lock/release, tachometer, digital clock, cargo cover, front storage tray, rear intermittent wiper/washer, 205/70R14 all-season tires. **Expo AWD** adds permanent 4-wheel drive.

Optional Equipment:

Anti-lock brakes (NA LRV base)	976	800	866
Air conditioning	829	680	736
Power Pkg., Expo	894	715	785
LRV base	719	575	631

Power windows and locks, cruise control, remote keyless entry. LRV base adds: power mirrors and requires automatic transmission.

Convenience Pkg., LRV base	596	477	523

Rear cargo cover, digital clock, center armrest, upgraded door trim, power door locks, power tailgate release, rear intermittent wiper/washer.

Luggage rack	274	178	220
CD player, Expo	626	407	504
Power sunroof (NA LRV Sport or Expo AWD)	685	548	601
Cargo Kit, LRV	99	70	82
Cargo tray and net.			
AM/FM stereo, LRV base	334	217	269
AM/FM cassette	466	312	380
Floormats, LRV	73	47	59
Expo	85	55	68
Mud guards (front and rear)	84	54	67
Wheel locks, Expo	37	24	30
Alloy wheels, Expo	291	233	256

Mitsubishi Mighty Max

Mitsubishi Mighty Max regular-cab with sport package

Side door guard beams and a center high-mounted stoplamp are among the few additions to these compact pickups.

Dodge for several years had marketed a similar Mitsubishi-made compact pickup as the Ram 50, but that model has been dropped for 1994.

Body Styles/Chassis

Mighty Max comes as a regular-cab and as the Macrocab extended-cab model. Regular-cabs have a 105.1-inch wheelbase; Macrocabs a 116.1-inch wheelbase. Both use a 6-foot cargo bed.

A 3-place bench seat is standard; buckets are unavailable. The Macrocab lacks rear seating, but adds 11 inches of storage space and a covered stowage box behind its 60/40 split front seat.

The regular-cab model is offered with 2- or 4-wheel drive; the Macrocab comes only with 2WD. Rear-wheel anti-lock brakes are fitted to only the 4WD Mighty Max. The other models have a load-sensing proportioning valve that automatically adjusts rear brake pressure to accommodate varying cargo loads.

Maximum payload, 1700 pounds, is found on the manual-transmission 4WD model. The Macrocab's payload ceiling is 1560 pounds.

For 1994, the optional air conditioning system uses CFC-free refrigerant.

Powertrains

A 116-horsepower 2.4-liter 4-cylinder is the only engine on 2WD models. Standard on the 4x4 is a 151-horsepower 3.0-liter V-6.

A 5-speed manual transmission is standard on all Mighty Maxes; a 4-speed overdrive automatic is available only on 2WD models.

Mitsubishi's 4WD is an on-demand, part-time (not for use on dry pavement) system that includes automatic locking front hubs. The vehicle has to be stopped to lock the hubs before 4WD can be engaged, however, and it also must be stopped to shift out of 4WD and then reversed to unlock the hubs.

All models can tow up to 3500 pounds if the trailer has brakes, and up to 1000 pounds if it does not.

Mitsubishi

Evaluation

These aren't among the best compact pickups, but base prices are reasonable, and Mitsubishi dealers should be discounting.

The regular cabs have only a narrow storage space behind the seats for hiding small items, so—as with most regular-cab compact pickups—you're forced to travel light if you don't want to throw things into the cargo bed.

Macrocab is without rear seating, but it is more practical than the regular-cab because it has a generous amount of interior storage space, including a concealed aft storage compartment. Instruments and controls are well laid out and head and leg room is good even for tall people, though bucket seats aren't offered.

Mitsubishi's 4-cylinder runs smoothly, but is lethargic with automatic transmission. The smoother V-6 delivers much better all-round performance. That helps Mighty Max in the towing department, though its trailering limit is still about half that of the Ford Ranger and Chevrolet S10/GMC Sonoma. Payloads are competitive for light-duty chores.

Mitsubishi Mighty Max Macrocab with Sport Package

Though the 4WD lacks shift-on-the-fly, once it's engaged, it allows intermittent use of 4WD, so you can shift between 2WD and 4WD High. However, if you reverse directions or make a tight U-turn, the hubs will unlock and you'll have to stop to engage 4WD again. That's inconvenient.

Might Max 4x4s have a firm suspension and tough tires that make for stiff, bouncy passage on paved roads and a jolting ride over rough roads. Models with the Sport Package option are nicely furnished sport trucks, with good interior assembly and a full set of gauges.

Specifications

	Regular cab	Macrocab
Wheelbase, in.	105.1	116.1
Overall length, in.	177.2	188.2
Overall width, in.	65.7	65.7
Overall height, in.	58.3	59.6
Turn diameter, ft.	35.4	38.7
Curb weight, lbs.	2600[1]	2780
Fuel capacity, gal.	13.7[2]	18.2

1. 3250 lbs., 4WD. 2. 15.7 gals., 4WD.

Passenger Area Dimensions

Seating capacity	3	3
Front head room, in.	38.8	38.9
Rear head room, in.	—	—
Front leg room, in.	41.9	43.4
Rear leg room, in.	—	—

Cargo Dimensions and Payloads

Cargo area length, in.	72.0	72.0
Cargo area width, in.	59.0	59.0
Cargo area width between wheels, in.	NA	NA
Cargo area height, in.	15.8	15.8
Max. payload, lbs.	1700	1560
Max. trailer weight, lbs.	3500	3500

Engines

	ohc I-4	ohc V-6
Size, liters/cu. in.	2.4/143	3.0/181
Horsepower @ rpm	116 @ 5000	151 @ 5000
Torque (lbs./ft.) @ rpm	136 @ 3500	174 @ 4000
Availability	S	S[1]

EPA city/highway mpg

5-speed OD manual	21/25	17/22
4-speed OD automatic	19/23	

1. Mighty Max 4WD.

Built in Japan.

KEY: Dimensions and capacities are supplied by the manufacturers. **Curb Weight:** base models, not including optional equipment. **Max. payload, lbs.** = gross amount; net payload may be lower due to optional equipment. **Engines:** ohv = overhead valve; ohc = overhead cam; **I** = inline cylinders; **V** = cylinders in V configuration; **flat** = horizontally opposed cylinders; **rpm** = revolutions per minute; **OD** = overdrive transmission; **S** = standard; **O** = optional; **NA** = not available.

Prices

Mitsubishi Mighty Max

	Retail Price	Dealer Invoice	Fair Price
2WD regular cab, 5-speed	$9429	$8512	$8712
2WD regular cab, automatic	10349	9109	9309
2WD Macrocab, 5-speed	10899	9595	9795
2WD Macrocab, automatic	11579	10192	10392
4WD regular cab, 5-speed	14219	12510	12710
Destination charge	420	420	420

Standard Equipment:

2.4-liter 4-cylinder engine, 5-speed manual or 4-speed automatic transmission, cloth and vinyl bench seat, tinted glass, carpet, dual outside mirrors, tilt steering column, front air dam, cargo tie down-hooks, trip odometer, black front bumper, chrome grille, sport steering wheel, front stabilizer bar, behind seat storage compartment, keyless entry system, 13.7-gallon fuel tank, 195/75R14 tires, styled steel wheels. **Macrocab** adds: reclining split bench seat, cargo straps, concealed rear storage, rear quarter windows, 18.2-gallon fuel tank, 205/75R14 tires. **4WD** adds to 2WD regular cab: 3.0-liter V-6 engine, rear anti-lock brakes, automatic locking front hubs, power steering, skid plates, mud guards, front tow hooks, fender flares, 15.7-gallon fuel tank, 225/75R15 tires.

Optional Equipment:

Air conditioning	729	598	655
Power steering, 2WD	290	232	258
Sport Pkg., 2WD	445	356	396

Bright windshield molding, color-keyed front bumper, halogen headlights, upgraded door trim and carpeting, door map pockets, cloth bench seat, day/night mirror, Radio Accommodation Pkg., rear sliding window, full instrumentation, tachometer. Requires Value Pkg.

| Value Pkg., 2WD | 759 | 759 | 759 |

Air conditioning, color-keyed rear step bumper, AM/FM cassette, digital clock, striping. Requires Sport Pkg.

Radio Accommodation Pkg. with two speakers,

regular cab	47	33	40
with four speakers, Macrocab	76	53	64
Limited-slip differential, 4WD	226	181	201
Black rear step bumper	162	113	136
Color-keyed front bumper, 4WD	38	30	34
Color-keyed rear bumper, 4WD	204	143	171

Requires color-keyed front bumper.

Mitsubishi

	Retail Price	Dealer Invoice	Fair Price
Chrome bumper	$201	$141	$169
Not available Sport Pkg.			
Digital clock	92	60	75
Dual chrome sport mirrors, 4WD	118	77	96
Bodyside moldings, 2WD	111	72	90
AM/FM radio, 2WD	321	210	262
AM/FM cassette, 4WD	481	327	399
Sliding rear window, 4WD	89	71	79
Wheel trim rings, 4WD	76	49	62
Floormats	52	34	42

Mitsubishi Montero

Mitsubishi Montero SR

A standard driver-side air bag, a larger available engine, and standard 7-passenger seating are among changes to Mitsubishi's sport-utility vehicle.

Body Styles/Chassis

Montero continues as a 5-door wagon with a side-hinged swing-open rear door. The lineup has been trimmed from four models to two. Discontinued are last year's base and RS models. Surviving are the LS and SR models.

Both Monteros have 4-wheel disc brakes as standard. Anti-lock brakes (ABS) that work in both 2WD and 4WD are optional on the LS and are now standard on the SR. Mitsubishi says the anti-lock system, which it calls Multi-Mode ABS, adjusts braking according to whether the vehicle is in 2WD or 4WD.

Montero's suspension has been revised for 1994 and is no longer is available with the optional driver-adjusted shock absorbers that could be set for hard, medium, or soft damping.

Both models now have double-pane sliding rear side windows, a running change made during model-year '93.

The LS's optional alloy wheels have been restyled. The SR also gets new alloy wheels, but drops the 31x10.5R15 tires it came with last year in favor of 265/70R15 all-season tires. Heated outside-mirrors also are newly standard on the SR.

Powertrains

The LS retains the 151-horsepower 3.0 V-6 that previously was Montero's only engine. The SR comes standard with a new engine, a twin-cam 3.5-liter V-6 rated at 215 horsepower.

LS models are available with either a 5-speed manual transmission or a 4-speed automatic. SRs come only with the automatic.

Mitsubishi labels Montero's standard 4-wheel drive system "Active-Trac 4WD." It's an on-demand setup that can be used on dry pavement. It has shift-on-the-fly between 2WD and 4WD High up to 62 mph. In 4WD, engine torque is normally divided 50/50 front/rear, but a viscous coupling unit can automatically split it up to 30/70 when traction needs demand. The SR is also available with an air-actuated locking rear differential.

Maximum towing capacity is 4000 pounds.

Accommodations

The standard driver-side air bag is housed in a new leather-wrapped 4-spoke steering wheel.

To the carried-over front-bucket seats and 3-place double-fold rear bench is added a third-row of seats for 7-passenger capacity. The new seats are individual units

Specifications	5-door wagon
Wheelbase, in.	107.3
Overall length, in.	185.2
Overall width, in.	66.7
Overall height, in.	73.4
Turn diameter, ft.	38.7
Curb weight, lbs.	4190
Fuel capacity, gal.	24.3

Passenger Area Dimensions	
Seating capacity	7
Front head room, in.	40.9
Rear head room, in.	40.0
Front leg room, in.	40.3
Rear leg room, in.	37.6

Cargo Dimensions and Payloads	
Cargo area length, in.	66.1
Cargo area width, in.	50.4
Cargo area width between wheels, in.	38.6
Cargo area height, in.	45.5
Cargo vol., cu. ft.	72.7
Max. payload, lbs.	NA
Max. trailer weight, lbs.	4000

Engines	ohc V-6	dohc V-6
Size, liters/cu. in.	3.0/181	3.5/213
Horsepower @ rpm	151 @ 5000	215 @ 5500
Torque (lbs./ft.) @ rpm	174 @ 4000	228 @ 3000
Availability	S	S[1]

EPA city/highway mpg		
5-speed OD manual	15/18	
4-speed OD automatic	15/18	14/17

1. *Montero SR.*

Built in Japan.

KEY: Dimensions and capacities are supplied by the manufacturers. **Curb Weight:** base models, not including optional equipment. **Max. payload, lbs.** = gross amount; net payload may be lower due to optional equipment. **Engines: ohv** = overhead valve; **ohc** = overhead cam; **I** = inline cylinders; **V** = cylinders in V configuration; **flat** = horizontally opposed cylinders; **rpm** = revolutions per minute; **OD** = overdrive transmission; **S** = standard; **O** = optional; **NA** = not available.

Mitsubishi

equipped with headrests and are hinged to fold up to the sides for maximum cargo room.

Also for '94, the previously optional Power Package of electric windows/door locks/door mirrors, plus cruise control has been made standard. And a power driver's seat is newly included with the optional leather-and-wood interior package. A new 6-speaker AM/FM/cassette stereo with graphic equalizer and compact disc changer pre-wiring is standard for SR and optional for LS.

An adjustable coil-sprung driver's "suspension" seat is again standard for SR, but is no longer offered on the LS. And the air conditioning system now uses CFC-free refrigerant.

Again standard is Mitsubishi's "Multi-Meter" compass/thermometer, inclinometer, and altimeter dashboard gauge group. A remote keyless entry system is now standard on the SR and remains an LS option.

Evaluation

Montero is a roomy, refined 4x4, but against the Jeep Grand Cherokee and the Ford Explorer, the best-selling models in this class, the Mitsubishi is no bargain.

Like other Japanese sport-utility models, it trails the domestic leaders in dollar value. Still, the addition of an air bag gives it a feature only the Grand Cherokee duplicates in this class, and few other compact sport-utility vehicle seat seven.

Mitsubishi's Active-Trac 4WD equals Jeep's Selec-Trac system for shift-on-the-fly convenience and can be left engaged to match Jeep's Quadra-Trac permanently engaged 4WD system. Our test Montero, however, wouldn't go from 2WD to 4WD High without some gear-grinding noise that was eliminated by shifting into Neutral before moving the transfer-case lever.

We haven't had an opportunity to try an SR with the new 3.5-liter engine. Unfortunately, it's available only in the pricey SR model, which means most Montero buyers will likely be saddled with the smaller engine.

The 3.0-liter V-6 is one of the smoothest and quietest truck engines, but it needs more muscle in this rather heavy rig. We timed the automatic LS at 13.2 seconds 0-60, fully 3 seconds slower than a similar Grand Cherokee. With automatic, steep upgrades caused noticeable slowing and lots of busy shifting—and that's with two aboard; a full passenger/cargo load bogs down mid-range passing ability even on the flat. At least the automatic's shifts are neither syrupy nor harsh. Fuel economy is just average at about 16.5 mpg in our city/highway driving.

Montero's "Multi-Mode ABS" provides consistently short, straight stops regardless of the drive mode.

Ride comfort rivals the Grand Cherokee's, though handling doesn't. Montero is stable yet somewhat ponderous in corners, with marked body lean and a slight tipsy feeling, plus vague on-center steering feel. And being relatively large, it's no joy on crowded urban streets or overgrown forest paths.

There's ample room for five adults, but getting in or out isn't as easy as in the Grand Cherokee because there's a higher step up into the interior. Montero has a spacious middle seat, but the new third seat is cramped. The attractive dash makes everything easy to see, reach, and use.

Equally nice are such amenities as the standard fitted tool kit in the rear door, a trouble light that recharges itself in the left rear trim panel, and two extra cigarette-lighter electrical outlets. The Multi Meter and available coil-spring "suspension seat" are mere gimmicks.

Much higher prices have dampened demand for the latest Montero, so you should be able to get a deep discount on one. But don't forget the more car-like Grand Cherokee and Ford's hot-selling Explorer.

Prices

Mitsubishi Montero	Retail Price	Dealer Invoice	Fair Price
LS 5-door wagon, 5-speed	$23975	$20505	$20905
LS 5-door wagon, automatic	24825	21219	21619
SR 5-door 4WD wagon, automatic	31475	26290	26690
Destination charge	445	445	445

Standard Equipment:

LS: 3.0-liter V-6, 5-speed manual transmission or 4-speed automatic transmission, full-time 4-wheel drive, 4-wheel disc brakes, driver-side air bag, power steering, tilt steering column, digital clock, trip odometer, cloth reclining front bucket seats, tachometer, oil pressure gauge, voltmeter, inclinometer, AM/FM cassette, front and rear tow hooks, remote fuel door release, front and rear mud guards, storage console with cup holders, power mirrors, power windows and door locks, cruise control, rear defogger, intermittent wipers, rear wiper/washer, tinted glass, skid plates, map lights, cargo tie-down hooks, rear door mounted tool kit, rear seat heater ducts, passenger-side visor mirrors, front and rear stabilizer bars, reclining and folding rear seat, 235/75R15 tires. **SR** adds: 3.5-liter DOHC V-6 engine, 4-speed automatic transmission, anti-lock brakes, air conditioning, remote keyless entry, driver's suspension seat, power heated mirrors, LCD compass, altimeter, inclinometer, interior and exterior thermometer, AM/FM cassette with equalizer, power diversity antenna, headlamp washers, wide body fender flares, spare tire cover, 265/70R15 all-weather tires, alloy wheels.

Optional Equipment:

Anti-lock brakes, LS	1188	950	1069
Rear differential lock, SR	400	320	360

Left: Montero has a driver-side air bag and 7-passenger seating. Above: Multi Meter gauges are standard on SR model.

Mitsubishi • Nissan

	Retail Price	Dealer Invoice	Fair Price
CD auto changer, SR	$899	$598	$749
Includes cargo mat and net.			
Leather and Wood Pkg., SR	1748	1398	1573
Includes: leather seats, leather-wrapped assist grip, burled wood instrument panel accents, power driver's seat.			
Pkg. A, LS	754	754	754
Air conditioning, remote keyless entry system, single play CD player, roof rack, cargo mat and net, spare tire cover.			
Pkg. B, LS	1337	1337	1337
Pkg. A plus graphic equalizer, CD auto changer, power diversity antenna.			
Power sunroof	688	550	619
Fog lights	228	148	188
Cargo cover	108	70	89
Side step	335	218	277
Roof rack, SR	277	180	229
Sliding rear quarter window	125	100	113
Chrome wheels, SR	625	500	563
Alloy wheels with locks, LS	331	265	298

Nissan Pathfinder

Nissan Pathfinder LE

Nissan tries to cash in on the growing demand for luxuriously equipped sport-utility vehicles with a new top-shelf LE Pathfinder model. These wagons also get a new dashboard.

Body Styles/Chassis

All Pathfinders are 5-door wagons with a swing-up tailgate and separate-opening rear window.

Base-level XE models come in 2- and 4-wheel drive. The better-equipped SE version has 4WD, as does the new LE model.

Front-disc/rear-drum brakes with rear anti-lock control are standard on XE and SE models. The LE has standard 4-wheel discs. The 4-wheel discs are included in the new SE Off-Road package along with a limited-slip rear differential, dual-rate shock absorbers, and black exterior trim.

The LE also dresses up with running boards and new 6-spoke alloy wheels as standard. New standard equipment for the SE series includes a removable glass sunroof, alloy wheels, 31x10.5R15 tires, outside mounted spare tire, fog lights, and side step rails. All of those features were options last year.

All models have a maximum payload rating of 1150 pounds.

Powertrains

All models use a 153-horsepower 3.0-liter V-6. XE and SE come with a choice of 5-speed manual or optional 4-speed automatic transmissions. The LE comes with automatic only.

Pathfinder's on-demand 4WD system is not for use on dry pavement. It features automatic-locking front hubs and limited shift-on-the-fly capability. Though you can move from rear drive to 4WD High at speeds up to 25 mph, you must stop and then back up a few feet to disengage 4WD.

Maximum trailering weight is 3500 pounds.

Accommodations

Reclining front bucket seats are standard, as is a folding rear bench with 60/40 split reclining backrest. SE and LE models add folding outboard rear armrests and a driver's-seat cushion-tilt and 3-stage lumbar-support adjustments.

The new instrument panel replaces an upright, angular design with a more modern, flowing design. And a 4-spoke steering wheel also is new.

Standard equipment on the LE includes leather upholstery, heated front seats, luggage rack, semi-automatic air conditioning, and a compact disc player.

Evaluation

Pathfinder bowed for 1987 (the 5-door debuted for 1990) and is one of the older compact sport-utility designs. It also is well down the sales charts, mainly because of its high prices and truck-like demeanor compared to the newer Ford Explorer and Jeep Grand Cherokee, the class leaders.

Specific problems begin with performance—or rather lack of it—compared with rivals from Jeep, Ford, and General Motors. Though off-the-line acceleration is decent, Pathfinder is shy on low-end torque for strong pull up steep hills, especially with heavy loads. And overall fuel economy was dismal in our test: 14.7 mpg with automatic.

The 4WD system is another minus. Without full shift-on-the-fly, it's far less convenient than most competitive part-time systems.

On a happier note, Pathfinder is as capable off-road as on, with predictable, benign handling responses and a pleasant day-to-day driving feel with notably precise steering. The suspension copes fairly well with small disturbances, but the ride turns stiff and bouncy over freeway expansion joints and broken-up urban thoroughfares.

Pathfinder also trails most 5-door rivals in the interior space race. Most 5-door competitors have longer wheelbases and larger rear door openings. Climbing aboard Pathfinder dictates a fairly high step-up, and rear doorways are unusually narrow, requiring some extra contortions to negotiate.

Inside, back-seaters don't get much foot room, but there's ample leg room all-round. A low ceiling leaves little rear head clearance for taller adults.

The cargo deck is wide but not that long with the rear seat up. The rear seatbacks fold flat to extend floor length, but you first have to tilt the cushion forward through 90 degrees, then remove the rear headrests and not use all the available front-seat travel. Those headrests clutter aft vision, as do the roof pillars and, where fitted, the bulky exterior-mount spare, though the spare robs a lot of cargo space when riding inside.

The new dash looks far more modern than the old, but it really doesn't improve on a functional design that presents clear analog gauges and mostly logical, easy-to-reach secondary controls. One item left unimproved is the location of the stereo, which sits just ahead of the shift lever—too low

Nissan

for safe fiddling while driving because it requires a long look away from the road.

The new steering wheel also looks more up-to-date, but Pathfinder fails to match the Grand Cherokee and Mitsubishi Montero by providing a driver-side air bag.

To its credit, Pathfinder has solid construction, thorough Japanese workmanship, good-looking interior materials, and proven engineering. But it lacks the kind of roomy, car-like comfort that upscale sport-utility buyers have come to demand. You should be able to negotiate a good deal on Nissan's 4x4.

Specifications

	5-door wagon
Wheelbase, in.	104.3
Overall length, in.	171.9
Overall width, in.	66.5
Overall height, in.	65.7
Turn diameter, ft.	35.4
Curb weight, lbs.	3885
Fuel capacity, gal.	20.4

Passenger Area Dimensions

Seating capacity	5
Front head room, in.	39.3
Rear head room, in.	36.8
Front leg room, in.	42.6
Rear leg room, in.	33.1

Cargo Dimensions and Payloads

Cargo area length, in.	65.2
Cargo area width, in.	55.1
Cargo area width between wheels, in.	38.0
Cargo area height, in.	34.3
Cargo vol., cu. ft.	80.2
Max. payload, lbs.	1150
Max. trailer weight, lbs.	3500

Engines

	ohc V-6
Size, liters/cu. in.	3.0/181
Horsepower @ rpm	153 @ 4800
Torque (lbs./ft.) @ rpm	180 @ 4000
Availability	S
EPA city/highway mpg	
5-speed OD manual	15/18
4-speed OD automatic	15/18

Built in Japan.

KEY: Dimensions and capacities are supplied by the manufacturers. **Curb Weight:** base models, not including optional equipment. **Max. payload, lbs.** = gross amount; net payload may be lower due to optional equipment. **Engines: ohv** = overhead valve; **ohc** = overhead cam; **I** = inline cylinders; **V** = cylinders in V configuration; **flat** = horizontally opposed cylinders; **rpm** = revolutions per minute; **OD** = overdrive transmission; **S** = standard; **O** = optional; **NA** = not available.

Prices

Nissan Pathfinder	Retail Price	Dealer Invoice	Fair Price
XE 2WD 5-door wagon, 5-speed	$19429	$17043	$17443
XE 2WD 5-door wagon, automatic	20649	18113	18513
XE 4WD 5-door wagon, 5-speed	21099	18508	18908
XE 4WD 5-door wagon, automatic	22469	19709	20109
SE 4WD 5-door wagon, 5-speed	25009	21938	22338
SE 4WD 5-door wagon, automatic	26109	22903	23303
LE 4WD 5-door wagon, automatic	28999	25438	25838

Pathfinder's dashboard and steering wheel are redesigned for 1994, but no air bag is offered. Outside-mount spare tire frees up cargo space.

	Retail Price	Dealer Invoice	Fair Price
Destination charge	$380	$380	$380

Standard Equipment:

XE: 3.0-liter V-6, 5-speed manual or 4-speed automatic transmission, anti-lock rear brakes, power steering, part-time 4WD with automatic locking front hubs (4WD), cloth reclining front bucket seats, split folding and reclining rear seat, tachometer, coolant temperature gauge, trip odometer, digital clock, rear wiper/washer, tinted glass, dual outside mirrors, front tow hooks, AM/FM cassette with diversity antenna, tilt steering column, rear defogger, front door map pockets, remote fuel door release, cargo tiedown

CONSUMER GUIDE® 145

Nissan

hooks, skid plates, fender flares and mud guards (4WD), 235/75R15 tires, chrome wheels. **SE** adds: power windows and locks, cruise control, variable-intermittent wipers, heated power mirrors, remote rear window release, voltmeter, rear quarter privacy glass, upgraded upholstery, flip-up removable sunroof, lighted visor mirrors, map lights, driver's seat height and lumbar support adjustments, folding rear armrests, step rail, fog lamps, rear wind deflector, outside spare tire carrier, 31x10.5R15 tires, alloy wheels, remote security system. **LE** adds: 4-speed automatic transmission, 4-wheel disc brakes, air conditioning, running board and splash guards, heated leather front seats, CD player.

Optional Equipment:	Retail Price	Dealer Invoice	Fair Price
Air conditioning, XE and SE	$995	$843	$897
XE Convenience Pkg.	1550	1313	1397

Cruise control, power windows and door locks, heated power mirrors, map lights, variable-intermittent wipers, remote vehicle security system. Requires air conditioning.

| XE Sport Pkg. | 860 | 728 | 775 |

Includes outside spare tire carrier, spare tire cover, fender flares (2WD), fog lights, limited-slip differential (4WD), cargo net. Requires XE Convenience Pkg.

| Leather Trim Pkg., SE | 1255 | 1063 | 1131 |

Includes leather seats, leather-wrapped steering wheel, shift knob and parking brake handle, heated front seats with individual controls. Requires air conditioning.

| SE Off-Road Pkg. | 750 | 635 | 676 |

Limited-slip rear differential, dual-rate adjustable shock absorbers, rear disc brakes, black exterior trim, luggage rack.

| 2-tone paint, LE | 300 | 254 | 270 |

Nissan Quest

RECOMMENDED

Nissan Quest XE

Nissan's front-drive minivan gets a standard driver-side air bag as its major addition for 1994. Installation of air bags didn't begin until late November, so early 1994 Quests won't have them.

Quest is built from the same design as the Mercury Villager, which also gets the air bag. Both vehicles were designed by Nissan but are built at a Ford plant in Ohio.

Body Styles/Chassis

Quest's body is the conventional minivan configuration: a sliding right-rear door and a liftgate with separate-opening window.

Neither Mercury nor Nissan offers an extended-length body style. And Nissan this year drops the cargo version of the Quest, which was visually identical to the passenger versions except for its dark-tint windows.

Anti-lock brakes were optional on both the base XE and more-expensive GXE models last year. This year, they're standard on the GXE. Other changes include a CFC-free refrigerant for the standard air conditioning and a heavy-duty radiator.

Maximum payload is 1594 pounds.

Powertrains

The only engine is a Nissan-built 3.0-liter V-6. It's rated at 151 horsepower and is shared with the Villager. The only

Specifications	4-door wagon
Wheelbase, in.	112.2
Overall length, in.	189.9
Overall width, in.	73.7
Overall height, in.	65.6
Turn diameter, ft.	39.9
Curb weight, lbs.	3783
Fuel capacity, gal.	20.0

Passenger Area Dimensions	
Seating capacity	7
Front head room, in.	39.4
Rear head room, in.	39.7
Front leg room, in.	39.9
Rear leg room, in.	34.8

Available Seating

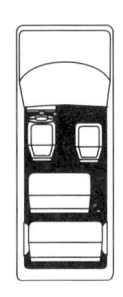

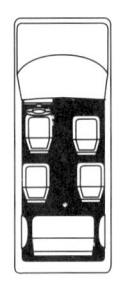

Cargo Dimensions and Payloads	
Cargo area length, in.	83.4
Cargo area width, in.	48.3
Cargo area width between wheels, in.	49.5
Cargo area height, in.	48.1
Cargo vol., cu. ft.	114.8
Max. payload, lbs.	1594
Max. trailer weight, lbs.	3500

Engines	ohc V-6
Size, liters/cu. in.	3.0/181
Horsepower @ rpm	151 @ 4800
Torque (lbs./ft.) @ rpm	174 @ 4400
Availability	S

EPA city/highway mpg

| 4-speed OD manual | 17/23 |

Built in Avon Lake, Ohio.

KEY: Dimensions and capacities are supplied by the manufacturers. **Curb Weight:** base models, not including optional equipment. **Max. payload, lbs.** = gross amount; net payload may be lower due to optional equipment. **Engines: ohv** = overhead valve; **ohc** = overhead cam; **I** = inline cylinders; **V** = cylinders in V configuration; **flat** = horizontally opposed cylinders; **rpm** = revolutions per minute; **OD** = overdrive transmission; **S** = standard; **O** = optional; **NA** = not available.

Nissan

transmission is an electronically controlled 4-speed automatic.

Quest's standard towing limit is 2000 pounds. An optional Extra Performance Package increases the limit to 3500 pounds and includes a heavy duty battery and cooling, revised shock absorbers, and springs, and 215/70R15 tires, among other items.

Accommodations

Seats for seven are standard, with two front buckets, a removable 2-place middle bench, and a 3-place rear bench. (Last year, the XE came with seating for five, with the middle seat as an option.)

An optional Luxury Package for GXE models replaces the middle bench with two removable captain's chairs.

The 3-place rear bench in both the Quest and Villager is unique in the minivan arena. It can be moved along an integrated track from the rear of the vehicle to the middle. Outboard shoulder belts are provided at both positions. The bench also double-folds to rearrange cargo space and can be slid just behind the front seats for maximum carrying capacity. The middle seatbacks, meanwhile, can be dropped to form table-like platforms with molded-in beverage holders.

Quest and Villager have a high-mounted third brake light and side-guard door beams. They previously met all passenger-car safety standards with motorized front shoulder belts as the passive restraint system. The 1994 models equipped with the air bag retain these motorized belts.

A Premium Audio Package with a compact disc player and eight speakers is a new option for the GXE.

Evaluation

Like the Villager, Quest is a roomy family vehicle that's easy to drive and has flexible seating and luggage accommodations.

On the road, Quest, like Villager, labors some up steep hills, but is pleasantly quick otherwise. The engine is smooth, transmission response prompt. Body roll is noticed in hard turns, but isn't excessive.

The Extra Performance Package has stabilizer bars and wider tires for slightly flatter cornering and better grip, but any Quest handles with poise, has good crosswind stability, and ample braking power.

We've tested Nissan and Mercury versions of this minivan and the Quests have had slightly better ride quality. They felt more stable on the highway and more absorbent on rough roads.

On the other hand, anti-lock brakes remain optional on Quest's base model, while all Villagers have them as standard. Villager offers optional digital instrumentation, Quest stays with analog gauges. Both manufacturers offer 3-year, 36,000-mile bumper-to-bumper warranties, but Nissan adds 5-year, 60,000-mile coverage for the powertrain and major systems.

Both vehicles have a user-friendly interior with a low step-in that allows easy entry/exit, a comfortable driving position, good visibility, and an ample supply of cup holders and cub-

Clockwise front top left: Quest gains a driver-side air bag for 1994. This upscale minivan comes in a single body length. Middle seats fold (center buckets are a GXE option), and when removed, allow the rear bench to slide forward on floor tracks.

Nissan

bies. However, the shift lever interferes some with the switch pod to the right of the gauge cluster, the stereo is mounted too low for easy tuning while driving, and most dashboard controls look so much alike it's hard to find a particular one in a hurry.

Passenger room is generous in front but a tad tight behind for really large persons. There's also scant cargo room with the third seat in place.

We like the sliding rear bench, but to take advantage of it, you have the difficult task of removing the heavy middle seat or seats. And the bothersome motorized front shoulder belts hamper movement of the front-seat occupants.

As upscale people movers, Villager and Quest are tough to beat. By contrast, the Chrysler Corporation minivans offer extended-body versions that, along with the new Ford Windstar, are more versatile at hauling people and cargo.

Prices

Nissan Quest	Retail Price	Dealer Invoice	Fair Price
XE 7-passenger	$18529	$16065	$17729
GXE 7-passenger	23039	19975	22239
Destination charge	380	380	380

Standard Equipment:

XE: 3.0-liter V-6 engine, 4-speed automatic transmission, driver-side air bag, motorized front shoulder belts, front air conditioning, power steering, cloth reclining front bucket seats, 2-passenger middle bench seat and 3-passenger rear bench seat, Quest Trac flexible seating, remote fuel door release, rear defogger, tilt steering column, dual mirrors, tachometer, trip odometer, variable intermittent wipers, rear intermittent wiper/washer, color-keyed bodyside moldings, visor mirrors, cornering lamps, door map pockets, AM/FM cassette, tinted glass, carpeted front and rear floormats, console with cassette/CD storage, tilt-out middle and rear quarter windows, cargo area net, cargo area mat, full wheel covers, 205/75R15 all-season tires. **GXE** adds: anti-lock brakes, rear air conditioning, rear heater controls, cruise control, power driver's seat, power locks and windows, power rear quarter windows, upgraded upholstery and door trim panels, power mirrors, illuminated visor mirrors, upgraded radio with rear controls, leather-wrapped steering wheel, power antenna, dual liftgate with opening window, side and rear privacy glass, map light, lockable underseat storage, alloy wheels.

Optional Equipment:

Extra Performance Pkg., XE	950	805	903
GXE	525	445	499

Heavy duty battery and radiator, tuned springs, shock absorbers and rear stabilizer bar, full-size spare tire, 215/70HR15 tires, alloy wheels (XE), 3500 lb. towing capacity.

Power Pkg., XE	825	699	784

Power windows, locks, and mirrors.

Convenience Pkg., XE	800	677	760

Cruise control, upgraded radio with power antenna, leather-wrapped steering wheel, privacy rear glass, lighted right visor mirror, luggage rack, lockable underseat storage. Requires Power Pkg.

Rear air conditioning, XE	625	529	594

Requires Power Pkg.

Anti-lock brakes, XE	700	593	665
2-tone paint, GXE	300	254	285
Power sunroof, GXE	825	699	784

GXE Extra Performance Pkg. is required when power sunroof and Leather Trim Pkg. are combined.

Leather Trim Pkg., GXE	1000	847	950

Leather upholstery. Requires Luxury Pkg.

Luxury Pkg., GXE	800	677	760

Power passenger seat, middle row captain's chairs, illuminated Digital Touch System, automatic headlamp control.

Premium Audio Pkg., GXE	1015	859	864

AM/FM cassette/CD player, subwoofer, eight speakers.

Nissan Truck

Nissan SE V-6 King Cab 4WD

Nissan's compact pickup trucks get a new mid-line XE price series and a redesigned dashboard for 1994.

Called the Nissan Truck, these pickups were designed in Nissan's California studio and are built at the Japanese company's plant in Tennessee.

Body Styles/Chassis

The Nissan Truck comes as a regular-cab with short- and long-bed cargo boxes and as the extended-cab King Cab.

Regular-cab short-bed models have a 104.3-inch wheelbase and a 6-foot cargo bed. Regular-cab long-beds have a 116.1-inch wheelbase and a 7.5-foot bed. King Cabs combine the 116.1-inch wheelbase with the 6-foot bed.

Last year, the lineup consisted of base and uplevel SE models. The new XE model slots between the base and SE versions.

Base models come only in the regular-cab body style, but with both short- and long-bed cargo boxes. XE and SE models come with either cab. Base models come only with 2-wheel-drive. XE and SE models are available with 2- or 4-wheel-drive.

Regular-cab models use a 3-place bench seat. King Cabs get front buckets and two inward-facing folding rear jump seats.

New for XE models is a value option package that includes such features as a chrome grille and exterior trim, bodyside graphics, chrome wheels, and a stereo with cassette player.

XE and SE models with 4-wheel-drive and the V-6 engine also have fender flares.

Rear anti-lock brakes are standard on 4WD models.

Base payload is 1400 pounds except on 2-wheel-drive long-beds, where it's 2000 pounds.

Powertrains

Two engines are offered, a 2.4-liter 4-cylinder with 134 horsepower and a 3.0-liter V-6 with 153.

The 4-cylinder engine is available with 2WD or 4WD and in all body styles except the regular-cab long-bed. That model uses the V-6 and comes only with 2WD. All other V-6 models are King Cabs with either 2WD or 4WD.

A 5-speed manual transmission is standard with both engines and is mandatory on the base regular cab models. A 4-speed overdrive automatic is available on all other Nissan Trucks.

Nissan

Nissan's 4WD is an on-demand system not for use on dry pavement. All 4x4s have manual locking front hubs except the XE and SE King Cabs with the V-6. They have automatic locking hubs that allow limited shift-on-the-fly: You can shift from 2WD to 4WD High below 25 mph, but you must to stop and then back up a few feet to disengage 4WD.

The regular-cab long-bed can tow up to 5000 pounds. Maximum trailer weight for all other models is 3500 pounds.

Evaluation

Though the price of the base-level Nissan Truck is up by more than $450 compared to a year ago, other models have seen more modest increases. And the new mid-line XE model, particularly with the value option package, seems the best buy of all in this line.

Still, despite the new dashboard and a reputation for reliability, Nissan's pickups feel decidedly old next to the newer, more refined Ford Ranger/Mazda B-Series and the Chevrolet S10/GMC Sonoma.

That was apparent in the XE 4WD King Cab we tested. Its 4-cylinder engine had a gruff, agricultural feel and a coarse sound. And while the pickup's body was stout, it did little to isolate the cabin from the engine's buzz and vibration.

Acceleration was adequate with the 5-speed manual. Though the available 3.0-liter V-6 isn't significantly faster than Nissan's big 4-cylinder, the six is a much smoother runner, especially at higher engine speeds, and feels more responsive with automatic transmission.

The rounded new dashboard, shared with the Pathfinder sport-utility vehicle, replaces a dated squared-off design. It retains the old dash's clear gauges and the placement of most controls remains logical. But the radio is still too low, forcing the driver to look away from the road and stretch to reach its small buttons.

The 116.1-inch wheelbase models, even with 4WD, provide a reasonably comfortable ride, and corners can be taken with good control and relatively little body lean. Braking is sure, with good resistance to rear-wheel lockup. And fit and finish are more than up to snuff.

On the downside, payload and towing capacities aren't

Specifications

	Short bed	Long bed	King Cab
Wheelbase, in.	104.3	116.1	116.1
Overall length, in.	174.6	190.0	190.0
Overall width, in.	65.0	65.0	65.0
Overall height, in.	62.0	62.0	62.0
Turn diameter, ft.	33.5	36.7	36.7
Curb weight, lbs.	2970	3115	2885
Fuel capacity, gal.	15.9	21.1	15.9

Passenger Area Dimensions

Seating capacity	3	3	4
Front head room, in.	39.3	39.3	39.3
Rear head room, in.	—	—	NA
Front leg room, in.	42.2	42.2	42.6
Rear leg room, in.	—	—	NA

Cargo Dimensions and Payloads

Cargo area length, in.	73.8	89.2	74.6
Cargo area width, in.	59.8	59.8	59.8
Cargo area width between wheels, in.	41.7	41.7	41.7
Cargo area height, in.	17.1	17.1	17.1
Max. payload, lbs.	1400	2000	1400
Max. trailer weight, lbs	3500	5000	3500

Engines

	ohc I-4	ohc V-6
Size, liters/cu. in.	2.4/146	3.0/181
Horsepower @ rpm	134 @ 5200	153 @ 4800
Torque (lbs./ft.) @ rpm	154 @ 3600	180 @ 4000
Availability	S	S[1]

EPA city/highway mpg

5-speed OD manual	23/27	19/23
4-speed OD automatic	21/26	18/24

1. Long Bed and King Cab SE.

Built in Smyrna, Tenn.

KEY: Dimensions and capacities are supplied by the manufacturers. **Curb Weight:** base models, not including optional equipment. **Max. payload, lbs.** = gross amount; net payload may be lower due to optional equipment. **Engines: ohv** = overhead valve; **ohc** = overhead cam; **I** = inline cylinders; **V** = cylinders in V configuration; **flat** = horizontally opposed cylinders; **rpm** = revolutions per minute; **OD** = overdrive transmission; **S** = standard; **O** = optional; **NA** = not available.

Top: Nissan's pickups get a redesigned dashboard and a new steering wheel for 1994. Middle and above: The new mid-range model is the XE, here shown as a 2WD regular-cab long-bed.

Nissan • Oldsmobile

among the best for this class; automatic locking front hubs are available only on the XE and SE V-6 King Cabs; and true 4WD shift-on-the-fly is unavailable.

But the real problem is that Ford and GM have shown how compact pickups can be both workhorses and satisfyingly car-like. The Nissan Truck isn't up to that standard.

Prices

Nissan Pickup	Retail Price	Dealer Invoice	Fair Price
Base 2WD regular cab short bed, 5-speed	$9459	*	*
XE 2WD regular cab short bed, 5-speed	10529	*	*
XE 2WD regular cab short bed, automatic	11844	*	*
Base V-6 2WD regular cab long bed, 5-speed	11589	*	*
XE 2WD King Cab, 5-speed	11979	*	*
XE 2WD King Cab, automatic	13294	*	*
SE V-6 2WD King Cab, 5-speed	14679	*	*
SE V-6 2WD King Cab, automatic	15679	*	*
XE 4WD regular cab, 5-speed	14069	*	*
XE 4WD King Cab, 5-speed	15409	*	*
XE V-6 4WD King Cab, 5-speed	16479	*	*
XE V-6 4WD King Cab, automatic	17479	*	*
SE V-6 4WD King Cab, 5-speed	16379	14368	14668
SE V-6 4WD King Cab, automatic	17379	15245	15545
Destination charge	380	380	380

Standard Equipment:

Base short bed: 2.4-liter 4-cylinder engine, 5-speed manual or 4-speed automatic transmission, vinyl front bench seat, tinted glass, left black outside mirror, front stabilizer bar, 195/75R14 tires. **Base long bed** adds: 3.0-liter V-6 engine, power steering, dual outside mirrors, door map pockets, cigarette lighter, LT195/75R14 tires. **XE 2WD** adds to Base short bed: power steering (4-speed automatic models), cloth upholstery, reclining front bucket seats (King Cab), sport steering wheel, black painted rear step bumper, cigarette lighter, door map pockets, full door panel trim, styled steel wheels, carpet. **XE 4WD** adds to XE 2WD: anti-lock rear brakes, power steering, manual locking front hubs, skid plates, tow hooks, 235/75R15 tires, titanium finish steel wheels. **XE V-6 King Cab** adds to XE 4WD King Cab: 3.0-liter V-6 engine, rear jump seats, bedliner, fender flares. **SE V-6 King Cab** adds to XE King Cab: 3.0-liter V-6 engine, power steering, cruise control, automatic locking front hubs (4WD), power mirrors, reclining power driver's seat, rear jump seats (std. 4WD), trip odometer, visor mirrors, bedliner, tachometer, tilt steering column, AM/FM cassette player, diversity antenna system, digital clock, intermittent wipers, center console, chrome bumpers and grille, 215/75R14 tires, chrome wheels.

Optional Equipment:

Air conditioning	995	843	912
Power steering, Base short bed, XE 2WD 5-speed	315	266	288
Chrome Pkg., XE regular cab	500	423	137

Chrome grille, bumpers, and mirrors, chrome exterior trim, chrome wheels, bodyside graphics. Requires power steering.

Power Pkg., SE V-6 King Cab	500	423	458

Power windows and door locks, power mirrors. 2WD requires air conditioning.

Convenience Pkg., XE regular cab	300	254	275

Power mirrors, variable-intermittent wipers, locking glove box, full-size spare tire (4WD). Requires Chrome Pkg.

Jump Seat Pkg. SE V-6 King Cab	225	191	206

Rear folding jump seats. Requires Value Truck Pkg.

Sport Pkg., SE V-6 2WD King Cab	1300	1101	1192
SE V-6 4WD King Cab	1875	1587	1718

Alloy wheels, flip-up glass sunroof. 4WD adds limited-slip differential, 31x10.5R15 tires, 235/75R15 spare tire. Requires air conditioning.

Sport/Power Pkg., SE V-6 2WD King Cab	1440	1219	1320
SE V-6 4WD King Cab	1975	1672	1810

Sport Pkg. and Power Pkg. require air conditioning.

	Retail Price	Dealer Invoice	Fair Price
Value Truck Pkg. XE regular cab	$995	$843	$912
XE King Cab and XE V-6 4WD King Cab	995	843	912

Chrome grille, bumpers, and power mirrors, chrome exterior trim, chrome wheels, bodyside graphics, variable-intermittent wipers, AM/FM cassette player, diversity antenna system, visor mirrors, locking glove box, center console, cigarette lighter and ashtray lights, tachometer, trip odometer, digital clock. 4WD models also include: full-size spare tire, tilt steering column (V-6), cruise control (V-6). 2WD models with 5-speed manual transmission require power steering.

Bedliner	280	128	202
Metallic or pearl paint, Base short bed	100	85	92
Metallic or pearl paint, regular cab 2WD short bed w/5-speed (NA 4WD)	100	85	92
All other 2WD models	NC	NC	NC

Oldsmobile Bravada

Oldsmobile Bravada

Oldsmobile's sport-utility vehicle gets some new safety features as it heads into its last model year before taking the 1995 season off.

Bravada is based on the same design as the Chevrolet S10 Blazer and GMC Jimmy, which are scheduled to be redesigned for 1995.

Initial plans did not include an Olds version of the 1995 S10 Blazer and Jimmy. Instead, Olds was considering marketing a version of the Japanese-built Isuzu Trooper. The rise in the value of the yen against the dollar and potential union objections scrapped that plan, but not in time for Olds to secure an edition of the 1995 Chevy/GMC sport-utility.

So there won't be a 1995 Bravada. Instead, Olds will come back with a 1996 model of the GM sport-utility, though it is uncertain whether that vehicle will retain the Bravada name.

Body Styles/Chassis

Olds eschews the 3-door version of its Chevy/GMC cousin for the 5-door wagon with its drop-down tailgate and separate swing-up window. Visual differences are the Olds-style split grille, front airdam with integral foglamps, body-color bumpers and specific wheels. A roof luggage rack is standard. Four-wheel anti-lock brakes (ABS) with front discs and rear drums are standard.

No off-road suspension is available, Bravada being marketed as a luxury road vehicle with the superior poor-weather traction of permanently engaged 4-wheel drive. Olds

Some dealer invoice and fair prices not available at time of publication.

Oldsmobile

says Bravada's 7.7-inch ground clearance is adequate for "limited off-road use."

For '94, Bravada is available two ways. There is a base model with a suggested retail price of $25,995 and a new one-price Special Edition for $24,995 (including the $475 destination charge). The Special Edition includes gold exterior trim and all-season tires.

Changes for 1994 on Bravada include guard beams in the four side doors and a center high-mounted stoplamp as new standard features. Softer shock absorbers this year are supposed to produce a more comfortable ride.

Maximum payload is 1069 pounds.

Powertrains

Standard is a 200-horsepower 4.3-liter V-6 engine and a 4-speed automatic transmission with electronic shift controls.

While Blazer and Jimmy offer on-demand, part-time 4-wheel drive, Bravada comes standard with permanently engaged 4WD, which is part of its "Smart Trak" system (the 4-wheel ABS is the other part). Torque is normally split 35/65 percent front/rear, but a viscous center differential can automatically vary that according to which axle has the greater traction.

Towing capacity is 2000 pounds standard, 5000 pounds with the optional trailering package.

Accommodations

Dual front buckets and a 3-place rear bench with 1-piece fold-down backrest are standard. So is air conditioning and a front console with cupholders and auxiliary electrical outlet.

The 1995 S10 Blazer and Jimmy will get a driver-side air bag, and possibly a passenger-side air bag, as well. For 1994, none of GM's sport-utility vehicles has an air bag.

Evaluation

Bravada's previous claim to fame as the only 4x4 in this price range with permanent 4WD is now matched by the Jeep Grand Cherokee. Nonetheless, the system does furnish outstanding traction regardless of the condition of the road surface and doesn't require that the driver make any decisions or work any buttons or levers.

Bravada's 200-horsepower V-6 provides ample power, though the engine fan is loud in acceleration. The electronically controlled automatic changes gears smoothly and is quick to downshift for passing or merging.

Overall, however, Bravada's acceleration is no better than the Jeep Grand Cherokee's or Ford Explorer's. The 4.3-liter V-6 consumes lots of gas, though the same can be said of the engines used in the Grand Cherokee and Explorer. Expect 15 mpg or less in the city and around 20 mpg on the highway.

Though ride quality is a little better this year, it's still not as good as the Grand Cherokee's. It is better than Blazer's,

Specifications

	5-door wagon
Wheelbase, in.	107.0
Overall length, in.	178.9
Overall width, in.	65.2
Overall height, in.	65.5
Turn diameter, ft.	37.1
Curb weight, lbs.	4031
Fuel capacity, gal.	20.0

Passenger Area Dimensions

Seating capacity	5
Front head room, in.	39.1
Rear head room, in.	38.8
Front leg room, in.	42.5
Rear leg room, in.	36.5

Cargo Dimensions and Payloads

Cargo area length, in.	74.3
Cargo area width, in.	52.5
Cargo area width between wheels, in.	38.4
Cargo area height, in.	39.1
Cargo vol., cu. ft.	74.3
Max. payload, lbs.	1069
Max. trailer weight, lbs.	5000

Engines

	ohv V-6
Size, liters/cu. in.	4.3/262
Horsepower @ rpm	200 @ 4500
Torque (lbs./ft.) @ rpm	260 @ 3600
Availability	S

EPA city/highway mpg

4-speed OD automatic	16/21

Built in Moraine, Ohio.

KEY: Dimensions and capacities are supplied by the manufacturers. **Curb Weight:** base models, not including optional equipment. **Max. payload, lbs.** = gross amount; net payload may be lower due to optional equipment. **Engines: ohv** = overhead valve; **ohc** = overhead cam; **I** = inline cylinders; **V** = cylinders in V configuration; **flat** = horizontally opposed cylinders; **rpm** = revolutions per minute; **OD** = overdrive transmission; **S** = standard; **O** = optional; **NA** = not available.

Bravada's dashboard looks and feels old-fashioned compared to newer rivals. Rear seats fold, but standard inside-mounted spare tire takes up a good amount of cargo space.

Oldsmobile

mostly because the Chevy is set up to go off road and the Olds isn't. Unfortunately, Bravada's softer suspension allows too much bounce over wavy pavement.

The 4-wheel ABS isn't a Bravada exclusive, but it does deliver straight, sure, fairly short stops with secure steering control. Alas, pedal feel is spongy and pedal travel too long.

Bravada's inherited dashboard is an unattractive mishmash of odd shapes, cheap-looking gray plastic, and needlessly complicated minor controls. The last are at least mounted high up and easy enough to reach. Forget the optional electronic instruments: hard to read and an unnecessary extra expense.

We'd stick with the standard cloth upholstery because the slick texture and lack of side bolstering on the optional leather seats has occupants sliding around in turns. The rear seat is wide enough for three and there's plenty of head room, but the seat cushion is low to the floor, making tall passengers ride with their knees up high. We'd also opt for the outside spare tire carrier because the standard full-size spare takes up a lot of space in the cargo area.

Despite absence of the air bag, a high level of standard equipment and the Smart Tac system help justify Bravada's lofty price. And the Bravada Special Edition is competitively priced against the upscale versions of the Grand Cherokee and Explorer, but Explorer and Grand Cherokee are higher on our shopping list.

Prices

Oldsmobile Bravada

	Retail Price	Dealer Invoice	Fair Price
5-door 4WD wagon	$26320	$23819	$24269
Special Edition 5-door 4WD wagon	25295	24178	*
Destination charge	475	475	475

Special Edition price includes destination charge. Additional "value-priced" models may also be available in California.

Standard Equipment:

4.3-liter V-6, 4-speed automatic transmission, permanent 4-wheel drive, anti-lock brakes, power steering, air conditioning, power driver's seat, driver and passenger power lumbar adjustment, center console with cup holders and electrical outlets, overhead console with compass, outside temperature readout and reading lamps, folding rear seat with armrest, solar control tinted windshield and front door glass, deep-tint rear windows, cruise control, power windows, power locks with remote control, power mirrors, rear wiper/washer, intermittent wipers, rear defogger, coolant temperature and oil pressure gauges, voltmeter, trip odometer, fog lamps, remote tailgate release, roof luggage rack, AM/FM cassette with equalizer, tilt steering wheel, leather-wrapped steering wheel, lighted visor mirrors, map lights, floormats, 235/75R15 tires, alloy wheels, full-size spare tire. **Special Edition** adds: custom leather trim, electronic instruments, exterior spare tire carrier, towing package.

Optional Equipment:

Custom leather trim	650	559	579
CD player	134	115	119
Towing Pkg.	255	219	227
Electronic instruments	195	168	174
235/75R15 white outline			
letter tires	133	114	118
Special Edition	NC	NC	NC
Exterior spare tire carrier	159	137	142
Engine block heater	33	28	29
Gold Pkg.	60	52	53
Special Edition	NC	NC	NC

Gold-tinted exterior emblems, gold-tinted cast aluminum wheels with black ports.

Oldsmobile Silhouette

RECOMMENDED

Oldsmobile Silhouette

Oldsmobile's version of General Motors' front-drive minivan gains some new safety features that include a driver-side air bag. And a power sliding rear door is a new option.

The same features are available on the similar Chevrolet Lumina Minivan and Pontiac Trans Sport, which are covered in separate reports.

Oldsmobile also has added a one-price Special Edition model that lists for $19,995, including the $530 destination charge—less than a base Silhouette with fewer standard features.

Body Styles/Chassis

Like the Trans Sport and Lumina Minivan, Silhouette comes in a single body length with a traditional sliding side door and one-piece liftgate. It uses a steel inner "space-frame" skeleton to which outer body panels of plastic-type materials are bonded or bolted on.

For 1994, the Chevy and Pontiac versions get new, shorter front ends. Silhouette does not, but it does share with its siblings a new a center high-mounted stoplamp, and the Olds also gets a deeper tint to side windows aft of the front doors. Plus, the optional power door locks this year can be programmed to either remain locked or automatically unlock when the transmission is shifted into park.

The power-operated sliding side door is an industry first and is optional on all three front-drive GM vans. A motor in the right-rear fender pulls the door open and pushes it closed at the command of buttons on the overhead console, on the right-side door pillar, and on the remote key fob. The door also responds to the door handle itself. The door will open only with the transmission in park and is designed to stop and reverse direction if an object blocks its path.

Silhouette's brakes are front discs and rear drums with standard 4-wheel anti-lock control. Electronic self-leveling is part of a Touring Suspension option.

In addition to the base model and the new Special Edition version, Olds offers a special one-price model to buyers in California. The California model has the same base price as the Special Edition but more standard equipment.

Maximum payload rating is 1186 pounds.

Powertrains

Standard on Silhouette and its corporate cousins is a 120-horsepower 3.1-liter V-6 and a 3-speed automatic transmission.

152 *Some dealer invoice and fair prices not available at time of publication.* CONSUMER GUIDE®

Oldsmobile

A 170-horsepower 3.8-liter V-6 is optional on the base Silhouette and is standard on the Special Edition and California models. The 3.8 V-6 uses an electronically controlled 4-speed overdrive automatic transmission.

A traction control system is a new option. It reduces engine power and applies the brakes as needed to restore traction when there is wheel slip.

Silhouette's maximum trailering limit is 3000 pounds.

Specifications

	4-door van
Wheelbase, in.	109.8
Overall length, in.	194.7
Overall width, in.	73.9
Overall height, in.	65.7
Turn diameter, ft.	43.0
Curb weight, lbs.	3679
Fuel capacity, gal.	20.0

Passenger Area Dimensions

Seating capacity	7
Front head room, in.	39.2
Rear head room, in.	35.6
Front leg room, in.	40.0
Rear leg room, in.	36.1

Available Seating

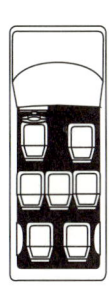

Cargo Dimensions and Payloads

Cargo area length, in.	86.0
Cargo area width, in.	56.0
Cargo area width between wheels, in.	42.5
Cargo area height, in.	45.3
Cargo vol., cu. ft.	112.6
Max. payload, lbs.	1186
Max. trailer weight, lbs.	3000

Engines

	ohv V-6	ohv V-6
Size, liters/cu. in.	3.1/191	3.8/231
Horsepower @ rpm	120 @ 4400	170 @ 4800
Torque (lbs./ft.) @ rpm	175 @ 2200	225 @ 3200
Availability	S	O

EPA city/highway mpg

3-speed automatic	19/23	
4-speed OD automatic		17/25

Built in Tarrytown, N.Y.

KEY: Dimensions and capacities are supplied by the manufacturers. **Curb Weight:** base models, not including optional equipment. **Max. payload, lbs.** = gross amount; net payload may be lower due to optional equipment. **Engines: ohv** = overhead valve; **ohc** = overhead cam; **I** = inline cylinders; **V** = cylinders in V configuration; **flat** = horizontally opposed cylinders; **rpm** = revolutions per minute; **OD** = overdrive transmission; **S** = standard; **O** = optional; **NA** = not available.

Accommodations

Silhouette comes standard with the 7-bucket seating package that's optional on the Trans Sport and Lumina Minivan. All seats in the middle row of three buckets and the rear row of two buckets can be removed without tools.

A new option for base models is a pair of child safety seats integrated into the outboard middle-row buckets. The safety seats fold out from the otherwise-standard backrests, contain a 5-point harness, and are designed for youngsters weighing between 20 and 40 pounds.

Evaluation

Oldsmobile previously positioned the Silhouette as a luxury minivan, but this year's Special Edition looks more like a practical family vehicle that offers good value for the money.

Silhouette drives much like a mid-size car, with good ride control and competent cornering ability. The standard anti-lock brakes and air bag and optional traction control are additional lures.

The 3.8-liter engine accelerates easily through traffic and provides stress-free highway passing. By comparison, the 3.1-liter V-6 struggles to muster adequate acceleration and makes more noise than power.

Passenger room is good, though hauling anything larger than a few grocery bags requires removing the rearmost seats. Luckily no minivan has seats that are easier to remove or rearrange than the lightweight buckets on the GM entries. They weigh just 34 pounds each.

Low door sills make climbing in and out easy, the plastic body panels resist dings, and the standard anti-lock brakes provide sure stops.

And, the price is right on the Special Edition: $19,995, with no haggling necessary. A limited number of options are available on the Special Edition and unfortunately the new integrated child seats aren't among them.

Visibility remains a sore spot with Silhouette. The droopy-nose styling and enormous dashtop render the front fenders invisible to the driver, while thick front windshield pillars, huge triangular front side windows, and wide center pillars create some annoying obstructions.

The Lumina Minivan and Trans Sport retain the large dashtop and their shorter new nose does not significantly reduce the problem.

The new automatic door is a convenience for families in loading and unloading children. It opens and closes at a moderate speed, but parents will want to be comfortable with its ability to stop and change direction when it meets an obstacle. It costs a reasonable $295, but you have to buy a $1660 option package to get it. And it's unavailable on the Special Edition or California models.

Among minivans, we rate Chrysler Corporation's entries as the best choices and list the Mercury Villager and Nissan Quest second. The moderately priced Silhouette Special Edition also deserves consideration.

Prices

Oldsmobile Silhouette

	Retail Price	Dealer Invoice	Fair Price
4-door van	$20365	$18430	$18830
Special Edition 4-door van with Pkg. R7B	20195	19310	*
Special Edition 4-door van with Pkg. R7c	21995	21029	*
Destination charge	530	530	530

*Some dealer invoice and fair prices not available at time of publication.

Oldsmobile • Plymouth

Special Edition price include destination charge. Additional "value-priced" models may also be available in California.

Standard Equipment:

Base: 3.1-liter V-6, 3-speed automatic transmission, anti-lock brakes, driver-side air bag, power steering, front air conditioning, 4-way adjustable driver's seat, 7-passenger seating (front bucket seats, three middle and two rear modular seats), center console with locking storage, power mirrors, tachometer, coolant temperature and oil pressure gauges, voltmeter, trip odometer, AM/FM radio, tilt steering wheel, tinted glass, intermittent wipers, rear wiper/washer, rear defogger, fog lamps, visor mirrors, floormats, 205/70R15 tires, alloy wheels. **California model** adds: 3.8-liter V-6 engine, power windows and locks, cruise control, remote keyless entry system, cassette player, roof luggage carrier, cargo area net. **Special Edition** adds to base: 3.8-liter V-6 engine, 4-speed automatic transmission, Option Pkg. 1SB.

Optional Equipment:

	Retail Price	Dealer Invoice	Fair Price
3.8-liter V-6 engine, base	$800	$688	$716
Includes 4-speed automatic transmission.			
Traction control system, base	350	301	313
Requires FE3 Touring Suspension and 3.8-liter V-6, or Option Pkg. 1SC.			
Option Pkg. 1SB, base	1660	1428	1486
Convenience Pkg., AM/FM cassette, Remote Lock Control Pkg., deep-tinted glass, roof luggage carrier, overhead console with compass and temperature readout, cargo area net.			
Option Pkg. 1SC, base	3270	2812	2927
Base with sunroof	3095	2662	2770
Option Pkg. 1SB plus 3.8-liter V-6 engine, 4-speed automatic transmission, power driver's seat, power sliding door, steering wheel touch controls, leather-wrapped steering wheel.			
Convenience Pkg., base	800	688	716
Power windows, programmable power door locks with sliding door delay, cruise control.			
Integrated dual child seats, base	225	194	201
Rear air conditioning	450	387	403
Base requires Option Pkg. 1SB plus 3.8-liter V-6 engine, or Option Pkg. 1SC.			
Power driver's seat	270	232	242
Base requires Option Pkg. 1SB.			
Power sliding door, base	295	254	264
Requires Option Pkg. 1SB.			
FE3 Touring Suspension, base	205	176	183
Includes eletronic level control, air inflation kit, 205/70R15 touring tires. Requires Option Pkg. 1SB or 1SC.			
Towing Pkg., base	355	305	318
Requires 3.8-liter V-6 engine or Option Pkg. 1SC. Includes FE3 Touring Suspension and traction control system.			
Cassette player, base	140	120	125
Base with Option Pkg. 1SB	30	26	27
AM/FM radio and CD player,			
Base with Option Pkg. 1SB	256	256	256
Base with Option Pkg. 1SC	226	194	202
Sunroof, base	350	301	313
Requires Option Pkg. 1SC.			
Custom leather trim, base and Special Edition	870	748	779
Base with Option Pkg. 1SC	780	671	698

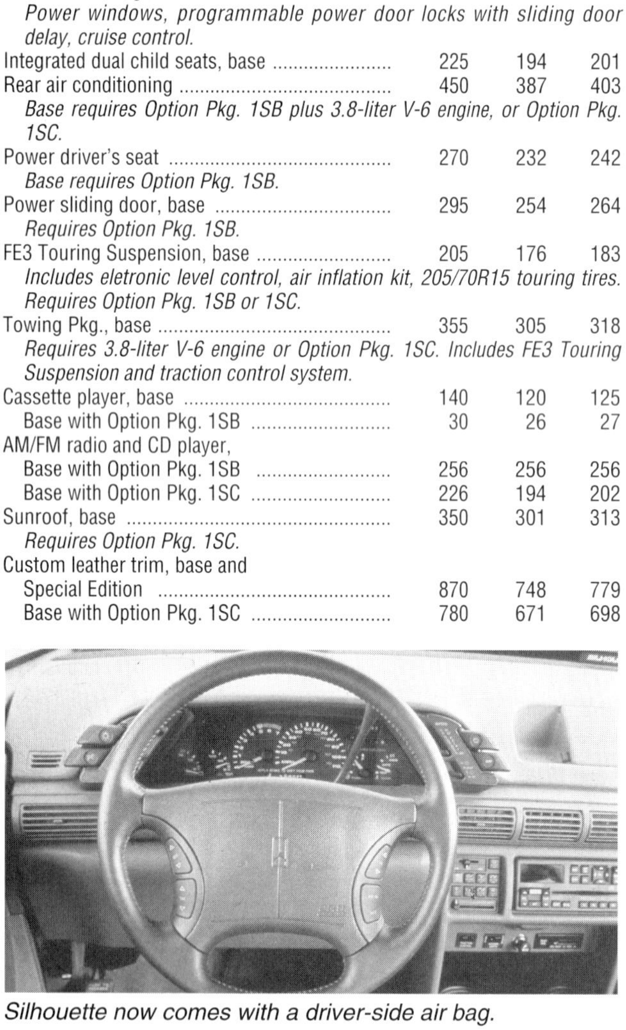

Silhouette now comes with a driver-side air bag.

Plymouth Colt Vista

Plymouth Colt Vista

A driver-side air bag heads the list of changes to this high-built subcompact wagon that's marketed as a "mini minivan."

Colt Vista is built in Japan by Mitsubishi from the same design used for the Eagle Summit Wagon and the Mitsubishi Expo LRV (see separate reports.)

Body Styles/Chassis

Badges, colors, and minor trim differences separate Colt Vista from the Eagle Summit Wagon. Like the Expo LRV, both have two conventional front doors, a one-piece tailgate, and a van-like curbside rear door that slides open and closed on a unique hidden track. (Mitsubishi also offers a larger iteration with four conventional side doors under the just-plain-Expo label.)

Colt Vista comes in base and SE models, which have front-wheel drive, and as the Colt Vista AWD, the suffix signifying All-Wheel Drive.

An anti-lock braking system with 4-wheel discs is optional in place of the standard front-disc/rear-drum setup.

For 1994, power steering is made standard on all Colt Vistas and base and AWD models get body-colored fascias. The optional air conditioning now uses a CFC-free refrigerant.

Powertrains

The base model comes with a 113-horsepower 1.8-liter 4-cylinder engine.

The SE and AWD models have a 136-horsepower 2.4-liter 4-cylinder engine. This engine was optional last year on the AWD Colt Vista.

Each engine teams with a standard 5-speed manual or optional 4-speed automatic transmission.

The AWD model has permanently engaged 4WD.

Towing capacity with the 1.8-liter engine is 1500 pounds. Rated capacity with the 2.4-liter is 2000 pounds on the SE and 2500 pounds on the AWD.

Accommodations

Vista again follows Summit/LRV form in having twin front bucket seats and a standard 3-place rear bench that tumbles forward and can be removed.

With the air bag, all Colt Vistas gain a manual 3-point seat belt with a height adjustment for the driver. A motorized

Plymouth

shoulder belt with a manual lap belt remains for the front passenger.

Also for '94, base and AWD models get new front-door panels with map pockets and all models gain a new 4-spoke steering wheel.

See the Eagle Summit Wagon report for our evaluation of the Colt Vista.

Specifications

	4-door wagon
Wheelbase, in.	99.2
Overall length, in.	168.5
Overall width, in.	66.7
Overall height, in.	62.1
Turn diameter, ft.	33.5
Curb weight, lbs.	2734[1]
Fuel capacity, gal.	14.5

1. 3064 lbs. 4WD.

Passenger Area Dimensions

Seating capacity	5
Front head room, in.	40.0
Rear head room, in.	38.6
Front leg room, in.	40.8
Rear leg room, in.	36.1

Available Seating

Cargo Dimensions and Payloads

Cargo area length, in.	67.8
Cargo area width, in.	41.3
Cargo area width between wheels, in.	39.0
Cargo area height, in.	43.4
Cargo vol., cu. ft.	79.0
Max. payload, lbs.	NA
Max. trailer weight, lbs.	2500

Engines

	ohc I-4	ohc I-4
Size, liters/cu. in.	1.8/112	2.4/143
Horsepower @ rpm	113 @ 6000	136 @ 5500
Torque (lbs./ft.) @ rpm	116 @ 4500	145 @ 4250
Availability	S	S[1]

EPA city/highway mpg

5-speed OD manual	24/29	22/27
4-speed OD automatic	24/29	20/26

1. SE and AWD models.

Built in Japan.

KEY: Dimensions and capacities are supplied by the manufacturers. **Curb Weight:** base models, not including optional equipment. **Max. payload, lbs.** = gross amount; net payload may be lower due to optional equipment. **Engines:** ohv = overhead valve; **ohc** = overhead cam; **I** = inline cylinders; **V** = cylinders in V configuration; **flat** = horizontally opposed cylinders; **rpm** = revolutions per minute; **OD** = overdrive transmission; **S** = standard; **O** = optional; **NA** = not available.

Prices

Plymouth Colt Vista

	Retail Price	Dealer Invoice	Fair Price
Base 4-door wagon	$12979	$12036	$12579
SE 4-door wagon	14194	13130	13694
AWD 4-door wagon	14884	13751	14384
Destination charge	430	430	430

Standard Equipment:

Base: 1.8-liter 4-cylinder engine, 5-speed manual transmission, driver-side air bag, motorized front passenger shoulder belt, power steering, cloth/vinyl reclining front bucket seats with center console, folding and removable rear seat, rear seat heater ducts, coolant temperature gauge, trip odometer, tilt steering column, remote fuel door release, dual outside mirrors, intermittent wipers, passenger-side visor mirror, 185/75R14 tires. **SE** adds: 2.4-liter 4-cylinder engine, cloth seats with armrests, split folding and removable rear seat with reclining back, power mirrors, tinted glass, driver-side visor mirror, power locks, remote tailgate lock, rear wiper/washer, 2-tone paint, wheel covers. **AWD** adds to base: 2.4-liter 4-cylinder engine, full-time 4-wheel drive, power mirrors, driver-side visor mirror, rear wiper/washer, 205/70R14 tires, wheel covers.

Optional Equipment:

Pkg. 21C/22C, base	1156	994	1017

Air conditioning, tinted glass, rear defogger, rear wiper/washer, power mirrors, AM/FM radio, power tailgate lock, rear stabilizer bar, wheel covers. Pkg. 22C requires automatic transmission.

Pkg. 21D/22D/24D, base	1796	1545	1580

Pkg. 21C plus power locks, cruise control, cassette player, floormats. Pkg. 22D requires automatic transmission. Pkg. 24D requires 2.4-liter engine, automatic transmission.

Pkg. 23K/24K, SE	1609	1384	1416

Air conditioning, rear defogger, power windows, cruise control, remote keyless entry, cassette player, cargo area cover, floormats. Pkg. 24K requires automatic transmission.

Pkg. 23S/24S, AWD	673	579	592

Tinted glass, rear defogger, remote keyless entry, AM/FM radio, floormats, full cloth seats, split back reclining rear seat, upgraded interior trim. Pkg. 24S requires automatic transmission.

Pkg. 23W/24W	2138	1839	1881

Pkg. 23S plus air conditioning, power windows, cruise control, AM/FM cassette, tachometer. Pkg. 24W requires automatic transmission.

2.4-liter 4-cylinder engine, base	181	156	159
4-speed automatic transmission	723	622	636
Anti-lock brakes	699	601	615
Includes rear disc brakes.			
Air conditioning, AWD	790	679	695
Rear defogger	66	57	58
Roof rack	151	130	133
AM/FM radio, base and AWD	288	248	253
AM/FM cassette, base and AWD	181	156	159

Colt Vista gains a driver-side air bag for 1994.

Plymouth

Plymouth Voyager

✓ **BEST BUY**

Plymouth Grand Voyager LE

Voyager and the other Chrysler Corporation minivans were redesigned just two years ago but still get several major changes this year.

New safety features include a passenger-side air bag and side door guard beams that enable Voyager to meet all passenger car safety requirements through 1998. There's also a new engine.

Voyager shares its design with the Chrysler Town & Country and Dodge Caravan, which also get the new engine and safety features and are covered in separate reports.

Body Styles/Chassis

As with Caravan, Voyager comes as a regular-length model (112.3-inch wheelbase, 178.1-inch-long body) and as an extended-length "Grand" version (119.3-inch wheelbase, 192.8-inch body).

Regular-length models come in base, SE, LE, and LX trim levels. Grand models come in base, SE, and LE form. All these models have front-wheel drive.

Both body lengths previously were available with permanently engaged all-wheel-drive, but this year only Grand Voyagers get that system. So equipped, they are offered as the SE AWD and LE AWD models. Unlike Caravan, Voyager has no cargo model.

Grand Voyagers with AWD now come standard with rear anti-lock brakes. Four-wheel anti-lock brakes are optional on all Voyagers except the base models.

All models have new bumper fascias and body moldings and also get guard beams in the front and side doors.

Maximum payload is 2000 pounds for either body length.

Powertrains

A 100-horsepower 2.5-liter 4-cylinder engine is available only on standard-size Voyagers.

A 142-horsepower 3.0-liter V-6 is available on standard-size SE and LE models and on the base Grand.

A 3.3-liter V-6 is standard on Grand SE models and AWD models. It's rated at 162 horsepower, 12 more than last year.

A 3.8-liter V-6 is a new option on Grand LE models. Like the 3.3-liter V-6, the 3.8 is rated at 162 horsepower. However, the 3.8 produces more torque than the 3.3, 213 pounds/feet to 194.

A 5-speed manual is the standard transmission with the 4-cylinder engine. The V-6s use either a 3- or a 4-speed automatic, depending on the model. The 4-speed automatic transmission now has a switch to lock out overdrive.

AWD models normally send about 90 percent of their engine power to the front wheels, but when one axle loses traction, a viscous center coupling reapportions engine

Specifications	4-door van	4-door van
Wheelbase, in.	112.3	119.3
Overall length, in.	178.1	192.8
Overall width, in.	72.0	72.0
Overall height, in.	66.0	66.7
Turn diameter, ft.	41.0	43.0
Curb weight, lbs.	3306	3574[1]
Fuel capacity, gal.	20.0[2]	20.0[2]

1. 4008 lbs., AWD. 2. 18.0 gal. with AWD.

Passenger Area Dimensions

Seating capacity	7	7
Front head room, in.	39.1	39.1
Rear head room, in.	38.6	38.5
Front leg room, in.	38.3	38.3
Rear leg room, in.	37.6	37.7

Available Seating

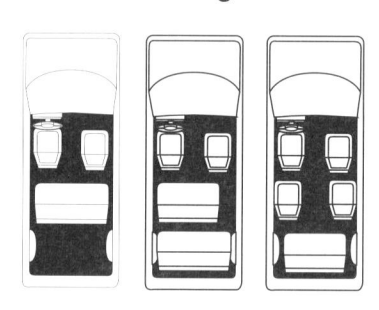

Cargo Dimensions and Payloads

Cargo area length, in.	81.9	96.4
Cargo area width, in.	59.0	59.0
Cargo area width between wheels, in.	50.9	50.9
Cargo area height, in.	48.0	48.4
Cargo vol., cu. ft.	133.0	160.0
Max. payload, lbs.	2000	2000
Max. trailer weight, lbs.	3500	3500

Engines	ohv I-4	ohc V-6	ohv V-6	ohv V-6
Size, liters/cu. in.	2.5/153	3.0/181	3.3/201	3.8/230
Horsepower @ rpm	100 @ 4800	142 @ 5000	162 @ 4800	162 @ 4000
Torque (lbs./ft.) @ rpm	135 @ 2800	173 @ 2400	194 @ 3600	213 @ 3600
Availability	S	O	O[1]	O[2]

EPA city/highway mpg

5-speed OD manual	20/27			
3-speed automatic	20/24	19/23		
4-speed OD automatic		19/23	18/23	16/22

1. Std., Grand Voyager SE and AWD models. 2. Grand LE.

Built in St. Louis, Mo., and Canada.

KEY: Dimensions and capacities are supplied by the manufacturers. **Curb Weight:** base models, not including optional equipment. **Max. payload, lbs.** = gross amount; net payload may be lower due to optional equipment. **Engines:** ohv = overhead valve; ohc = overhead cam; **I** = inline cylinders; **V** = cylinders in V configuration; **flat** = horizontally opposed cylinders; **rpm** = revolutions per minute; **OD** = overdrive transmission; **S** = standard; **O** = optional; **NA** = not available.

power to the wheels with the best grip until traction is restored.

Maximum trailer weight is 1750 pounds with the 4-cylinder engine, 2000 with the V-6s, and 3500 with a V-6 and the optional trailering package.

Accommodations

Regular-length models have seating for five or seven. Grands seat seven.

Integrated child safety seats are an option on 7-passenger models. So equipped, the 2-place middle bench seat can be used as a regular seat or converted for use by two toddlers weighing between 20 and 40 pounds by folding out sections of the backrest. Toddlers are secured by a built-in 5-point lap/shoulder harness.

A reclining seatback is added to the child-safety-seat bench for 1994.

On 7-passenger models, a Quad-Command option replaces the middle bench with a pair of reclining buckets.

The passenger-side air bag joins a driver-side air bag. The dashboard is slightly revised and now includes a knee bolster.

Evaluation

Chrysler's minivans are best in class because they are car-like to drive and offer a range of models and features that no rival matches.

Still, competition has forced dealers to offer big discounts on these vans. That doesn't mean they're inexpensive, but there is fine value here.

Acceleration is subpar with the 4-cylinder engine. The V-6s furnish power that escalates from adequate with the 3.0 through outstanding with the new 3.8.

Part of the cost of running these vehicles is in fuel; none of the V-6s will average more than 15-17 mpg in everyday driving.

The AWD models improve on the good traction of the front-drive versions, but AWD adds weight that reduces fuel economy and diminishes ride quality.

Climbing in or out of the front or middle seats is as easy as in most cars. The Quad-Command option includes a tilt-forward right-side bucket, but getting to the rearmost seat in any Voyager requires some contortions.

The standard-size model has less leg room for the middle and rear seats than the Grand, though there's enough for most adults to fit without being cramped.

Cargo space also is skimpier in the standard-size model: With the rear seat in place, there's only enough room at the back for one row of grocery bags. The rear seat of both models can be removed, but it's heavy and hard to squeeze out the rear door without scratching the side interior panels.

The well-designed dashboard has clear gauges and well-marked controls that are mounted high, where they're easy to see and reach while driving. And added sound insulation has reduced road noise this year.

Overall, no manufacturer's minivans have more all-round attributes than Chrysler's. Don't buy without first checking out a Caravan or Voyager.

Prices

Plymouth Voyager	Retail Price	Dealer Invoice	Fair Price
Base SWB	$14919	$13629	$14329
Base Grand	18178	16522	17222
SE SWB	18139	16462	17162

Plymouth

	Retail Price	Dealer Invoice	Fair Price
Grand SE	$19304	$17513	$18413
Grand SE AWD	21982	19869	20769
LE SWB	21963	19827	20727
Grand LE	22883	20662	21562
Grand LE AWD	25560	23017	23917
LX SWB	22472	20275	21175
Destination charge	560	560	560

SWB denotes standard wheelbase; AWD denotes All-Wheel Drive.

Standard Equipment:

Base: 2.5-liter 4-cylinder engine, 5-speed manual transmission, driver- and passenger-side air bags, power steering, cloth front bucket seats, 3-passenger middle bench seat, tinted glass, trip odometer, coolant temperature gauge, dual outside mirrors, visor mirrors, AM/FM radio, intermittent wipers, rear wiper/washer, 195/75R14 tires, wheel covers. **Base Grand** adds: 3.0-liter V-6 engine, 3-speed automatic transmission, 7-passenger seating (front buckets and 2-place middle and 3-place rear bench seats), rear trim panel storage and cup holders, 205/70R15 tires. **SE** adds to Base: 3.0-liter V-6 engine, 3-speed automatic transmission, cruise control, power mirrors, cassette player, power remote tailgate release, tilt steering wheel, front passenger lockable underseat storage drawer, striping, dual note horn. **Grand SE** adds to Base Grand: 3.3-liter V-6 engine, 4-speed automatic transmission, cruise control, power mirrors, cassette player, power remote tailgate release, tilt steering wheel, front passenger lockable underseat storage drawer, striping, dual note horn. **LE** adds to SE: front air conditioning, front storage console, overhead console with trip computer, rear defogger, power rear quarter vent windows, power door locks, remote keyless entry system, tachometer, oil pressure gauge, voltmeter, heated power mirrors, lighted visor mirrors, illuminated entry system, headlamp time delay, floormats, 205/70R15 tires. **Grand LE** adds to Grand SE: front air conditioning, front storage console, overhead console with trip computer, rear defogger, power rear quarter vent windows, power door locks, remote keyless entry system, tachometer, oil pressure gauge, voltmeter, heated power mirrors, lighted visor mirrors, illuminated entry system, headlamp time delay, floormats. **LX** adds to LE SWB: LX Decor Group. **AWD** models have permanently engaged all-wheel drive.

Quick Order Packages:

Pkgs. 21T, 22T, 24T Base SWB and
26T Base SWB, Base Grand 213   181   196
Air conditioning, map and cargo lights, power remote liftgate release, front passenger underseat lockable storage drawer, bodyside molding, dual horns. Pkg. 22T requires 3-speed automatic transmission; Pkg. 24T requires 3.0-liter engine and 3-speed automatic transmission; Pkg. 26T requires 3.0-liter engine and 4-speed transmission.

Pkg. 26B SE SWB and Pkg. 28B SE SWB,
Grand SE, Grand SE AWD 213   181   196
Pkgs. 24B-28B add to SE standard equipment: air conditioning, map and cargo lights, rear defogger. SE SWB Pkg. 24B requires 4-speed automatic transmission; SE SWB Pkg. 28B requires 3.3-liter engine and 4-speed automatic transmission.

Pkg. 26D SE SWB, and Pkg. 28D SE SWB,
Grand SE, Grand SE AWD 1159   985   1066
Pkgs. 26D-28D add to Pkgs. 26B-28B forward and overhead consoles, oil pressure and voltage gauges, tachometer, lighted visor mirrors, Light Group, power door locks and rear quarter vent windows, floormats, deluxe insulation. SE SWB Pkg. 26D requires 4-speed automatic transmission; SE SWB Pkg. 28D requires 3.3-liter engine and 4-speed automatic transmission.

Pkg. 26K LE SWB, and Pkg. 28K LE SWB,
Grand LE, Grand LE AWD and Pkg. 29K
Grand LE, Grand LE AWD 306   260   282
Pkgs. 26K-29K add to LE standard equipment: power driver's seat, power windows, AM/FM radio with cassette player, equalizer and six Infinity speakers, sunscreen glass. LE SWB Pkg. 26K requires 4-speed automatic transmission; LE SWB Pkg. 28K requires 3.3-liter engine and 4-speed automatic transmission; Grand LE and Grand LE AWD require 3.8-liter engine.

Pkg. 28L and 29L Grand LE,
Grand LE AWD 962   818   885
Pkgs. 28L-29L add to 28K-29K: Woodgrain Decor Group (woodgrain trim and moldings, front and rear body-color fascias, luggage rack, whitewall tires, alloy wheels). Requires 3.8-liter engine.

Plymouth

Top left: Voyager adds a passenger-side air bag to its driver-side air bag for '94. Above: The right-middle Quad Command bucket tilts to ease rear-seat access. Left: A regular-length Voyager SE.

	Retail Price	Dealer Invoice	Fair Price
Pkgs. 26M-28M LX SWB	$431	$366	$397

Pkgs. 26M-29M add to 26K-28K LX SWB: LX Decor Group (body-color fascia, cladding, and grille, fog lamps, alloy wheels), Sport Handling Group (heavy duty brakes, firmer front and rear sway bars and front struts and rear shocks, 205/70R15 tires, alloy wheels). LX SWB Pkg. 26M requires 4-speed automatic transmission; LX SWB Pkg. 28M requires 3.3-liter engine and 4-speed automatic transmission.

Individual Options:

	Retail	Dealer	Fair
3.0-liter V-6, Base SWB	767	652	706
Requires 3-speed automatic transmission.			
3.3-liter V-6, SE, LE, and ES SWB	102	87	94
Requires 4-speed automatic transmission.			
3.8-liter V-6, Grand LE, and Grand LE AWD	302	257	278
Includes 4-speed transmission.			
3-speed automatic transmission, Base SWB	601	511	553
4-speed automatic transmission, SE, LE, LX SWB and Base Grand	198	168	182
Anti-lock brakes: SE SWB with Pkgs. 26-28B or 26-28D	687	584	632
SE SWB with Pkgs. 26-28B or 26-28D and alloy wheels, Trailer Tow, Sport Handling, Gold Special Edition, or Sport Wagon Groups; Grand SE with Pkgs. 28B or 28D	599	509	551
LE SWB with Pkgs. 26-28K or 26-28M; Grand LE with Pkgs. 26-28K, 26-28L or 26-28M	599	509	551
Front air conditioning, Base SWB and Base Grand	857	728	788
Front air conditioning with sunscreen glass, Base SWB with Pkg. 26T, SE SWB with Pkg. 26-28B and 26-28D, Base Grand with Pkg. 26T and SE Grand with Pkg. 28B and 28D	414	352	381
Not available with Sport Wagon Decor Group.			
Sunscreen glass, Grand SE AWD with Pkg. 28B and 28D	414	352	381
Rear air conditioning with rear heater and sunscreen glass, Base Grand with Pkg. 26T, Grand SE with Pkg. 28B, Grand SE AWD with Pkg. 28B	988	840	909
Grand SE and Grand SE AWD with Pkg. 28B and Sport Wagon Decor Group	574	488	528
with Trailer Towing Group	925	786	851
with Sport Wagon Decor Group and Trailer Towing Group	511	434	470
Grand SE and Grand SE AWD with Pkg. 28D	880	748	810
with Sport Wagon Decor Group	466	396	429
with Trailer Towing Group	818	695	753
with Sport Wagon Decor Group and Trailer Towing Group	404	343	372
Grand LE and Grand LE AWD with Pkgs. 28-29K, 28-29L, or 28-29M	466	396	429
with Trailer Towing Group	404	343	372
Requires rear defogger.			
Rear bench seat, Base SWB	346	294	318
7-passenger seating with integrated child seat, Base SWB	570	485	524
SE, LE and LX SWB, Grand, Grand AWD	225	191	207
Quad Command Seating, SE, LE and LX	597	507	549
Two front and two middle bucket seats, 3-passenger rear bench seat.			
Converta-Bed 7-passenger seating, SE, LE and LX	553	470	509
Leather trim, LX	865	735	796
Not available with integrated child seat.			
Heavy Duty Trailer Towing Group, SE SWB with Pkgs. 26-28B and 26-28D	556	473	512
with Gold Special Edition Group	442	376	407
LE SWB with Pkgs. 26-28K, Grand SE with Pkgs. 28B and 28D and Grand LE with Pkgs. 28-29K and 28-29L	442	376	407
SE SWB with Pkgs. 26-28B and 26-28D, LE SWB with Pkgs. 26-28K, LX SWB with Pkgs. 26-28M, Grand SE with Pkgs. 28B and 28D, Grand LE with Pkgs. 28-29K and 28-29L	410	349	377

Plymouth • Pontiac

Pontiac Trans Sport

RECOMMENDED

Pontiac Trans Sport SE

A driver-side air bag and a new, shorter nose are changes for Pontiac's version of General Motors' front-drive minivan.

Trans Sport shares its design and plastic body panels with the Chevrolet Lumina Minivan and Oldsmobile Silhouette; all three gain an air bag for '94, but only Silhouette retains last year's elongated front-end styling.

Body Styles/Chassis

Trans Sport returns in a single body style with a sliding right-side door and a one-piece liftgate. As with the Silhouette and Lumina Minivan, plastic outer-body panels are attached to a steel skeleton frame. Anti-lock brakes are standard.

The new front end is shorter than last year's by two inches and includes integral fog lamps. A center high-mounted brake light is added at the rear.

A power sliding side door was promised as a mid-year option for 1993, but was not available until the start of the 1994 model year.

Trans Sport's maximum payload is 1257 pounds.

Powertrains

Again standard is a 120-horsepower 3.1-liter V-6 engine and a 3-speed automatic transmission.

Optional is a 170-horsepower 3.8-liter V-6 and 4-speed automatic. Pontiac says a traction-control system will be added to the options list later in the model year.

Towing capacity is 2000 pounds with the 3.1-liter engine and 3000 pounds with the 3.8-liter.

Accommodations

Trans Sport returns in a single SE price level with standard seating for five. Last year's 6-bucket-seat offering is dropped, leaving a 7-bucket arrangement as the only seating option.

Seven-seat models can be ordered with up to two integrated child seats. The optional child seats fold from the backrest of an otherwise-ordinary outboard middle-row bucket and contain a 5-point safety harness. They are for children weighing between 20 and 40 pounds.

Automatic power door locks are new for 1994, and seats anchored in the rearmost positions gain a fold-and-stow feature.

	Retail Price	Dealer Invoice	Fair Price
Grand SE AWD with Pkgs. 28B and 28D, Grand LE AWD with Pkgs. 28-29K, 28-29L and 28-29M	$373	$317	$343
Heavy duty brakes, battery, load suspension and radiator, trailer towing wiring harness, 205/70R15 all-season tires, conventional spare tire.			
Sport Handling Group, SWB SE with Pkg. 26-28B and 26-28D	239	203	220
Grand SE with Pkg. 28B and 28D, Grand LE with Pkg. 28-29L	125	106	115
Heavy duty brakes, front and rear sway bars, 205/70R15 tires. Not available with Sport Wagon Decor Pkg.			
LE SWB with Pkg. 26-28K and Grand LE with Pkg. 28-29K	488	415	449
Heavy duty brakes, front and rear sway bars, 205/70R15 tires, alloy wheels.			
Convenience Group I, Base SWB and Base Grand	372	316	342
Cruise control, tilt steering wheel.			
Convenience Group II, Base SWB and Base Grand	694	590	638
SE SWB with Pkg. 26-28B and Grand SE with 28B	265	225	244
Convenience Group I plus power mirrors and door locks.			
Convenience Group III, SE SWB with Pkg. 26-28B and Grand SE with Pkg. 28B	673	572	619
SE SWB with Pkg. 26-28D and Grand SE with Pkg. 28D	408	347	375
Convenience Group II plus power windows and remote keyless entry system.			
AWD Convenience Group I, Grand SE AWD with Pkg. 28B	265	225	244
Power mirrors and door locks.			
AWD Convenience Group II, Grand SE AWD with Pkg. 28B	673	572	619
with Pkg. 28D	408	347	375
AWD Convenience Group I plus power windows and remote keyless entry system.			
Gold Special Edition Group, SE	250	213	230
Gold striping, moldings and badging, 205/70R15 tires, gold-color alloy wheels.			
Sport Wagon Decor Group, SE	750	638	690
Sunscreen glass, front and rear fascias, leather-wrapped steering wheel, fog lamps, Sport Handling Group, alloy wheels.			
Rear defogger	168	143	155
Power door locks	265	225	244
Luggage rack	143	122	132
Cassette player	170	145	156
AM and FM stereo with CD player, equalizer and six Infinity speakers, SE SWB with Pkg. 26-28D, Grand SE with Pkg. 28D, Grand SE AWD with Pkg. 28D, LE SWB with Pkg. 26-28K and 26-28L, Grand LE with Pkg. 28-29K, 28-29L, 28-29M, Grand LE AWD with Pkg. 28-29K, 28-29L, 28-29M	501	426	461
	170	145	156
Infinity speaker system, SE	202	172	186
Firm Ride Heavy Load Suspension, 2WD	178	151	129
with Sport Handling Group	146	124	105
Includes conventional spare tire.			
205/70R14 whitewall tires, Base SWB and SWB	143	122	132
205/70R15 whitewall tires, SWB SE, SWB LE, Base Grand, Grand SE, Grand LE, Grand SE AWD, Grand LE AWD	69	59	63
Not available with Sport Handling, Gold Special Edition, Sport Wagon Groups.			
Conventional spare tire	109	93	100
15-inch alloy wheels, LE SWB with Pkg. 26-28K, Grand LE with Pkg. 28-29K, Grand LE AWD with Pkg. 28-29K	363	309	334
Extra-cost paint	97	82	89

CONSUMER GUIDE® 159

Pontiac

Trans Sport's standard air bag fits into a new steering wheel that also has redundant radio controls. The dashboard layout is unchanged, but a new terraced panel on top of the instrument panel is designed to visually "shorten" Trans Sport's long dashtop shelf.

Evaluation

Futuristic styling has always set Trans Sport apart from the crowd, and the shorter new nose doesn't change that.

Specifications	4-door van
Wheelbase, in.	109.8
Overall length, in.	192.2
Overall width, in.	74.6
Overall height, in.	65.7
Turn diameter, ft.	42.5
Curb weight, lbs.	3540
Fuel capacity, gal.	20.0

Passenger Area Dimensions	
Seating capacity	7
Front head room, in.	39.2
Rear head room, in.	39.0
Front leg room, in.	40.1
Rear leg room, in.	36.1

Available Seating

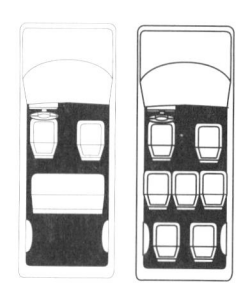

Cargo Dimensions and Payloads	
Cargo area length, in.	86.0
Cargo area width, in.	56.0
Cargo area width between wheels, in.	42.5
Cargo area height, in.	45.3
Cargo vol., cu. ft.	112.6
Max. payload, lbs.	1257
Max. trailer weight, lbs.	3000

Engines	ohv V-6	ohv V-6
Size, liters/cu. in.	3.1/191	3.8/231
Horsepower @ rpm	120 @ 4400	170 @ 4800
Torque (lbs./ft.) @ rpm	175 @ 2200	225 @ 3200
Availability	S	O

EPA city/highway mpg		
3-speed automatic	18/23	
4-speed automatic		17/25

Built in Tarrytown, N.Y.

KEY: Dimensions and capacities are supplied by the manufacturers. **Curb Weight:** base models, not including optional equipment. **Max. payload, lbs.** = gross amount; net payload may be lower due to optional equipment. **Engines: ohv** = overhead valve; **ohc** = overhead cam; **I** = inline cylinders; **V** = cylinders in V configuration; **flat** = horizontally opposed cylinders; **rpm** = revolutions per minute; **OD** = overdrive transmission; **S** = standard; **O** = optional; **NA** = not available.

Neither does it help improve visibility from the driver's seat.

The view forward is cluttered by extra roof pillars and made daunting by a dashtop that's still the longest of any vehicle, despite this year's "terraced" treatment.

That said, Trans Sport performs admirably as a sporty people mover. It drives, rides, and stops much like a midsize car, thanks to a capable suspension and standard anti-lock brakes. And the standard air bag brings it abreast of most other minivans in safety features, though the leaders in this class from the Chrysler Corporation, as well as the Toyota Previa and new Ford Windstar, now have dual air bags.

Trans Sport's standard 3.1-liter V-6 gives adequate acceleration unless the van is loaded with passengers and/or cargo—but that is why people buy this type of vehicle. With the 3.8-liter V-6, Trans Sport has no trouble handling most any chore.

There's little cargo room with all seats in place. But we really like the removable bucket seats, which are lighter than any rival's.

The optional power sliding side door is a convenience that only GM's vans offer. It is operated by controls in the interior and on the key fob for the optional remote keyless entry system. It opens only when the transmission is in park, but parents will want to be confident of it's ability to stop and reverse direction if an object blocks its path.

Trans Sport now has a driver-side air bag. The optional power sliding door is designed to stop and reverse direction when it encounters an obstruction.

Prices

Pontiac Trans Sport

	Retail Price	Dealer Invoice	Fair Price
SE 4-door van	$17469	*	*
Destination charge	530	530	530

Additional "value-priced" models may be available in California.

Standard Equipment:

SE: 3.1-liter V-6 engine, 3-speed automatic transmission, anti-lock brakes, driver-side air bag, power steering, 4-way adjustable driver's seat, front reclining bucket seats, 3-passenger middle seat, cloth upholstery, tinted glass with solar-control windshield, tachometer, coolant temperature and oil pressure gauges, voltmeter, trip odometer, AM/FM radio, Lamp Group (includes overhead console map lights, rear reading lights, cargo area lights, underhood light), left remote and right manual mirrors, door and seatback pockets, intermittent wipers, fog lamps, rear wiper/washer, visor mirrors, front and rear floormats, 205/70R15 tires, wheel covers. **California model** adds: 3.8-liter V-6 engine, 4-speed automatic transmission, cruise control, front air conditioning, AM/FM cassette player, power door locks, windows and mirrors, remote keyless entry system, 7-passenger seating, 6-way power driver's seat, cargo area net, deep-tint glass, luggage carrier, 205/70R15 touring tires, alloy wheels.

Optional Equipment:

	Retail	Dealer	Fair
3.8-liter V-6 engine	819	704	734
Includes 4-speed automatic transmission.			
Front air conditioning	830	714	744
Front and rear air conditioning with rear heater	1280	1101	1147
with Group 1SB, 1SC, 1SD, or 1SE	450	387	403
Requires automatic level control and deep-tint glass.			
Automatic level control	200	172	179
Includes rear saddle bags.			
Option Group 1SB	1388	1194	1244
Front air conditioning, cruise control, cassette player, power mirrors, tilt steering wheel.			
Option Group 1SC	2483	2135	2225
Group 1SB plus automatic power door locks, power windows with driver-side express down, rear defogger, 7-passenger seating, deep-tint glass.			
Option Pkg. 1SD	3033	2608	2718
Group 1SC plus 6-way power driver's seat, remote keyless entry system, luggage rack.			
Option Pkg. 1SE	4008	3447	3592
Group 1SD plus automatic level control, cassette player with equalizer, self-sealing touring tires, alloy wheels.			
Rear defogger	170	146	152
Deep-tint glass	245	211	220
Pop-up glass sunroof	300	258	269
Power mirrors	48	41	43
Automatic power locks	300	258	269
6-way power driver's seat	270	232	242
Power windows with driver-side express down	275	237	246
Requires automatic power door locks.			
Power sliding side door	295	254	264
Requires automatic power door locks.			
Remote keyless entry system	135	116	121
Cassette player	140	120	125
Cassette player with equalizer, with Group 1SD	315	271	282
Includes steering wheel radio controls and leather-wrapped steering wheel.			
CD player with equalizer, with Group 1SD	541	465	485
with Group 1SE	206	177	185
Includes steering wheel radio controls and leather-wrapped steering wheel.			
7-passenger seating	705	606	632
Three second row and two third row modular seats, cargo area net.			
7-passenger seating with leather upholstery, with Group 1SD or 1SE	870	748	780
Integral child seat	125	108	112
Requires 7-passenger seating.			

Pontiac • Suzuki

	Retail Price	Dealer Invoice	Fair Price
Two integral child seats	$225	$194	$202
Requires 7-passenger seating.			
Traction control	350	301	314
Alloy wheels	275	237	246

Suzuki Samurai

Suzuki Samurai

The pioneer of mini-4x4s in the U.S. loses its 2-wheel-drive base model and gains a high-mounted center stoplamp for 1994.

Though the basic design is now more than two decades old, Suzuki keeps Samurai in the lineup so it can claim rights to the lowest-priced, most fuel-efficient sport-utility vehicle on the market.

Body Styles/Chassis

The only body is a 2-door semi-convertible with spare tire mounted on a right-hinged swing-open tailgate.

Discontinued is the rear-drive JA model. The sole surviving version is the 4-wheel-drive JL. A full fold-up canvas top is standard on the JL, but had been optional on the JA.

Anti-lock brakes are not available. Maximum payload capacity is 845 pounds.

Powertrains

Samurai's sole engine is a 66-horsepower 1.3-liter 4-cylinder that mates exclusively to a 5-speed overdrive manual transmission.

Standard is a part-time 4-wheel-drive system (not for use on dry pavement). It has manual front hubs that must be locked by hand before 4WD can be used.

Towing limit is 1000 pounds.

Accommodations

A pair of front buckets are the only seats.

Evaluation

We cannot recommend the purchase of a Samurai. Its doors close with a tinny clang, interior trim is low-buck unattractive, and the flimsy top is a hassle to put up or down. Adding insult to these injuries, resale values are in the cellar.

And the price is no longer bargain-basement, the JL having increased nearly $1100, or more than 12 percent, over a year ago, due mostly to the rise in the value of the Japanese yen against the U.S. dollar.

Samurai made a splash nine years ago, but the advent of more "adult" mini-4x4s—namely Suzuki's own Sidekick and Geo Tracker—quickly pushed Samurai out of the spotlight even before it became the target of allegations that it was

*Dealer invoice and fair price not available at time of publication.

161

Suzuki

prone to roll over in turns. Federal investigators concluded that Samurai was no more prone to tip in corners than other mini-4x4s, which as a class suffer high rollover rates.

The fact remains that even among open 4x4s, Samurai's track (the width between wheels on the same axle) is unusually narrow for its height. Specifically, track here is 13.4 inches less than height. With most other small 4WDs, the track is around 11 inches less than height, and difference in the Suzuki-built Sidekick/Tracker is at 9.9 inches.

The result in the Samurai is copious body lean in even moderately hard cornering, plus the kind of bouncy, bangy ride expected in a stiffly sprung short-wheelbase rig. Adding to the suffering is an assault by wind, road, and engine noise.

The engine is too small and weak to cope with the higher urban speeds and longer cross-country driving distances in America versus those of its native Japan.

Safe merging into freeway traffic requires shrewd advance planning. The same might be said for braking: reasonably short in panic situations but not at all directionally stable, with unwanted slewing and, at times, sudden wheel locking.

Buy a used Wrangler if you simply must have a raucous runabout, or stretch for the more refined Sidekick or Tracker. Just pass on this one.

Specifications

	2-door conv.
Wheelbase, in.	79.9
Overall length, in.	135.0
Overall width, in.	60.6
Overall height, in.	64.6
Turn diameter, ft.	33.5
Curb weight, lbs.	2046
Fuel capacity, gal.	10.6

Passenger Area Dimensions

Seating capacity	2
Front head room, in.	40.2
Rear head room, in.	—
Front leg room, in.	38.5
Rear leg room, in.	—

Cargo Dimensions and Payloads

Cargo area length, in.	32.5
Cargo area width, in.	43.7
Cargo area width between wheels, in.	NA
Cargo area height, in.	41.2
Cargo vol., cu. ft.	33.9
Max. payload, lbs.	845
Max. trailer weight, lbs.	1000

Engines

	ohc I-4
Size, liters/cu. in.	1.3/79
Horsepower @ rpm	66 @ 6000
Torque (lbs./ft.) @ rpm	76 @ 3500
Availability	S

EPA city/highway mpg

5-speed OD manual	28/29

Built in Japan.

KEY: Dimensions and capacities are supplied by the manufacturers. **Curb Weight:** base models, not including optional equipment. **Max. payload, lbs.** = gross amount; net payload may be lower due to optional equipment. **Engines: ohv** = overhead valve; **ohc** = overhead cam; **I** = inline cylinders; **V** = cylinders in V configuration; **flat** = horizontally opposed cylinders; **rpm** = revolutions per minute; **OD** = overdrive transmission; **S** = standard; **O** = optional; **NA** = not available.

Prices

Suzuki Samurai	Retail Price	Dealer Invoice	Fair Price
JL 4WD 2-door convertible	$9689	*	*
Destination charge	330	330	330

Standard Equipment:
1.3-liter 4-cylinder engine, 5-speed manual transmission, floor mounted transfer case, free-wheeling manual locking front hubs, vinyl reclining front bucket seats, dual outside mirrors, trip odometer, fuel tank skid plate, rear-mounted spare-tire carrier with full-size spare tire, tinted glass, intermittent wipers, carpeting, soft canvas top, mud flaps, 205/70R15 tires.

Options are available as dealer-installed accessories.

Suzuki Sidekick

Suzuki Sidekick JLX 5-door

Suzuki's larger mini sport-utility vehicles gain a center high-mounted stoplamp, a tilt steering column, and an anti-theft alarm as standard equipment for 1994.

The Sidekick convertible is duplicated at Chevrolet dealers as the Geo Tracker (see separate report). Tracker also offers a 3-door hardtop wagon, but Suzuki retains exclusive rights to the longer 5-door wagon body style.

Body Styles/Chassis

Sidekick's 2-door semi-convertible has an 86.6-inch wheelbase. The 5-door wagon has an 11-inch longer wheelbase and a body 16 inches longer overall. Both body types have a right-hinged tailgate.

The soft-top models come in JS and JX trim, each with a choice of 2- or 4-wheel drive. The wagons offer a JS model with 2WD and JX and top-line JLX models with 4WD.

All have front-disc/rear-drum brakes with standard rear anti-lock control.

Payload is 800 pounds for convertibles and 880 pounds for wagons.

Powertrains

All Sidekicks have a 1.6-liter 4-cylinder engine. Convertibles use an 8-valve version with 80 horsepower. Wagons have a 16-valve variant with 95 horsepower.

A 5-speed manual is standard on all models and is the only transmission available on 2WD wagon models. The

*Dealer invoice and fair price not available at time of publication.

Suzuki

able automatic on the convertibles is a 3-speed unit. Exclusive to wagons is an electronically controlled 4-speed overdrive automatic with "Normal" and "Power" shift modes.

Sidekick's 4WD system is an on-demand part-time setup that's not for use on dry pavement. Automatic-locking front hubs are standard. The vehicle must be stopped and shifted from 2WD to 4WD to automatically lock the front hubs, but once locked, it can be shifted between 2WD and 4WD high at any speed if the front wheels are straight. The vehicle must be stopped again and backed up a few feet to unlock the front hubs.

Towing limits are 1000 pounds on convertibles, 1500 on wagons.

Accommodations

All Sidekicks seat four via twin reclining front buckets and a 2-place bench behind. Rear seats are double-fold affairs with one-piece backrests on convertibles and a 50/50 split on wagons.

For '94, Sidekicks receive new contoured front seats with thicker padding and the JLX wagon gets cruise control as standard.

Evaluation

Sidekick's convertible model is so similar to its Tracker cousin that we'll refer you to the Geo report for comments on that model. Here we'll focus on the 5-door.

Compared to the base 1.6-liter engine, the 16-valver has a difference you can feel in most every driving situation. Still, Sidekick lags behind most larger rivals in performance. Our automatic took 16 seconds to 60 mph and its 21.4-mpg average was nothing special even for a compact 4x4. And torque is relatively meager, so the automatic tends to "hunt" annoyingly between third and fourth gears in medium-speed driving. The 5-speed we tested did not accelerate discernably quicker, but was far more responsive to the throttle at mid-range speeds and returned a more respectable 25.3 mpg.

The automatic's overdrive fourth gear allows 60 mph cruising at a fairly relaxed 2800 rpm, versus a busy 3500 rpm with the 3-speed automatic still offered on the open 4WD models. Overall noise levels are lower too, but still relatively high for a closed 4x4.

Despite the standard rear anti-lock brakes, our test models tended to sudden back-wheel lockup in panic stops—plus occasional front-wheel locking to the detriment of steering control.

Marked body lean is the rule in tight corners, though the 5-door doesn't feel nearly as tippy as the convertibles or 3-door Tracker. Nor does the "big" Suzuki bounce so much on

Specifications	2-door conv.	5-door wagon
Wheelbase, in.	86.6	97.6
Overall length, in.	142.5	158.7
Overall width, in.	64.2	64.6
Overall height, in.	65.2	66.5
Turn diameter, ft.	32.2	35.4
Curb weight, lbs.	2253	2571
Fuel capacity, gal.	11.1	14.5

Passenger Area Dimensions		
Seating capacity	4	4
Front head room, in.	39.5	40.6
Rear head room, in.	39.0	40.0
Front leg room, in.	42.1	42.1
Rear leg room, in.	31.7	32.7

Cargo Dimensions and Payloads		
Cargo area length, in.	27.8	38.2
Cargo area width, in.	50.4	51.2
Cargo area width between wheels, in.	41.2	41.2
Cargo area height, in.	40.6	40.5
Cargo vol., cu. ft.	32.9	46.0
Max. payload, lbs.	800	880
Max. trailer weight, lbs.	1000	1500

Engines	ohc I-4	ohc I-4
Size, liters/cu. in.	1.6/97	1.6/97
Horsepower @ rpm	80 @ 5400	95 @ 5600
Torque (lbs./ft.) @ rpm	94 @ 3000	98 @ 4000
Availability	S[1]	S[2]

EPA city/highway mpg		
5-speed OD manual	25/27	23/26
3-speed automatic	23/24	
4-speed automatic		22/26

1. Convertible. 2. Wagon.

Built in Canada.

KEY: Dimensions and capacities are supplied by the manufacturers. **Curb Weight:** base models, not including optional equipment. **Max. payload, lbs.** = gross amount; net payload may be lower due to optional equipment. **Engines: ohv** = overhead valve; **ohc** = overhead cam; **I** = inline cylinders; **V** = cylinders in V configuration; **flat** = horizontally opposed cylinders; **rpm** = revolutions per minute; **OD** = overdrive transmission; **S** = standard; **O** = optional; **NA** = not available.

Top: The same dashboard design is used in both Sidekick body styles. Above: A 2WD JS convertible.

Suzuki • Toyota

rougher roads, though ride is definitely truck-like and, at times, harsh.

Seats are comfortable enough for a compact sport-utility, though the rear bench is barely wide enough for two adults. All-round head room is abundant, but pushing the front seats fully aft forces rear-seaters to ride knees-up. Entry/exit is no picnic. Step-up is rather high, rear doorways quite narrow at the bottom.

The cargo area is just four feet wide and less than 20 inches long from rear seat to load sill. At least it's tall, and you can double volume by folding up the back seat, though even that nets you only 46 cubic feet total. The exterior-mount spare tire helps, but it hinders driver vision rearward. On the up side, the 5-door has the same convenient dash as Sidekick/Tracker convertibles.

Sidekick's size, relatively lightweight construction, and limited performance don't reassure us from a safety standpoint. Plus, prices are up over a year ago, from $450 on the 2WD JS convertible to a whopping $1570 on the top JLX model, which now approaches $17,000.

Mini-4x4s suffer too many shortcomings compared to cars of the same price. But as a second or third utility hauler that can double as an off-road fun machine, the Suzuki wagon makes more sense than most.

Prices

Suzuki Sidekick

	Retail Price	Dealer Invoice	Fair Price
JS 2WD 2-door conv., 5-speed	$11449	$10762	$10962
JS 2WD 2-door conv., 5-speed (New York and California)	11749	11044	11244
JS 2WD 2-door conv., automatic	12049	11326	11526
JS 2WD 2-door conv., automatic (New York and California)	12349	11608	11808
JX 4WD 2-door conv., 5-speed	12849	11821	12021
JX 4WD 2-door conv., 5-speed (New York and California)	13149	12097	12297
JX 4WD 2-door conv., automatic	13449	12373	12573
JX 4WD 2-door conv., automatic (New York and California)	13749	12649	12849
JS 2WD 5-door, 5-speed	12999	*	*
JX 4WD 5-door, 5-speed	14309	*	*
JX 4WD 5-door, automatic	15259	*	*
JLX 4WD 5-door, 5-speed	15719	*	*
JLX 4WD 5-door, automatic	16669	*	*
Destination charge, 2-door	330	330	330
5-door	350	350	350

Standard Equipment:

JS 2-door: 1.6-liter 4-cylinder engine, 5-speed manual transmission or 3-speed automatic transmission, rear-wheel drive, anti-lock rear brakes, cloth reclining front bucket seats and folding rear seat, center console, front door map pockets, fuel tank skid plate, folding canvas top, tinted glass, dual outside mirrors, intermittent wipers, trip odometer, carpeting, 195/75R15 tires. **JX 2-door** adds: part-time 4WD, 5-speed manual or 3-speed automatic transmission, automatic locking front hubs, 2-speed transfer case, power steering, power mirrors, tachometer, 205/75R15 tires. **JS 5-door** adds: 1.6-liter DOHC engine, 5-speed manual transmission, rear-wheel drive, power steering, power mirrors, rear defogger, child-safety rear door locks, carpeting, center console, locking fuel door, tinted glass, front map pockets, AM/FM cassette, reclining front bucket seats, cloth upholstery, split folding rear seat, fuel tank skid plate, tachometer, intermittent wipers, 195/75R15 tires. **JX 5-door** adds: 5-speed manual or 4-speed automatic transmission, part-time 4WD, automatic locking front hubs, 2-speed transfer case, 205/75R15 tires. **JLX 5-door** adds: tilt steering column, power windows and locks, cruise control, map lights, rear wiper/washer, remote fuel door release, deluxe upholstery, locking spare tire case, 205/75R15 outline white letter mud and snow tires, chrome wheels.

Options are available as dealer-installed accessories.

Toyota Land Cruiser

Toyota Land Cruiser

This big luxury sport-utility wagon from Japan is a virtual rerun this year. The only changes involve nine instead of five speakers for the standard audio system and adoption of safety belts with an automatic locking retractor feature for all passenger positions.

Body Styles/Chassis

Land Cruiser is a 5-door wagon with a drop-down tailgate and separate top-hinged rear window. Side door guard beams and a center high-mounted stoplamp are included.

Four-wheel anti-lock brakes are available as a $1180 extra-cost item, or as part of a $1930 option package that includes locking differentials (see below). Rear discs replace drums when the anti-lock system is fitted.

Payload capacity is 1765 pounds.

Powertrains

The only engine is a 212-horsepower 4.5-liter inline 6-cylinder with dual overhead camshafts and 4 valves per cylinder.

Land Cruiser's sole transmission is a 4-speed overdrive automatic with electronic shift controls.

Permanently engaged 4-wheel-drive is standard, as is a 2-speed transfer case, with a "Low" range for maximum traction in difficult off-road situations.

Optional are locking front and rear differentials operated by a dashboard switch. The system can be engaged when in low range and allows two opposing wheels to receive equal power and turn at the same speed for more traction capability.

A 5000-pound towing capacity is standard.

Accommodations

Land Cruiser has standard seating for five on reclining front buckets and a 3-place 50/50 split rear bench that double-folds for extra cargo space.

An optional 3-person third seat, also split 50/50, increases passenger capacity to eight. This seat also folds, but each half is hinged at the side to swing up for vertical stowage via straps secured to the rear-roof passenger assist grips. Deep-tinted privacy glass is included with the optional third-seat package.

No air bag is available.

*5-door dealer invoice and fair price not available at time of publication.

Toyota

Evaluation

Land Cruiser is an enormously capable sport-utility vehicle. It has the excellent assembly quality typical of Toyota products. And since Toyota sells all 8000 or so that it imports annually, a limited supply means it has a dash of exclusivity about it.

The price is enormous, too, when compared to the Ford Explorer and Jeep Grand Cherokee, which offer similar mechanical features at lower cost.

The Grand Cherokee, for instance, isn't as roomy but is available with a V-8 engine, permanently engaged 4WD, and a driver-side air bag.

Still, there's much to like about the Land Cruiser. With dual overhead cams and four valves per cylinder, its 4.5-liter engine is somewhat exotic for this class. But it gets the job done by supplying enough power and torque to move this rig's considerable weight.

The 4.5 gets the 4762-pound wagon off the line smartly, though with a heavy passenger/cargo load, Land Cruiser's pace slows noticeably going up hill or when trying to pass quickly. Weight remains the enemy of fuel economy, which probably won't be much above the abysmal 13 mpg we averaged.

Land Cruiser's permanent 4WD is a great convenience. It does the job without any input from the driver, and the available locking differentials furnish superb off-road traction.

A wide stance imparts stable cornering behavior, though body lean is noticed in this high-built wagon. Ride remains firm, almost stiff, but appropriate to the Cruiser's tough, truck-like character, though it can be uncomfortable on a long drive.

There's plenty of space in a surprisingly car-like interior, and both the second and optional third seats pack up easily to enlarge cargo volume to a generous 91 cubic feet.

We'd like to see anti-lock brakes made standard in a vehicle that starts at over $35,000, though.

Prices

Toyota Land Cruiser	Retail Price	Dealer Invoice	Fair Price
5-door 4WD wagon	$35298	*	*
Destination charge	385	385	385

Fair price not available at time of publication. Prices are for vehicles distributed by Toyota Motor Sales, U.S.A., Inc. The dealer invoice, fair price, and destination charge may be higher in areas served by independent distributors.

Standard Equipment:

4.5-liter DOHC 6-cylinder engine, 4-speed automatic transmission, permanent 4-wheel drive, power steering, air conditioning, cruise control, cloth reclining front bucket seats, middle seat center armrests, folding rear seat, power windows and locks, power mirrors, rear step bumper, console with storage, rear defogger and intermittent wiper/washer, remote fuel door release, tinted glass, rear heater, AM/FM cassette, digital clock with stopwatch and alarm, auto-off headlamps, skid plates for fuel tank and transfer case, tilt steering column, front and rear tow hooks, tachometer, voltmeter, oil pressure and coolant temperature gauges, trip odometer, variable intermittent wipers, passenger-side lighted visor mirror, transmission oil cooler, trailer towing wiring harness, 275/70R16 tires.

Optional Equipment:

Anti-lock disc brakes	1180	968	—
Premium AM/FM cassette w/CD player	800	600	—
Leather Trim Pkg.	4030	3224	—

Leather seats and door trim, leather-wrapped steering wheel, headrests, transmission lever, transfer case knob, leather covered center console, power seats, Third Seat Pkg.(Requires AM/FM cassette with CD.)

Differential locks	1930	1568	—

Lockable front and rear differentials, viscous coupling transfer case, full floating axle, anti-lock disc brakes.

Power moonroof	1150	920	—
Third Seat Pkg.	1395	1116	—

Includes split folding rear third seat, rear 3-point seat belts, cloth headrests, privacy glass, rear assist grips, sliding rear quarter windows.

Alloy wheels	515	412	—
2-tone paint	260	208	—

Specifications

	5-door wagon
Wheelbase, in.	112.2
Overall length, in.	188.2
Overall width, in.	76.0
Overall height, in.	70.3
Turn diameter, ft.	40.4
Curb weight, lbs.	4762
Fuel capacity, gal.	25.1

Passenger Area Dimensions

Seating capacity	8
Front head room, in.	40.7
Rear head room, in.	40.0
Front leg room, in.	42.2
Rear leg room, in.	33.6

Cargo Dimensions and Payloads

Cargo area length, in.	63.3
Cargo area width, in.	53.3
Cargo area width between wheels, in.	44.0
Cargo area height, in.	42.2
Cargo vol., cu. ft.	91.1
Max. payload, lbs.	1765
Max. trailer weight, lbs.	5000

Engines

	dohv I-6
Size, liters/cu. in.	4.5/275
Horsepower @ rpm	212 @ 4600
Torque (lbs./ft.) @ rpm	275 @ 3200
Availability	S

EPA city/highway mpg

4-speed OD automatic	12/15

Built in Japan.

KEY: Dimensions and capacities are supplied by the manufacturers. **Curb Weight:** base models, not including optional equipment. **Max. payload, lbs.** = gross amount; net payload may be lower due to optional equipment. **Engines: ohv** = overhead valve; **ohc** = overhead cam; **I** = inline cylinders; **V** = cylinders in V configuration; **flat** = horizontally opposed cylinders; **rpm** = revolutions per minute; **OD** = overdrive transmission; **S** = standard; **O** = optional; **NA** = not available.

Cabin is roomy and car-like, but lacks a driver-side air bag.

Dealer invoice and fair price not available at time of publication.

Toyota

Toyota Pickup

Toyota 2WD pickup

Toyota's line of compact pickups returns for 1994 without a long-bed body style but with new safety features for the remaining regular-cab and extended-cab models.

This is the second consecutive year Toyota has trimmed its compact pickup lineup in deference to its larger T100 pickup, which was introduced last year and is covered in a separate report.

Body Styles/Chassis

Regular-cab models have a 103-inch wheelbase. The stretched-cab Xtracab has a 121.9-inch wheelbase. Both have cargo beds 6.2 feet long. The discontinued long-bed regular-cab model had a 112-inch wheelbase and 7.2-foot bed.

Both 2- and 4-wheel-drive models come in Deluxe (DX), DX V-6, and SR5 V-6 trim. All SR5 V-6 models are Xtracabs, and there's also a base-level 2WD model in the regular-cab body style.

Regular-cab models have a 3-place bench seat. DX Xtracab models have front bucket seats; Xtracab SR5 V-6s come with a 60/40 split front bench and buckets are optional. Also on Xtracabs, dual forward-facing rear jump seats are standard on the 4WD SR5 V-6 model, optional on the others. Flip-out rear side windows are Xtracab standards and so are rear shoulder belts when the jump seats are fitted.

New safety features on the 1994 models include side door guard beams and a center high-mounted stoplamp, both of which are required on trucks this year.

Rear-wheel anti-lock brakes (ABS) are standard on SR5 V-6s and optional on all other models when power steering is ordered. This is because unlike conventional anti-lock systems, which draw power from engine vacuum, Toyota's system uses the power steering pump to activate the brake actuator. On 4x4s, ABS operates only in 2WD.

Top payload for 2WD models is 1895 pounds, on the regular-cab short bed with manual transmission. Top payload for 4x4s is 2015 pounds, on the regular-cab DX with manual transmission.

Powertrains

A 116-horsepower 2.4-liter 4-cylinder engine is the base engine. A 150-horsepower 3.0-liter V-6 is standard on SR5 V-6 models and is available on DX Xtracabs and on a 4WD DX regular-cab model.

Both engines are available with either a 5-speed manual transmission or a 4-speed automatic.

Two on-demand 4WD systems are used; both employ a floor-mounted transfer-case lever and neither is for use on dry pavement. The base system has manual locking hubs and requires that the truck be stopped before engagement. Available at additional cost is Toyota's 4WDemand. This has automatic locking front hubs and permits shift-on-the-fly between 2WD and 4WD High at any speed below 50 mph.

All of Toyota's compact pickups can tow trailers up to 3500 pounds. However, 2WD models with the automatic transmission have a standard 2000-pound towing limit. An optional towing package is required to reach the 3500-pound maximum.

Evaluation

Toyota continues to pare back its compact-pickup line where it might overlap the new T100, which is a larger, heavier, costlier pickup with a bigger cargo bed, but no available stretched cab.

Specifications

	Short bed	Xtracab
Wheelbase, in.	103.0	121.9
Overall length, in.	174.4	193.1
Overall width, in.	66.5	66.5
Overall height, in.	60.8	61.0
Turn diameter, ft.	35.4	41.3
Curb weight, lbs.	2690[1]	2970[2]
Fuel capacity, gal.	13.7	17.2

1. 3365 lbs., 4WD. 2. 3550 lbs., 4WD.

Passenger Area Dimensions

Seating capacity	3	5
Front head room, in.	38.3	38.6
Rear head room, in.	—	37.4
Front leg room, in.	41.5	43.7
Rear leg room, in.	—	NA

Cargo Dimensions and Payloads

Cargo area length, in.	75.0	75.0
Cargo area width, in.	59.7	59.7
Cargo area width between wheels, in.	41.0	41.0
Cargo area height, in.	15.9	15.9
Max. payload, lbs.	2015	1820
Max. trailer weight, lbs.	3500	3500

Engines

	ohc I-4	ohc V-6
Size, liters/cu. in.	2.4/144	3.0/181
Horsepower @ rpm	116 @ 4800	150 @ 4800
Torque (lbs./ft.) @ rpm	140 @ 2800	180 @ 3400
Availability	S	O

EPA city/highway mpg

5-speed OD manual	22/27	16/21
4-speed OD automatic	22/25	18/22

Built in Fremont, Calif., and Japan.

KEY: Dimensions and capacities are supplied by the manufacturers. **Curb Weight:** base models, not including optional equipment. **Max. payload, lbs.** = gross amount; net payload may be lower due to optional equipment. **Engines: ohv** = overhead valve; **ohc** = overhead cam; **I** = inline cylinders; **V** = cylinders in V configuration; **flat** = horizontally opposed cylinders; **rpm** = revolutions per minute; **OD** = overdrive transmission; **S** = standard; **O** = optional; **NA** = not available.

Toyota

Last year, Toyota shelved the long-bed 4x4 and the 2WD long-bed workhorse One Ton model. The latter had a payload of 2520 pounds, just 50 pounds less than the heftiest T100 model, and its 5000-pound towing limit matched that of the base T100.

This year, it kills the compact pickup's 7.2-foot cargo bed, which threatened to infringe on the 8-foot bed of the T100.

Toyota's is the best-selling import-brand compact pickup in the U.S. The company expects current owners to form the core of its T100 audience, and eliminating any potential overlap may help encourage them to move up to the larger truck.

Such brand loyalty is a good bet because independent surveys show that owners of Toyota's pickups are among the most satisfied in this market segment.

Indeed, we've been impressed by these trucks' quality design and assembly. Unfortunately, they also can be costly. Our test 5-speed 4WD Xtracab SR5 V-6 with a host of options had a price just shy of $20,000. That's a lot for a compact pickup.

Toyota's V-6 is a little smoother than Nissan's, the import sales runner-up. But neither has the muscle of the larger Ford or General Motors V-6s. Nonetheless, our SR5 V-6 ran 0-60 mph in 13.1 seconds—not bad for a curb weight of more than 3800 pounds. Braking also was laudable, with short stopping distances and good resistance to rear-wheel locking.

Cab comfort, quietness, and driving ease also rate high. And the ride is reasonably comfortable, even on the tautly sprung 4x4s. Cornering is stable and assured, and the 4WDemand system is easy to use and much more convenient than the basic Toyota system.

Less impressive is the tighter rear seat room in Toyota's Xtracab versus the Nissan King Cab or Isuzu's Spacecab. And step-in height of the 4x4 is a bit taller than most. Payload and towing capacities are about the Japanese norm, but below the domestics.

Toyota builds a fine compact pickup, but it's not a great value unless you buy only the equipment you really need and will use.

Prices

Toyota 2WD Pickups

	Retail Price	Dealer Invoice	Fair Price
Short bed, 5-speed	$10118	*	*
DX short bed, 5-speed	10998	*	*
DX short bed, automatic	11718	*	*
DX Xtracab short bed, 5-speed	12568	*	*
DX Xtracab short bed, automatic	13288	*	*
DX V-6 Xtracab short bed, 5-speed	13718	*	*
DX V-6 Xtracab short bed, automatic	14698	*	*
SR5 V-6 Xtracab short bed, 5-speed	15698	*	*
SR5 V-6 Xtracab short bed, automatic	16659	*	*
Destination charge	385	385	385

Prices are for vehicles distributed by Toyota Motor Sales, U.S.A., Inc. The dealer invoice, fair price, and destination charge may be higher in areas served by independent distributors.

Standard Equipment:

2.4-liter 4-cylinder engine, 5-speed manual transmission, vinyl tilt forward bench seat, coolant temperature gauge, one-touch tailgate release, black left outside mirror, cargo bed tie down hooks, cup holder, 195/75R14 tires, full-

Top: Most models have a simple dashboard and a cloth-covered bench seat; Xtracabs can have front buckets. Middle: Xtracab models can also get two rear jump seats; they're standard on 4WD SR5 V-6 models like this one. Above: The 7.2-foot long cargo box is dropped, so Toyota's compact pickups all have a 6.2-foot bed. Shown is a regular-cab 4x4.

*Dealer invoice and fair price not available at time of publication.

Toyota

size spare. **DX** adds: 2.4-liter 4-cylinder engine or 3.0-liter V-6 engine, 5-speed manual or 4-speed automatic transmission, power steering (V-6), dual outside mirrors, tinted windshield glass, cloth upholstery, upgraded door trim, day/night rearview mirror, cigarette lighter, full carpet, full wheel covers. **Xtracab** adds: reclining bucket seats, flip-out rear quarter windows, rear cab storage compartments, rear mud guards, 205/75R14 all-season tires. **SR5** adds: 3.0-liter V-6 engine, anti-lock rear brakes, 60/40 split folding seat, dual foward-facing rear jump seats, power steering, tilt steering column, digital clock, tachometer, oil pressure and coolant temperature gauges, trip odometer, AM/FM radio, variable intermittent wipers, door map pockets, passenger-side visor mirror.

Optional Equipment:

	Retail Price	Dealer Invoice	Fair Price
Anti-lock rear brakes	$300	$255	$275
Requires power steering.			
Power steering (std. V-6)	290	246	266
Chrome Pkg., DX	180	144	161
SR5	160	128	143
Chrome front bumper, grille, windshield moldings and door handles.			
Comfort Pkg., DX Xtracab	270	216	241
60/40 split bench seat, cloth rear jump seats.			
Cruise Control Pkg.,			
DX Xtracab	265	212	237
SR5 Xtracab	385	308	344
Cruise control, variable speed intermittent wipers; SR5 adds leather-wrapped steering wheel.			
Power Pkg., SR5	735	588	657
Power windows and locks, power mirrors, power antenna; requires Cruise Control Pkg.			
Sports Pkg., SR5	310	248	277
Rear quarter privacy glass, cloth sport seats with head restraints, rear storage console; requires Chrome Pkg.			
Touring Pkg., DX 5-speed	115	92	103
Tachometer, trip odometer, halogen headlamps.			
Alloy Wheel Pkg., SR5	765	612	683
215/65R15 tires on alloy wheels, chrome wheel opening moldings; requires Chrome Pkg.			
Value Pkg., DX	414	373	391
Xtracab	534	481	504
DX V-6 Xtracab	344	310	325
SR5 Xtracab	405	365	382
Sliding rear window, power steering, Chrome Pkg., chrome rear bumper, rear jump seat with 3-point seatbelts (Xtracab), 60/40 front split bench seat (Xtracab), AM/FM radio, floormats.			
Window Pkg.	200	160	179
Front vent windows, sliding rear window.			
Cloth Pkg., base	105	84	94
Cloth bench seat, carpet, day/night rearview mirror, cigarette lighter.			
Front vent windows	65	52	58
Metallic paint, base	120	76	97
AM/FM radio	240	180	208
AM/FM cassette, DX regular cab			
(2 speakers)	455	341	395
DX Xtracab (4 speakers)	555	416	482
SR5 Xtracab (4 speakers)	315	236	273
Premium AM/FM cassette, SR5	630	472	547
Moonroof, SR5	380	304	339
Tilt steering column, DX	155	132	142
Includes variable intermittent wipers.			
All Weather Guard Pkg.	65	55	60
Towing Pkg., 2.4/automatic	50	40	45
3.0/automatic	65	52	58

Toyota 4WD Pickups

	Retail Price	Dealer Invoice	Fair Price
DX short bed, 5-speed	$14448	$12642	$12942
DX short bed, automatic	15348	13429	13729
DX Xtracab, 5-speed	15988	13750	14250
DX V-6 short bed, 5-speed	15698	13736	14236
DX V-6 Xtracab, 5-speed	17218	14807	15307
DX V-6 Xtracab, automatic	18448	15865	16365
SR5 V-6 Xtracab, 5-speed	$19148	$16180	$16880
SR5 V-6 Xtracab, automatic	20368	17211	17711
Destination charge	385	385	385

Prices are for vehicles distributed by Toyota Motor Sales, U.S.A., Inc. The dealer invoice, fair price, and destination charge may be higher in areas served by independent distributors.

Standard Equipment:

DX: 2.4-liter 4-cylinder engine or 3.0-liter V-6, 5-speed manual or 4-speed automatic transmission, power steering (V-6), manual locking front hubs, cloth bench seat, locking fuel door, cargo area tie down hooks, cup holders, coolant temperature gauge, skid plates, carpeting, tinted glass, dual outside mirrors, intermittent wipers, front and rear mudguards, 225/75R15 mud and snow tires. **Xtracab models** add: reclining front bucket seats, flip-out rear quarter windows, rear cab storage compartments, 31X10.5 mud and snow tires (V-6). **SR5** adds: 3.0-liter V-6 engine, anti-lock rear brakes, 4WDemand, power steering, 60/40 split bench seat, digital clock, halogen headlights, tachometer, oil pressure gauge, voltmeter, trip odometer, AM/FM radio, tilt steering column, variable speed intermittent wipers.

Optional Equipment:

	Retail	Dealer	Fair
Anti-lock rear brakes	300	255	275
Requires power steering.			
4Wheel Demand, DX V-6	210	178	193
Power steering (std. V-6)	290	246	266
Chrome Pkg.	180	144	161
Chrome front bumper, grille, windshield moldings and door handles.			
Comfort Pkg., DX Xtracab	270	216	241
60/40 split bench seat, cloth rear jump seats.			
Cruise Control Pkg., DX Xtracab	265	212	237
SR5	385	308	344
Cruise control, variable speed intermittent wipers; SR5 adds leather-wrapped steering wheel.			
Power Pkg., SR5	735	588	657
Power windows and locks, power mirrors, power antenna; requires Cruise Control Pkg.			
Sports Pkg., SR5	310	248	277
Rear quarter privacy glass, cloth sport seats with head restraints, rear storage console; requires Chrome Pkg.			
Touring Pkg., V-6	115	92	103
4-cylinder	155	124	138
Tachometer, trip odometer, halogen headlamps.			
Wheel Pkg., SR5	885	708	791
10.5R15 tires on steel wheels, wheel opening moldings; requires Chrome Pkg.			
Styled steel wheels, DX V-6	580	464	518
10.5R15 tires, silversteel wheels, larger wheel opening moldings.			
Value Pkg., DX	464	418	438
Xtracab	534	481	504
DX V-6	244	202	221
DX V-6 Xtracab	344	310	325
SR5 Xtracab	405	365	382
Sliding rear window, power steering, Chrome Pkg., chrome rear bumper, rear jump seat with 3-point seatbelts (Xtracab), 60/40 front split bench seat (Xtracab), AM/FM radio, floormats.			
Window Pkg.	200	160	179
Front vent windows, sliding rear window.			
Front vent windows	65	52	58
Metallic paint, base	120	76	97
AM/FM radio	240	180	208
AM/FM cassette, DX regular cab			
(2 speakers)	455	341	395
DX Xtracab (4 speakers)	555	416	482
SR5 Xtracab (4 speakers)	315	236	273
Premium AM/FM cassette, SR5	630	472	547
Moonroof, SR5	380	304	339
Tilt steering column, DX	155	132	142
Includes variable intermittent wipers.			
All Weather Guard Pkg.	65	55	60

Toyota Previa

Toyota Previa LE

Toyota's minivan adds a standard passenger-side air bag and an available supercharged engine for '94. Plus, all models get a slightly restyled front bumper and spoiler.

Previa became the first minivan to meet all passenger-car safety requirements in 1992 when it gained a driver-side air bag and other features.

Body Styles/Chassis

Previa comes in a single body length with a sliding right-rear door and a one-piece liftgate. A pull-down strap on the inside of the liftgate is a new feature this year.

Two trim levels, DX (Deluxe) and LE continue, each offered with rear-wheel drive or "All-Trac" permanently engaged all-wheel drive (see below). Models with the supercharged engine are due in showrooms in February and will be offered in the LE trim only. They'll be tagged the LE S/C and LE S/C All-Trac.

Previa's unusual "front/mid-engine" layout puts the engine beneath the floor between and slightly behind the front seats.

Anti-lock brakes (ABS) are optional on all models. When ordered on the DX versions, ABS includes rear disc brakes to match the 4-wheel-disc arrangement that's standard on the LE models.

Maximum payload rating is 1760 pounds.

Powertrains

The base engine remains a 138-horsepower 2.4-liter 4-cylinder.

Adding a supercharger to this engine results in a rating of 161 horsepower, an increase of 16 percent over the naturally aspirated engine. The supercharged engine also delivers a 24-percent increase in torque, from 154 pounds/feet to 201.

Both these engines employ a remote accessory drive that puts radiator fan, air-conditioner compressor, alternator, and power steering components in the nose beneath a small hatch for service access from outside the vehicle. Also housed up front are the air filter, battery and major fluid reservoirs, including a translucent 2-liter oil tank from which the engine is automatically replenished when needed.

The engine itself is reached from inside through a small floor panel or from underneath the vehicle. To minimize the need for that, Toyota specifies long-life and low-maintenance engine components such as platinum-tipped 60,000-mile spark plugs.

A 5-speed manual transmission that had been standard on 2WD DX models is discontinued, so all Previas come only with an electronically controlled 4-speed overdrive automatic transmission with column shift.

Specifications

	4-door van
Wheelbase, in.	112.8
Overall length, in.	187.0
Overall width, in.	70.8
Overall height, in.	68.7
Turn diameter, ft.	37.4
Curb weight, lbs.	3610[1]
Fuel capacity, gal.	19.8

1. All-Trac, 3830 lbs.

Passenger Area Dimensions

Seating capacity	7
Front head room, in.	39.4
Rear head room, in.	38.9
Front leg room, in.	40.1
Rear leg room, in.	36.6

Available Seating

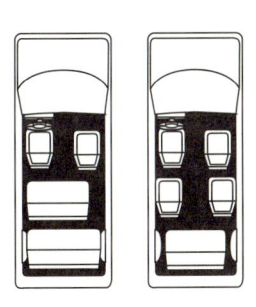

Cargo Dimensions and Payloads

Cargo area length, in.	96.9
Cargo area width, in.	64.0
Cargo area width between wheels, in.	48.4
Cargo area height, in.	45.7
Cargo vol., cu. ft.	157.8
Max. payload, lbs.	1760
Max. trailer weight, lbs.	3500

Engines

	dohc I-4	Supercharged dohc I-4
Size, liters/cu. in.	2.4/149	2.4/149
Horsepower @ rpm	138 @ 5000	161 @ 5000
Torque (lbs./ft.) @ rpm	154 @ 4000	201 @ 3600
Availability	S	S[1]

EPA city/highway mpg
4-speed OD automatic ... 17/22   NA

1. LE S/C and LE S/C All-Trac.

Built in Japan.

KEY: Dimensions and capacities are supplied by the manufacturers. **Curb Weight:** base models, not including optional equipment. **Max. payload, lbs.** = gross amount; net payload may be lower due to optional equipment. **Engines: ohv** = overhead valve; **ohc** = overhead cam; **I** = inline cylinders; **V** = cylinders in V configuration; **flat** = horizontally opposed cylinders; **rpm** = revolutions per minute; **OD** = overdrive transmission; **S** = standard; **O** = optional; **NA** = not available.

Toyota

A passenger-side air bag joins Previa's driver-side air bag for '94. Rearmost seats hinge to stow against the walls.

All-Trac models have permanently engaged 4-wheel drive. They use an electronically controlled viscous-coupling center differential. This normally divides engine torque 50/50 front/rear, but can bias the split according to whichever axle has greater grip.

Maximum towing capacity is 3500 pounds on all models.

Accommodations

Seats for seven are standard. DX models have a 2-place middle bench and a non-removable 3-passenger third seat. Still exclusive to LEs is a 4-seat "captain's chair" option with middle buckets that swivel 180 degrees.

All middle seats have fore/aft adjustment and are removable via quick-release clamps. Third seats have reclining backrests and are side-hinged to fold up against the cabin walls, secured by straps, for extra cargo space.

The passenger-side air bag joins the standard driver-side air bag. Among other changes are a new steering wheel and new front bucket seats with adjustable headrests. A 6-speaker stereo is now standard on DX models. CFC-free refrigerant is now used in the air conditioning system.

Evaluation

Standard dual air bags and other safety features make this roomy, versatile minivan attractive as a family vehicle. And the supercharged engine makes it even more attractive.

However, there's still too much engine noise and Previa remains priced at the very top of this class, where well-equipped Chrysler Corporation minivans with smoother V-6 engines are better values.

We clocked a rear-drive Previa LE at 12.4 seconds to 60 mph. That's respectable for a 4-cylinder minivan and acceleration is fairly brisk from low speeds. But there's not enough torque for confident passing above about 40 mph, and the engine sounds harsh all the time and feels coarse during hard acceleration.

A prototype LE S/C we tested was more responsive off the line and felt more capable in passing or merging situations. The supercharged engine was still raspy, however, unlike the smoother V-6s in most rivals.

All-Trac models are heavier and thus a bit less responsive. But on slippery pavement, their unobtrusive 4WD provides a dimension of security unmatched by the rear-drive versions.

Previa's overall length falls between the long and short versions of the popular front-drive Dodge Caravan/Plymouth Voyager, but the Toyota is taller than most every other minivan. Previa thus seems a tad bulky in the urban grind, but compensates with ample passenger room and good cargo space even with all seats in place. Wind noise is higher than the slick styling implies. But tire rumble is muted, the ride is comfortable, and braking is good.

Previa boasts Toyota's reputation for reliability and solid workmanship. High prices remain a sore point—and they're up an average of $3100 over last year at this time for the naturally aspirated models. The new supercharged versions add another $1580 on top of that. The best bet is to stay with a DX model and go easy on the extras.

Prices

Toyota Previa	Retail Price	Dealer Invoice	Fair Price
DX 2WD	$22818	*	*
LE 2WD	26578	*	*
LE S/C 2WD	28158	*	*
LE S/C All-Trac	26148	*	*
DX All-Trac	29718	*	*
LE S/C All-Trac	31298	*	*
Destination charge	385	385	385

Dealer invoice, fair price and LE S/C standard equipment and options not available at time of publication.

Prices are for vehicles distributed by Toyota Motor Sales, U.S.A., Inc. The dealer invoice, fair price, and destination charge may be higher in areas served by independent distributors.

Standard Equipment:

DX: 2.4-liter DOHC 4-cylinder engine, 4-speed automatic transmission, driver- and passenger-side air bags, power steering, tilt steering column, cloth reclining front bucket seats, 2-passenger center seat, 3-passenger split-folding rear seat, AM/FM radio, rear defogger, variable intermittent wipers, rear intermittent wiper/washer, auto-off headlamps, tinted glass, digital clock, dual outside mirrors, tilt-out rear quarter windows, wheel covers, 215/65R15 all-season tires, full-size tire. **LE** adds: dual air conditioners, 4-wheel disc brakes, cruise control, power windows and door locks, power mirrors, AM/FM cassette, upgraded upholstery and interior trim, passenger-side lighted visor mirror. **All-Trac** adds permanently engaged 4-wheel drive.

Optional Equipment:

Anti-lock brakes, DX	1100	899	1000
Includes rear disc brakes.			
Anti-lock brakes, LE	950	779	865
Dual air conditioners, DX	1685	1348	1517
Power Pkg., DX	745	596	671
Power windows and locks, power mirrors.			
Privacy glass, LE	385	308	347
Cruise control, DX	275	220	248
AM/FM cassette, DX	170	127	149
Premium AM/FM cassette, LE	435	326	381
Premium AM/FM cassette with CD, LE	1275	956	1116
Dual power moonroofs, LE 2WD	1550	1240	1395
Captain's chairs with armrests, LE	790	632	711
Theft deterrent system, DX	945	756	851
Includes Power Pkg.			
Theft deterrent system, LE	200	160	180
Alloy wheels, LE	420	336	378

Dealer invoice and fair price not available at time of publication.

Toyota T100

Toyota T100 2WD

A driver-side air bag and the addition of a 4-cylinder as the new base engine are among the changes in the T100's second model year.

This is the first Japanese pickup to break out of the compact class. It was designed specifically for the U.S. market and slots between the mid-size Dodge Dakota and the full-size trucks from Ford, General Motors, and Dodge.

Body Styles/Chassis

The T100 comes only as a regular cab model with a 121.8-inch wheelbase and 209-inch overall length. Its 8-foot-long cargo bed is wide enough so that 4-foot wide panels can lay flat on the floor. (By comparison, the base Ford F-150 has a wheelbase of 116.8 inches, an overall length of 197.1, and a 6.8-foot bed. The regular-cab F-150 with an 8-foot bed has a 133-inch wheelbase and a 213-inch overall length.)

The 4-cylinder model bows in a new entry-level T100 model available in 2-wheel-drive only. The V-6 models come in DX and SR5 trim in 2- and 4-wheel drive. Plus, there's a 2WD DX V-6 One-Ton model.

In addition to the driver-side air bag, all T100s gain side-door guard beams and a center high-mounted stoplamp. Cargo-bed tie-down hooks also are new for all models.

A 3-place bench seat is standard; SR5 models get a 60/40 split bench and a folding center armrest. There is a small storage space behind the seats, and the SR5 has a built-in tool box.

Last year, rear anti-lock brakes (ABS) were standard on all models. This year, rear ABS is optional on the 4-cylinder and DX models and standard only on the SR5s. The anti-lock system works only in 2WD.

Payload capacity is 1680 pounds on the 4-cylinder T100, 1650 on the base T100, and 2750 pounds on the One-Ton.

Powertrains

The new model uses a dual-overhead cam 2.7-liter 4-cylinder engine rated at 150 horsepower.

All others have a single-overhead cam 150-horsepower V-6, the same engine used in Toyota's compact pickups and the 4Runner sport-utility vehicle.

A 5-speed manual transmission is standard on all models and is the only transmission available on the 4-cylinder T100. A 4-speed automatic with a steering-column shift lever is available on all other models.

The 4x4s use the 4Wheel Demand system also available in the compact Toyota trucks. It's not for use on dry pavement, but has automatic locking front hubs and a floor-mounted transfer case lever for shifting between 2WD and 4WD High at speeds up to 50 mph.

Towing capacity is 5000 pounds for all 2WD models, 5500 pounds for 4x4s, and 6000 pounds for the One-Ton.

Evaluation

Toyota had hoped to sell 60,000 T100s in its first model year, but sales totaled only 21,171. Blame was cast in several directions, starting with a price that's higher than comparable 6-cylinder domestic trucks.

That remains an issue for 1994, as T100 prices increase from nearly $1000 on the base V-6 model to a whopping $2350 for the top-line 4WD SR5 compared to a year ago. Part of the problem is the 25-percent import tariff placed on the T100. The escalating value of the Japanese yen has also done its part to boost prices.

Several new "value" option packages bow for 1994 as a way to group popular extra-cost items at a discount. And

Specifications

	Regular cab
Wheelbase, in.	121.8
Overall length, in.	209.1
Overall width, in.	75.2
Overall height, in.	66.7
Turn diameter, ft.	38.7
Curb weight, lbs.	3320[1]
Fuel capacity, gal.	24.3

1. 3875 lbs., 4WD.

Passenger Area Dimensions

Seating capacity	3
Front head room, in.	39.6
Rear head room, in.	—
Front leg room, in.	41.3
Rear leg room, in.	—

Cargo Dimensions and Payloads

Cargo area length, in.	97.8
Cargo area width, in.	NA
Cargo area width between wheels, in.	49.2
Cargo area height, in.	NA
Max. payload, lbs.	2570
Max. trailer weight, lbs.	6000

Engines

	dohc I-4	ohc V-6
Size, liters/cu. in.	2.7/163	3.0/181
Horsepower @ rpm	150 @ 4800	150 @ 4800
Torque (lbs./ft.) @ rpm	177 @ 4000	180 @ 3400
Availability	S	S

EPA city/highway mpg

5-speed OD manual	NA	16/21
4-speed OD automatic		16/20

Built in Japan.

KEY: Dimensions and capacities are supplied by the manufacturers. **Curb Weight:** base models, not including optional equipment. **Max. payload, lbs.** = gross amount; net payload may be lower due to optional equipment. **Engines: ohv** = overhead valve; **ohc** = overhead cam; **I** = inline cylinders; **V** = cylinders in V configuration; **flat** = horizontally opposed cylinders; **rpm** = revolutions per minute; **OD** = overdrive transmission; **S** = standard; **O** = optional; **NA** = not available.

Toyota

at $12,998, the new price-leader 4-cylinder model starts at $1000 less than last year's base V-6. That still doesn't address another criticism of the T100, however.

Most full-size domestic pickups are sold with V-8s, and a V-8 has been a popular choice among buyers of the mid-size Dodge Dakota. Toyota says a V-8 is not currently planned for the T100.

Lack of an extended-cab body was another shortfall, though Toyota now says it will attempt to introduce one as early as the 1995 model year.

The company says it plans to shift the T100's sales pitch to an upscale audience. That may be appropriate, for what the T100 lacks in the brawn demanded by tradesmen and farmers it makes up for in finesse and refinement. It also carries Toyota's reputation for quality and reliability, and independent surveys of customer satisfaction rated it near the top among all pickups in its first year.

We haven't driven a 4-cylinder model, but take note that the four has the same horsepower rating as the V-6, and nearly the same torque.

Acceleration in a 2WD V-6 with the 5-speed manual transmission feels more than adequate and the engine operates smoothly and quietly. With automatic, the engine doesn't feel as lively, particularly in passing situations and when climbing hills. On the 4x4s, which weigh some 550 pounds more, progress is noticeably slower and the engine sounds strained in hard acceleration.

In other dynamic areas, the T100 is downright pleasant. The 2WD models absorb most bumps easily. There's too much bouncing on wavy roads with an empty cargo bed, but the T100 is more stable than a lot of big pickups. Steering and handling are better, too.

The additional weight in the 4WD models is noticed in ride and handling. Bumps seem more prominent, though there's less bouncing on uneven surfaces.

Wind noise is moderate and road noise is minimal.

The T100's interior earns high marks in most areas, but the narrow space behind the seats is only enough for a few hand tools, a lunch bucket, and such. Door map pockets, the glove box, and a small covered bin in the center armrest provide adequate storage for little stuff.

The interior is wide enough for three adults. The one in the middle, however, has to rest his feet on the transmission tunnel and sit with his knees an inch or two from the stereo. The dashboard is modern and convenient, though when the dual cupholders at the top of the dash are being used, you can't reach the climate controls.

The bottom line is that if you want more than a compact pickup, but don't need an extended cab or a V-8 engine and think refinement is worth paying for, the T100 is a great way to go.

Prices

Toyota T100	Retail Price	Dealer Invoice	Fair Price
2WD Half-ton, 4-cylinder 5-speed	$12998	*	*
2WD DX Half-ton, V-6 5-speed	14918	*	*
2WD DX Half-ton, V-6 automatic	15819	*	*
2WD SR5 Half-ton, V-6 5-speed	17018	*	*
2WD SR5 Half-ton, V-6 automatic	17918	*	*
2WD DX One-ton, V-6 5-speed	15665	*	*
2WD DX One-ton, V-6 automatic	16568	*	*
4WD DX Half-ton, V-6 5-speed	18438	*	*
4WD DX Half-ton, V-6 automatic	19338	*	*
4WD SR5 Half-ton, V-6 5-speed	20478	*	*
4WD SR5 Half-ton, V-6 automatic	21378	*	*

	Retail Price	Dealer Invoice	Fair Price
Destination charge	$385	$385	$385

2WD Half-ton 4-cylinder prices and options not available at time of publication. Prices are for vehicles distributed by Toyota Motor Sales, U.S.A., Inc. The dealer invoice, fair price, and destination charge may be higher in areas served by independent distributers.

Standard Equipment:

2.7-liter DOHC 4-cylinder engine, 5-speed manual transmission, driver-side air bag, vinyl bench seat with center armrest, tinted glass, intermittent wipers, cup holders, door map pockets, front and rear mud guards, 215/75R15 tires. **DX** adds: 3.0-liter V-6 engine, 5-speed manual or 4-speed automatic transmission, power steering, cloth bench seat with center armrest, carpeting, dual outside mirrors, skid plates (4WD), day/night mirror, front tow hooks (4WD), digital clock, cigarette lighter, trip odometer, wheel covers (2WD), styled steel wheels (4WD), 235/75R15 (4WD). **SR5** adds: anti-lock rear brakes, split 60/40 cloth bench seat with center storage armrest, tilt steering column, AM/FM radio, chrome front bumper, grille, windshield moldings, door and tailgate handles, upgraded door trim panels, tachometer, trip odometer, map lights, passenger-side visor mirror, sliding rear window, tool storage & cover, variable speed intermittent wipers, 235/75R15 tires.

Optional Equipment:

Anti-lock rear brakes, DX	300	255	278
Convenience Pkg., DX	445	367	406
with cruise control	730	595	663
Tilt steering column, sliding rear window, tachometer, oil pressure gauge, voltmeter, variable speed intermittent wipers.			
Cruise Control Pkg., DX	345	279	312
SR5	360	288	324
Cruise control, leather-wrapped steering wheel, variable-intermittent wipers.			
Power Pkg., SR5	735	588	662
Power windows and locks, dual chrome power mirrors, power antenna. Requires Cruise Control.			
Chrome Pkg., DX	150	120	135
Chrome front bumper, grille, windshield molding, door and tailgate handles.			
Value Pkg., DX One-ton and DX 4WD Half-ton	206	185	196
DX 2WD Half-ton	331	298	315
Air conditioning, Chrome Pkg., chrome rear bumper, bodyside moldings, carpeted floormats. DX 2WD Half-ton adds: 235/75R15 tires.			
Value Pkg., SR5	1401	1261	1331
Air conditioning, Power Pkg., chrome rear bumper, cruise control, variable intermittent wipers, leather-wrapped steering wheel, bodyside moldings, carpeted floormats.			
Value/Two-Tone Pkg., DX One-ton and DX 4WD Half-ton	436	392	414
DX 2WD Half-ton	561	505	533
SR5	1631	1468	1550
Value Pkg. plus 2-tone paint. Deletes bodyside moldings.			
2-tone paint, DX	400	320	360
SR5	330	264	297
Includes chrome front bumper (std. SR5).			
Chrome Pkg. and 2-tone paint, DX	480	384	432
Radio Prep Pkg., DX	50	37	44
Wheel Pkg., DX 4WD	265	212	239
31-10.5 tires, styled steel wheels.			
Alloy wheel Pkg., SR5 2WD	590	472	531
SR5 4WD	735	588	662
Alloy wheels, chrome wheel opening moldings, 235/75R15 tires (2WD), 31-10.5 tires (4WD).			
AM/FM radio, DX	240	180	210
AM/FM cassette, DX	615	461	538
SR5	170	127	149
Premium cassette player with equalizer, SR5	525	394	460
Premium 3-in-one combo, SR5	1325	994	1160
Premium AM/FM cassette & CD player, programmable equalizer, 7-speakers.			
Sliding rear window, DX 4WD	135	108	122
235/75R15 mud & snow tires, DX 2WD Half-ton	125	100	113

Dealer invoice and fair price not available at time of publication.

Toyota 4Runner

Toyota 4Runner V-6 4WD

An available 4-wheel anti-lock brake system highlights the changes to this compact sport-utility vehicle.

All 4Runners also gain a center high-mounted stoplamp and side door guard beams, which are required on truck-based vehicles this year.

Body Styles/Chassis

Toyota dropped the 3-door body style for 1993, so all 4Runners are 5-door wagons with a bottom-hinged tailgate with power drop-down window. The spare tire is carried in a rear underbody cradle.

The standard braking system consists of front discs and rear drums. Rear anti-lock control is standard on 6-cylinder 4Runners and a $300 option on 4-cylinder models.

The new 4-wheel anti-lock feature is available only on 4Runners with the V-6 engine and costs an additional $660.

Maximum payloads are 1610 pounds with 2WD, 1550 with 4WD.

Powertrains

The 4-cylinder 4Runner continues with 4WD and a 2.4-liter engine rated at 116 horsepower.

The V-6 models are available in 2WD or 4WD and use a 3.0-liter with 150 horsepower.

A 5-speed manual is the only transmission offered with the 4-cylinder engine and is available on the 4WD V-6 model. A 4-speed electronically controlled automatic is optional on the 4WD V-6 and is the only transmission available on the 2WD V-6.

Toyota's 4WDemand system is standard on 4x4 models. It is an on-demand part-time system not for use on dry pavement. A floor-mounted transfer-case lever and automatic locking front hubs allow shifting between 2WD and 4-wheel High up to 50 mph.

Maximum trailer weight is 3500 pounds across the board.

Accommodations

Like most sport-utility wagons, 4Runners are 5-seaters with twin reclining front buckets and a 3-place rear bench. The latter is split 50/50 and double-folds for added cargo space.

Leather upholstery is again optional on 4WD V-6 models and this year it's available in a new oak color with bronze privacy glass for the rear windows.

Evaluation

The 4Runner's chief attractions are tight, thorough assembly quality and a commendable reputation for reliability. It also scores highly in independent customer satisfaction surveys.

However, 4Runner is far more compact inside than the top-selling Ford Explorer and Jeep Grand Cherokee, with barely adequate space for four. Entry/exit is hurt by a higher than usual stance—nearly two feet off the ground. This is much higher than rivals from Ford, Jeep, and General Motors and an inconvenience that diminishes 4Runner's appeal as a family 4x4.

And with curb weights in the 4000-pound range, acceleration is nothing special even with the V-6, which is a smooth, quiet operator, but hard-pressed to break 13 seconds 0-60 mph with 5-speed and 4WD. Further, our automatic 4WD V-6 averaged just 13.8 mpg in suburban and expressway driving—and that was all in 2WD.

Ride quality is pleasant with the standard tires, but as with its rivals, the big 31-inch rubber makes the going jiggly over bumps and accentuates an inherently tippy feeling in tight turns.

Specifications

	5-door wagon
Wheelbase, in.	103.3
Overall length, in.	176.6
Overall width, in.	66.5
Overall height, in.	66.1
Turn diameter, ft.	37.4
Curb weight, lbs.	3825
Fuel capacity, gal.	17.2[1]

1. 18.8 gal. w/31 ×10.5 tire option.

Passenger Area Dimensions

Seating capacity	5
Front head room, in.	38.7
Rear head room, in.	38.3
Front leg room, in.	41.5
Rear leg room, in.	31.6

Cargo Dimensions and Payloads

Cargo area length, in.	69.8
Cargo area width, in.	52.2
Cargo area width between wheels, in.	36.2
Cargo area height, in.	35.6
Cargo vol., cu. ft.	78.3
Max. payload, lbs.	1610
Max. trailer weight, lbs.	3500

Engines

	ohc I-4	ohc V-6
Size, liters/cu. in.	2.4/144	3.0/181
Horsepower @ rpm	116 @ 4800	150 @ 4800
Torque (lbs./ft.) @ rpm	140 @ 2800	180 @ 3400
Availability	S	S

EPA city/highway mpg

5-speed OD manual	19/22	14/18
4-speed OD automatic		14/16

Built in Japan.

KEY: Dimensions and capacities are supplied by the manufacturers. **Curb Weight:** base models, not including optional equipment. **Max. payload, lbs.** = gross amount; net payload may be lower due to optional equipment. **Engines: ohv** = overhead valve; **ohc** = overhead cam; **I** = inline cylinders; **V** = cylinders in V configuration; **flat** = horizontally opposed cylinders; **rpm** = revolutions per minute; **OD** = overdrive transmission; **S** = standard; **O** = optional; **NA** = not available.

Toyota

Car-like describes the supportive front buckets and, unlike in the rear compartment, there's plenty of leg room for taller people. All-round head room is generous. Alas, all seats are right on the floor, which means a near straight-leg posture that some drivers won't find agreeable. Clear analog gauges and logical, slick-working minor controls are pluses. And with the spare tire stowed out of sight, drivers get a clear view directly aft.

4Runner's tall build partly results from a generous 9.1-inch ground clearance designed for off-roading. But it also means a high cargo floor and less floor-to-ceiling height than in most rivals. Load volume is good, all things considered, but not great.

Plus points include the convenient 4WDemand system, which permits on-the-fly shifting in and out of 4WD, and the new 4-wheel anti-lock system. Unfortunately, the 4-wheel anti-lock system is a $660 option instead of standard.

High prices remain one of the 4Runner's biggest problems. The 4-cylinder model starts at over $20,000 and the V-6 models at more than $21,000. Dress up a 4Runner with a few appearance and convenience options and the price can easily exceed $25,000.

We prefer the Explorer and Grand Cherokee, which have more room and better all-around performance for less money. In addition, the Grand Cherokee comes with a driver-side air bag, which isn't offered on the 4Runner.

Workmanship is great, but 4Runner is more compact inside than domestic rivals. Spare tire mounts beneath rear of body.

Prices

Toyota 4Runner

	Retail Price	Dealer Invoice	Fair Price
2WD 5-door wagon, V-6, automatic	$21348	*	*
4WD 5-door wagon, 5-speed	20308	*	*
4WD 5-door wagon, V-6, 5-speed	22278	*	*
4WD 5-door wagon, V-6, automatic	23328	*	*
Destination charge	385	385	385

Prices are for vehicles distributed by Toyota Motor Sales, U.S.A., Inc. The dealer invoice, fair price, and destination charge may be higher in areas served by independent distributors.

Standard Equipment:

2.4-liter 4-cylinder engine, 5-speed manual transmission, 4WDemand part-time 4WD (4WD models), power steering, cloth reclining front bucket seats with center console, split folding rear seat, tachometer, coolant temperature and oil pressure gauges, voltmeter, trip odometer, remote fuel door release, dual outside mirrors, tinted glass, power tailgate window, rear wiper/washer, digital clock, 225/75R15 all-season tires. **V6 models** add: 3.0-liter V-6, 5-speed manual or 4-speed automatic transmission, anti-lock rear brakes, intermittent wipers, rear defogger, AM/FM radio, tilt steering column, passenger-side visor mirror.

Optional Equipment:

Anti-lock rear brakes, 4-cylinder	300	255	278
4-wheel anti-lock brakes, V-6	660	541	601
Air conditioning	955	764	860
Tilt steering column, 4-cylinder	215	183	199
Rear heater	160	128	144
Chrome Pkg., 4-cylinder and V-6	245	196	221
Chrome grille, windshield molding, bumpers, and door handles.			
Cruise Control	375	300	338
Includes Lighting Pkg., leather-wrapped steering wheel.			
Power Pkg.	790	632	711
Power windows and locks, chrome power mirrors. Requires Cruise Control Pkg; Chrome Pkg. or alloy wheels.			
Sports Pkg.	450	360	405
with bronze glass	290	232	261
Cloth sport seats, rear privacy glass. Requires Chrome Pkg., or Value Pkg. 1 or 2 or alloy wheels.			
Bronze glass	160	128	144
Leather Seat Pkg., 4WD V-6	1680	1344	1512
Includes rear privacy glass, leather trimmed seats and door trim, 4-way adjustable headrests, Lighting Pkg., cruise control, variable intermittent wipers, leather-wrapped steering wheel.			
Value Pkg. 1, V-6	1436	1292	1364
4-cyl.	1991	1792	1892
Air conditioning, Chrome Pkg., Power Pkg., Lighting Pkg., cruise control, AM/FM cassette (4-cyl.), variable intermittent wipers, leather-wrapped steering wheel (4-cyl.), floormats.			
Value Pkg. 2, 4WD V-6	2281	2053	2167
Value Pkg. 1 plus alloy wheels, chrome rear bumper for wider tires.			
Value Pkg. 3, 4WD V-6	3586	3227	3407
Value Pkg. 2 plus Leather Trim Pkg.			
All Weather Guard Pkg.,			
4-cylinder	235	191	213
V-6	65	55	60
Includes rear defogger (std. V-6) and heavy duty battery (V-6 only), heavy duty wiper motor, distributor cover, starter motor. Requires rear heater.			
Power moonroof, V-6	810	648	729
AM/FM cassette, 4-cylinder	555	416	486
V-6	270	207	234
Premium AM/FM cassette, V-6	675	506	591
Includes power antenna, six speakers.			
Cassette and CD player, V-6	1475	1106	1291
Includes power antenna.			
Alloy wheels and 31-inch tires,			
4WD V-6	1090	872	981
Includes Chrome Pkg.			
Alloy wheels, V-6	470	376	423

Dealer invoice and fair price not available at time of publication.

Volkswagen EuroVan

1993 Volkswagen EuroVan GL

A revised EuroVan with dual air bags is due in April as an early 1995 model. Until then, VW dealers will be selling remaining 1993s, so there will be no 1994 edition of Volkswagen's front-drive minivan.

EuroVan was introduced for 1993 to replace the rear-engine/rear-drive Vanagon.

Body Styles/Chassis

EuroVan has two front doors, a sliding curb-side rear door, and a one-piece tailgate.

Anti-lock brakes are optional. Payload is 1750 pounds.

No air bag is available on the '93 models. The 1995 model is due to get driver- and passenger-side air bags, plus structural reinforcements designed to meet new federal side-impact requirements for 1997.

The model lineup will also be shuffled. The current entry-level CL model will be dropped. GL will become the new base model and a new GLS will take over from the GL as the mid-range offering. The MV will again top the line.

Powertrains

A transverse-mounted 2.5-liter inline-5-cylinder with 109 horsepower is the only engine and is expected to be retained for the '95 edition.

A 5-speed manual transmission is standard; a 4-speed overdrive automatic is optional. VW says it has not decided whether EuroVan will eventually have a 4-wheel drive system, as did the Vanagon.

EuroVan can tow a braked trailer weighing up to 4400 pounds, or a non-braked trailer weighing 1500 pounds.

Accommodations

All EuroVans come with seats for seven, including two front bucket seats, two middle seats, and a 3-passenger rear bench seat.

The '95 GLS will have dual forward-facing captain's chairs in the mid position. The MV will continue with a pair of rear-facing buckets and a swing-up table in the center, plus a rear bench that can be folded into a bed.

The Weekender Package available on the MV has a pop-up roof with an integral double bed, a refrigerator, and window screens.

Front and rear air conditioners were standard on GL models for '93, and optional on the base CL; for '95, they'll be standard across the board. Currently, the rear air conditioner is deleted when the Weekender Package is installed on the MV.

Evaluation

EuroVan has its attributes, but Volkswagen is well off target in delivering what most U.S. buyers desire in a minivan.

EuroVan is far more modern than the old rear-engine Vanagon and retains Volkswagen's traditional virtues of

Specifications

	4-door van
Wheelbase, in.	115.0
Overall length, in.	186.6
Overall width, in.	72.4
Overall height, in.	75.6
Turn diameter, ft.	38.4
Curb weight, lbs.	3806
Fuel capacity, gal.	21.1

Passenger Area Dimensions

Seating capacity	7
Front head room, in.	39.3
Rear head room, in.	41.7
Front leg room, in.	37.8
Rear leg room, in.	39.3

Available Seating

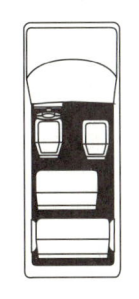

Cargo Dimensions and Payloads

Cargo area length, in.	97.8
Cargo area width, in.	63.7
Cargo area width between wheels, in.	NA
Cargo area height, in.	54.0
Cargo vol., cu. ft.	201.0
Max. payload, lbs.	1750
Max. trailer weight, lbs.	4400

Engines

	ohc I-5
Size, liters/cu. in.	2.5/150
Horsepower @ rpm	109 @ 4500
Torque (lbs./ft.) @ rpm	140 @ 2200
Availability	S

EPA city/highway mpg

5-speed OD manual	17/21
4-speed OD automatic	17/19

Built in Germany.

KEY: Dimensions and capacities are supplied by the manufacturers. **Curb Weight:** base models, not including optional equipment. **Max. payload, lbs.** = gross amount; net payload may be lower due to optional equipment. **Engines: ohv** = overhead valve; **ohc** = overhead cam; **I** = inline cylinders; **V** = cylinders in V configuration; **flat** = horizontally opposed cylinders; **rpm** = revolutions per minute; **OD** = overdrive transmission; **S** = standard; **O** = optional; **NA** = not available.

Volkswagen

Top: The 1995 dashboard will sport dual air bags. This is a '93 version. Middle: The optional Weekender package includes a pop-up camper top. Above: MV models come with a fold-out table.

ample room and utility in a compact package, but it lacks the contemporary styling and car-like comfort of minivan rivals.

In addition, most rivals have more power. Though acceleration is adequate for most tasks, you can't easily merge into freeway traffic or pass at will on 2-lane roads.

EuroVan's German character comes through in the very firm but supportive chair-like seats and in the absence of interior ornamentation.

It's also evident in a suspension that notices most every pavement flaw, but provides a relatively flat ride and fine overall control. Noise from engine and road also are quite evident, though wind rush is surprisingly low at highway speeds.

A higher step-in and some wheelarch intrusion keeps front-door entry from being as easy as most modern minivans, a problem compounded by the chair-height seat cushions. A mini-running board inside the sliding side-door opening provides a small toehold that's helpful when climbing aboard.

Drivers will find unobstructed gauges, but EuroVan's steering wheel is fixed at an awkward bus-like horizontal angle. It's a long reach to the stubby floor-mounted shift lever and there's a confusing array of climate controls that require deep study of the owner's manual. Visibility is nearly panoramic, though as many as five headrests can be visible through the rearview mirror, confusing the view aft.

The rear bench can be folded down for more space, or the seat can be unbolted to create room for a 4x8 sheet of plywood. Unfortunately, there are no quick-release latches for the rear seat.

Prices

1993 Volkswagen EuroVan	Retail Price	Dealer Invoice	Fair Price
CL 4-door van	$16640	$15325	$16125
GL 4-door van	20420	18279	19079
MV 4-door van	21850	19557	20357
Destination charge	490	490	490

Standard equipment:

CL: 2.5-liter PFI 5-cylinder engine, 5-speed manual transmission, power steering, height-adjustable front shoulder belts, reclining cloth front bucket seats, 2-place center bench seat, 3-place folding rear seat, cup holders, tinted glass, rear defogger, intermittent wipers, rear wiper/washer, dual outside mirrors, visor mirrors, rear heater, child safety rear door locks (hatch and side door), radio prep (speakers, wiring, antenna), full carpeting, clock, trip odometer, 205/65R15 tires. **GL** adds: front and rear air conditioners, front seat arm rests, upgraded interior trim, heated power mirrors, AM/FM cassette w/anti-theft circuitry, tachometer, lighted visor mirrors, body-color bumpers, wheel covers. **MV** adds: two center removable rear-facing seats with storage trays, rear 3-seat bench that folds out into a bed, folding table, storage locker, velour upholstery, privacy curtains.

Optional equipment:

4-speed automatic transmission	895	863	879
Anti-lock brakes	870	865	860
Popular Equipment Pkg., CL	2030	1746	1888
Front and rear air conditioners, AM/FM cassette.			
Convenience Group, GL, MV	765	658	712
Power windows and locks, cruise control.			
Popular Feature Pkg., CL	1860	1632	1746
Front and rear air conditioning, AM/FM cassette player.			
Weekender Pkg., MV	2530	2227	2379
Pop-up roof, window curtains and screens, refrigerator, second battery; deletes rear air conditioner.			
Compact disc changer	495	412	454
Metallic paint	170	146	158